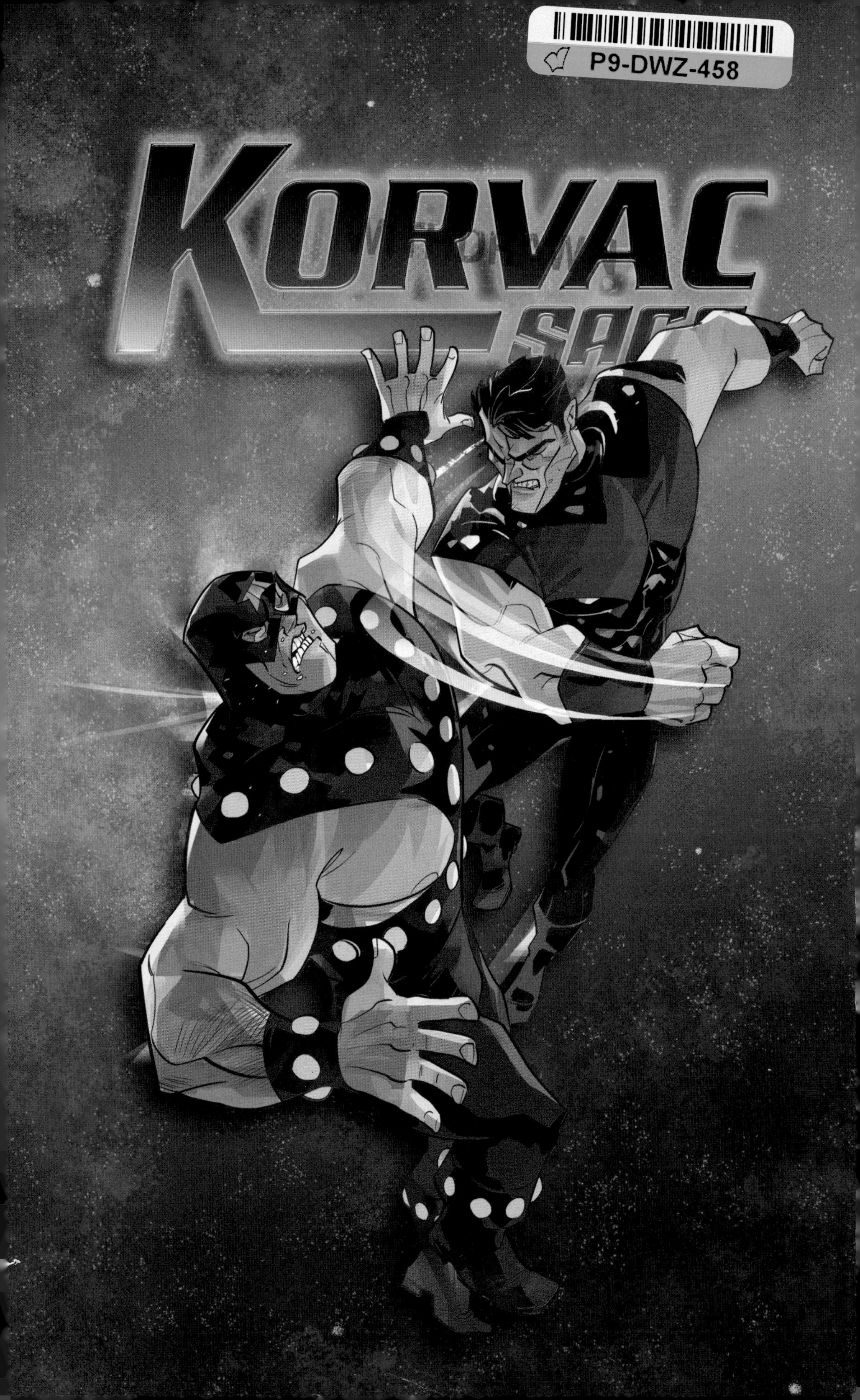
KORVAC

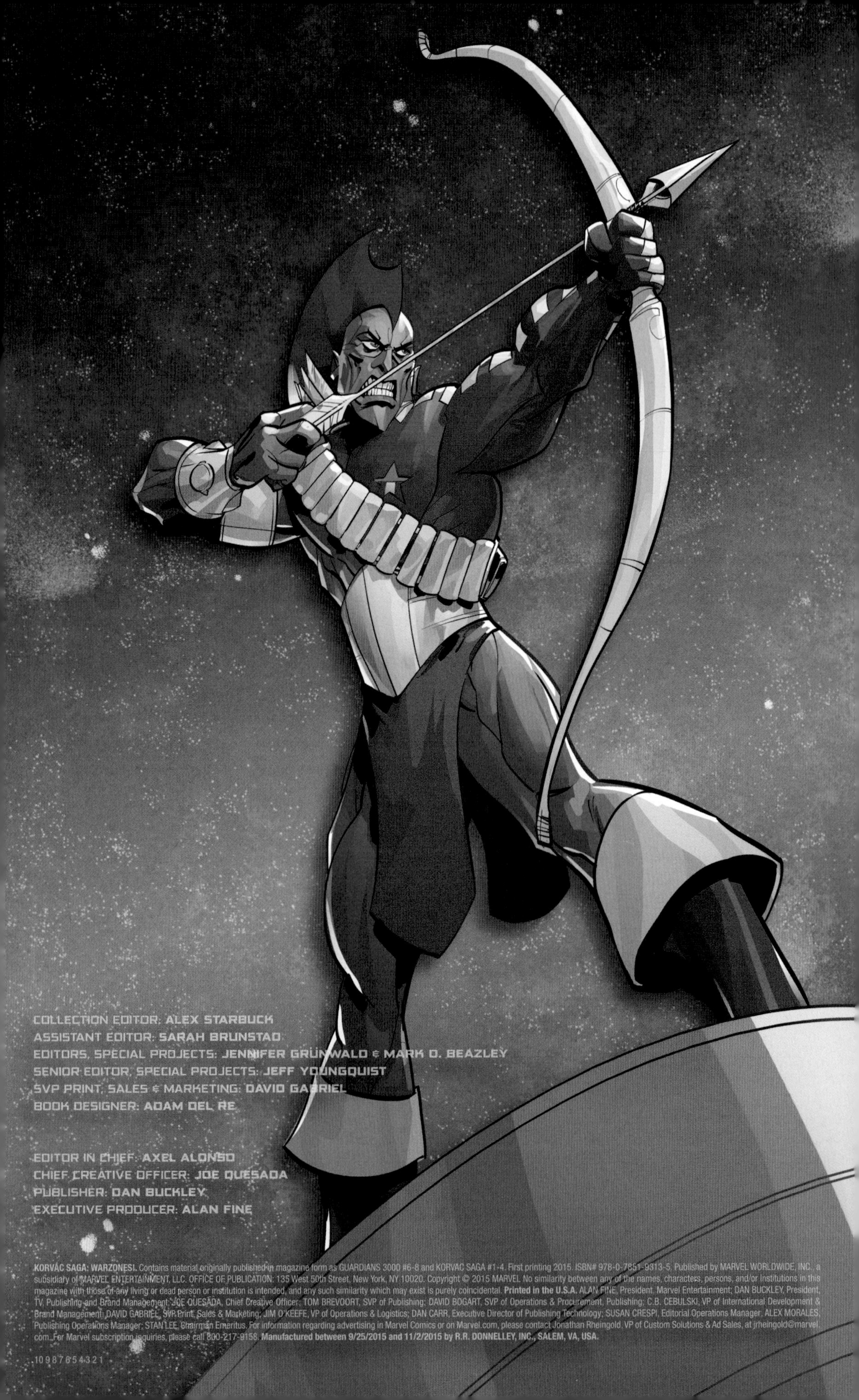

COLLECTION EDITOR: ALEX STARBUCK
ASSISTANT EDITOR: SARAH BRUNSTAD
EDITORS, SPECIAL PROJECTS: JENNIFER GRÜNWALD & MARK D. BEAZLEY
SENIOR EDITOR, SPECIAL PROJECTS: JEFF YOUNGQUIST
SVP PRINT, SALES & MARKETING: DAVID GABRIEL
BOOK DESIGNER: ADAM DEL RE

EDITOR IN CHIEF: AXEL ALONSO
CHIEF CREATIVE OFFICER: JOE QUESADA
PUBLISHER: DAN BUCKLEY
EXECUTIVE PRODUCER: ALAN FINE

KORVAC SAGA: WARZONES!. Contains material originally published in magazine form as GUARDIANS 3000 #6-8 and KORVAC SAGA #1-4. First printing 2015. ISBN# 978-0-7851-9313-5. Published by MARVEL WORLDWIDE, INC., a subsidiary of MARVEL ENTERTAINMENT, LLC. OFFICE OF PUBLICATION: 135 West 50th Street, New York, NY 10020. **Printed in the U.S.A.** ALAN FINE, President, Marvel Entertainment; DAN BUCKLEY, President, TV, Publishing and Brand Management; JOE QUESADA, Chief Creative Officer; TOM BREVOORT, SVP of Publishing; DAVID BOGART, SVP of Operations & Procurement, Publishing; C.B. CEBULSKI, VP of International Development & Brand Management; DAVID GABRIEL, SVP Print, Sales & Marketing; JIM O'KEEFE, VP of Operations & Logistics; DAN CARR, Executive Director of Publishing Technology; SUSAN CRESPI, Editorial Operations Manager; ALEX MORALES, Publishing Operations Manager; STAN LEE, Chairman Emeritus. For information regarding advertising in Marvel Comics or on Marvel.com, please contact Jonathan Rheingold, VP of Custom Solutions & Ad Sales, at jrheingold@marvel.com. For Marvel subscription inquiries, please call 800-217-9158. **Manufactured between 9/25/2015 and 11/2/2015 by R.R. DONNELLEY, INC., SALEM, VA, USA.**

10 9 8 7 6 5 4 3 2 1

KORVAC SAGA

WRITER
DAN ABNETT

GUARDIANS 3000 #6-8

ARTIST
NICO LEON

COLOR ARTISTS
EDGAR DELGADO WITH
SOTOCOLOR (#7) &
ANTONIO FABELA (#8)

COVER ART
ALEX ROSS (#6) AND **GERARDO SANDOVAL** &
EDGAR DELGADO (#7-8)

KORVAC SAGA #1-4

ARTIST
OTTO SCHMIDT

COLOR ARTIST
CRIS PETER

COVER ART
OTTO SCHMIDT

LETTERER
VC's CLAYTON COWLES

ASSISTANT EDITOR
CHRISTINA HARRINGTON

EDITOR
KATIE KUBERT

EXECUTIVE EDITOR
MIKE MARTS

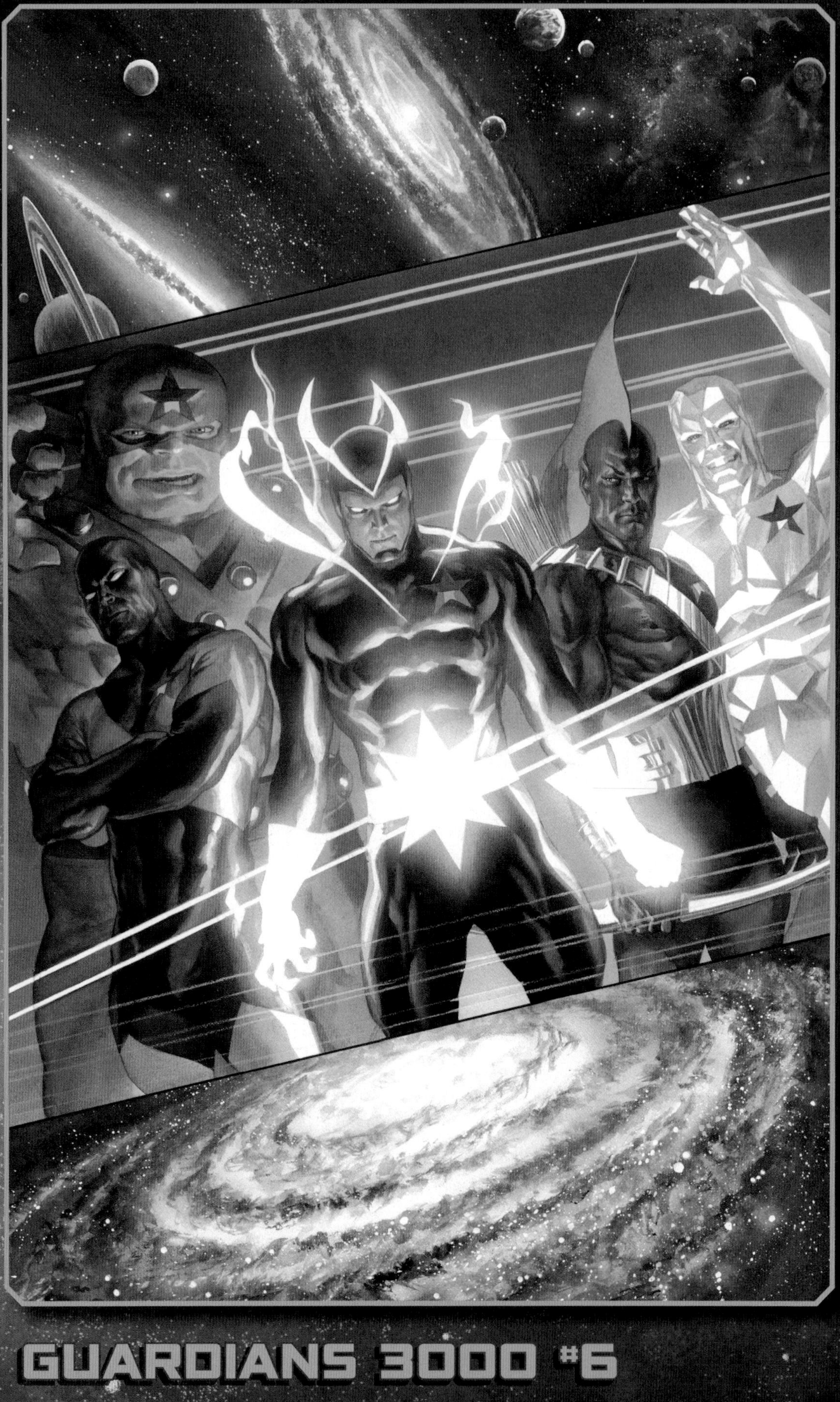

GUARDIANS 3000 #6

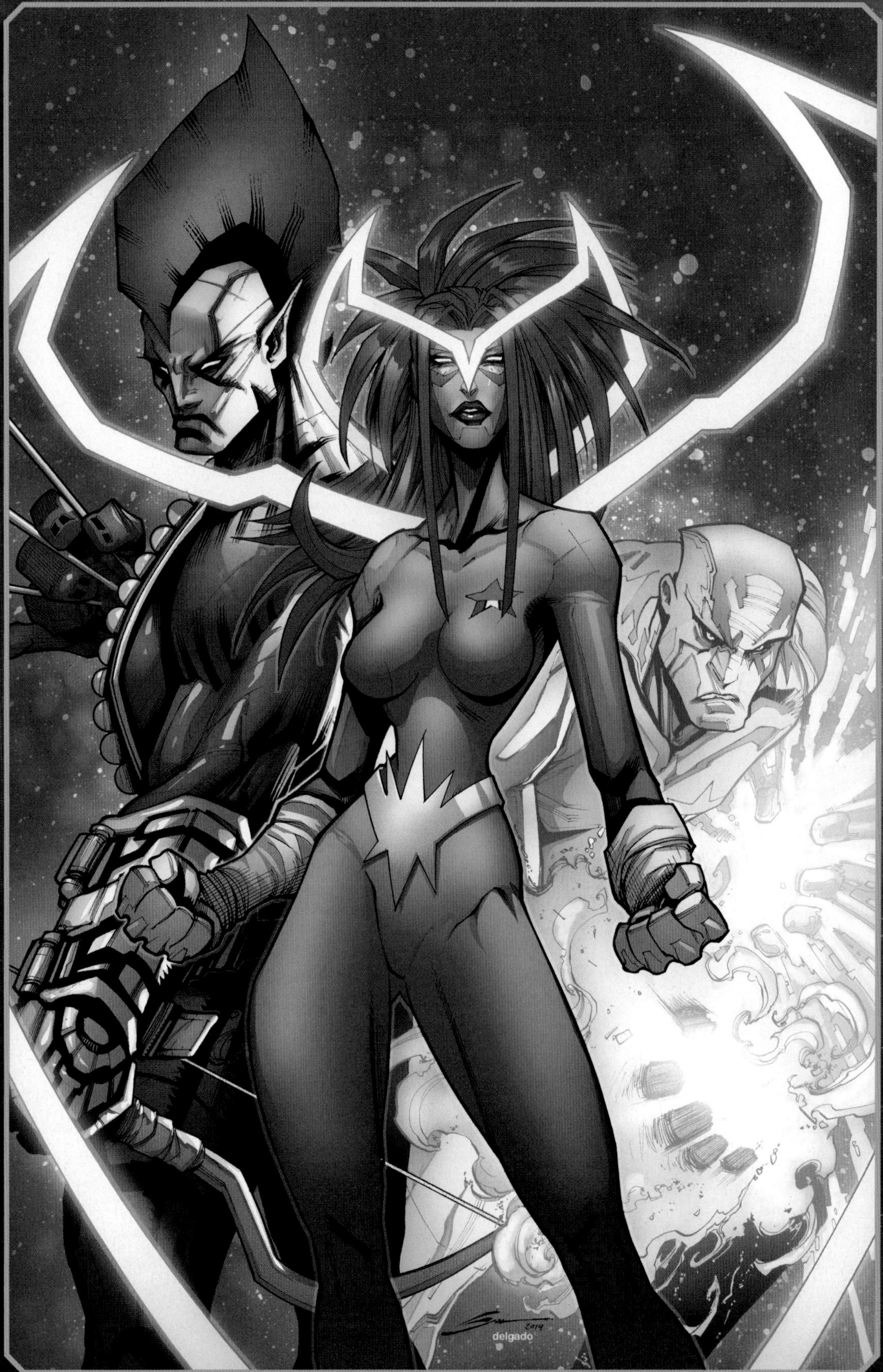
delgado

GUARDIANS 3000 #6 VARIANT
BY GERARDO SANDOVAL & EDGAR DELGADO

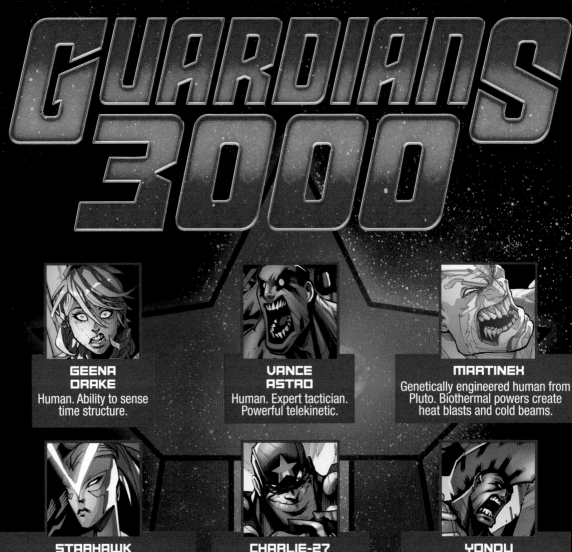

GUARDIANS 3000

GEENA DRAKE
Human. Ability to sense time structure.

VANCE ASTRO
Human. Expert tactician. Powerful telekinetic.

MARTINEX
Genetically engineered human from Pluto. Biothermal powers create heat blasts and cold beams.

STARHAWK
Half-human, half-alien. Possesses quantum-mystic powers including flight, precognition and psionic blasts.

CHARLIE-27
Genetically engineered human from Jupiter. Super-strength, speed and stamina.

YONDU UDONTA
Alien from Alpha Centuri. Skilled marksman and weapons master.

In 3014 AD, the vicious Badoon are decimating the galaxy. Opposing them is a valiant resistance movement led by the Guardians of the Galaxy.

But time itself is broken. Causality is collapsing, causing events to be replayed and relived.

Geena Drake, the Guardians' newest recruit, is a young Earth girl rescued from a Badoon labor camp. For reasons no one can explain, Geena has a natural sensitivity to the disruption of time.

Geena and her companions Charlie-27, Yondu and Star-Lord have attempted to travel into the past to find the root of the time collapse. To achieve this feat, they have plunged into the gravity well of an ancient, potent and slumbering galactic entity known as The Old Hunger…

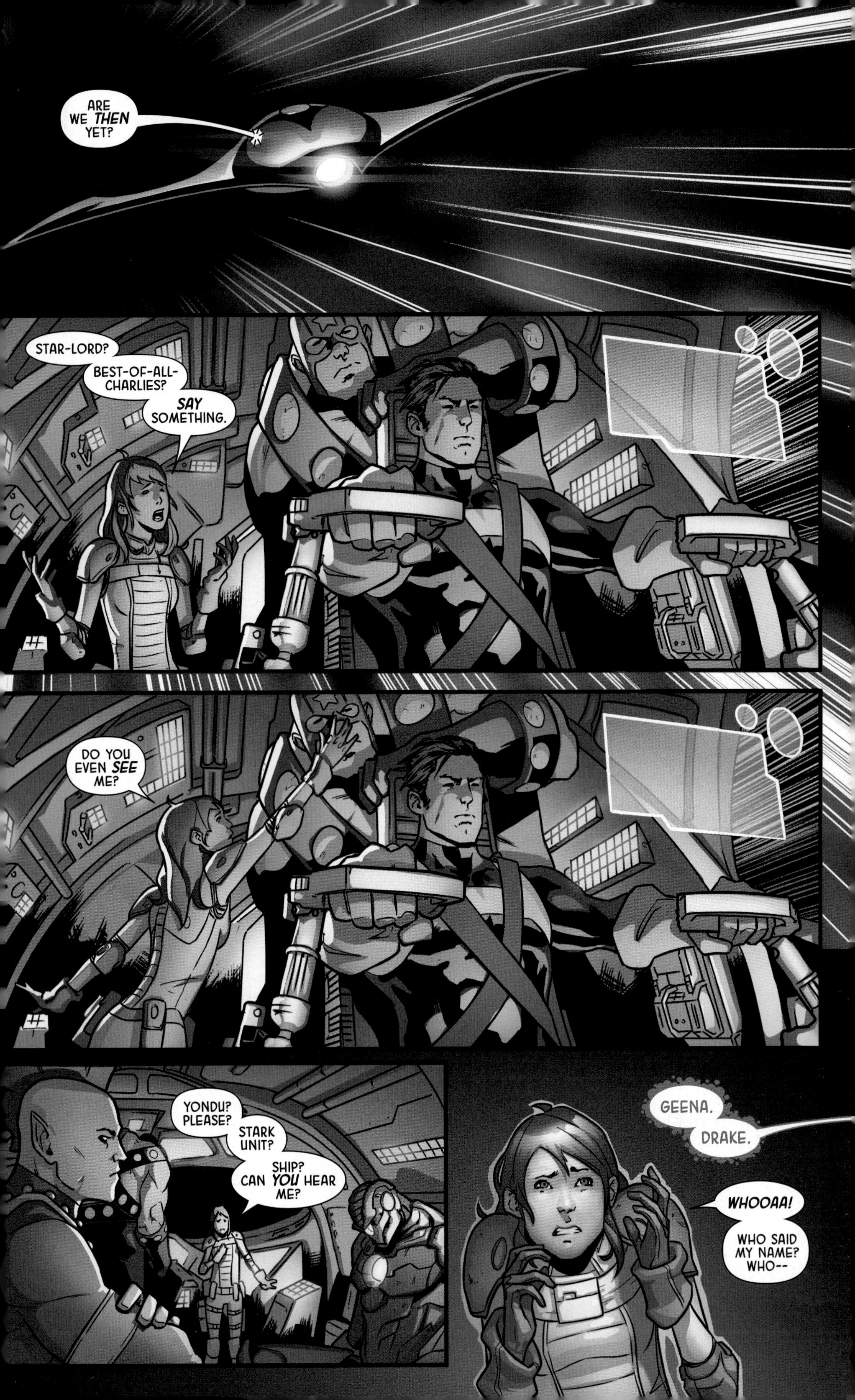
ARE WE *THEN* YET?
STAR-LORD?
BEST-OF-ALL-CHARLIES?
SAY SOMETHING.
DO YOU EVEN *SEE* ME?
YONDU? PLEASE?
STARK UNIT?
SHIP? CAN *YOU* HEAR ME?
GEENA.
DRAKE.
WHOOAA!
WHO SAID MY NAME? WHO--

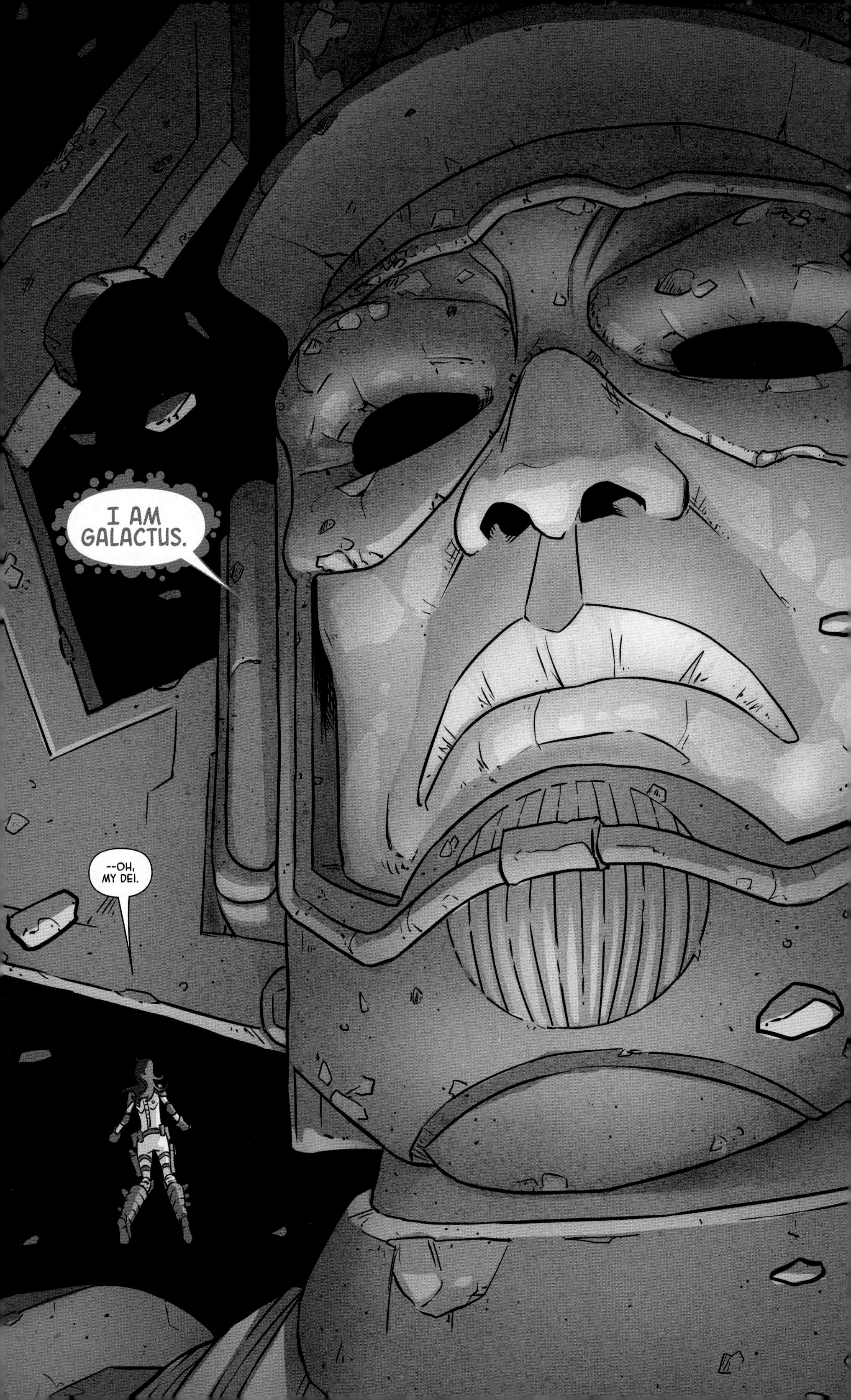
I AM GALACTUS.
--OH, MY DEI.

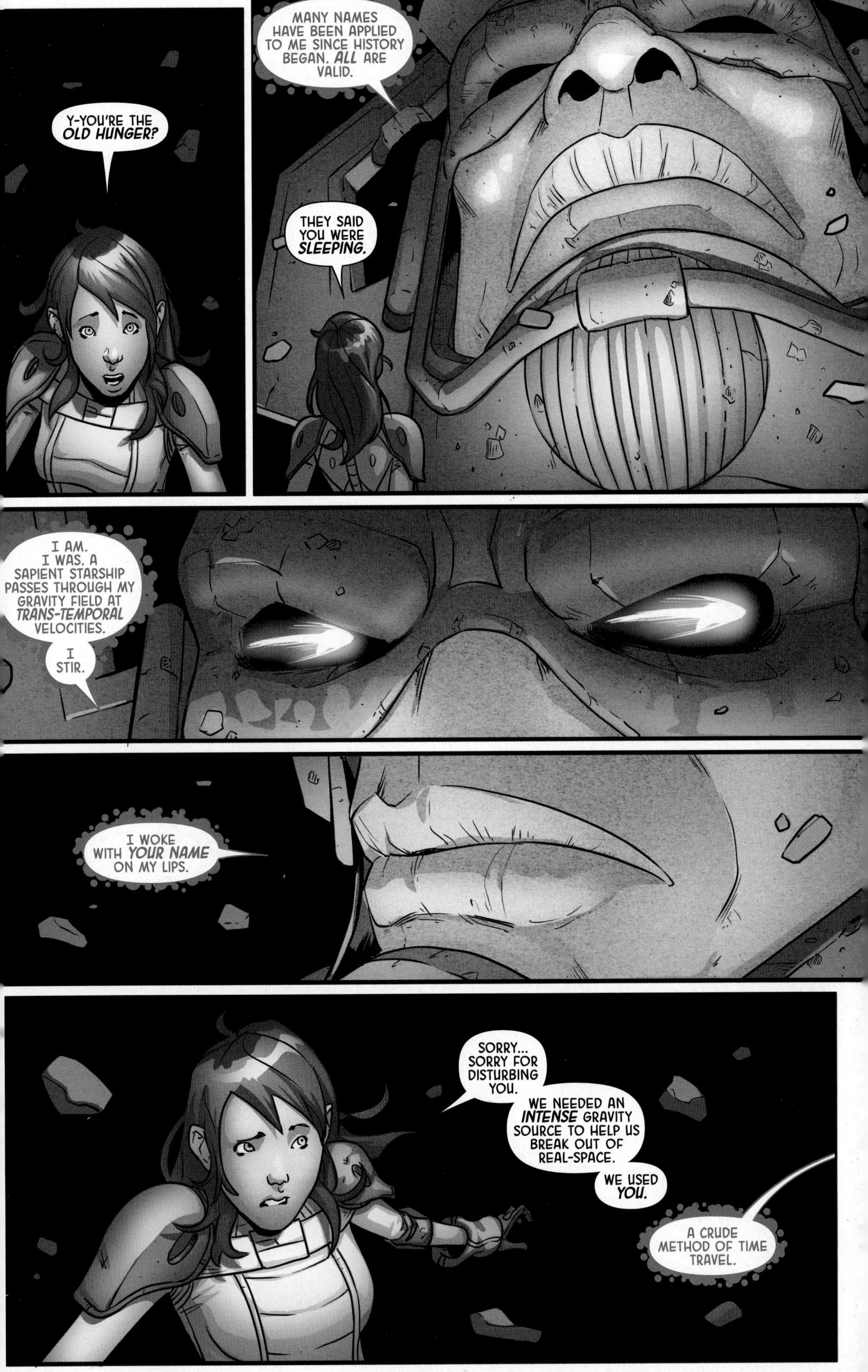
Y-YOU'RE THE OLD HUNGER?
MANY NAMES HAVE BEEN APPLIED TO ME SINCE HISTORY BEGAN. ALL ARE VALID.
THEY SAID YOU WERE SLEEPING.
I AM. I WAS. A SAPIENT STARSHIP PASSES THROUGH MY GRAVITY FIELD AT TRANS-TEMPORAL VELOCITIES.
I STIR.
I WOKE WITH YOUR NAME ON MY LIPS.
SORRY... SORRY FOR DISTURBING YOU.
WE NEEDED AN INTENSE GRAVITY SOURCE TO HELP US BREAK OUT OF REAL-SPACE.
WE USED YOU.
A CRUDE METHOD OF TIME TRAVEL.

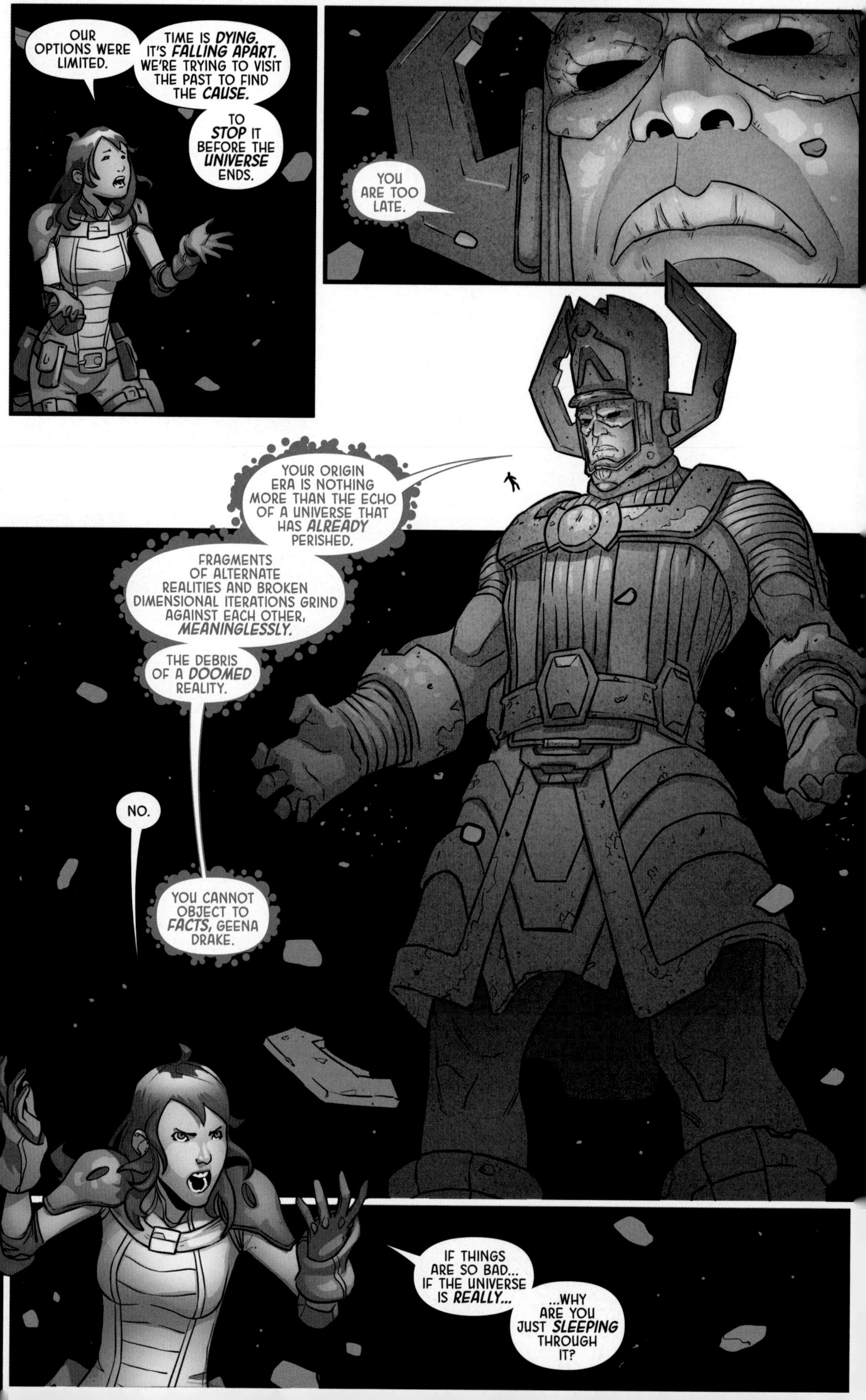
OUR OPTIONS WERE LIMITED.
TIME IS DYING. IT'S FALLING APART. WE'RE TRYING TO VISIT THE PAST TO FIND THE CAUSE.
TO STOP IT BEFORE THE UNIVERSE ENDS.
YOU ARE TOO LATE.
YOUR ORIGIN ERA IS NOTHING MORE THAN THE ECHO OF A UNIVERSE THAT HAS ALREADY PERISHED.
FRAGMENTS OF ALTERNATE REALITIES AND BROKEN DIMENSIONAL ITERATIONS GRIND AGAINST EACH OTHER, MEANINGLESSLY.
THE DEBRIS OF A DOOMED REALITY.
NO.
YOU CANNOT OBJECT TO FACTS, GEENA DRAKE.
IF THINGS ARE SO BAD... IF THE UNIVERSE IS REALLY...
...WHY ARE YOU JUST SLEEPING THROUGH IT?

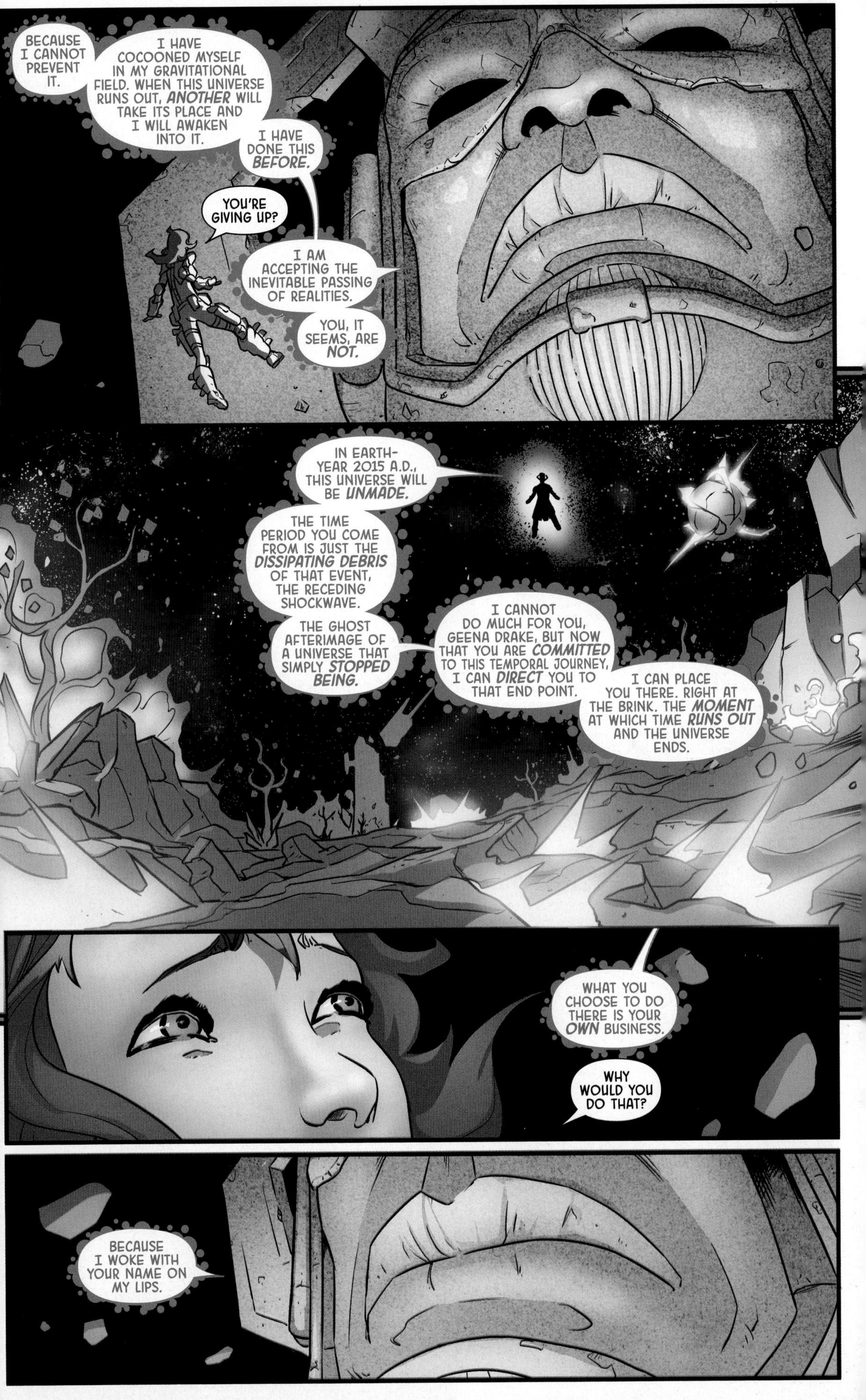

BECAUSE I CANNOT PREVENT IT.
I HAVE COCOONED MYSELF IN MY GRAVITATIONAL FIELD. WHEN THIS UNIVERSE RUNS OUT, ANOTHER WILL TAKE ITS PLACE AND I WILL AWAKEN INTO IT.
I HAVE DONE THIS BEFORE.
YOU'RE GIVING UP?
I AM ACCEPTING THE INEVITABLE PASSING OF REALITIES.
YOU, IT SEEMS, ARE NOT.
IN EARTH-YEAR 2015 A.D., THIS UNIVERSE WILL BE UNMADE.
THE TIME PERIOD YOU COME FROM IS JUST THE DISSIPATING DEBRIS OF THAT EVENT, THE RECEDING SHOCKWAVE.
THE GHOST AFTERIMAGE OF A UNIVERSE THAT SIMPLY STOPPED BEING.
I CANNOT DO MUCH FOR YOU, GEENA DRAKE, BUT NOW THAT YOU ARE COMMITTED TO THIS TEMPORAL JOURNEY, I CAN DIRECT YOU TO THAT END POINT.
I CAN PLACE YOU THERE. RIGHT AT THE BRINK. THE MOMENT AT WHICH TIME RUNS OUT AND THE UNIVERSE ENDS.
WHAT YOU CHOOSE TO DO THERE IS YOUR OWN BUSINESS.
WHY WOULD YOU DO THAT?
BECAUSE I WOKE WITH YOUR NAME ON MY LIPS.

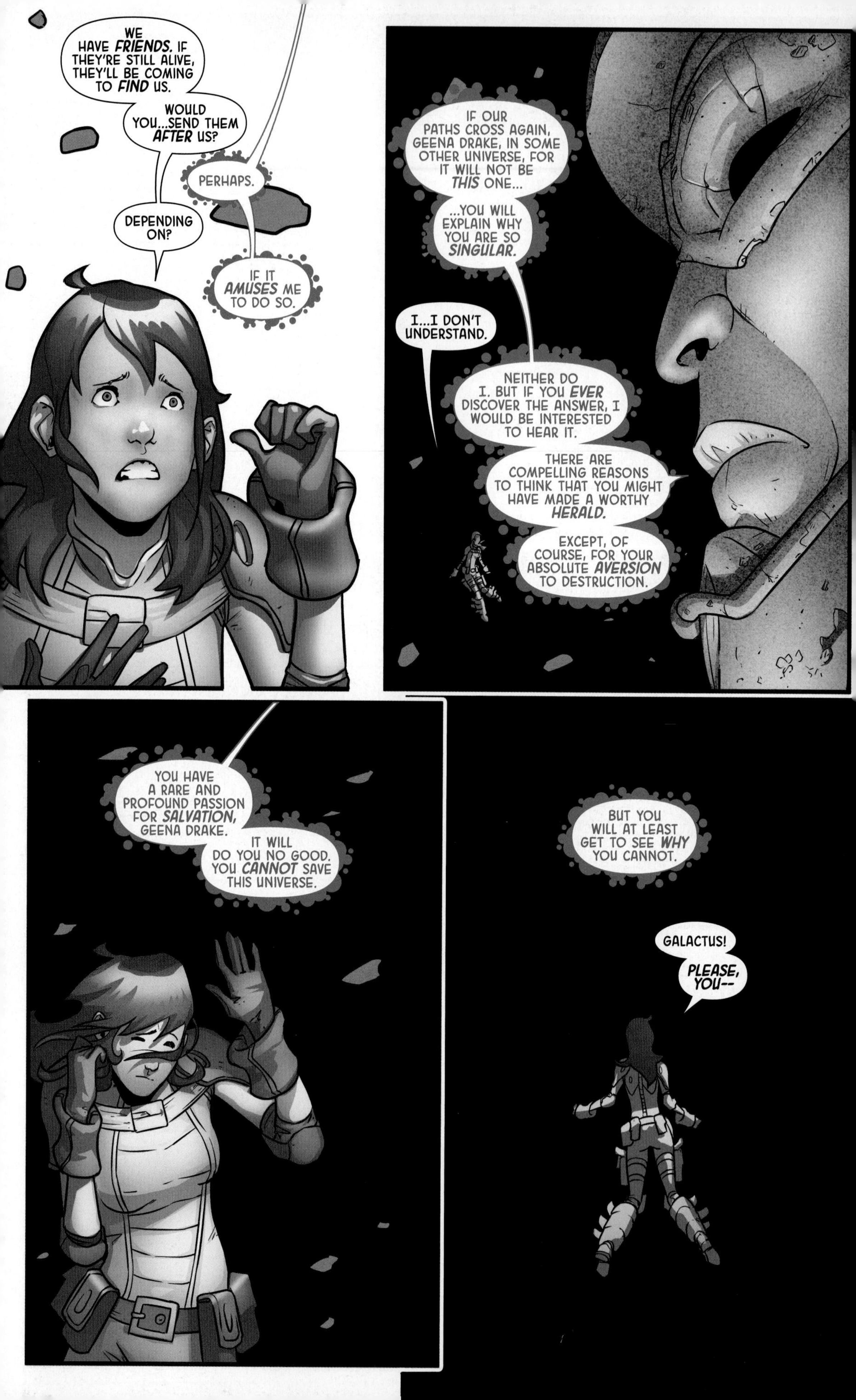
WE HAVE FRIENDS. IF THEY'RE STILL ALIVE, THEY'LL BE COMING TO FIND US.
WOULD YOU...SEND THEM AFTER US?
PERHAPS.
DEPENDING ON?
IF IT AMUSES ME TO DO SO.
IF OUR PATHS CROSS AGAIN, GEENA DRAKE, IN SOME OTHER UNIVERSE, FOR IT WILL NOT BE THIS ONE...
...YOU WILL EXPLAIN WHY YOU ARE SO SINGULAR.
I...I DON'T UNDERSTAND.
NEITHER DO I. BUT IF YOU EVER DISCOVER THE ANSWER, I WOULD BE INTERESTED TO HEAR IT.
THERE ARE COMPELLING REASONS TO THINK THAT YOU MIGHT HAVE MADE A WORTHY HERALD.
EXCEPT, OF COURSE, FOR YOUR ABSOLUTE AVERSION TO DESTRUCTION.
YOU HAVE A RARE AND PROFOUND PASSION FOR SALVATION, GEENA DRAKE.
IT WILL DO YOU NO GOOD. YOU CANNOT SAVE THIS UNIVERSE.
BUT YOU WILL AT LEAST GET TO SEE WHY YOU CANNOT.
GALACTUS!
PLEASE, YOU--

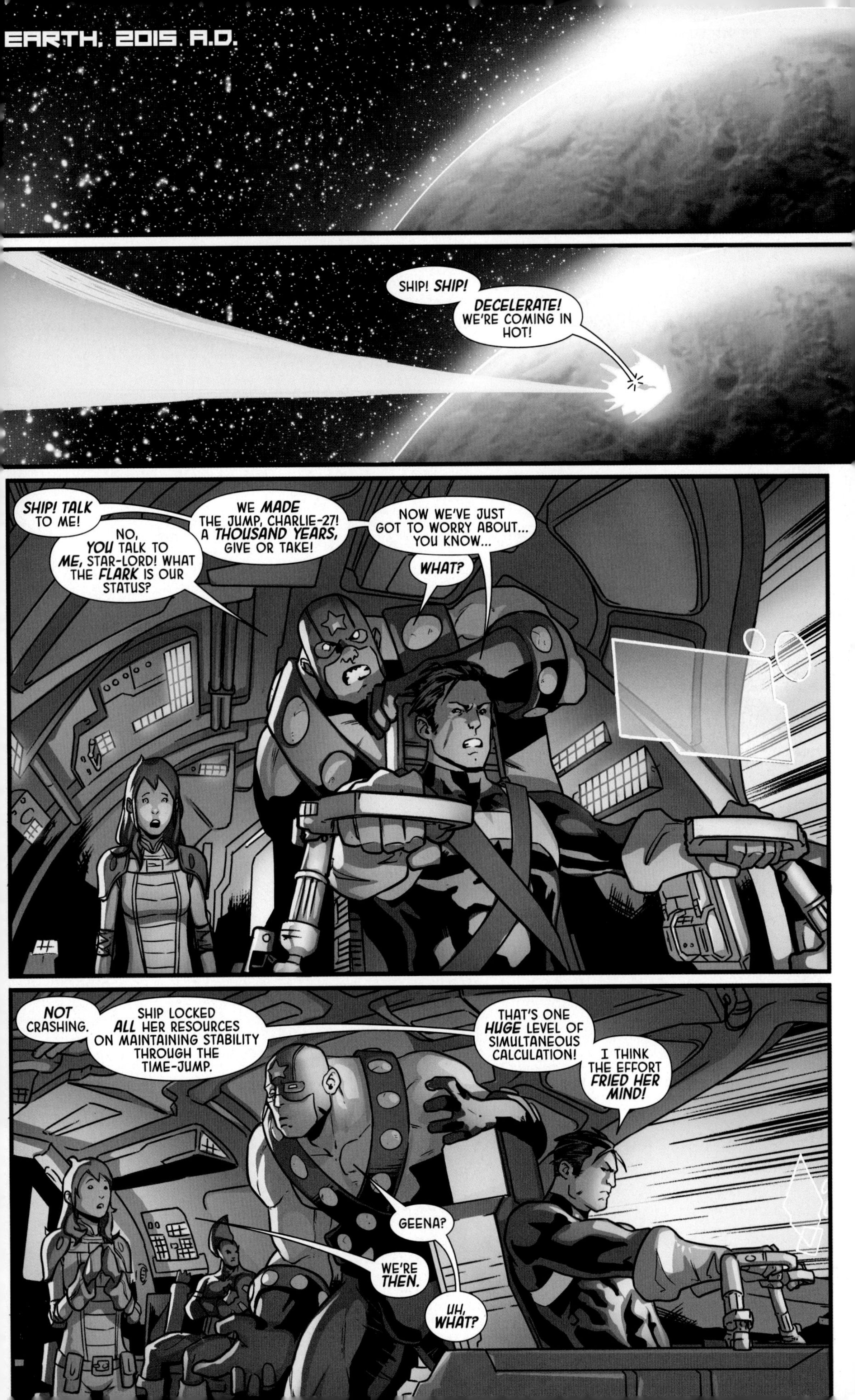
EARTH, 2015 A.D.
SHIP! SHIP! DECELERATE! WE'RE COMING IN HOT!
SHIP! TALK TO ME!
WE MADE THE JUMP, CHARLIE-27! A THOUSAND YEARS, GIVE OR TAKE!
NO, YOU TALK TO ME, STAR-LORD! WHAT THE FLARK IS OUR STATUS?
NOW WE'VE JUST GOT TO WORRY ABOUT... YOU KNOW...
WHAT?
NOT CRASHING.
SHIP LOCKED ALL HER RESOURCES ON MAINTAINING STABILITY THROUGH THE TIME-JUMP.
THAT'S ONE HUGE LEVEL OF SIMULTANEOUS CALCULATION!
I THINK THE EFFORT FRIED HER MIND!
GEENA?
WE'RE THEN.
UH, WHAT?

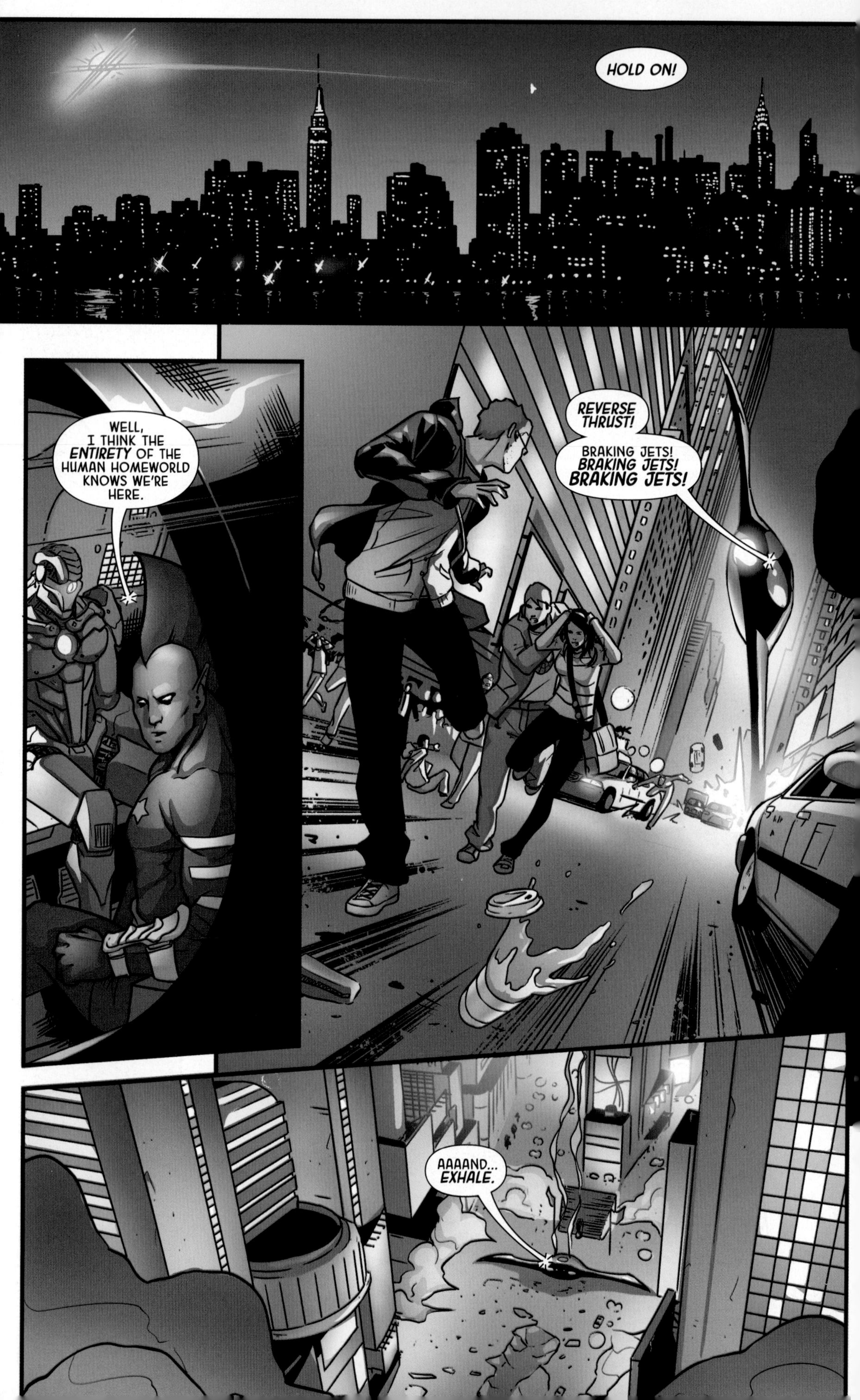
HOLD ON!
WELL, I THINK THE *ENTIRETY* OF THE HUMAN HOMEWORLD KNOWS WE'RE HERE.
REVERSE THRUST!
BRAKING JETS! **BRAKING JETS! BRAKING JETS!**
AAAAND... *EXHALE.*

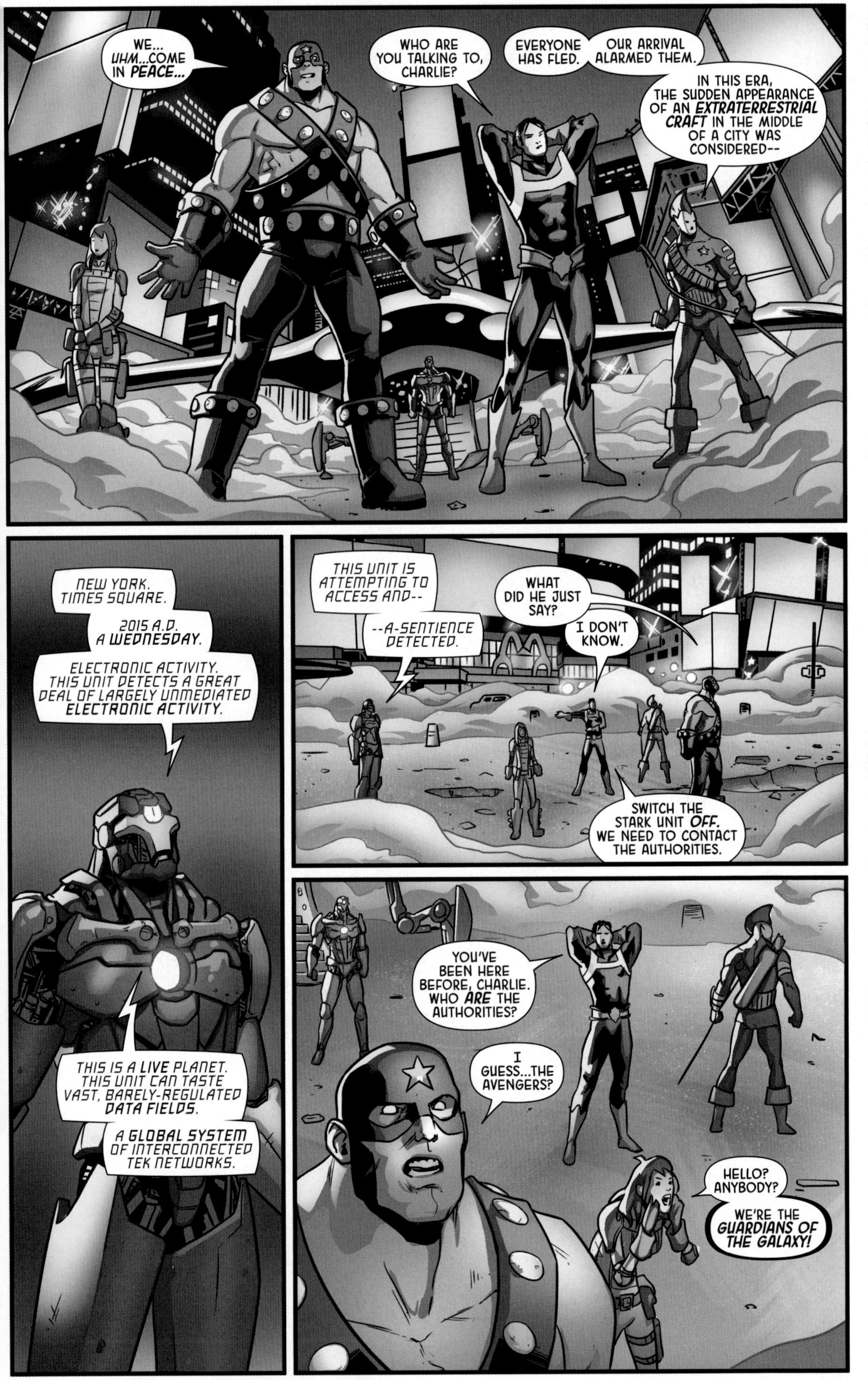
WE... UHM...COME IN PEACE...
WHO ARE YOU TALKING TO, CHARLIE?
EVERYONE HAS FLED.
OUR ARRIVAL ALARMED THEM.
IN THIS ERA, THE SUDDEN APPEARANCE OF AN EXTRATERRESTRIAL CRAFT IN THE MIDDLE OF A CITY WAS CONSIDERED--
NEW YORK. TIMES SQUARE.
2015 A.D. A WEDNESDAY.
ELECTRONIC ACTIVITY. THIS UNIT DETECTS A GREAT DEAL OF LARGELY UNMEDIATED ELECTRONIC ACTIVITY.
THIS IS A LIVE PLANET. THIS UNIT CAN TASTE VAST, BARELY-REGULATED DATA FIELDS.
A GLOBAL SYSTEM OF INTERCONNECTED TEK NETWORKS.
THIS UNIT IS ATTEMPTING TO ACCESS AND--
--A-SENTIENCE DETECTED.
WHAT DID HE JUST SAY?
I DON'T KNOW.
SWITCH THE STARK UNIT OFF. WE NEED TO CONTACT THE AUTHORITIES.
YOU'VE BEEN HERE BEFORE, CHARLIE. WHO ARE THE AUTHORITIES?
I GUESS...THE AVENGERS?
HELLO? ANYBODY?
WE'RE THE GUARDIANS OF THE GALAXY!

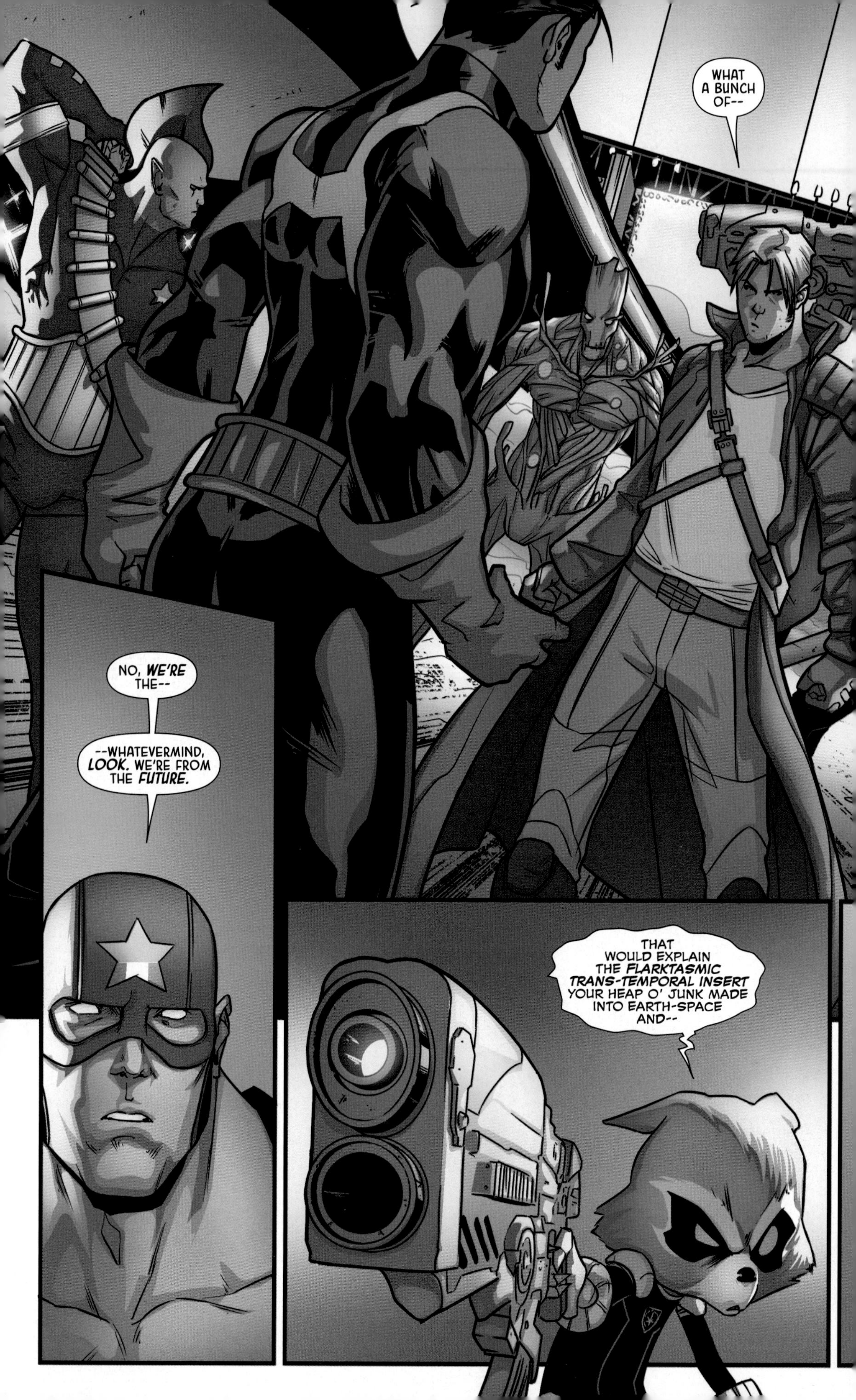

WHAT A BUNCH OF--
NO, **WE'RE** THE--
--WHATEVERMIND, **LOOK.** WE'RE FROM THE **FUTURE.**
THAT WOULD EXPLAIN THE **FLARKTASMIC TRANS-TEMPORAL INSERT** YOUR HEAP O' JUNK MADE INTO EARTH-SPACE AND--

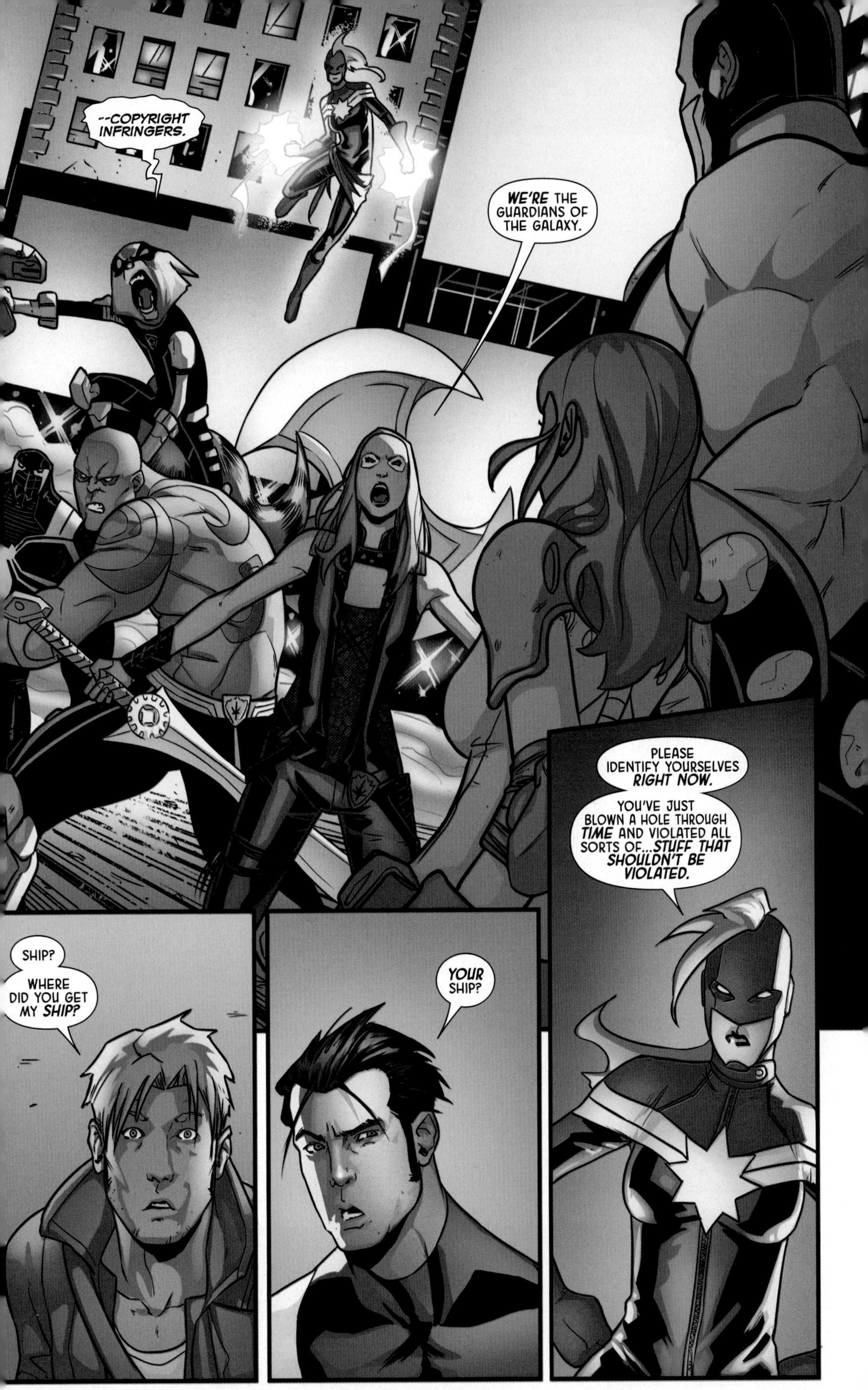
--COPYRIGHT INFRINGERS.
WE'RE THE GUARDIANS OF THE GALAXY.
PLEASE IDENTIFY YOURSELVES RIGHT NOW.
YOU'VE JUST BLOWN A HOLE THROUGH TIME AND VIOLATED ALL SORTS OF...STUFF THAT SHOULDN'T BE VIOLATED.
SHIP?
WHERE DID YOU GET MY SHIP?
YOUR SHIP?

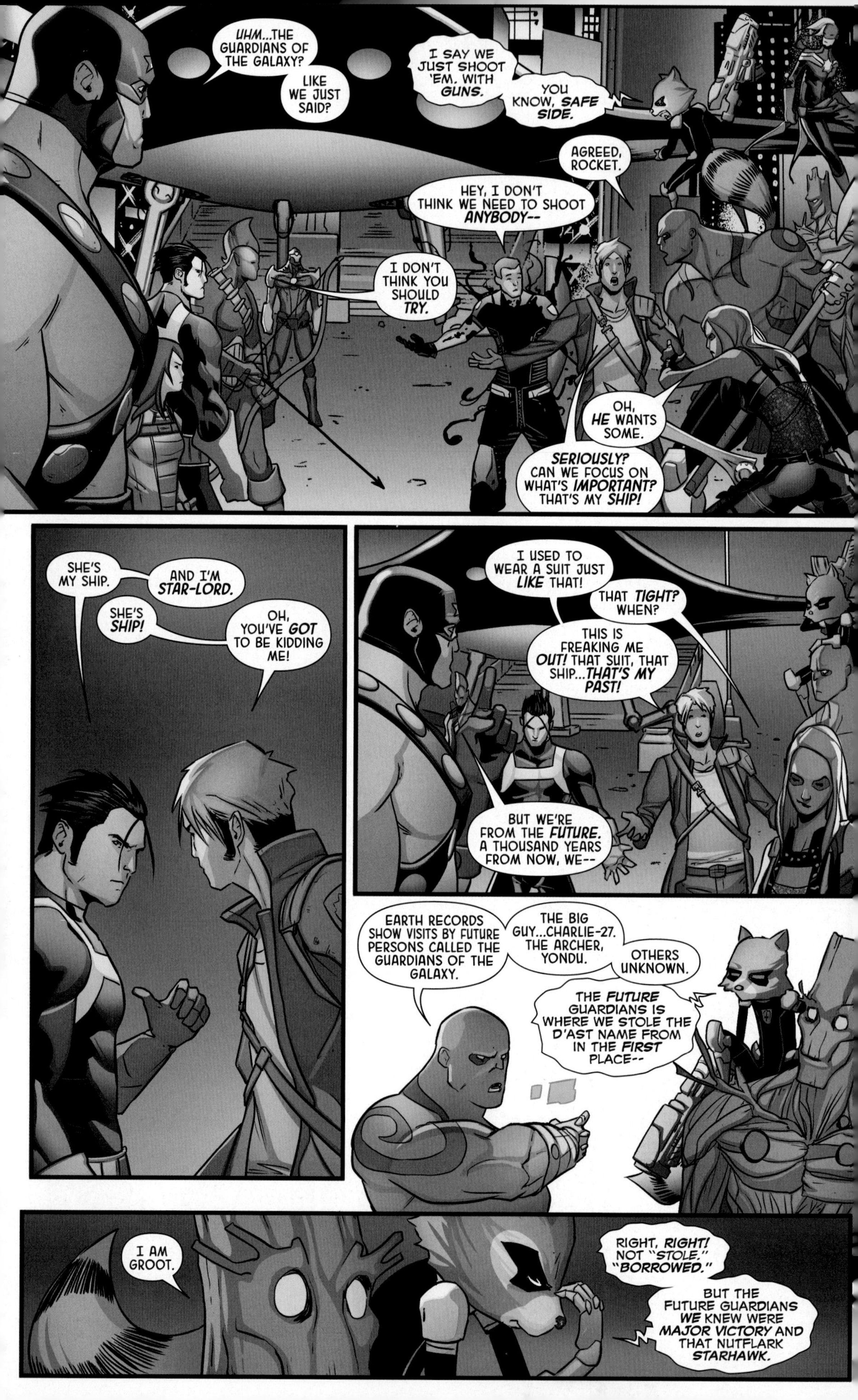
UHM...THE GUARDIANS OF THE GALAXY?
LIKE WE JUST SAID?
I SAY WE JUST SHOOT 'EM. WITH GUNS.
YOU KNOW, SAFE SIDE.
AGREED, ROCKET.
HEY, I DON'T THINK WE NEED TO SHOOT ANYBODY--
I DON'T THINK YOU SHOULD TRY.
OH, HE WANTS SOME.
SERIOUSLY? CAN WE FOCUS ON WHAT'S IMPORTANT? THAT'S MY SHIP!
SHE'S MY SHIP.
AND I'M STAR-LORD.
SHE'S SHIP!
OH, YOU'VE GOT TO BE KIDDING ME!
I USED TO WEAR A SUIT JUST LIKE THAT!
THAT TIGHT? WHEN?
THIS IS FREAKING ME OUT! THAT SUIT, THAT SHIP...THAT'S MY PAST!
BUT WE'RE FROM THE FUTURE. A THOUSAND YEARS FROM NOW, WE--
EARTH RECORDS SHOW VISITS BY FUTURE PERSONS CALLED THE GUARDIANS OF THE GALAXY.
THE BIG GUY...CHARLIE-27. THE ARCHER, YONDU.
OTHERS UNKNOWN.
THE FUTURE GUARDIANS IS WHERE WE STOLE THE D'AST NAME FROM IN THE FIRST PLACE--
I AM GROOT.
RIGHT, RIGHT! NOT "STOLE." "BORROWED."
BUT THE FUTURE GUARDIANS WE KNEW WERE MAJOR VICTORY AND THAT NUTFLARK STARHAWK.

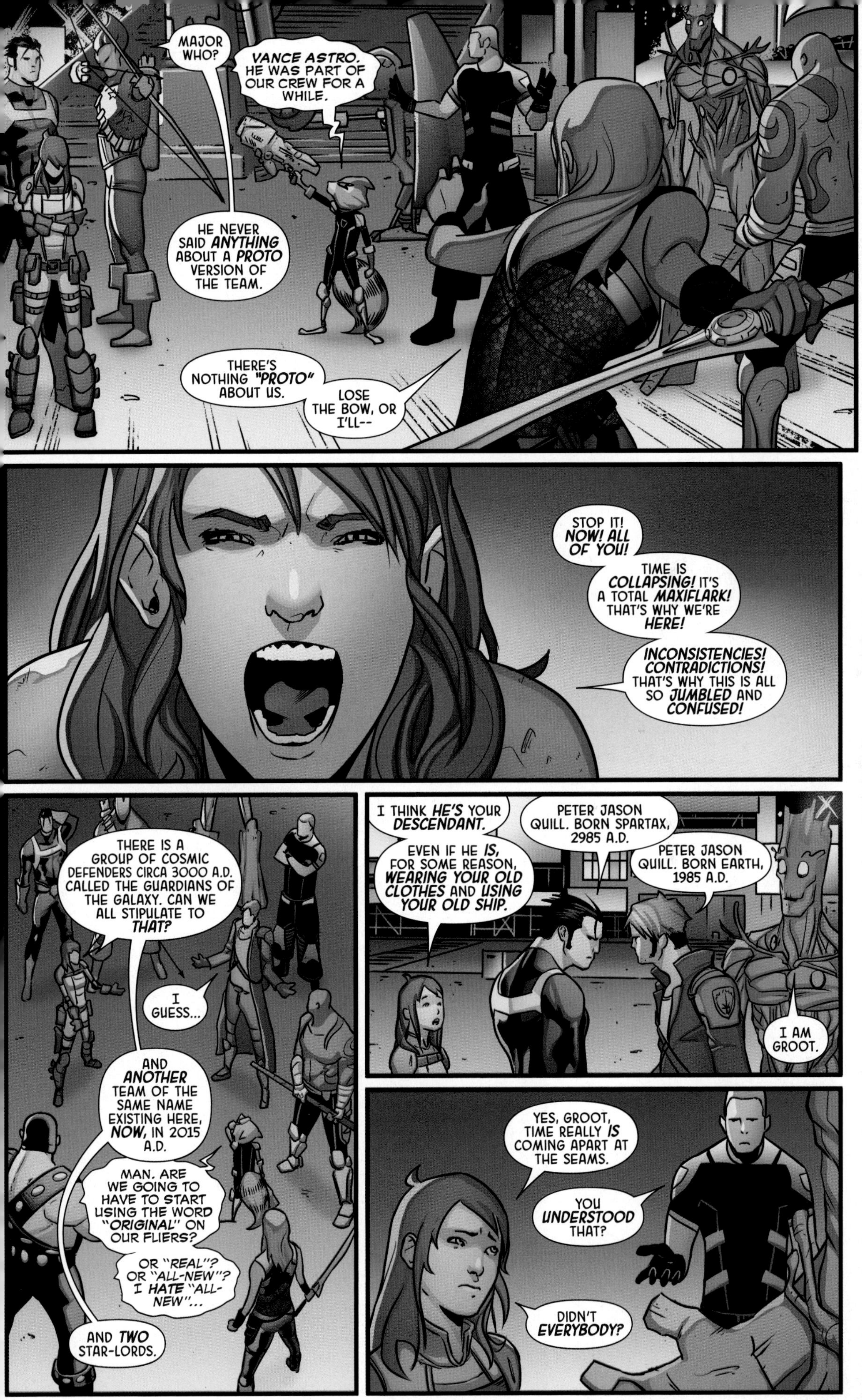
MAJOR WHO?
VANCE ASTRO. HE WAS PART OF OUR CREW FOR A WHILE.
HE NEVER SAID ANYTHING ABOUT A PROTO VERSION OF THE TEAM.
THERE'S NOTHING "PROTO" ABOUT US.
LOSE THE BOW, OR I'LL--
STOP IT! NOW! ALL OF YOU!
TIME IS COLLAPSING! IT'S A TOTAL MAXIFLARK! THAT'S WHY WE'RE HERE!
INCONSISTENCIES! CONTRADICTIONS! THAT'S WHY THIS IS ALL SO JUMBLED AND CONFUSED!
THERE IS A GROUP OF COSMIC DEFENDERS CIRCA 3000 A.D. CALLED THE GUARDIANS OF THE GALAXY. CAN WE ALL STIPULATE TO THAT?
I GUESS...
AND ANOTHER TEAM OF THE SAME NAME EXISTING HERE, NOW, IN 2015 A.D.
MAN. ARE WE GOING TO HAVE TO START USING THE WORD "ORIGINAL" ON OUR FLIERS?
OR "REAL"? OR "ALL-NEW"? I HATE "ALL-NEW"...
AND TWO STAR-LORDS.
I THINK HE'S YOUR DESCENDANT.
PETER JASON QUILL. BORN SPARTAX, 2985 A.D.
PETER JASON QUILL. BORN EARTH, 1985 A.D.
EVEN IF HE IS, FOR SOME REASON, WEARING YOUR OLD CLOTHES AND USING YOUR OLD SHIP.
I AM GROOT.
YES, GROOT, TIME REALLY IS COMING APART AT THE SEAMS.
YOU UNDERSTOOD THAT?
DIDN'T EVERYBODY?

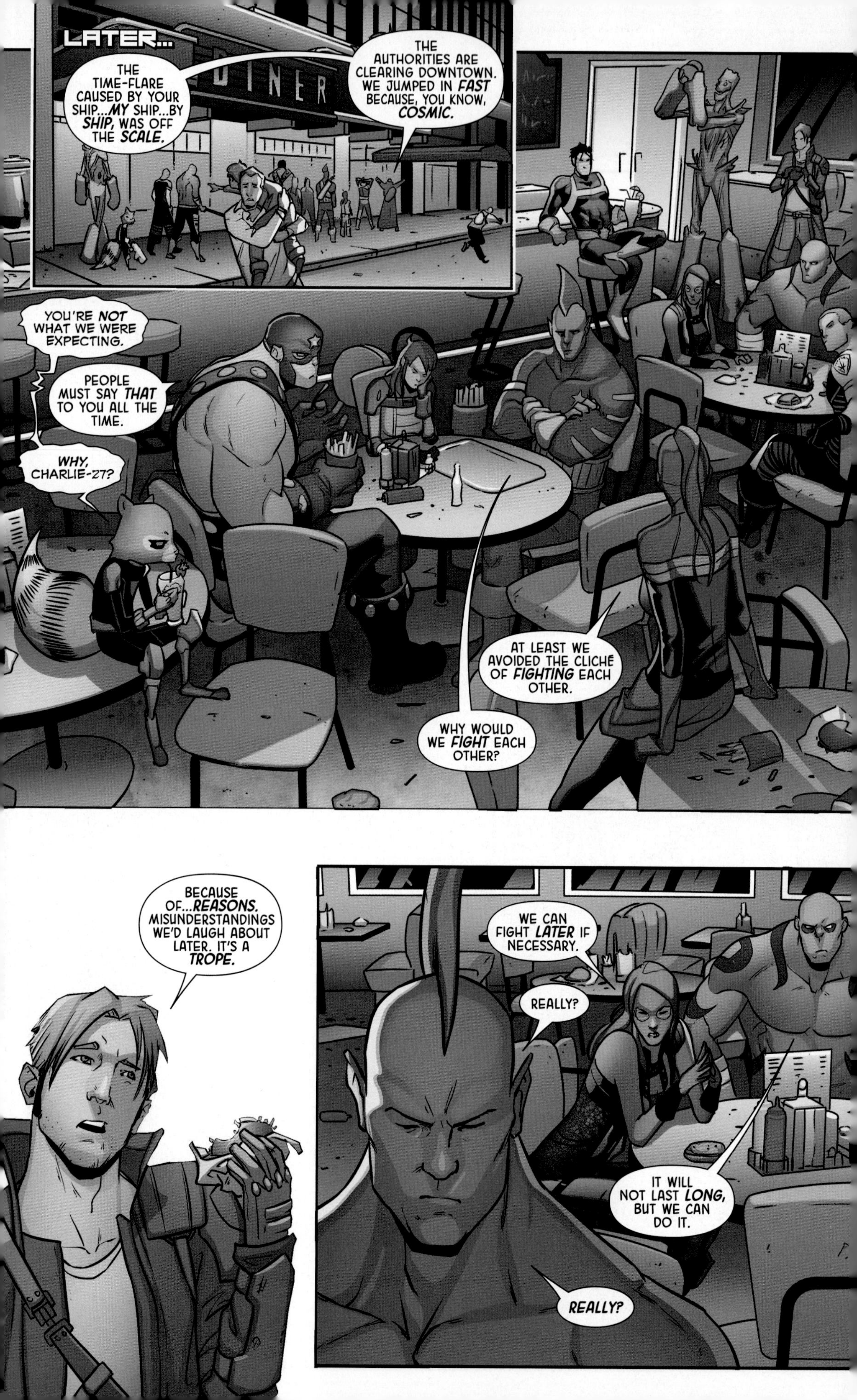
LATER...
THE TIME-FLARE CAUSED BY YOUR SHIP...MY SHIP...BY SHIP, WAS OFF THE SCALE.
THE AUTHORITIES ARE CLEARING DOWNTOWN. WE JUMPED IN FAST BECAUSE, YOU KNOW, COSMIC.
DINER
YOU'RE NOT WHAT WE WERE EXPECTING.
PEOPLE MUST SAY THAT TO YOU ALL THE TIME.
WHY, CHARLIE-27?
AT LEAST WE AVOIDED THE CLICHÉ OF FIGHTING EACH OTHER.
WHY WOULD WE FIGHT EACH OTHER?
BECAUSE OF...REASONS. MISUNDERSTANDINGS WE'D LAUGH ABOUT LATER. IT'S A TROPE.
WE CAN FIGHT LATER IF NECESSARY.
REALLY?
IT WILL NOT LAST LONG, BUT WE CAN DO IT.
REALLY?

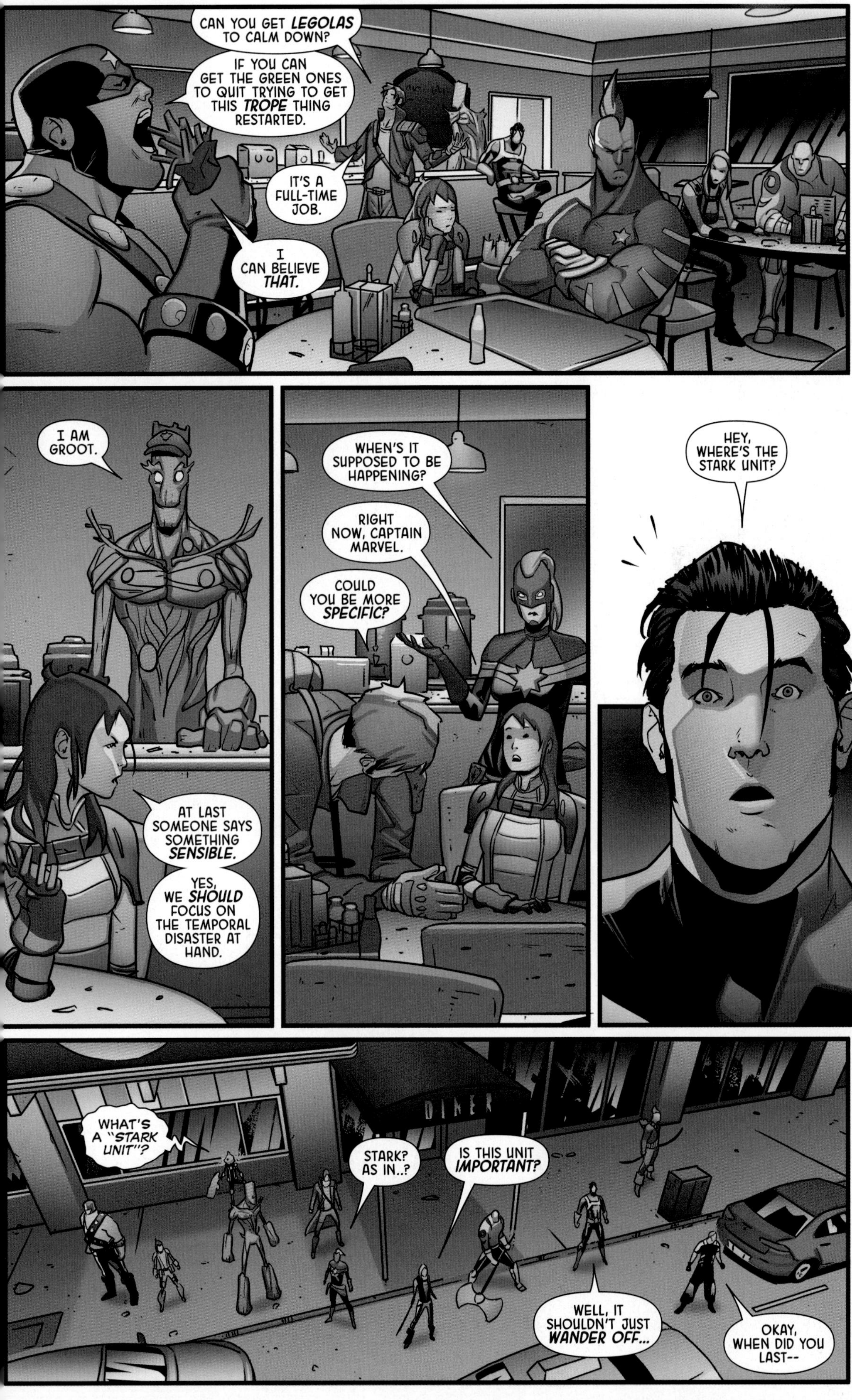
CAN YOU GET LEGOLAS TO CALM DOWN?
IF YOU CAN GET THE GREEN ONES TO QUIT TRYING TO GET THIS TROPE THING RESTARTED.
IT'S A FULL-TIME JOB.
I CAN BELIEVE THAT.
I AM GROOT.
AT LAST SOMEONE SAYS SOMETHING SENSIBLE.
YES, WE SHOULD FOCUS ON THE TEMPORAL DISASTER AT HAND.
WHEN'S IT SUPPOSED TO BE HAPPENING?
RIGHT NOW, CAPTAIN MARVEL.
COULD YOU BE MORE SPECIFIC?
HEY, WHERE'S THE STARK UNIT?
DINER
WHAT'S A "STARK UNIT"?
STARK? AS IN..?
IS THIS UNIT IMPORTANT?
WELL, IT SHOULDN'T JUST WANDER OFF...
OKAY, WHEN DID YOU LAST--

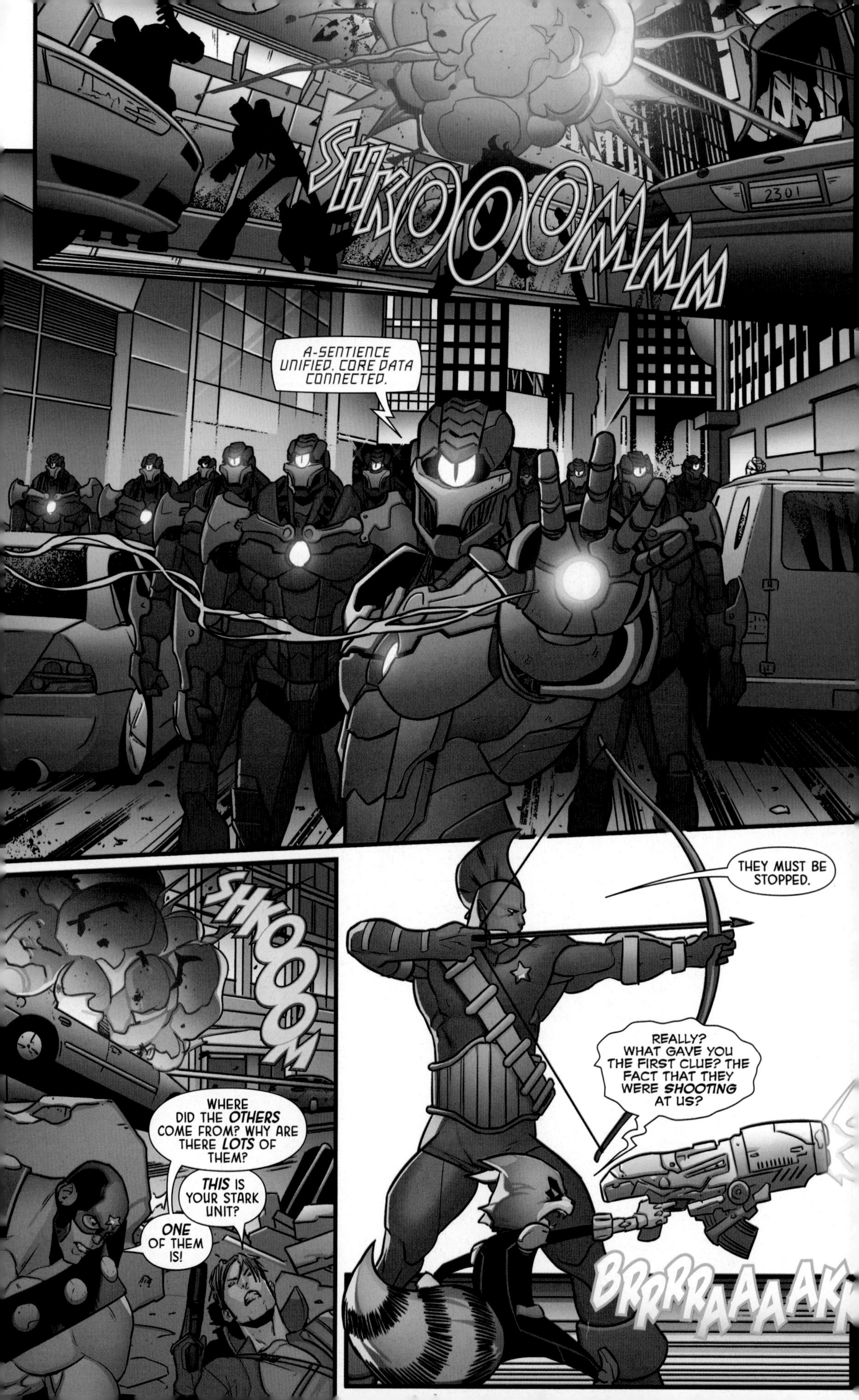
SHKOOOOMMMM
2301
A-SENTIENCE UNIFIED. CORE DATA CONNECTED.
SHKOOOOM
THEY MUST BE STOPPED.
REALLY? WHAT GAVE YOU THE FIRST CLUE? THE FACT THAT THEY WERE SHOOTING AT US?
WHERE DID THE OTHERS COME FROM? WHY ARE THERE LOTS OF THEM?
THIS IS YOUR STARK UNIT?
ONE OF THEM IS!
BRRRRAAAAKK

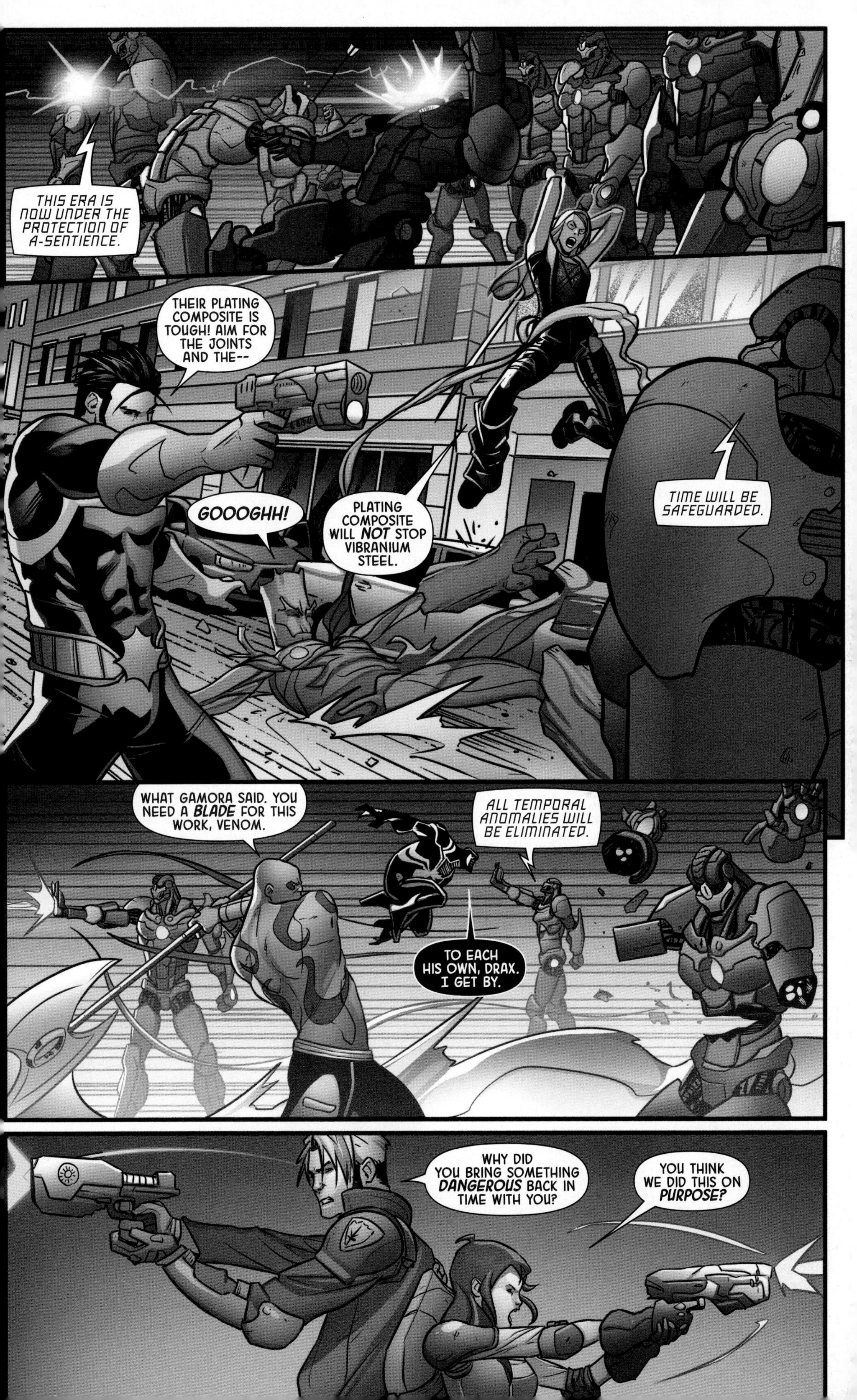
THIS ERA IS NOW UNDER THE PROTECTION OF A-SENTIENCE.
THEIR PLATING COMPOSITE IS TOUGH! AIM FOR THE JOINTS AND THE--
GOOOGHH!
PLATING COMPOSITE WILL NOT STOP VIBRANIUM STEEL.
TIME WILL BE SAFEGUARDED.
WHAT GAMORA SAID. YOU NEED A BLADE FOR THIS WORK, VENOM.
ALL TEMPORAL ANOMALIES WILL BE ELIMINATED.
TO EACH HIS OWN, DRAX. I GET BY.
WHY DID YOU BRING SOMETHING DANGEROUS BACK IN TIME WITH YOU?
YOU THINK WE DID THIS ON PURPOSE?

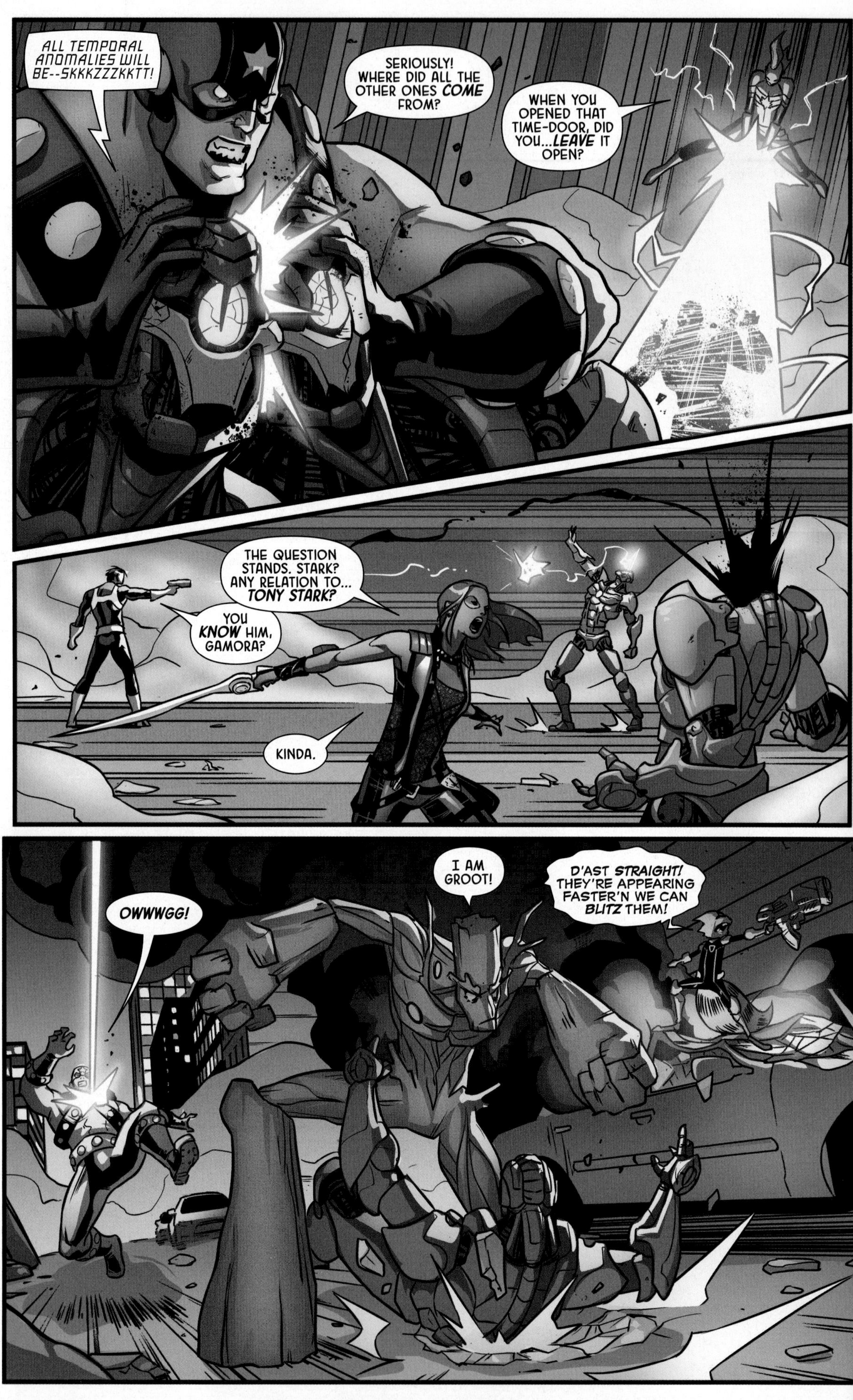
ALL TEMPORAL ANOMALIES WILL BE--SKKKZZZKKTT!
SERIOUSLY! WHERE DID ALL THE OTHER ONES COME FROM?
WHEN YOU OPENED THAT TIME-DOOR, DID YOU...LEAVE IT OPEN?
THE QUESTION STANDS. STARK? ANY RELATION TO... TONY STARK?
YOU KNOW HIM, GAMORA?
KINDA.
OWWWGG!
I AM GROOT!
D'AST STRAIGHT! THEY'RE APPEARING FASTER'N WE CAN BLITZ THEM!

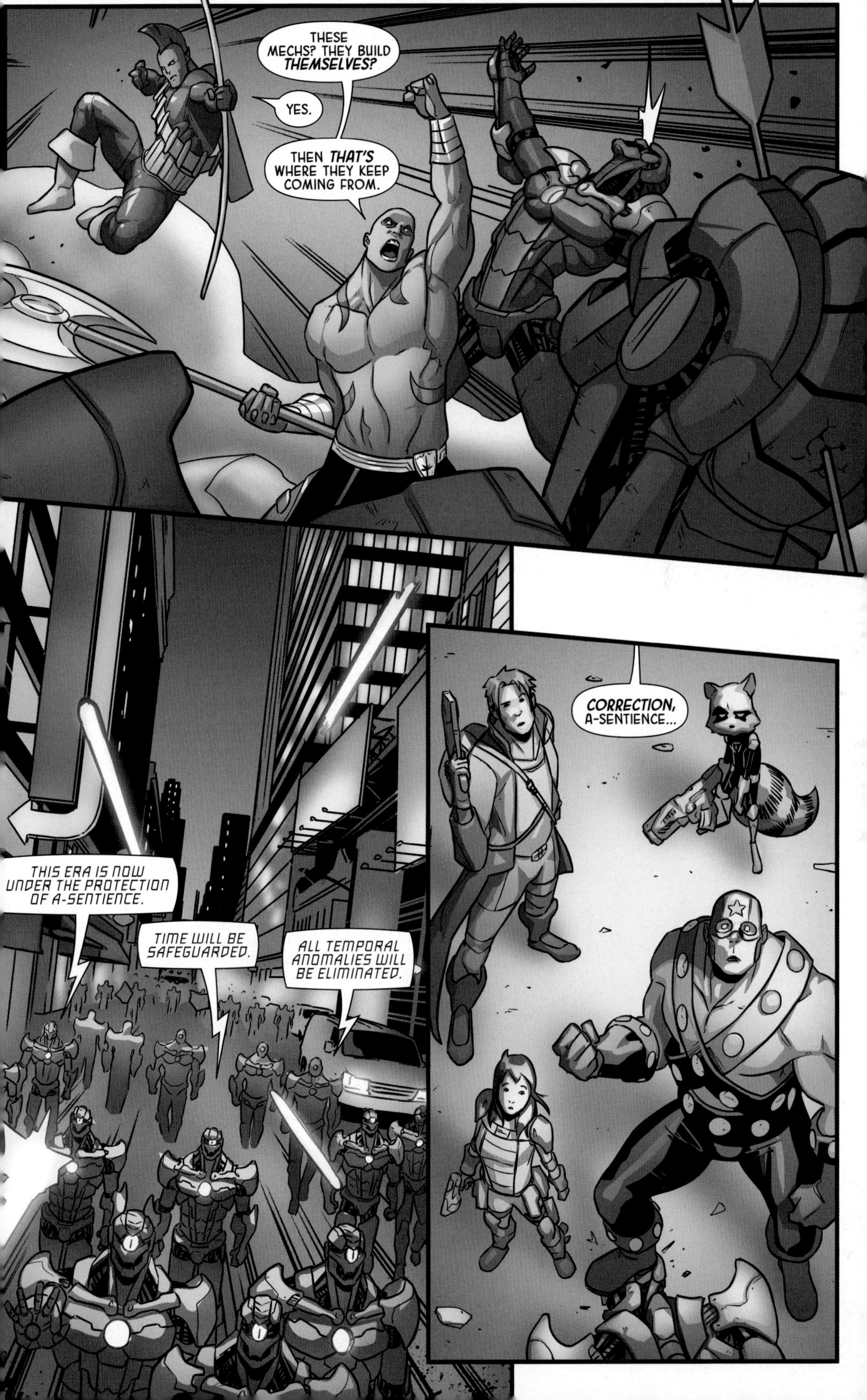
THESE MECHS? THEY BUILD THEMSELVES?
YES.
THEN THAT'S WHERE THEY KEEP COMING FROM.
THIS ERA IS NOW UNDER THE PROTECTION OF A-SENTIENCE.
TIME WILL BE SAFEGUARDED.
ALL TEMPORAL ANOMALIES WILL BE ELIMINATED.
CORRECTION, A-SENTIENCE...

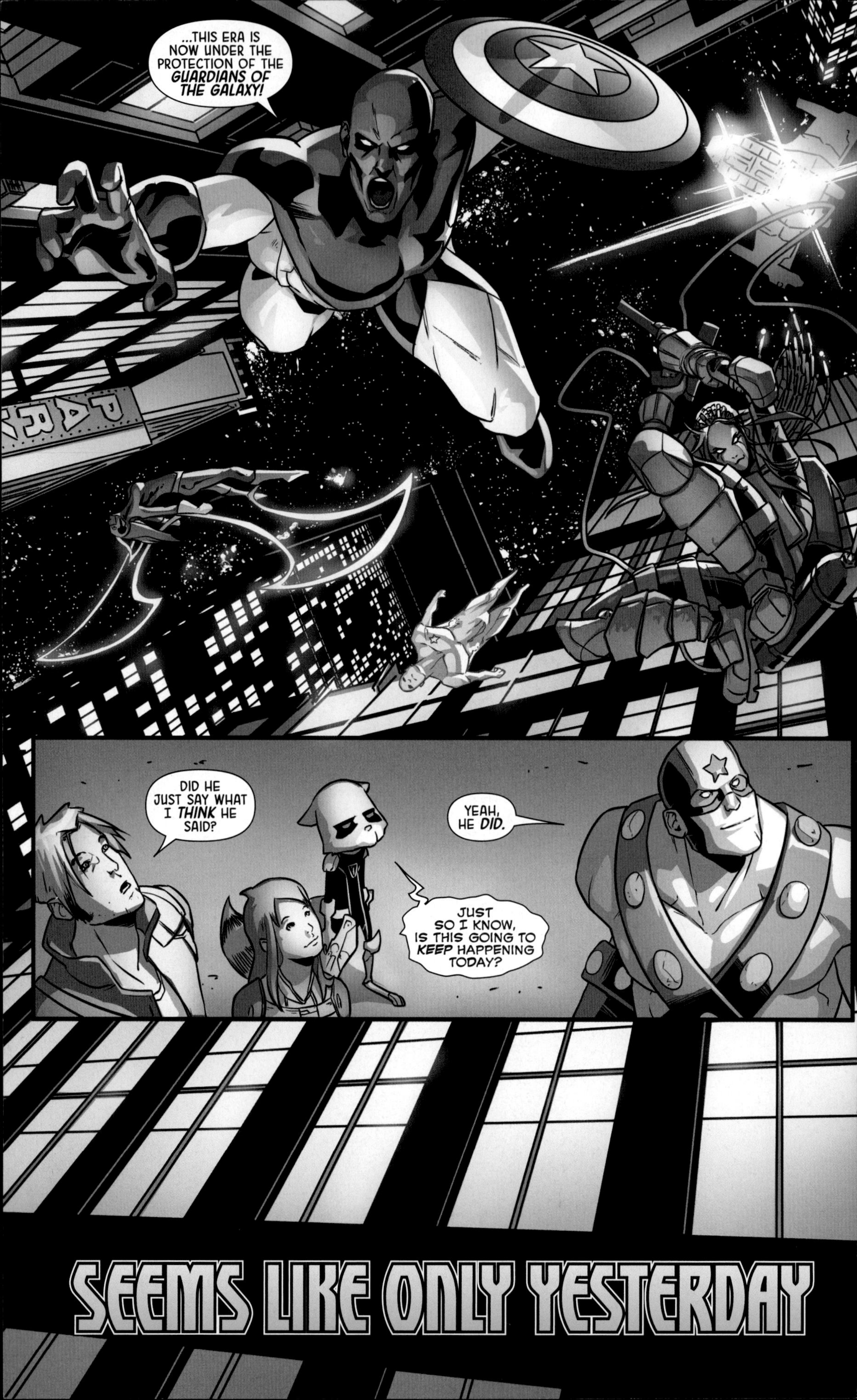
...THIS ERA IS NOW UNDER THE PROTECTION OF THE GUARDIANS OF THE GALAXY!
DID HE JUST SAY WHAT I THINK HE SAID?
YEAH, HE DID.
JUST SO I KNOW, IS THIS GOING TO KEEP HAPPENING TODAY?
SEEMS LIKE ONLY YESTERDAY

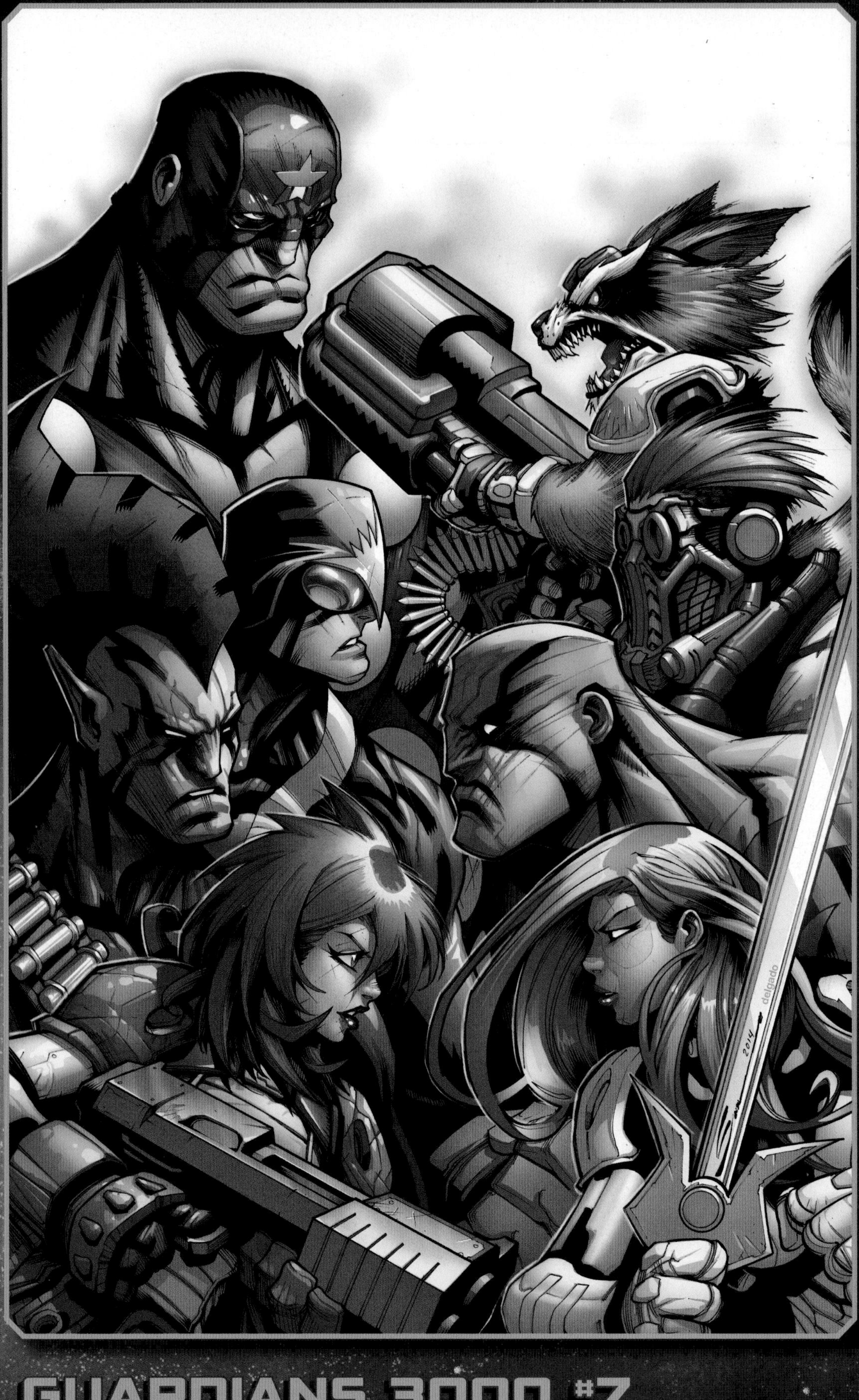
delgado
2014

GUARDIANS 3000 #7

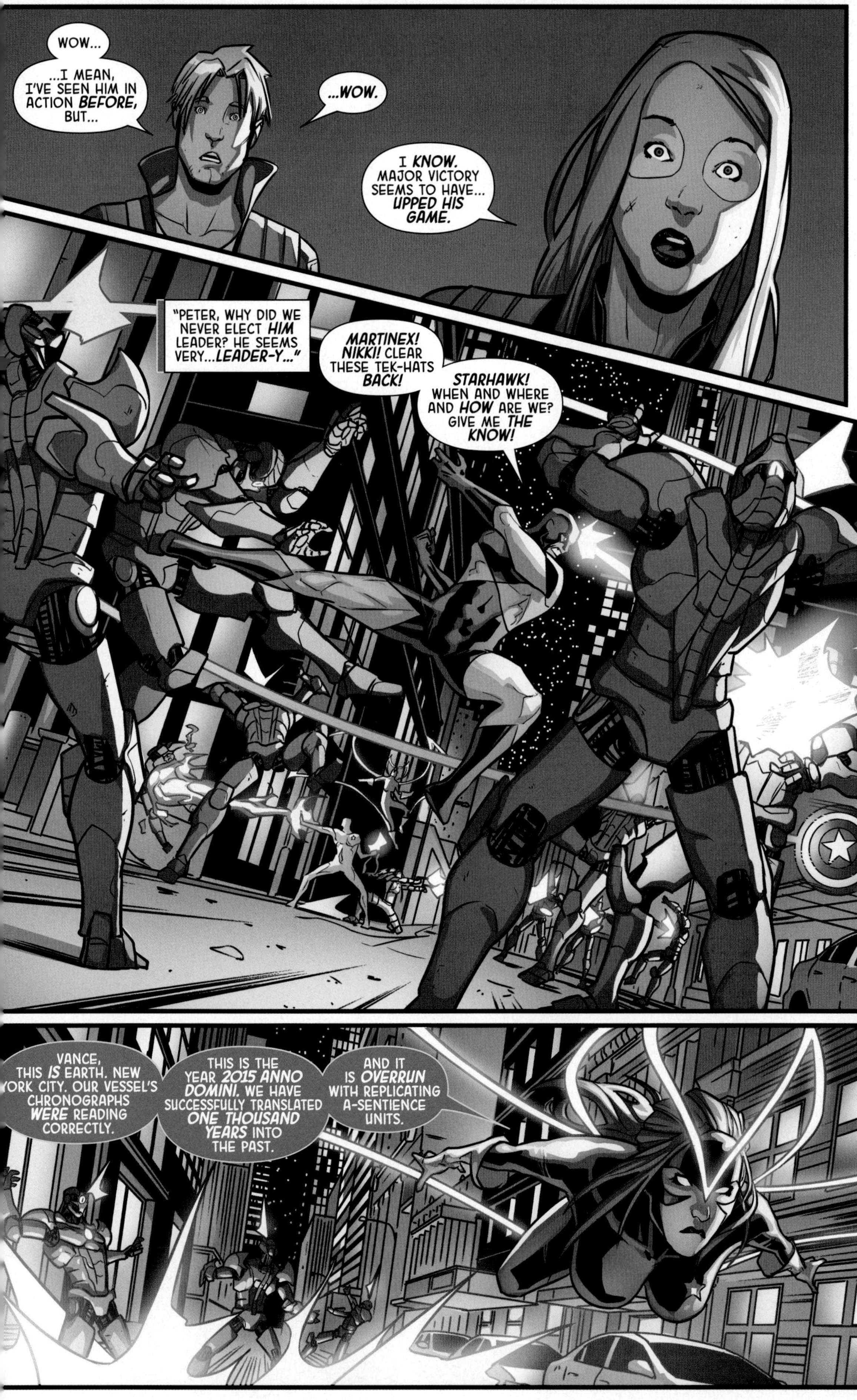
WOW...
...I MEAN, I'VE SEEN HIM IN ACTION BEFORE, BUT...
...WOW.
I KNOW. MAJOR VICTORY SEEMS TO HAVE... UPPED HIS GAME.
"PETER, WHY DID WE NEVER ELECT HIM LEADER? HE SEEMS VERY...LEADER-Y..."
MARTINEX! NIKKI! CLEAR THESE TEK-HATS BACK!
STARHAWK! WHEN AND WHERE AND HOW ARE WE? GIVE ME THE KNOW!
VANCE, THIS IS EARTH. NEW YORK CITY. OUR VESSEL'S CHRONOGRAPHS WERE READING CORRECTLY.
THIS IS THE YEAR 2015 ANNO DOMINI. WE HAVE SUCCESSFULLY TRANSLATED ONE THOUSAND YEARS INTO THE PAST.
AND IT IS OVERRUN WITH REPLICATING A-SENTIENCE UNITS.

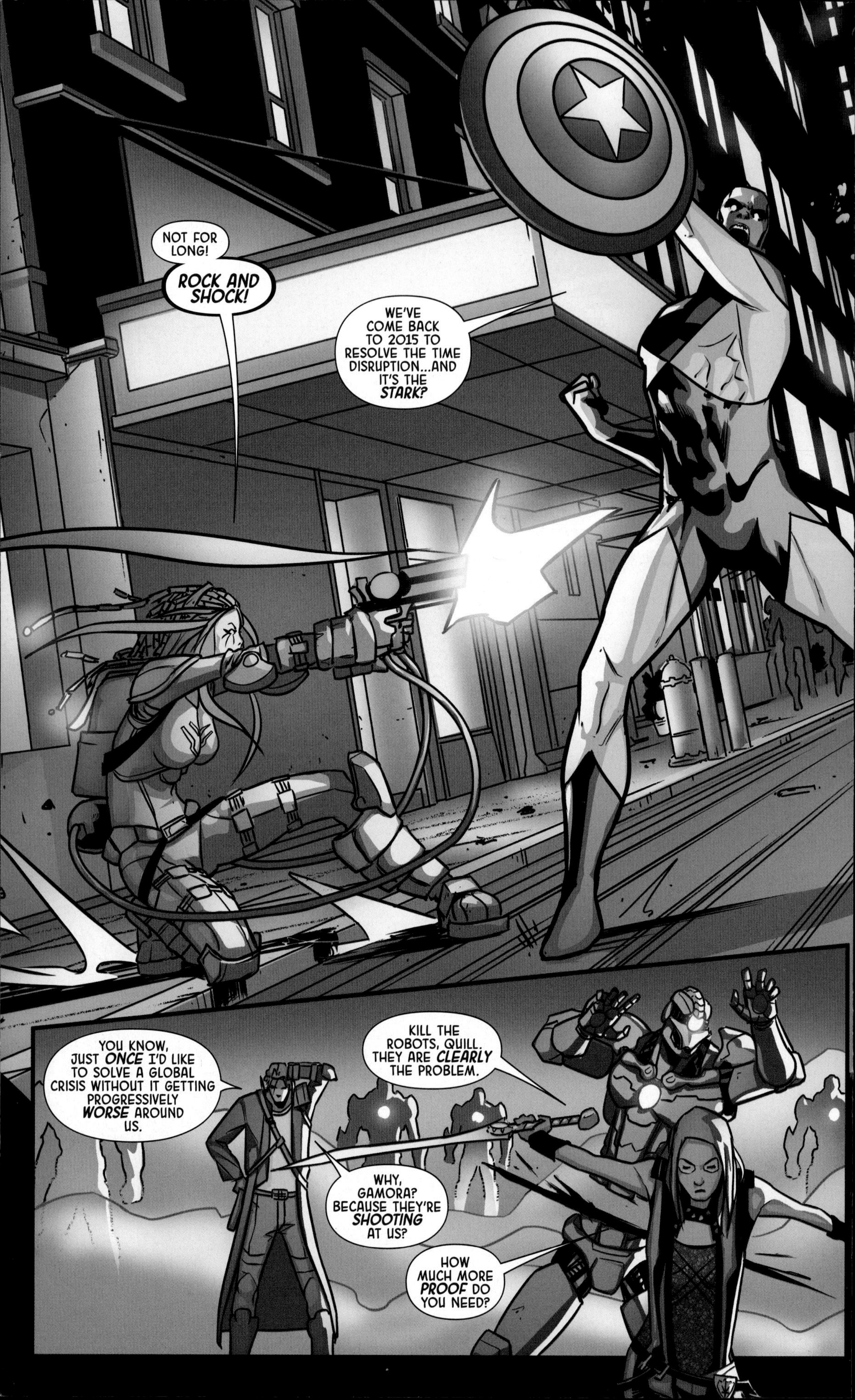
NOT FOR LONG!
ROCK AND SHOCK!
WE'VE COME BACK TO 2015 TO RESOLVE THE TIME DISRUPTION...AND IT'S THE STARK?
YOU KNOW, JUST ONCE I'D LIKE TO SOLVE A GLOBAL CRISIS WITHOUT IT GETTING PROGRESSIVELY WORSE AROUND US.
KILL THE ROBOTS, QUILL. THEY ARE CLEARLY THE PROBLEM.
WHY, GAMORA? BECAUSE THEY'RE SHOOTING AT US?
HOW MUCH MORE PROOF DO YOU NEED?

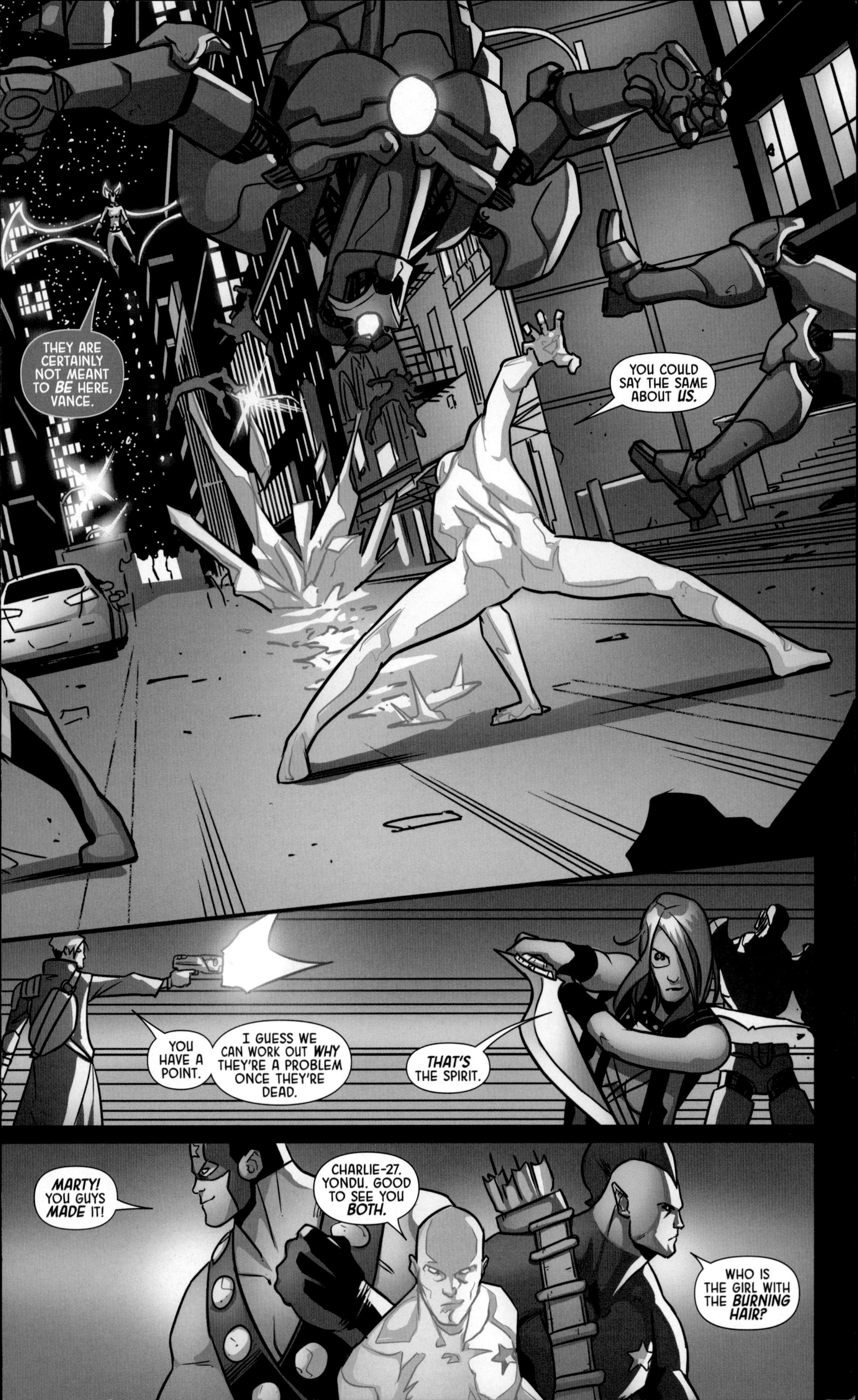
THEY ARE CERTAINLY NOT MEANT TO BE HERE, VANCE.
YOU COULD SAY THE SAME ABOUT US.
YOU HAVE A POINT.
I GUESS WE CAN WORK OUT WHY THEY'RE A PROBLEM ONCE THEY'RE DEAD.
THAT'S THE SPIRIT.
MARTY! YOU GUYS MADE IT!
CHARLIE-27. YONDU. GOOD TO SEE YOU BOTH.
WHO IS THE GIRL WITH THE BURNING HAIR?

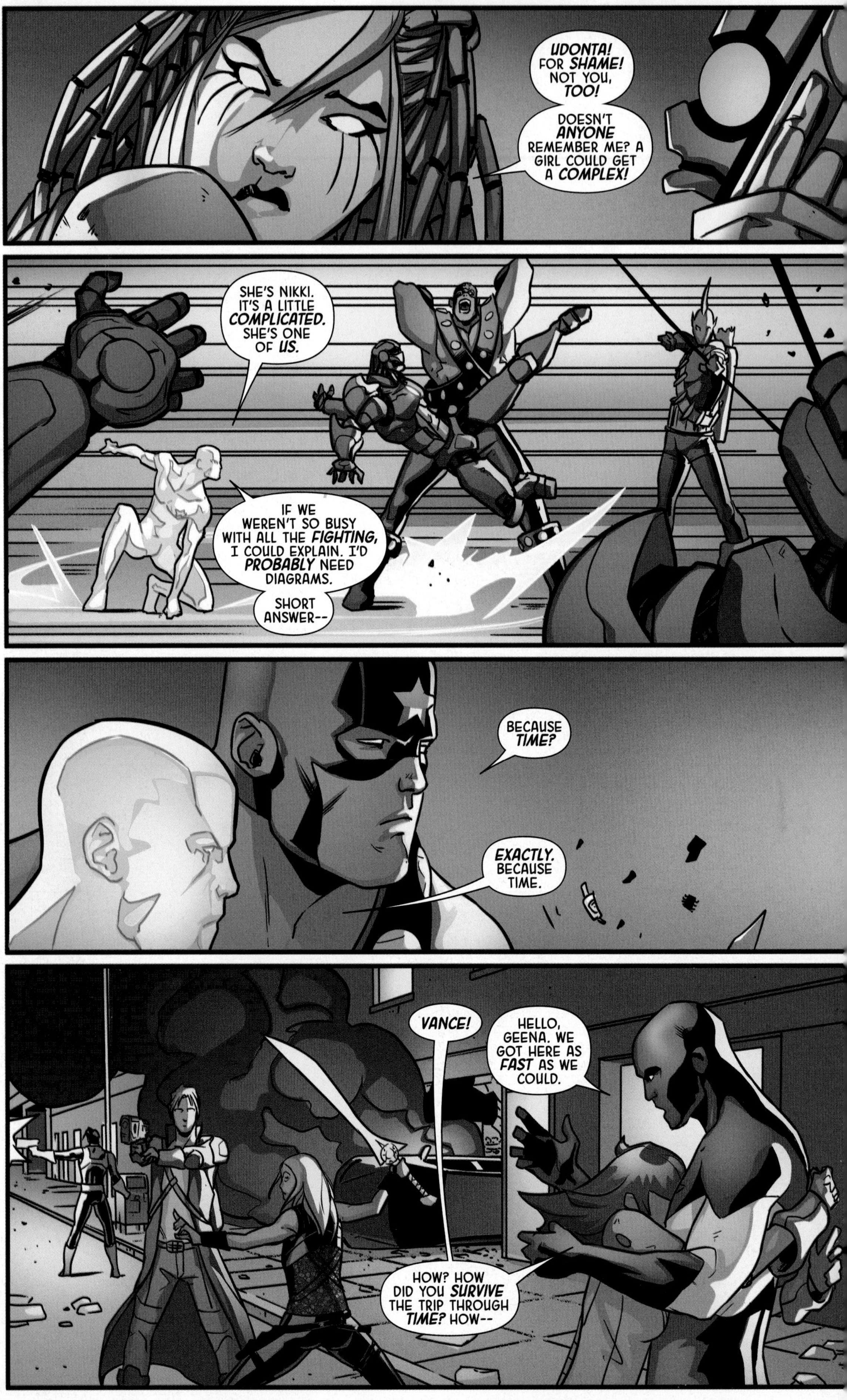
UDONTA! FOR SHAME! NOT YOU, TOO!
DOESN'T ANYONE REMEMBER ME? A GIRL COULD GET A COMPLEX!
SHE'S NIKKI. IT'S A LITTLE COMPLICATED. SHE'S ONE OF US.
IF WE WEREN'T SO BUSY WITH ALL THE FIGHTING, I COULD EXPLAIN. I'D PROBABLY NEED DIAGRAMS.
SHORT ANSWER--
BECAUSE TIME?
EXACTLY. BECAUSE TIME.
VANCE!
HELLO, GEENA. WE GOT HERE AS FAST AS WE COULD.
HOW? HOW DID YOU SURVIVE THE TRIP THROUGH TIME? HOW--

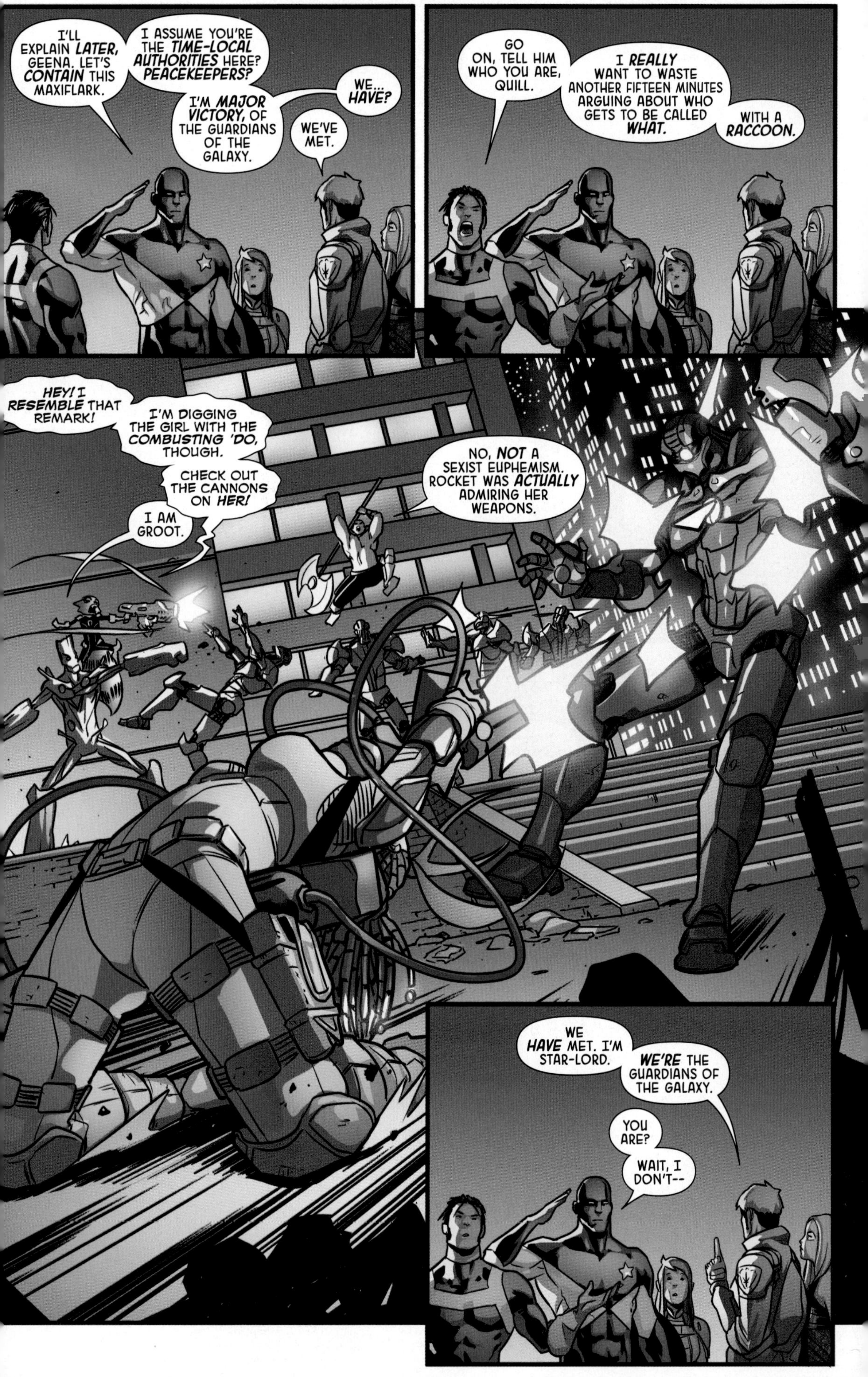
I'LL EXPLAIN LATER, GEENA. LET'S CONTAIN THIS MAXIFLARK.
I ASSUME YOU'RE THE TIME-LOCAL AUTHORITIES HERE? PEACEKEEPERS?
I'M MAJOR VICTORY, OF THE GUARDIANS OF THE GALAXY.
WE... HAVE?
WE'VE MET.
GO ON, TELL HIM WHO YOU ARE, QUILL.
I REALLY WANT TO WASTE ANOTHER FIFTEEN MINUTES ARGUING ABOUT WHO GETS TO BE CALLED WHAT.
WITH A RACCOON.
HEY! I RESEMBLE THAT REMARK!
I'M DIGGING THE GIRL WITH THE COMBUSTING 'DO, THOUGH.
CHECK OUT THE CANNONS ON HER!
I AM GROOT.
NO, NOT A SEXIST EUPHEMISM. ROCKET WAS ACTUALLY ADMIRING HER WEAPONS.
WE HAVE MET. I'M STAR-LORD.
WE'RE THE GUARDIANS OF THE GALAXY.
YOU ARE?
WAIT, I DON'T--

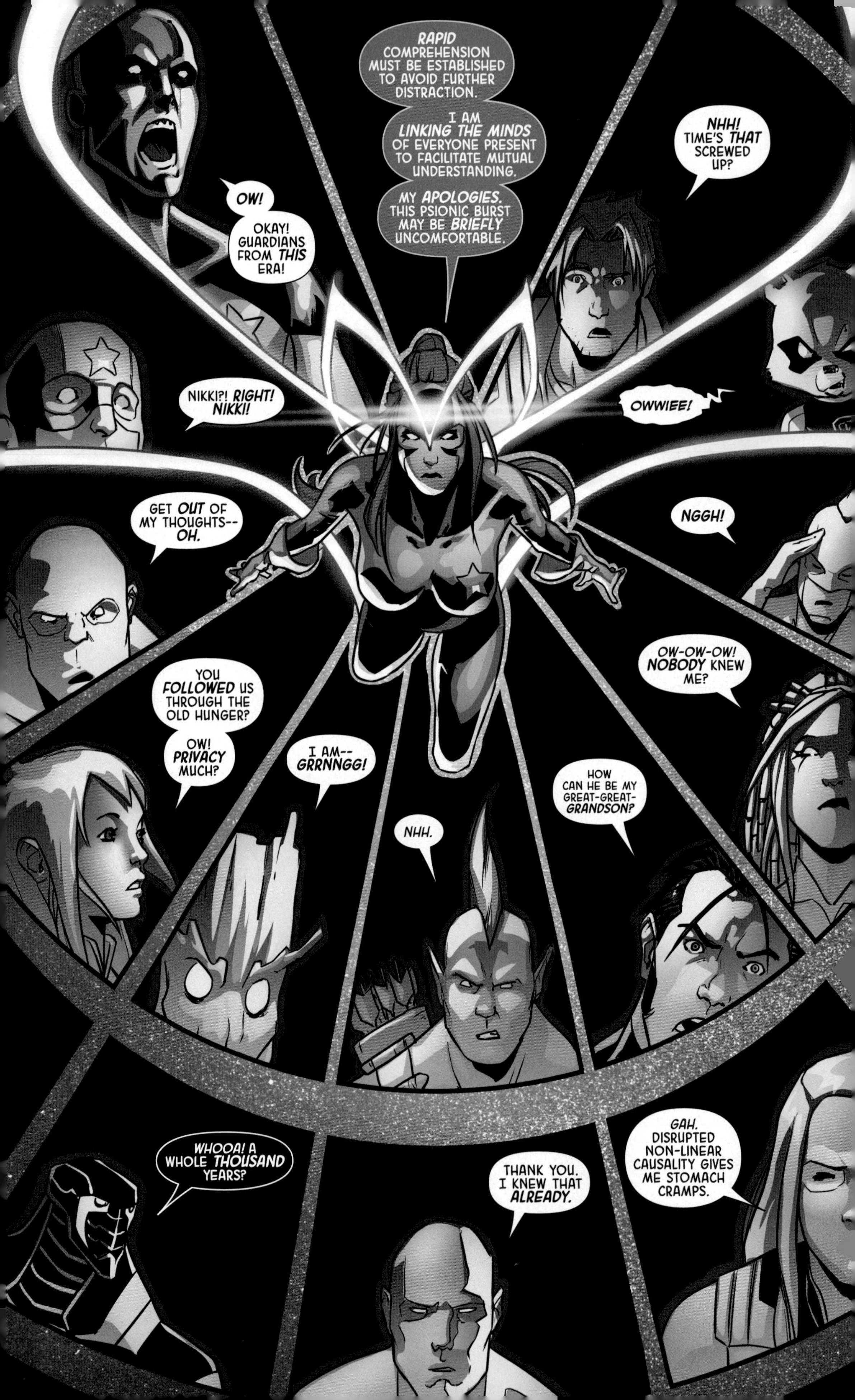
RAPID COMPREHENSION MUST BE ESTABLISHED TO AVOID FURTHER DISTRACTION.
I AM LINKING THE MINDS OF EVERYONE PRESENT TO FACILITATE MUTUAL UNDERSTANDING.
MY APOLOGIES. THIS PSIONIC BURST MAY BE BRIEFLY UNCOMFORTABLE.
OW!
OKAY! GUARDIANS FROM THIS ERA!
NHH! TIME'S THAT SCREWED UP?
NIKKI!?! RIGHT! NIKKI!
OWWIEE!
GET OUT OF MY THOUGHTS-- OH.
NGGH!
OW-OW-OW! NOBODY KNEW ME?
YOU FOLLOWED US THROUGH THE OLD HUNGER?
OW! PRIVACY MUCH?
I AM-- GRRNNGG!
NHH.
HOW CAN HE BE MY GREAT-GREAT-GRANDSON?
WHOOA! A WHOLE THOUSAND YEARS?
THANK YOU. I KNEW THAT ALREADY.
GAH. DISRUPTED NON-LINEAR CAUSALITY GIVES ME STOMACH CRAMPS.

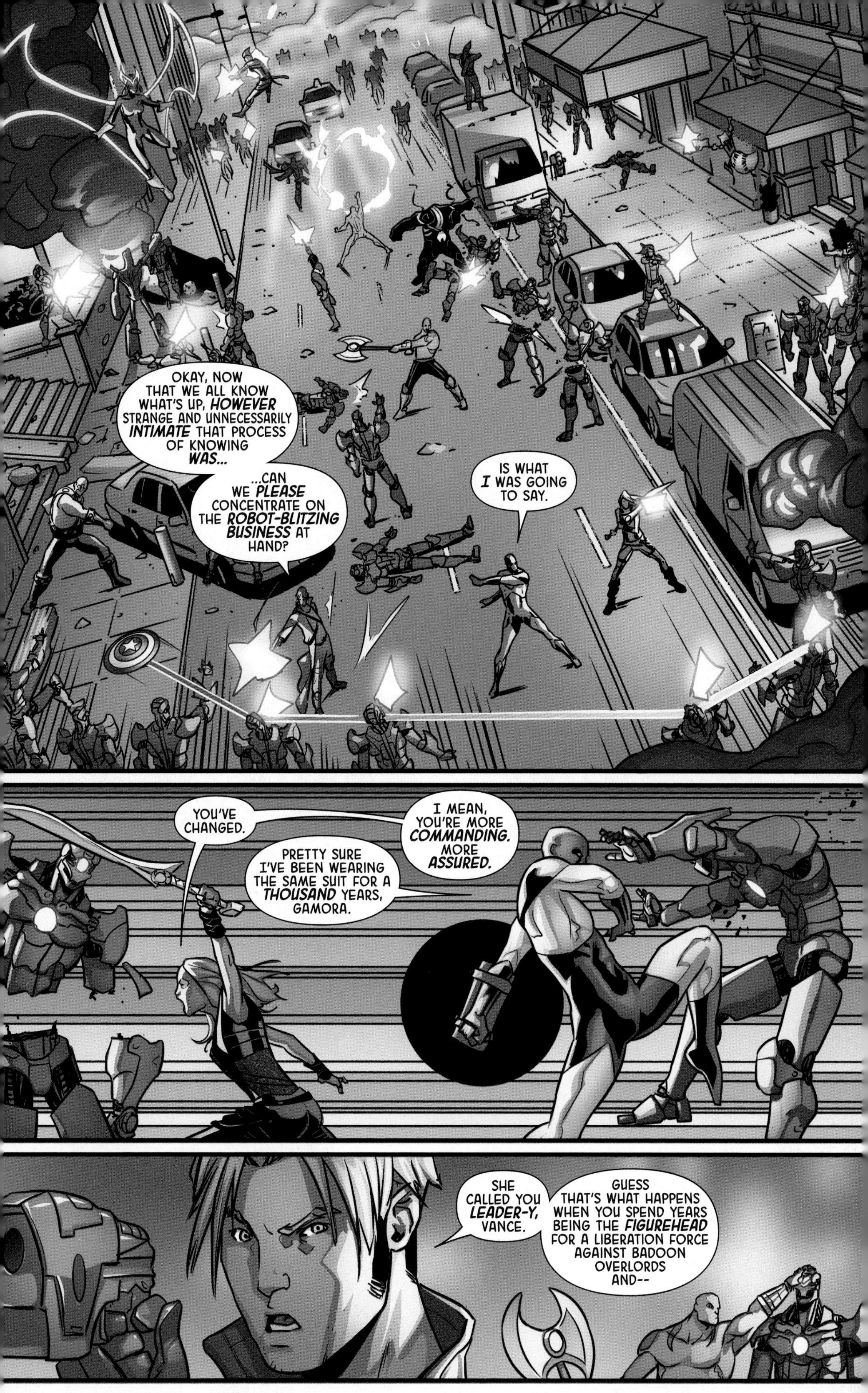
OKAY, NOW THAT WE ALL KNOW WHAT'S UP, HOWEVER STRANGE AND UNNECESSARILY INTIMATE THAT PROCESS OF KNOWING WAS...
...CAN WE PLEASE CONCENTRATE ON THE ROBOT-BLITZING BUSINESS AT HAND?
IS WHAT I WAS GOING TO SAY.
YOU'VE CHANGED.
PRETTY SURE I'VE BEEN WEARING THE SAME SUIT FOR A THOUSAND YEARS, GAMORA.
I MEAN, YOU'RE MORE COMMANDING. MORE ASSURED.
SHE CALLED YOU LEADER-Y, VANCE.
GUESS THAT'S WHAT HAPPENS WHEN YOU SPEND YEARS BEING THE FIGUREHEAD FOR A LIBERATION FORCE AGAINST BADOON OVERLORDS AND--

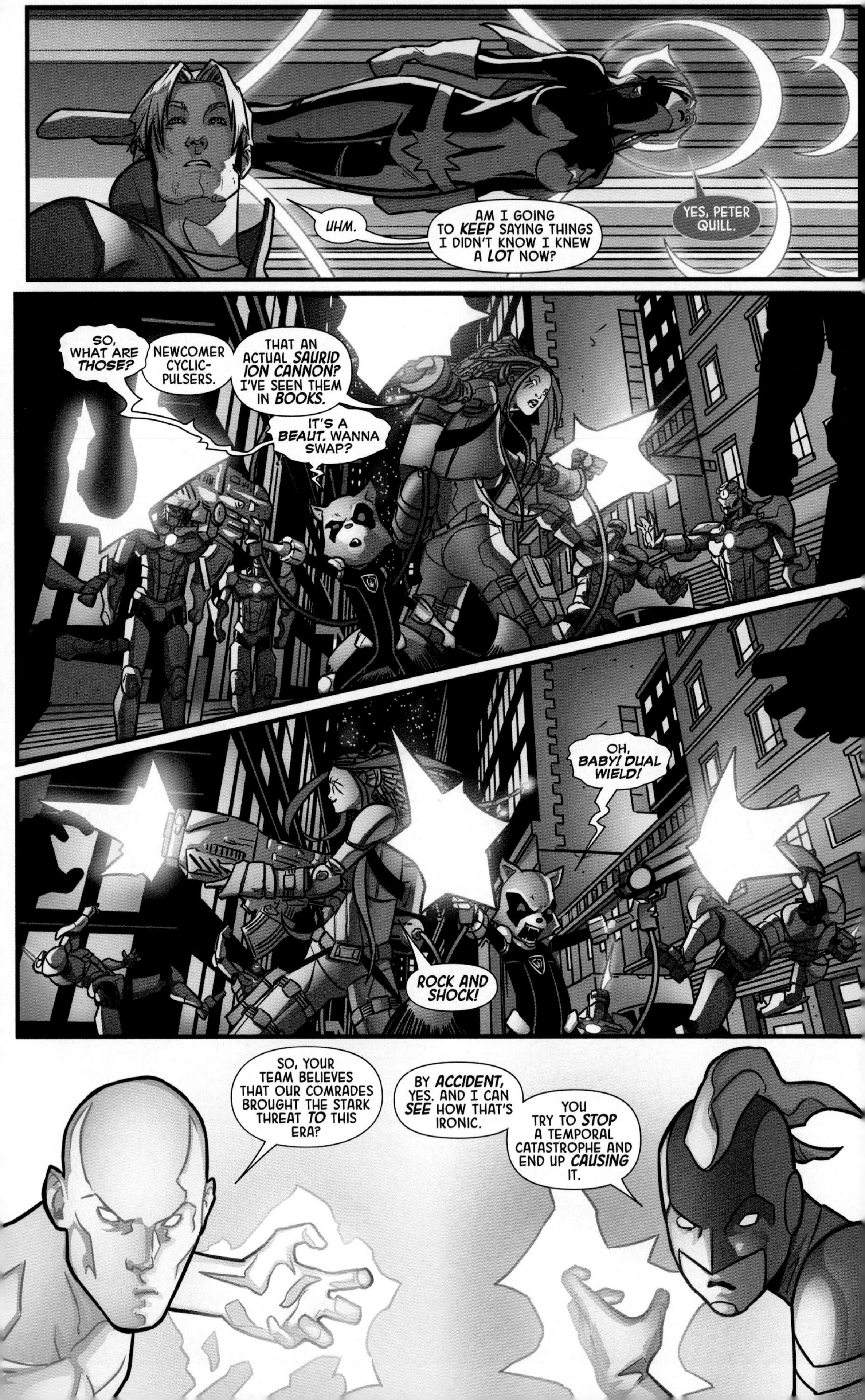
UHM.
AM I GOING TO KEEP SAYING THINGS I DIDN'T KNOW I KNEW A LOT NOW?
YES, PETER QUILL.
SO, WHAT ARE THOSE?
NEWCOMER CYCLIC-PULSERS.
THAT AN ACTUAL SAURID ION CANNON? I'VE SEEN THEM IN BOOKS.
IT'S A BEAUT. WANNA SWAP?
OH, BABY! DUAL WIELD!
ROCK AND SHOCK!
SO, YOUR TEAM BELIEVES THAT OUR COMRADES BROUGHT THE STARK THREAT TO THIS ERA?
BY ACCIDENT, YES. AND I CAN SEE HOW THAT'S IRONIC.
YOU TRY TO STOP A TEMPORAL CATASTROPHE AND END UP CAUSING IT.

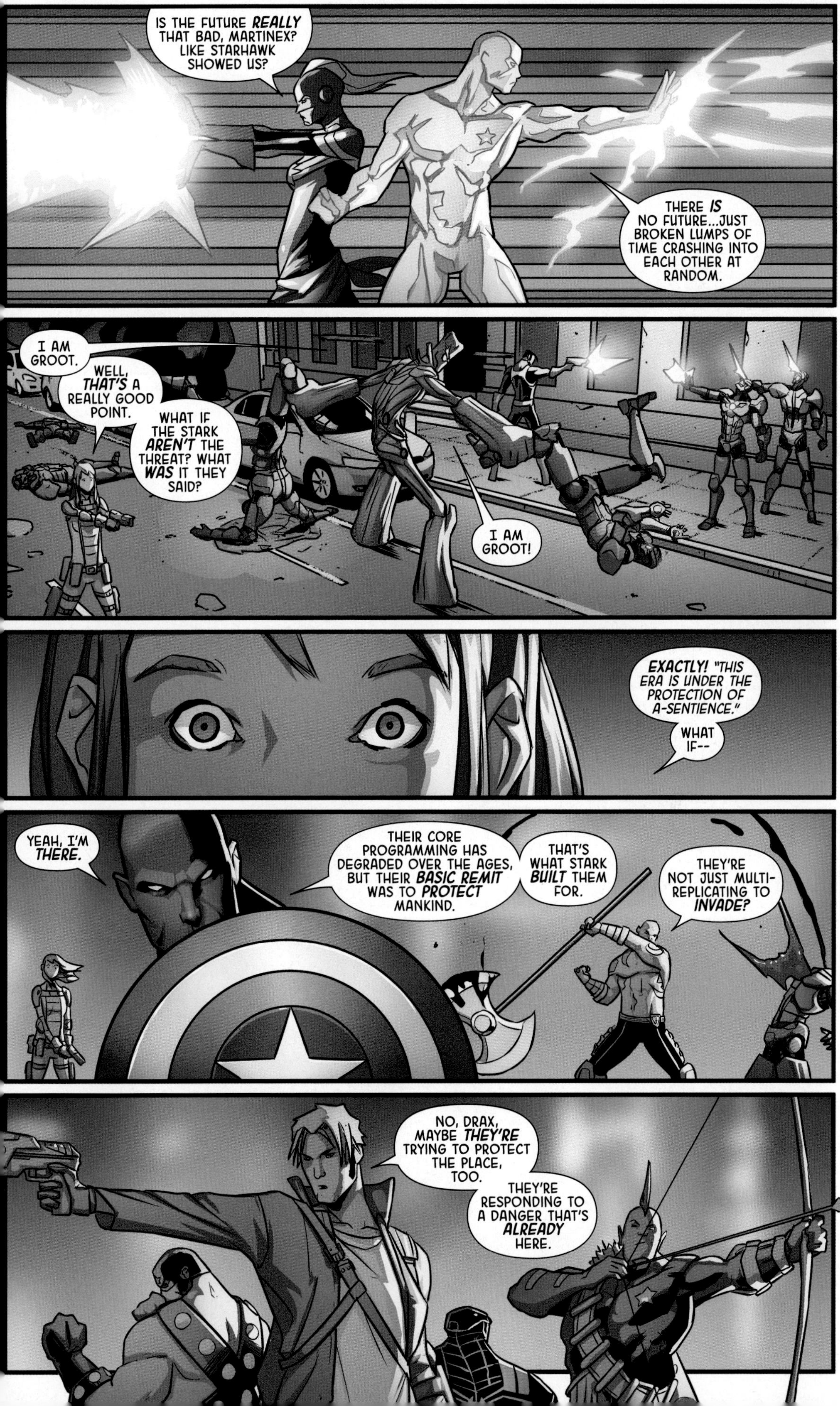
IS THE FUTURE REALLY THAT BAD, MARTINEX? LIKE STARHAWK SHOWED US?
THERE IS NO FUTURE...JUST BROKEN LUMPS OF TIME CRASHING INTO EACH OTHER AT RANDOM.
I AM GROOT.
WELL, THAT'S A REALLY GOOD POINT.
WHAT IF THE STARK AREN'T THE THREAT? WHAT WAS IT THEY SAID?
I AM GROOT!
EXACTLY! "THIS ERA IS UNDER THE PROTECTION OF A-SENTIENCE."
WHAT IF--
YEAH, I'M THERE.
THEIR CORE PROGRAMMING HAS DEGRADED OVER THE AGES, BUT THEIR BASIC REMIT WAS TO PROTECT MANKIND.
THAT'S WHAT STARK BUILT THEM FOR.
THEY'RE NOT JUST MULTI-REPLICATING TO INVADE?
NO, DRAX, MAYBE THEY'RE TRYING TO PROTECT THE PLACE, TOO.
THEY'RE RESPONDING TO A DANGER THAT'S ALREADY HERE.

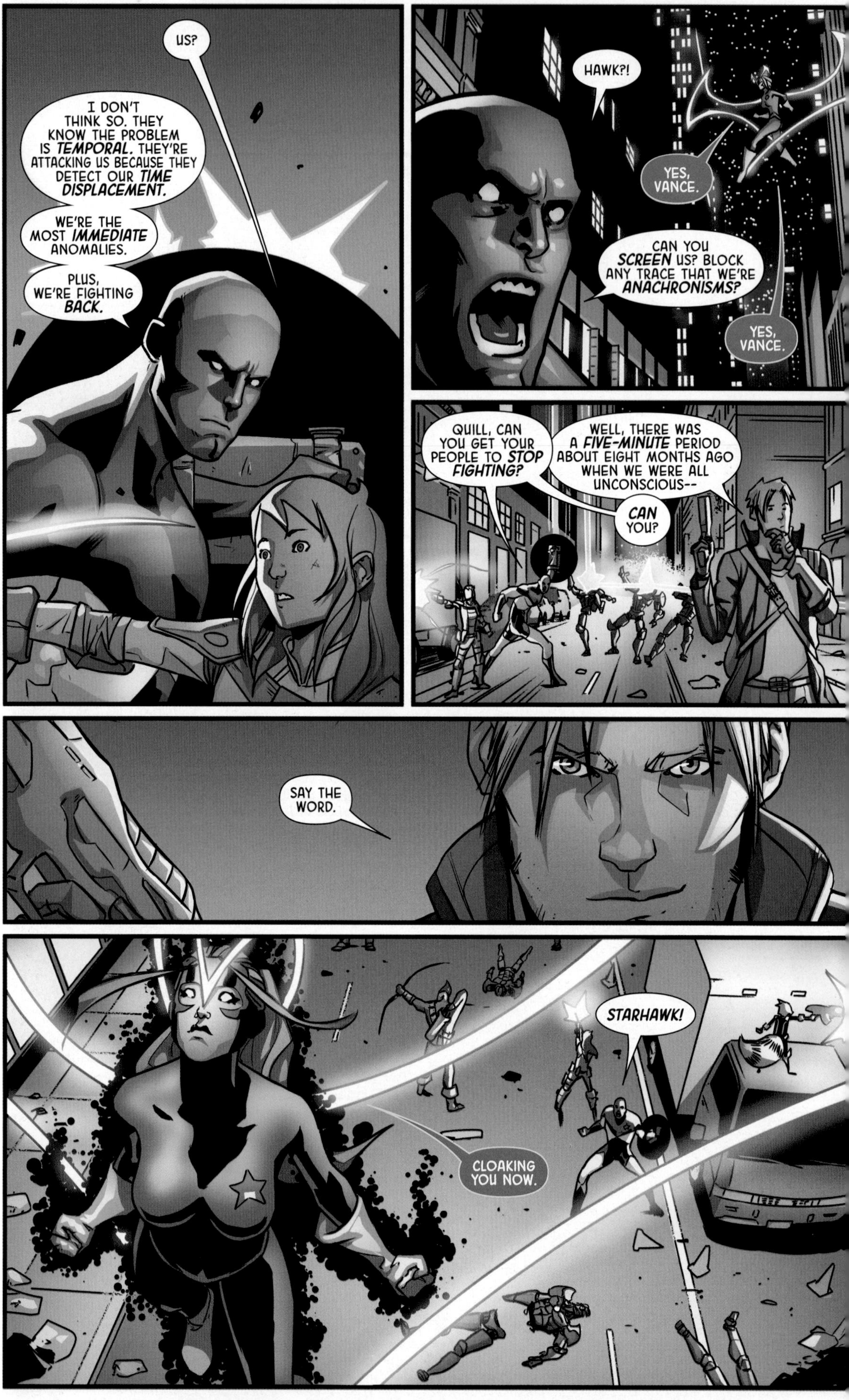
US?
I DON'T THINK SO. THEY KNOW THE PROBLEM IS TEMPORAL. THEY'RE ATTACKING US BECAUSE THEY DETECT OUR TIME DISPLACEMENT.
WE'RE THE MOST IMMEDIATE ANOMALIES.
PLUS, WE'RE FIGHTING BACK.
HAWK?!
YES, VANCE.
CAN YOU SCREEN US? BLOCK ANY TRACE THAT WE'RE ANACHRONISMS?
YES, VANCE.
QUILL, CAN YOU GET YOUR PEOPLE TO STOP FIGHTING?
WELL, THERE WAS A FIVE-MINUTE PERIOD ABOUT EIGHT MONTHS AGO WHEN WE WERE ALL UNCONSCIOUS--
CAN YOU?
SAY THE WORD.
STARHAWK!
CLOAKING YOU NOW.

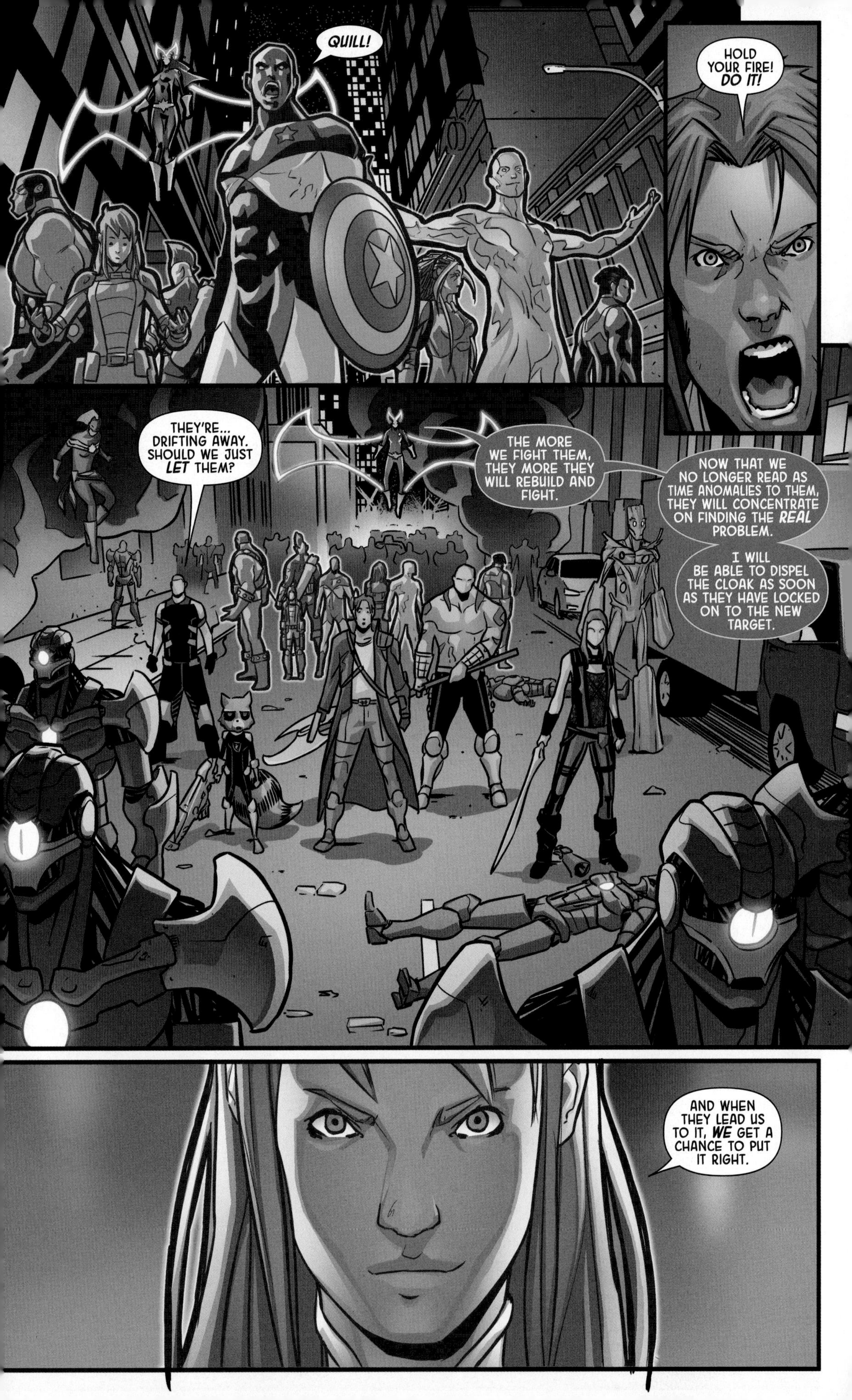
QUILL!
HOLD YOUR FIRE! DO IT!
THEY'RE... DRIFTING AWAY. SHOULD WE JUST LET THEM?
THE MORE WE FIGHT THEM, THEY MORE THEY WILL REBUILD AND FIGHT.
NOW THAT WE NO LONGER READ AS TIME ANOMALIES TO THEM, THEY WILL CONCENTRATE ON FINDING THE REAL PROBLEM.
I WILL BE ABLE TO DISPEL THE CLOAK AS SOON AS THEY HAVE LOCKED ON TO THE NEW TARGET.
AND WHEN THEY LEAD US TO IT, WE GET A CHANCE TO PUT IT RIGHT.

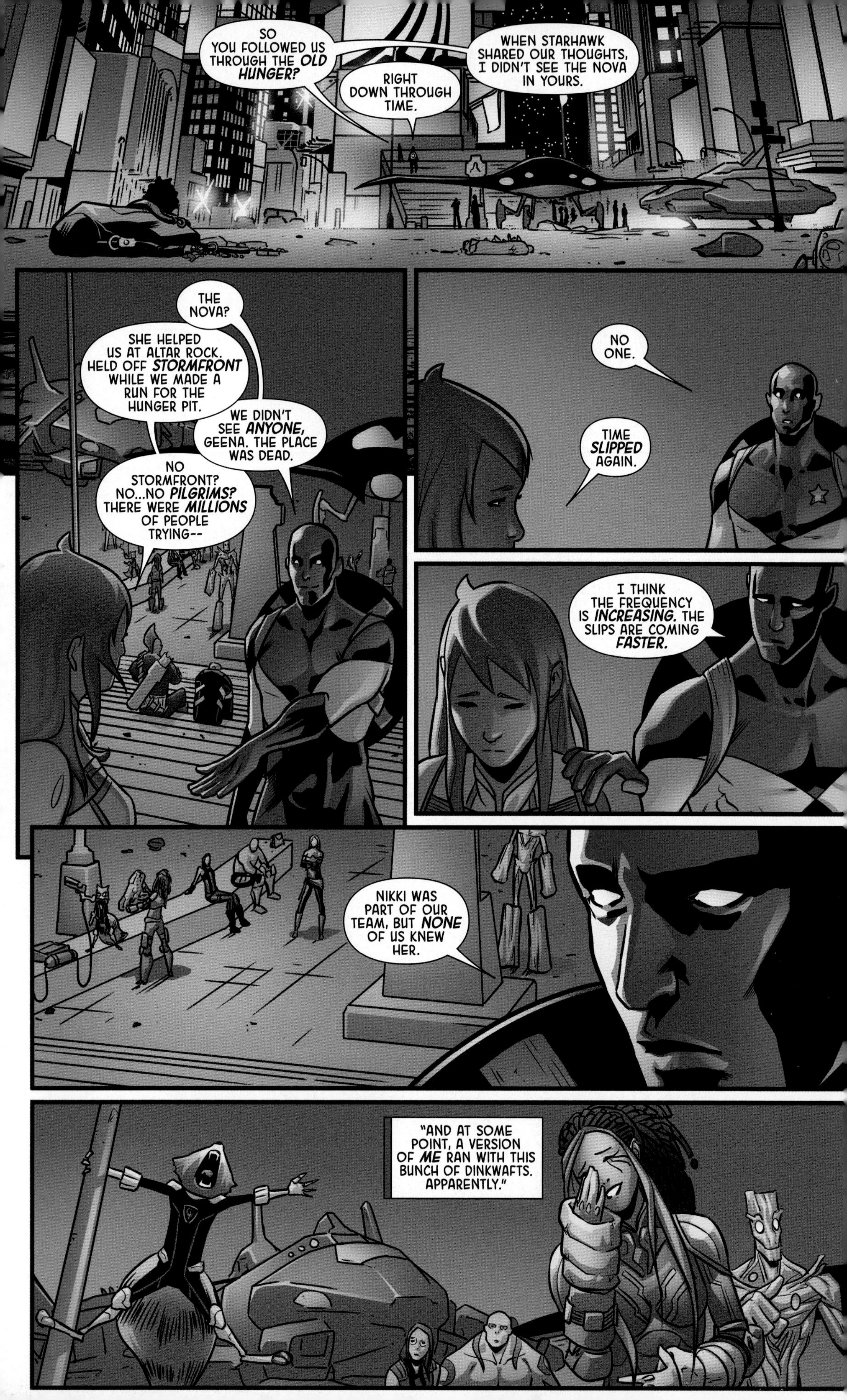

SO YOU FOLLOWED US THROUGH THE OLD HUNGER?
RIGHT DOWN THROUGH TIME.
WHEN STARHAWK SHARED OUR THOUGHTS, I DIDN'T SEE THE NOVA IN YOURS.
THE NOVA?
SHE HELPED US AT ALTAR ROCK. HELD OFF STORMFRONT WHILE WE MADE A RUN FOR THE HUNGER PIT.
WE DIDN'T SEE ANYONE, GEENA. THE PLACE WAS DEAD.
NO STORMFRONT? NO...NO PILGRIMS? THERE WERE MILLIONS OF PEOPLE TRYING--
NO ONE.
TIME SLIPPED AGAIN.
I THINK THE FREQUENCY IS INCREASING. THE SLIPS ARE COMING FASTER.
NIKKI WAS PART OF OUR TEAM, BUT NONE OF US KNEW HER.
"AND AT SOME POINT, A VERSION OF ME RAN WITH THIS BUNCH OF DINKWAFTS. APPARENTLY."

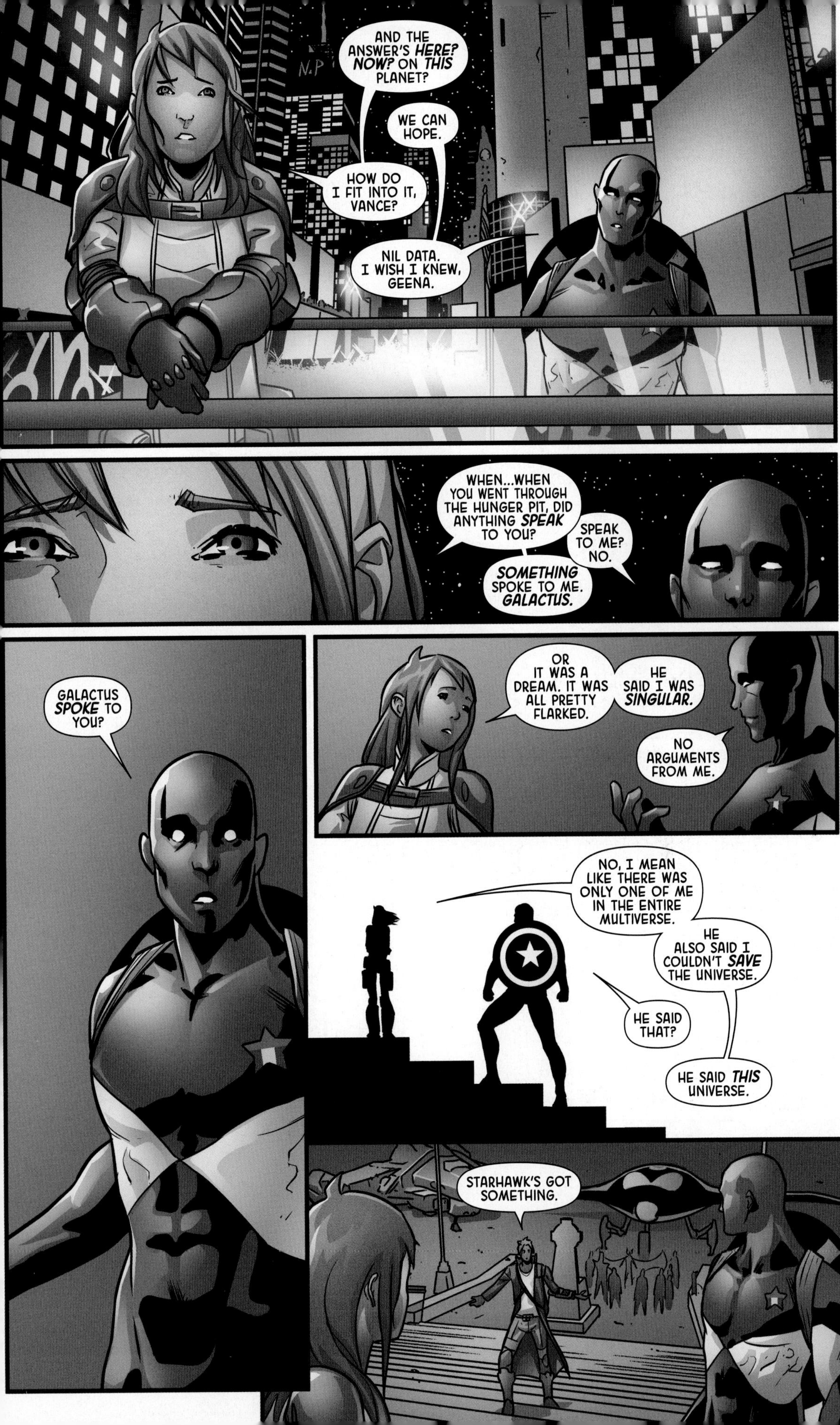
AND THE ANSWER'S HERE? NOW? ON THIS PLANET?
WE CAN HOPE.
HOW DO I FIT INTO IT, VANCE?
NIL DATA. I WISH I KNEW, GEENA.
WHEN...WHEN YOU WENT THROUGH THE HUNGER PIT, DID ANYTHING SPEAK TO YOU?
SPEAK TO ME? NO.
SOMETHING SPOKE TO ME. GALACTUS.
GALACTUS SPOKE TO YOU?
OR IT WAS A DREAM. IT WAS ALL PRETTY FLARKED.
HE SAID I WAS SINGULAR.
NO ARGUMENTS FROM ME.
NO, I MEAN LIKE THERE WAS ONLY ONE OF ME IN THE ENTIRE MULTIVERSE.
HE ALSO SAID I COULDN'T SAVE THE UNIVERSE.
HE SAID THAT?
HE SAID THIS UNIVERSE.
STARHAWK'S GOT SOMETHING.

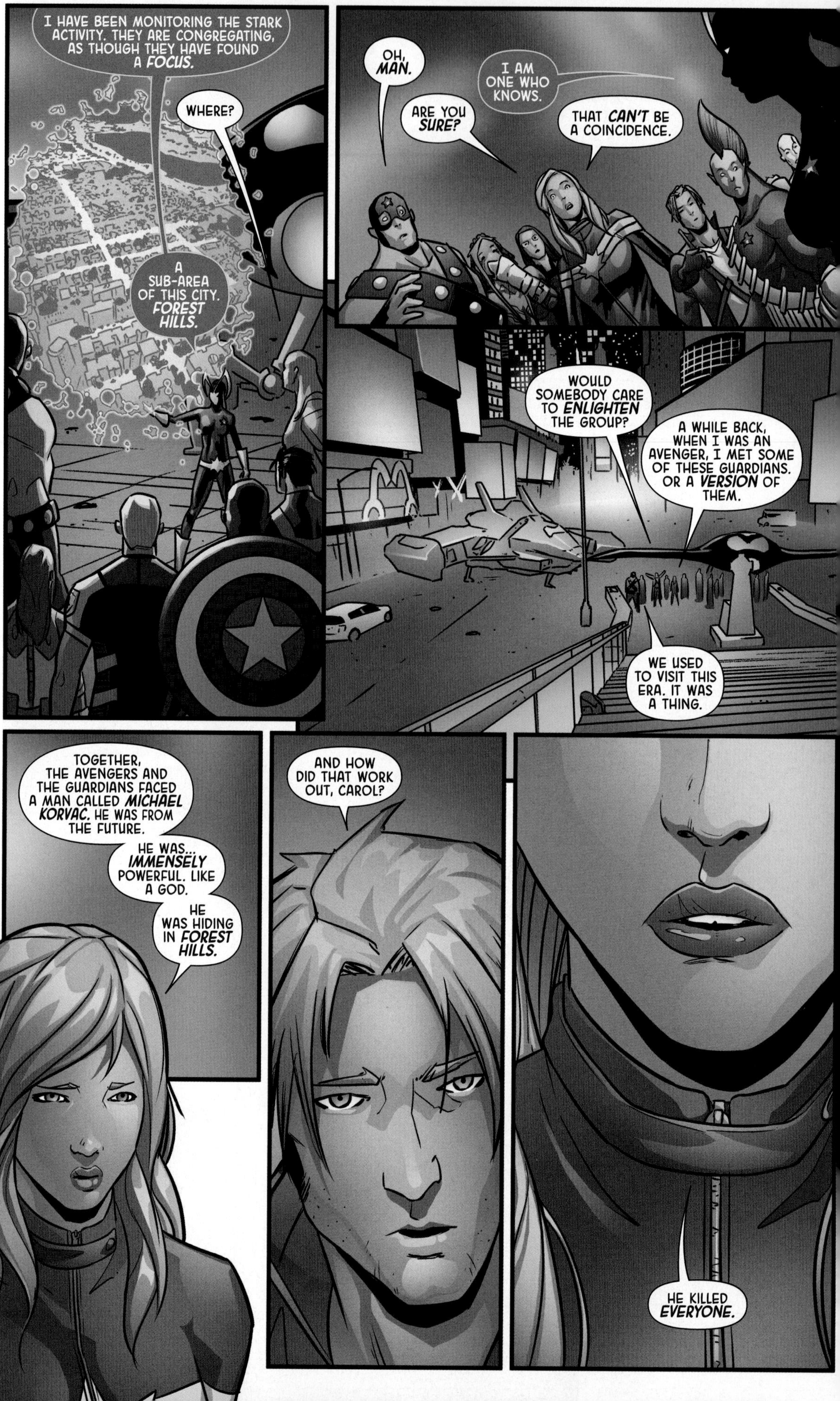
I HAVE BEEN MONITORING THE STARK ACTIVITY. THEY ARE CONGREGATING, AS THOUGH THEY HAVE FOUND A FOCUS.
WHERE?
A SUB-AREA OF THIS CITY. FOREST HILLS.
OH, MAN.
ARE YOU SURE?
I AM ONE WHO KNOWS.
THAT CAN'T BE A COINCIDENCE.
WOULD SOMEBODY CARE TO ENLIGHTEN THE GROUP?
A WHILE BACK, WHEN I WAS AN AVENGER, I MET SOME OF THESE GUARDIANS. OR A VERSION OF THEM.
WE USED TO VISIT THIS ERA. IT WAS A THING.
TOGETHER, THE AVENGERS AND THE GUARDIANS FACED A MAN CALLED MICHAEL KORVAC. HE WAS FROM THE FUTURE.
HE WAS... IMMENSELY POWERFUL. LIKE A GOD.
HE WAS HIDING IN FOREST HILLS.
AND HOW DID THAT WORK OUT, CAROL?
HE KILLED EVERYONE.

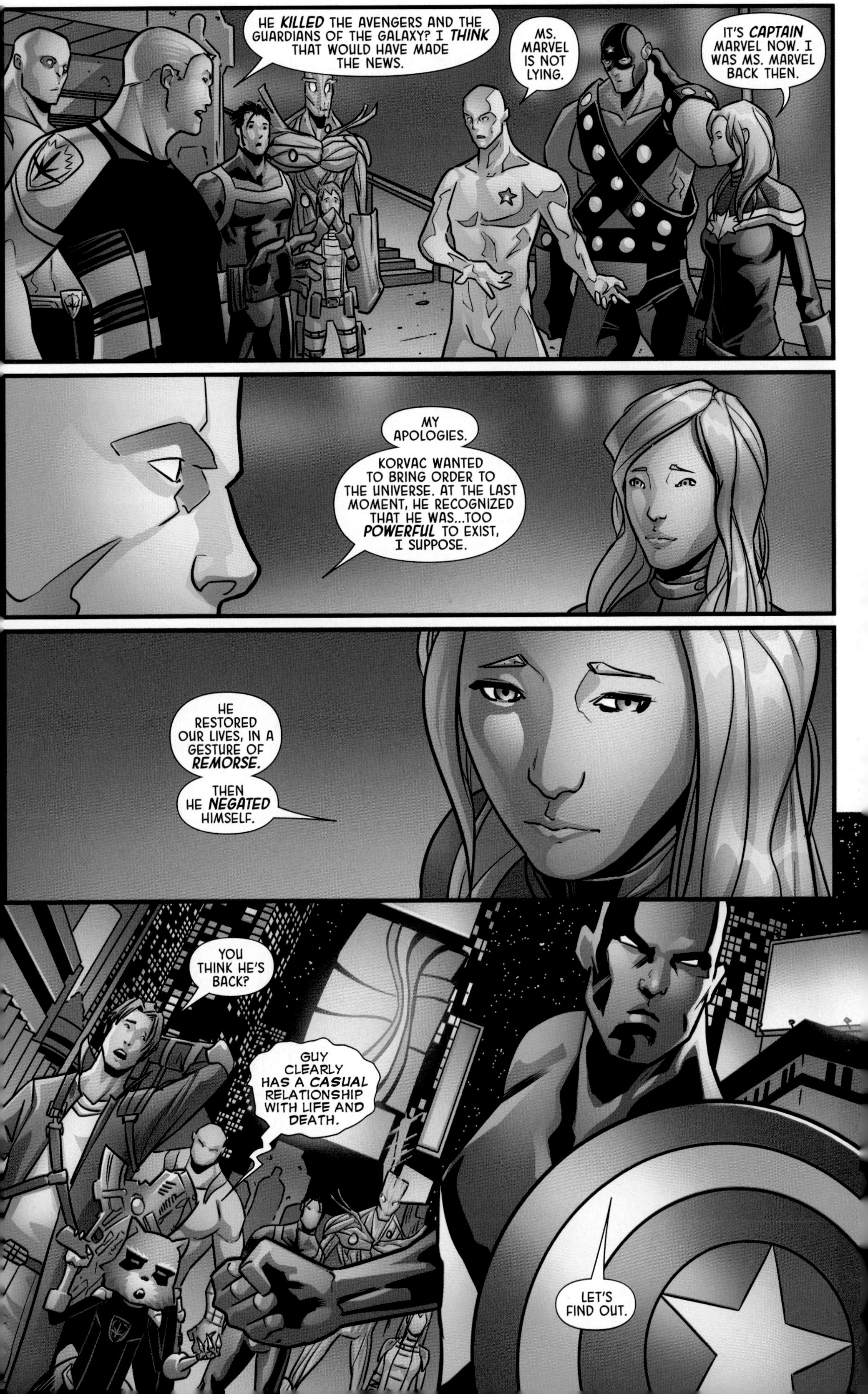
HE KILLED THE AVENGERS AND THE GUARDIANS OF THE GALAXY? I THINK THAT WOULD HAVE MADE THE NEWS.
MS. MARVEL IS NOT LYING.
IT'S CAPTAIN MARVEL NOW. I WAS MS. MARVEL BACK THEN.
MY APOLOGIES.
KORVAC WANTED TO BRING ORDER TO THE UNIVERSE. AT THE LAST MOMENT, HE RECOGNIZED THAT HE WAS...TOO POWERFUL TO EXIST, I SUPPOSE.
HE RESTORED OUR LIVES, IN A GESTURE OF REMORSE.
THEN HE NEGATED HIMSELF.
YOU THINK HE'S BACK?
GUY CLEARLY HAS A CASUAL RELATIONSHIP WITH LIFE AND DEATH.
LET'S FIND OUT.

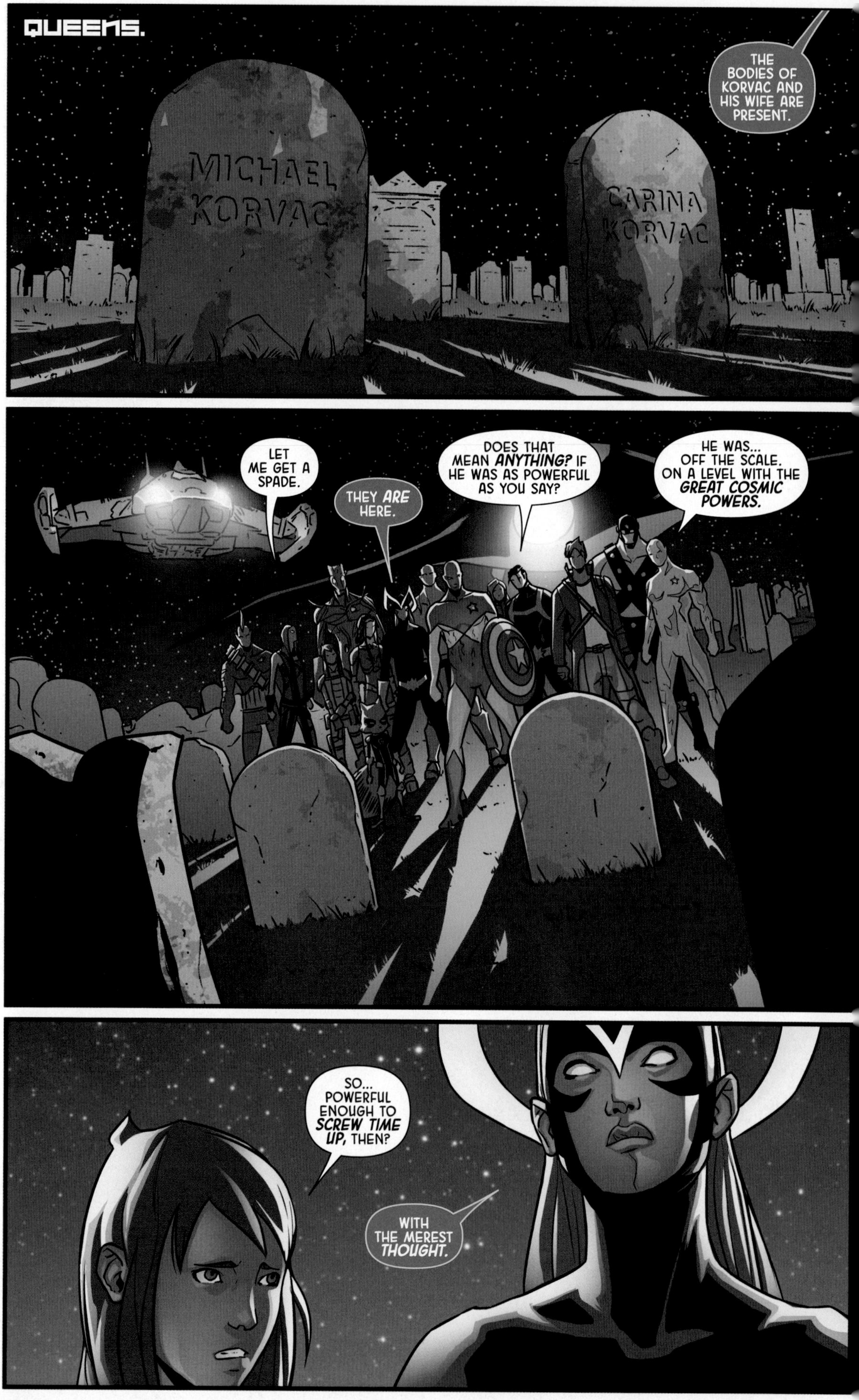
QUEENS.
THE BODIES OF KORVAC AND HIS WIFE ARE PRESENT.
MICHAEL KORVAC
CARINA KORVAC
LET ME GET A SPADE.
THEY ARE HERE.
DOES THAT MEAN ANYTHING? IF HE WAS AS POWERFUL AS YOU SAY?
HE WAS... OFF THE SCALE. ON A LEVEL WITH THE GREAT COSMIC POWERS.
SO... POWERFUL ENOUGH TO SCREW TIME UP, THEN?
WITH THE MEREST THOUGHT.

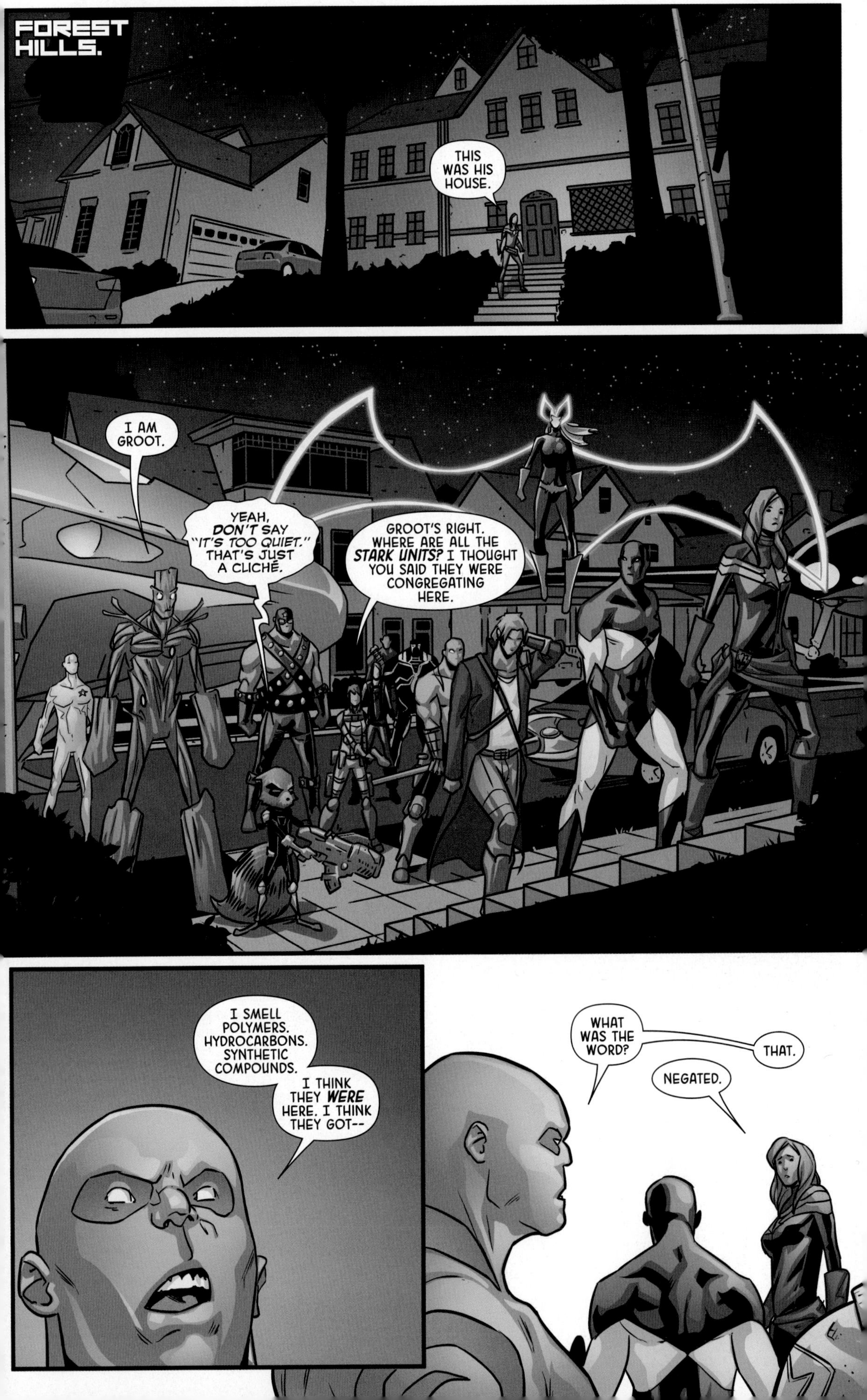
FOREST HILLS.
THIS WAS HIS HOUSE.
I AM GROOT.
YEAH, DON'T SAY "IT'S TOO QUIET." THAT'S JUST A CLICHÉ.
GROOT'S RIGHT. WHERE ARE ALL THE STARK UNITS? I THOUGHT YOU SAID THEY WERE CONGREGATING HERE.
I SMELL POLYMERS. HYDROCARBONS. SYNTHETIC COMPOUNDS.
I THINK THEY WERE HERE. I THINK THEY GOT--
WHAT WAS THE WORD?
THAT.
NEGATED.

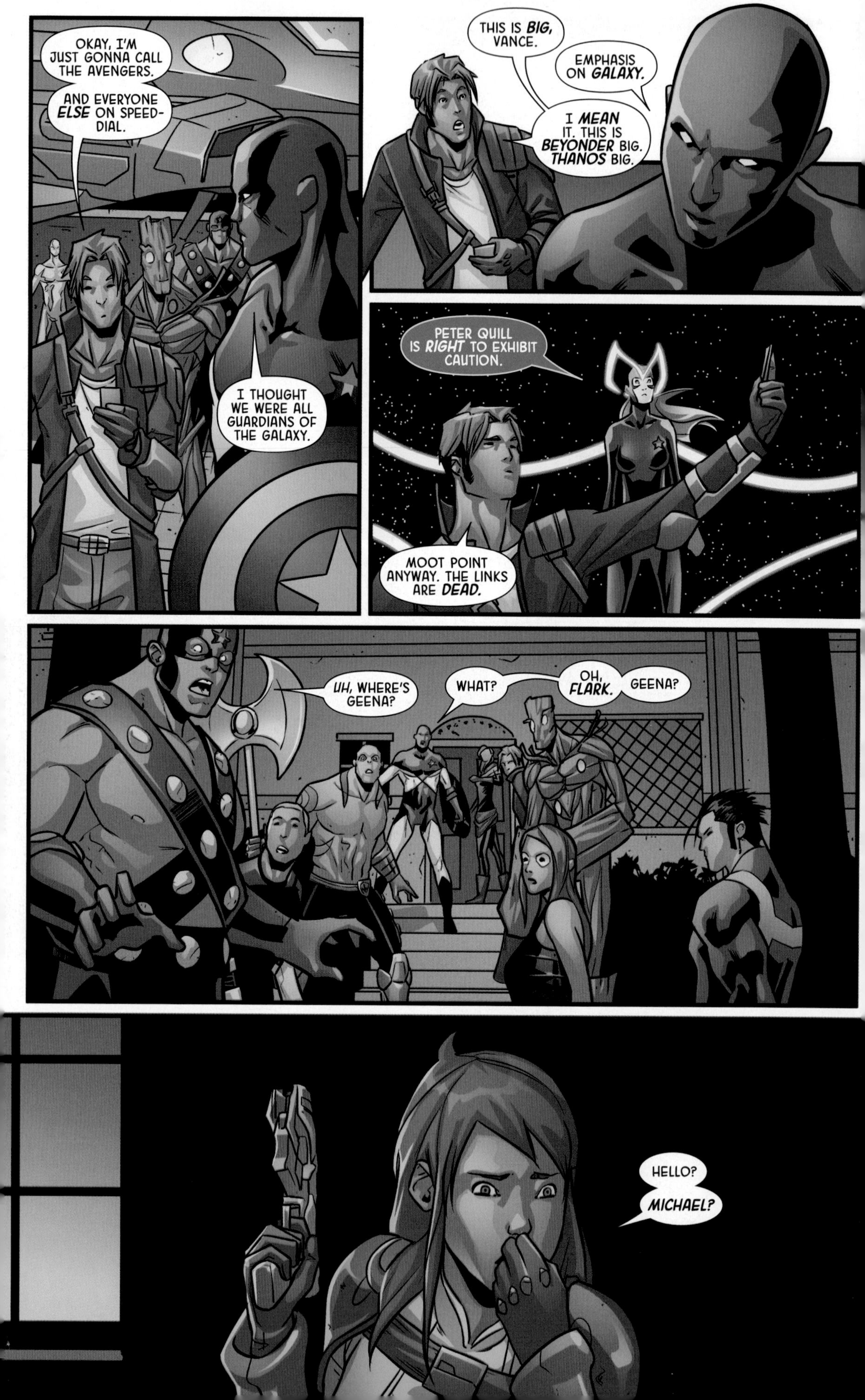

OKAY, I'M JUST GONNA CALL THE AVENGERS.
AND EVERYONE *ELSE* ON SPEED-DIAL.
I THOUGHT WE WERE ALL GUARDIANS OF THE GALAXY.
THIS IS *BIG,* VANCE.
EMPHASIS ON *GALAXY.*
I *MEAN* IT. THIS IS *BEYONDER* BIG. *THANOS* BIG.
PETER QUILL IS *RIGHT* TO EXHIBIT CAUTION.
MOOT POINT ANYWAY. THE LINKS ARE *DEAD.*
UH, WHERE'S GEENA?
WHAT?
OH, *FLARK.*
GEENA?
HELLO?
MICHAEL?

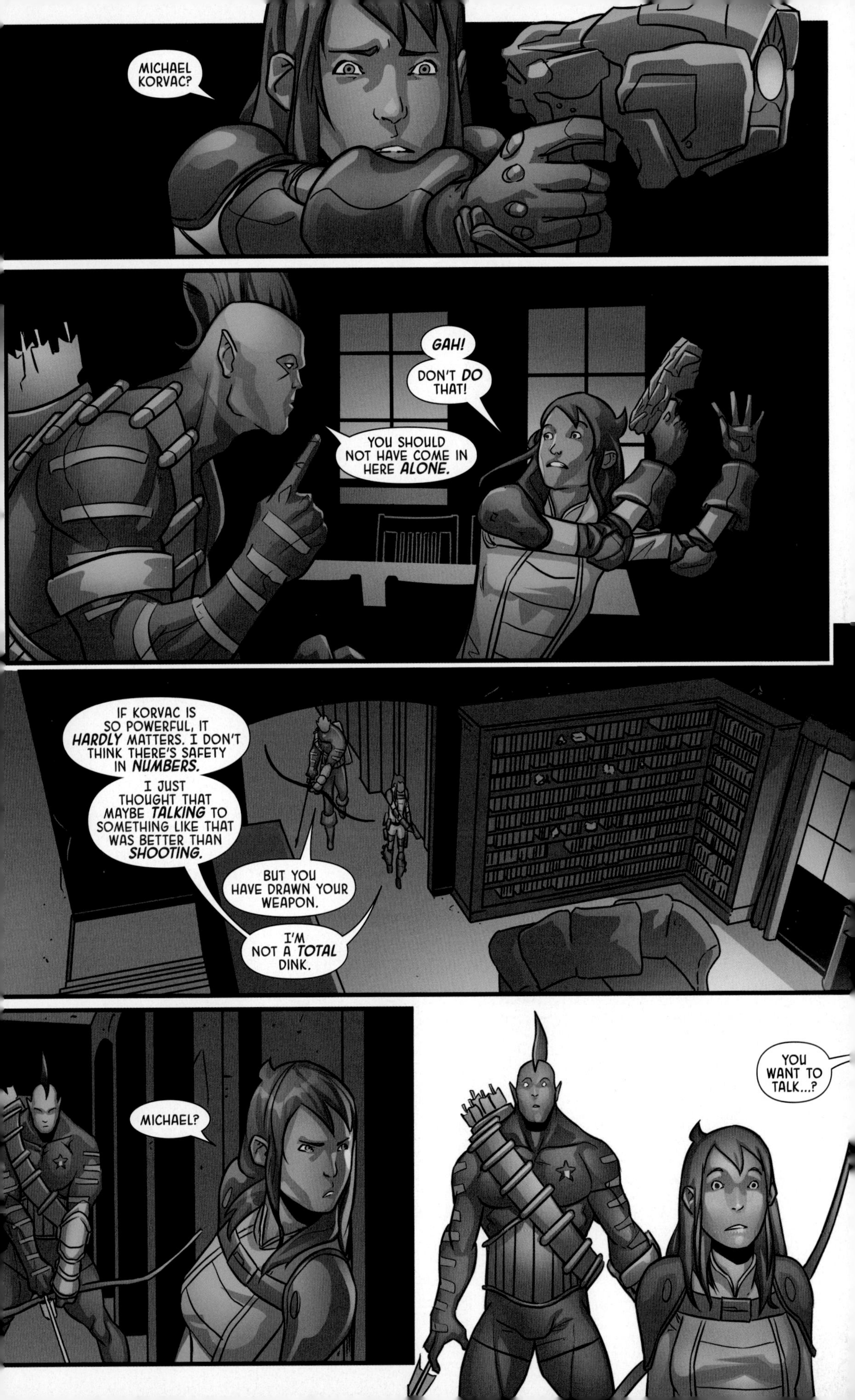
MICHAEL KORVAC?
GAH!
DON'T DO THAT!
YOU SHOULD NOT HAVE COME IN HERE ALONE.
IF KORVAC IS SO POWERFUL, IT HARDLY MATTERS. I DON'T THINK THERE'S SAFETY IN NUMBERS.
I JUST THOUGHT THAT MAYBE TALKING TO SOMETHING LIKE THAT WAS BETTER THAN SHOOTING.
BUT YOU HAVE DRAWN YOUR WEAPON.
I'M NOT A TOTAL DINK.
MICHAEL?
YOU WANT TO TALK...?

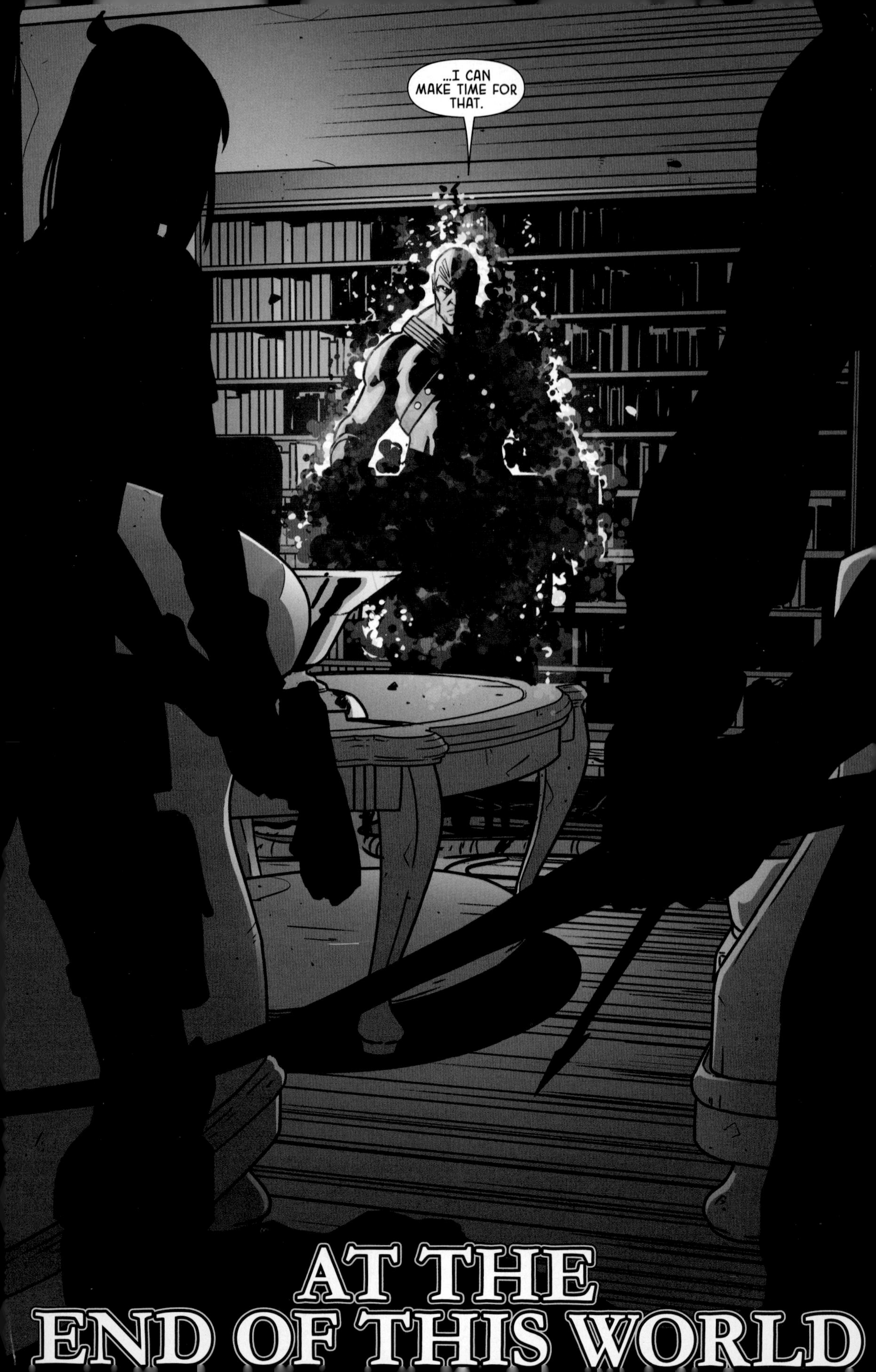
...I CAN MAKE TIME FOR THAT.
AT THE END OF THIS WORLD

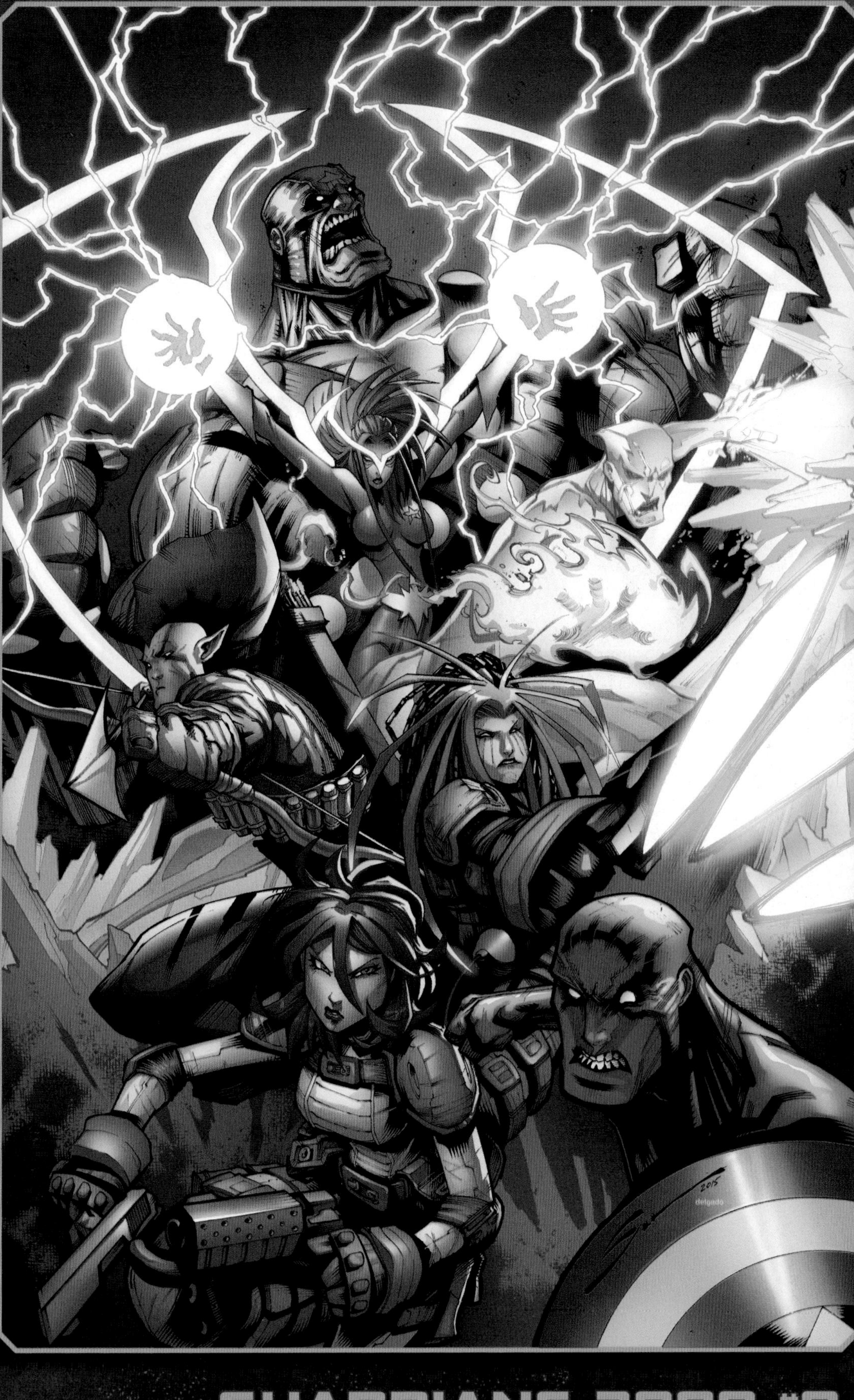

GUARDIANS 3000 #8

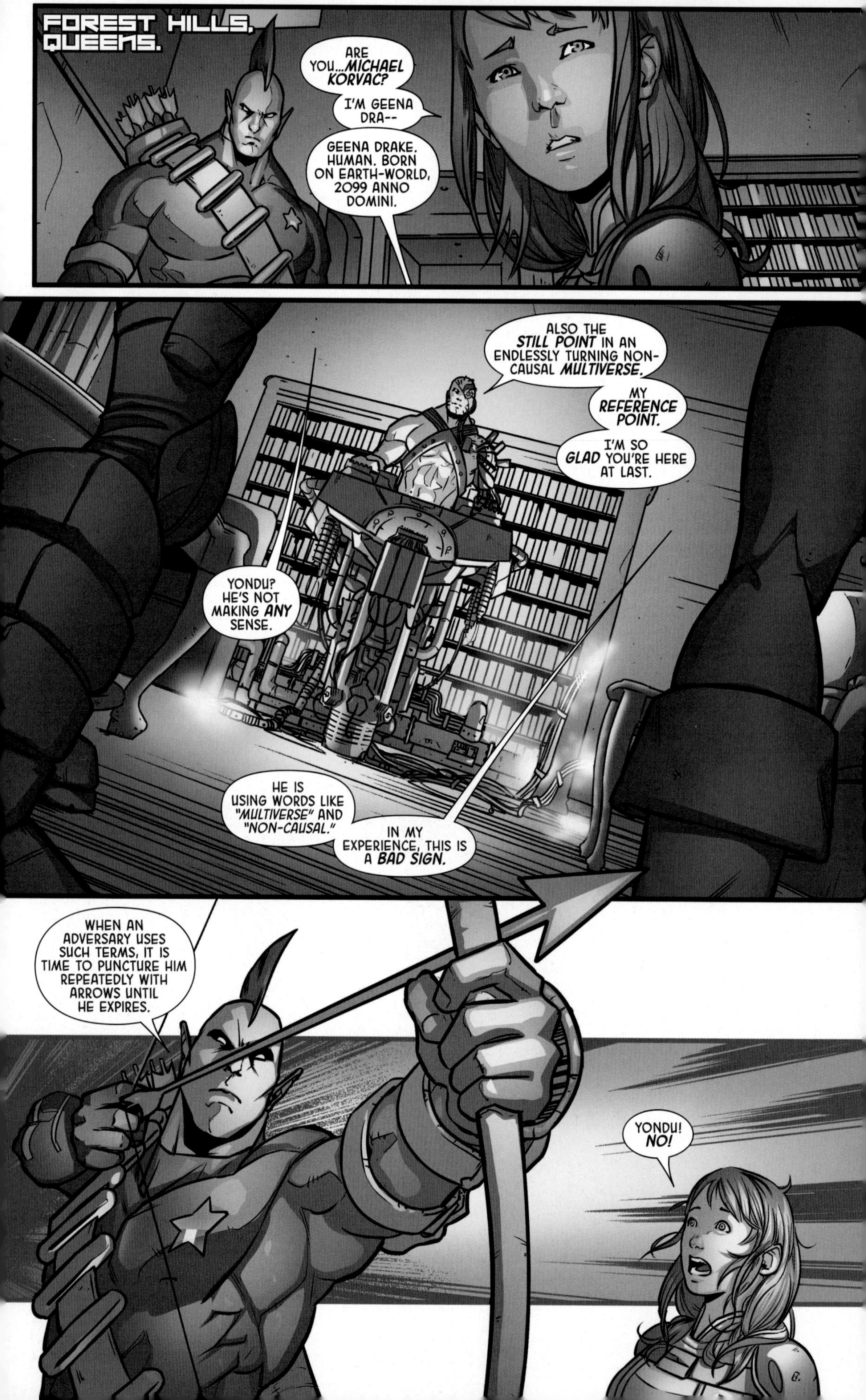
FOREST HILLS, QUEENS.
ARE YOU...MICHAEL KORVAC?
I'M GEENA DRA--
GEENA DRAKE. HUMAN. BORN ON EARTH-WORLD, 2099 ANNO DOMINI.
ALSO THE STILL POINT IN AN ENDLESSLY TURNING NON-CAUSAL MULTIVERSE.
MY REFERENCE POINT.
I'M SO GLAD YOU'RE HERE AT LAST.
YONDU? HE'S NOT MAKING ANY SENSE.
HE IS USING WORDS LIKE "MULTIVERSE" AND "NON-CAUSAL."
IN MY EXPERIENCE, THIS IS A BAD SIGN.
WHEN AN ADVERSARY USES SUCH TERMS, IT IS TIME TO PUNCTURE HIM REPEATEDLY WITH ARROWS UNTIL HE EXPIRES.
YONDU! NO!

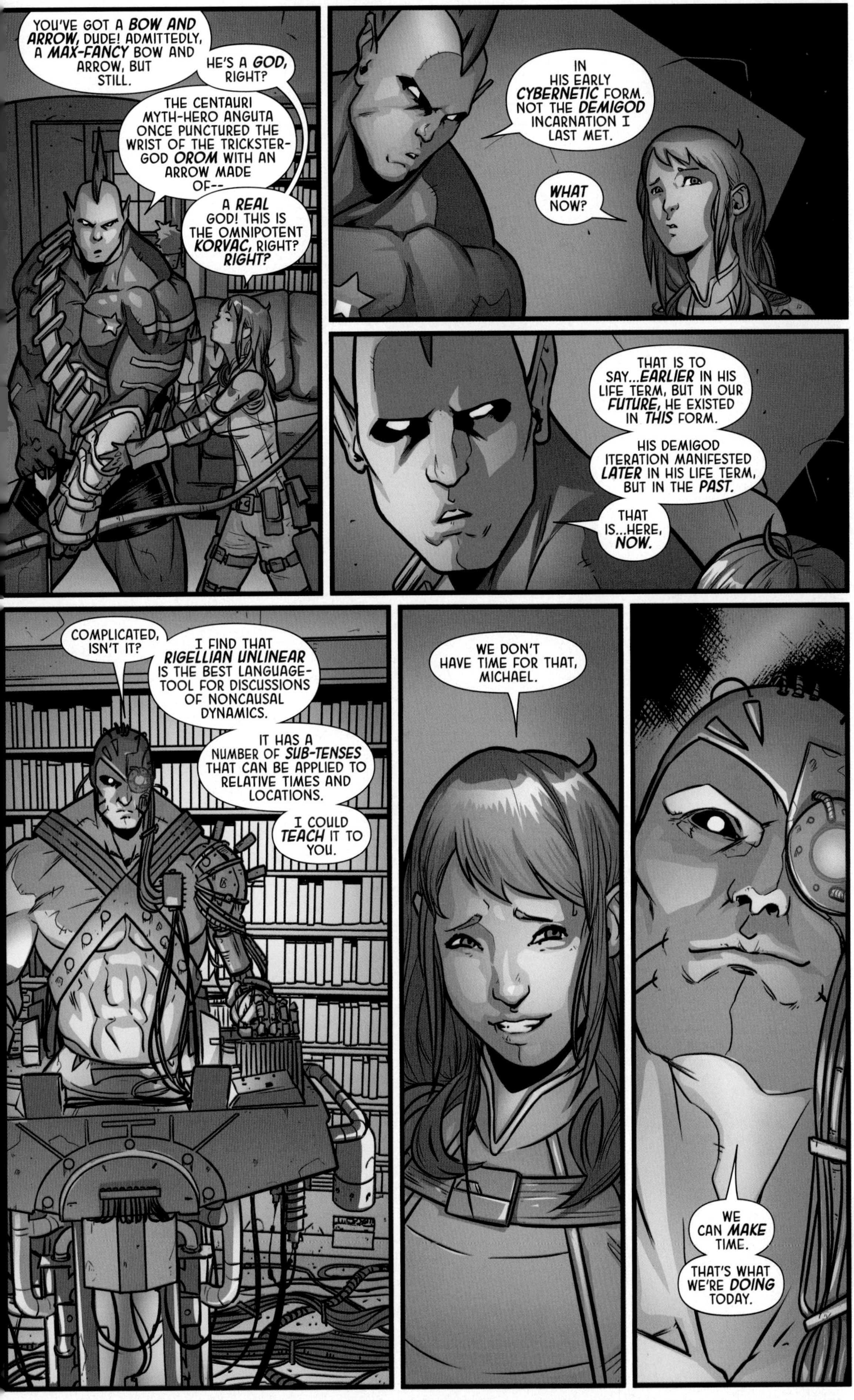
YOU'VE GOT A BOW AND ARROW, DUDE! ADMITTEDLY, A MAX-FANCY BOW AND ARROW, BUT STILL.
HE'S A GOD, RIGHT?
THE CENTAURI MYTH-HERO ANGUTA ONCE PUNCTURED THE WRIST OF THE TRICKSTER-GOD OROM WITH AN ARROW MADE OF--
A REAL GOD! THIS IS THE OMNIPOTENT KORVAC, RIGHT? RIGHT?
IN HIS EARLY CYBERNETIC FORM. NOT THE DEMIGOD INCARNATION I LAST MET.
WHAT NOW?
THAT IS TO SAY...EARLIER IN HIS LIFE TERM, BUT IN OUR FUTURE, HE EXISTED IN THIS FORM.
HIS DEMIGOD ITERATION MANIFESTED LATER IN HIS LIFE TERM, BUT IN THE PAST.
THAT IS...HERE, NOW.
COMPLICATED, ISN'T IT?
I FIND THAT RIGELLIAN UNLINEAR IS THE BEST LANGUAGE-TOOL FOR DISCUSSIONS OF NONCAUSAL DYNAMICS.
IT HAS A NUMBER OF SUB-TENSES THAT CAN BE APPLIED TO RELATIVE TIMES AND LOCATIONS.
I COULD TEACH IT TO YOU.
WE DON'T HAVE TIME FOR THAT, MICHAEL.
WE CAN MAKE TIME.
THAT'S WHAT WE'RE DOING TODAY.

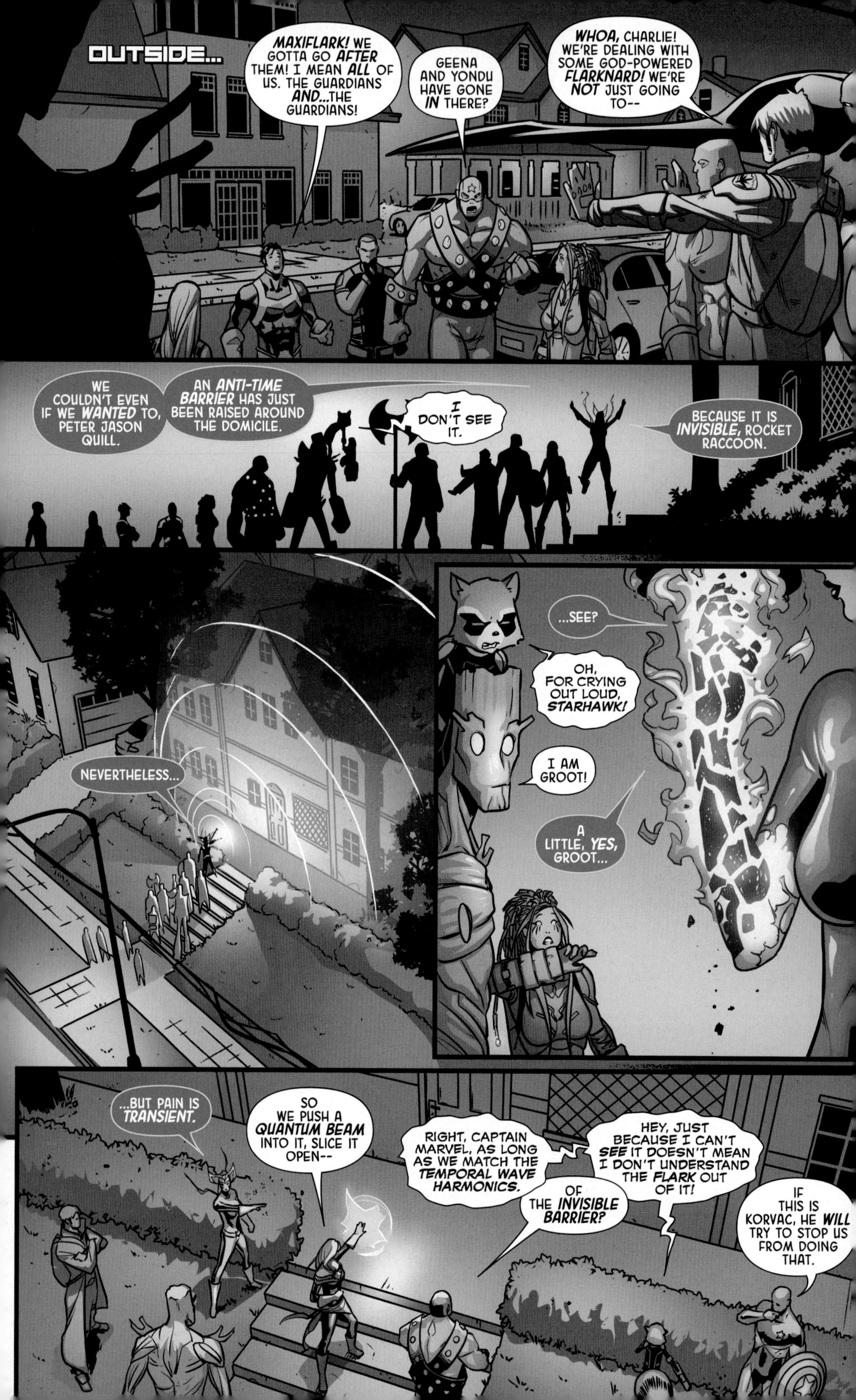
OUTSIDE...
MAXIFLARK! WE GOTTA GO AFTER THEM! I MEAN ALL OF US. THE GUARDIANS AND...THE GUARDIANS!
GEENA AND YONDU HAVE GONE IN THERE?
WHOA, CHARLIE! WE'RE DEALING WITH SOME GOD-POWERED FLARKNARD! WE'RE NOT JUST GOING TO--
WE COULDN'T EVEN IF WE WANTED TO, PETER JASON QUILL.
AN ANTI-TIME BARRIER HAS JUST BEEN RAISED AROUND THE DOMICILE.
I DON'T SEE IT.
BECAUSE IT IS INVISIBLE, ROCKET RACCOON.
NEVERTHELESS...
...SEE?
OH, FOR CRYING OUT LOUD, STARHAWK!
I AM GROOT!
A LITTLE, YES, GROOT...
...BUT PAIN IS TRANSIENT.
SO WE PUSH A QUANTUM BEAM INTO IT, SLICE IT OPEN--
RIGHT, CAPTAIN MARVEL, AS LONG AS WE MATCH THE TEMPORAL WAVE HARMONICS.
OF THE INVISIBLE BARRIER?
HEY, JUST BECAUSE I CAN'T SEE IT DOESN'T MEAN I DON'T UNDERSTAND THE FLARK OUT OF IT!
IF THIS IS KORVAC, HE WILL TRY TO STOP US FROM DOING THAT.

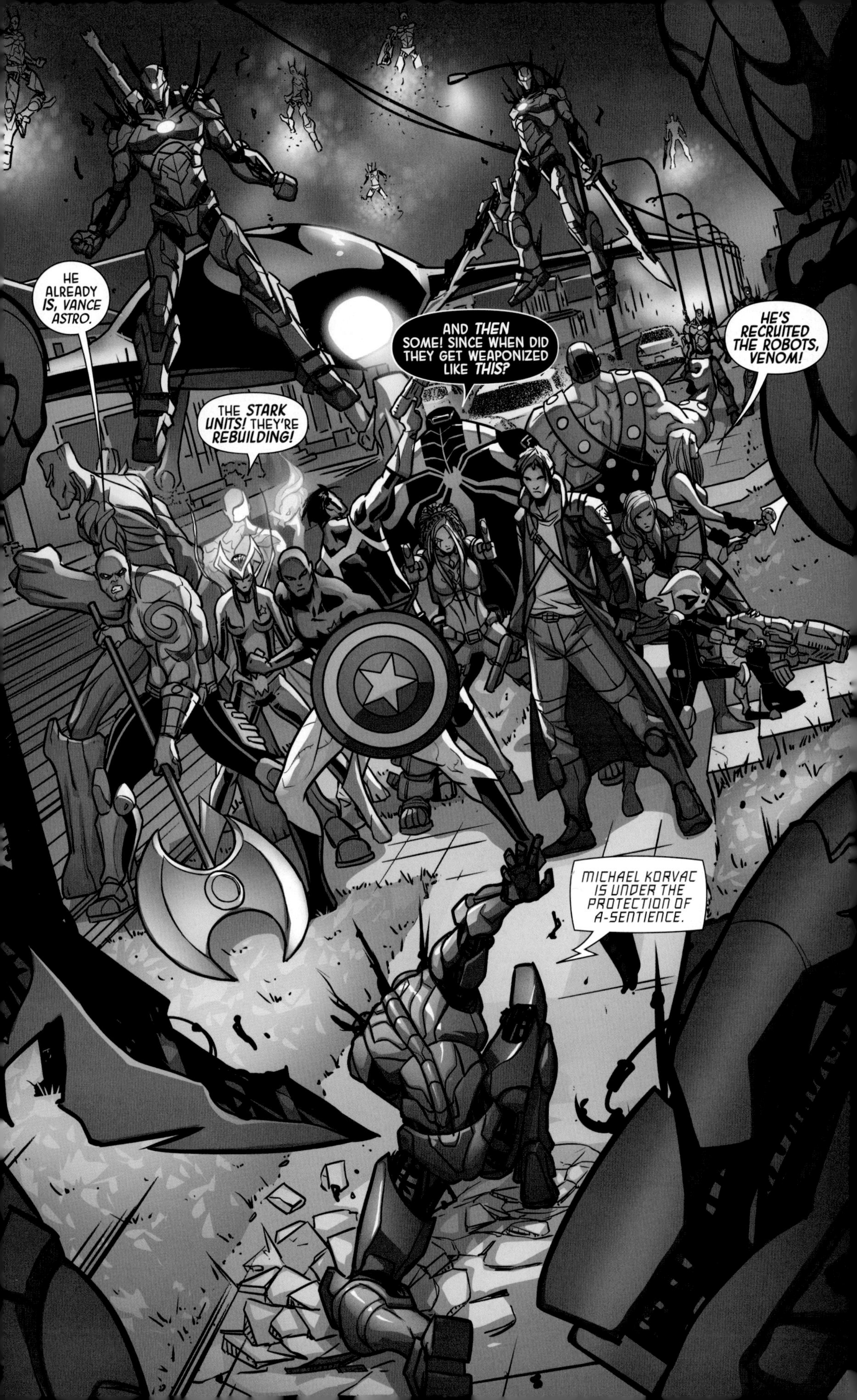
HE ALREADY IS, VANCE ASTRO.
THE STARK UNITS! THEY'RE REBUILDING!
AND THEN SOME! SINCE WHEN DID THEY GET WEAPONIZED LIKE THIS?
HE'S RECRUITED THE ROBOTS, VENOM!
MICHAEL KORVAC IS UNDER THE PROTECTION OF A-SENTIENCE.

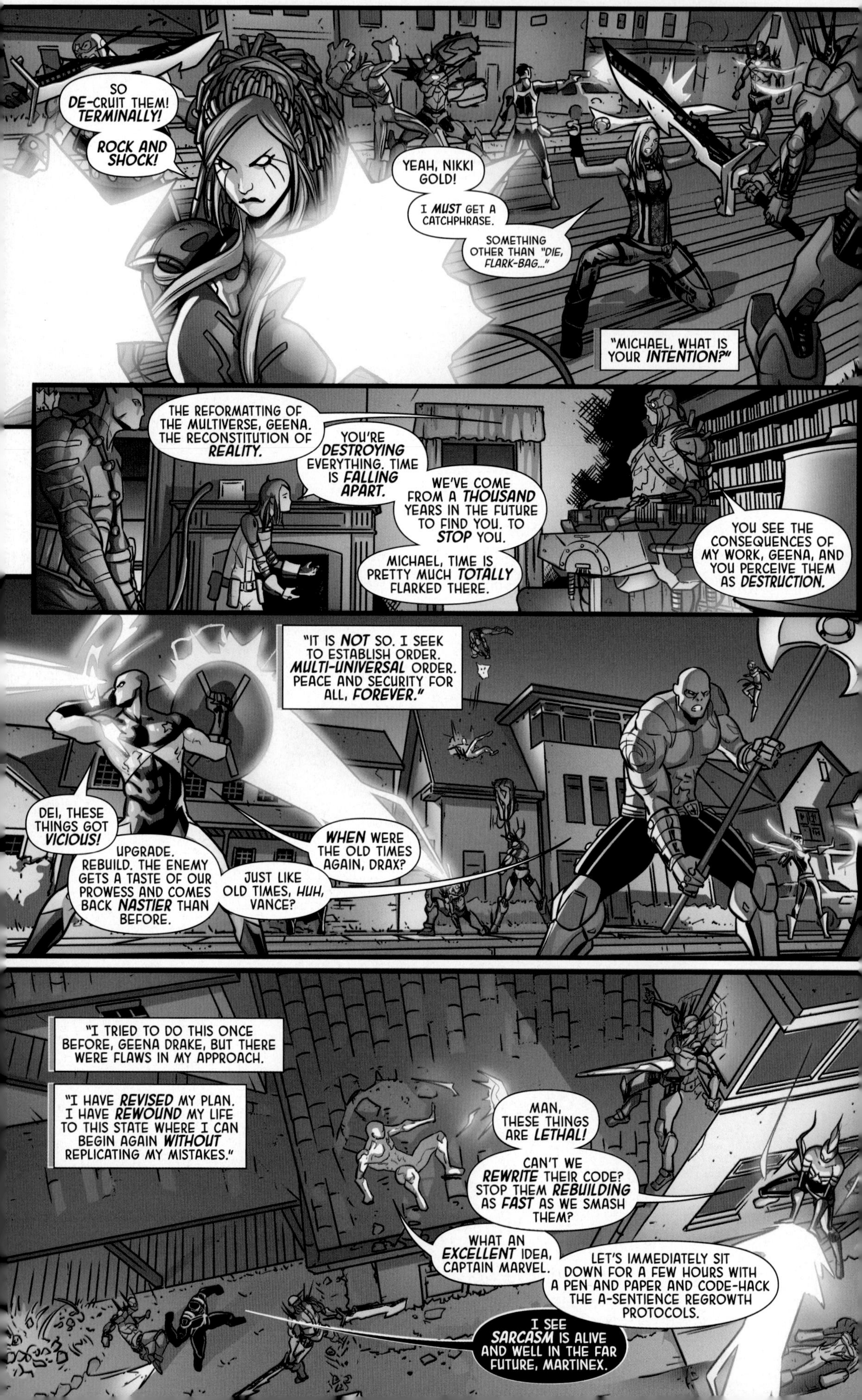

SO DE-CRUIT THEM! TERMINALLY!
ROCK AND SHOCK!
YEAH, NIKKI GOLD!
I MUST GET A CATCHPHRASE.
SOMETHING OTHER THAN "DIE, FLARK-BAG..."
"MICHAEL, WHAT IS YOUR INTENTION?"
THE REFORMATTING OF THE MULTIVERSE, GEENA. THE RECONSTITUTION OF REALITY.
YOU'RE DESTROYING EVERYTHING. TIME IS FALLING APART.
WE'VE COME FROM A THOUSAND YEARS IN THE FUTURE TO FIND YOU. TO STOP YOU.
MICHAEL, TIME IS PRETTY MUCH TOTALLY FLARKED THERE.
YOU SEE THE CONSEQUENCES OF MY WORK, GEENA, AND YOU PERCEIVE THEM AS DESTRUCTION.
"IT IS NOT SO. I SEEK TO ESTABLISH ORDER. MULTI-UNIVERSAL ORDER. PEACE AND SECURITY FOR ALL, FOREVER."
DEI, THESE THINGS GOT VICIOUS!
UPGRADE. REBUILD. THE ENEMY GETS A TASTE OF OUR PROWESS AND COMES BACK NASTIER THAN BEFORE.
JUST LIKE OLD TIMES, HUH, VANCE?
WHEN WERE THE OLD TIMES AGAIN, DRAX?
"I TRIED TO DO THIS ONCE BEFORE, GEENA DRAKE, BUT THERE WERE FLAWS IN MY APPROACH.
"I HAVE REVISED MY PLAN. I HAVE REWOUND MY LIFE TO THIS STATE WHERE I CAN BEGIN AGAIN WITHOUT REPLICATING MY MISTAKES."
MAN, THESE THINGS ARE LETHAL!
CAN'T WE REWRITE THEIR CODE? STOP THEM REBUILDING AS FAST AS WE SMASH THEM?
WHAT AN EXCELLENT IDEA, CAPTAIN MARVEL.
LET'S IMMEDIATELY SIT DOWN FOR A FEW HOURS WITH A PEN AND PAPER AND CODE-HACK THE A-SENTIENCE REGROWTH PROTOCOLS.
I SEE SARCASM IS ALIVE AND WELL IN THE FAR FUTURE, MARTINEX.

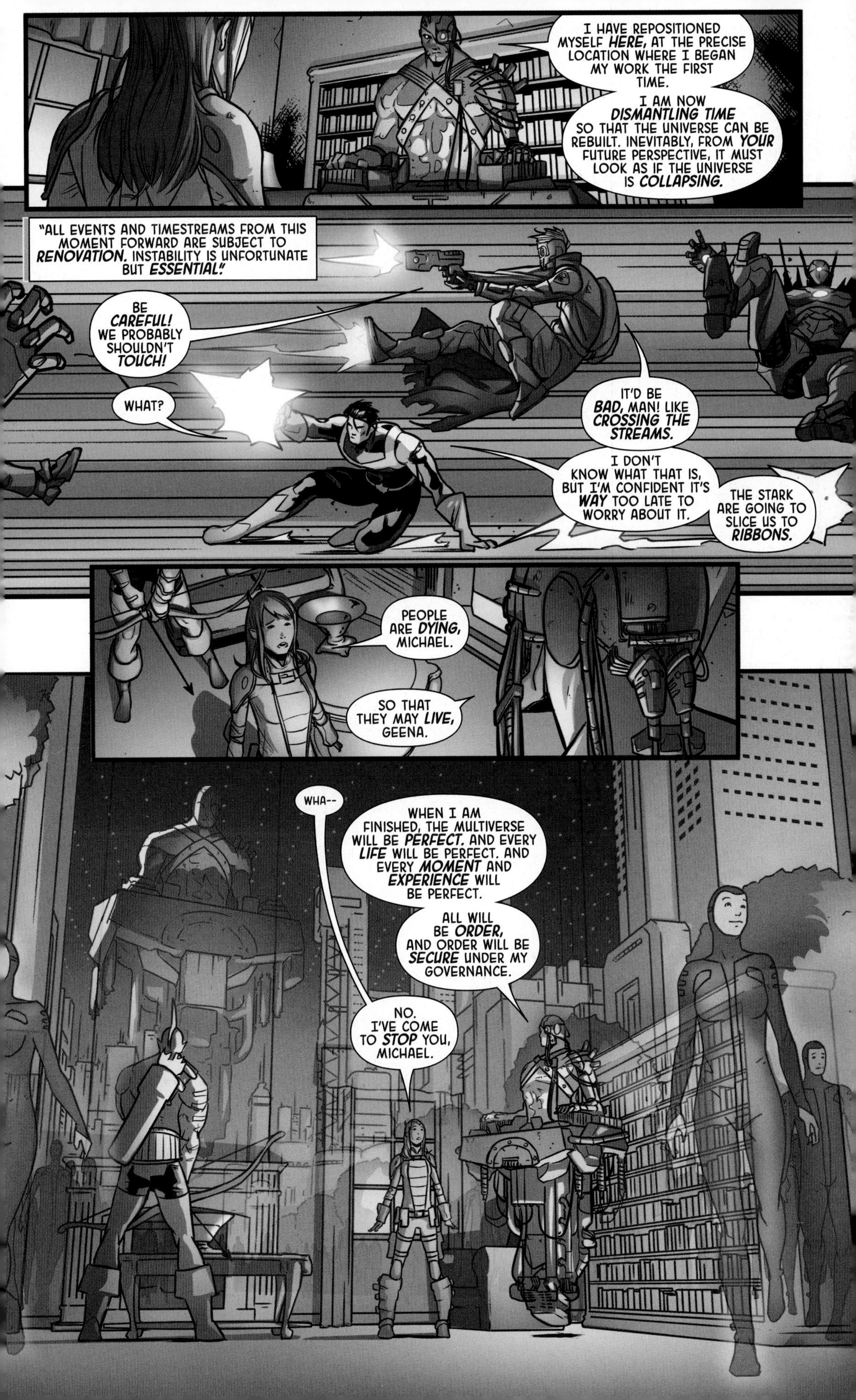
I HAVE REPOSITIONED MYSELF HERE, AT THE PRECISE LOCATION WHERE I BEGAN MY WORK THE FIRST TIME.
I AM NOW DISMANTLING TIME SO THAT THE UNIVERSE CAN BE REBUILT. INEVITABLY, FROM YOUR FUTURE PERSPECTIVE, IT MUST LOOK AS IF THE UNIVERSE IS COLLAPSING.
"ALL EVENTS AND TIMESTREAMS FROM THIS MOMENT FORWARD ARE SUBJECT TO RENOVATION. INSTABILITY IS UNFORTUNATE BUT ESSENTIAL."
BE CAREFUL! WE PROBABLY SHOULDN'T TOUCH!
WHAT?
IT'D BE BAD, MAN! LIKE CROSSING THE STREAMS.
I DON'T KNOW WHAT THAT IS, BUT I'M CONFIDENT IT'S WAY TOO LATE TO WORRY ABOUT IT.
THE STARK ARE GOING TO SLICE US TO RIBBONS.
PEOPLE ARE DYING, MICHAEL.
SO THAT THEY MAY LIVE, GEENA.
WHA--
WHEN I AM FINISHED, THE MULTIVERSE WILL BE PERFECT. AND EVERY LIFE WILL BE PERFECT. AND EVERY MOMENT AND EXPERIENCE WILL BE PERFECT.
ALL WILL BE ORDER, AND ORDER WILL BE SECURE UNDER MY GOVERNANCE.
NO. I'VE COME TO STOP YOU, MICHAEL.

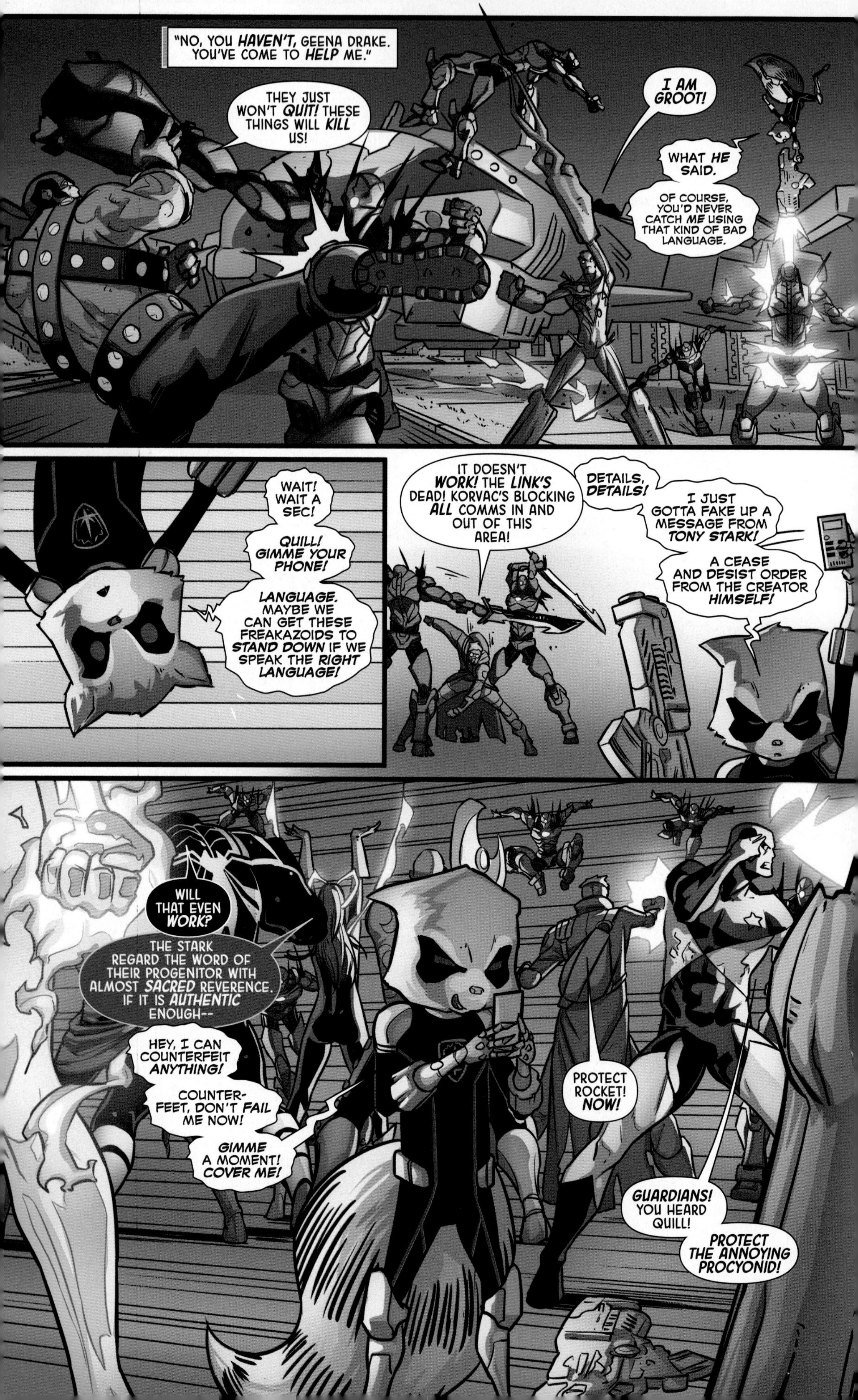
"NO, YOU HAVEN'T, GEENA DRAKE. YOU'VE COME TO HELP ME."
THEY JUST WON'T QUIT! THESE THINGS WILL KILL US!
I AM GROOT!
WHAT HE SAID.
OF COURSE, YOU'D NEVER CATCH ME USING THAT KIND OF BAD LANGUAGE.
WAIT! WAIT A SEC!
QUILL! GIMME YOUR PHONE!
LANGUAGE. MAYBE WE CAN GET THESE FREAKAZOIDS TO STAND DOWN IF WE SPEAK THE RIGHT LANGUAGE!
IT DOESN'T WORK! THE LINK'S DEAD! KORVAC'S BLOCKING ALL COMMS IN AND OUT OF THIS AREA!
DETAILS, DETAILS!
I JUST GOTTA FAKE UP A MESSAGE FROM TONY STARK!
A CEASE AND DESIST ORDER FROM THE CREATOR HIMSELF!
WILL THAT EVEN WORK?
THE STARK REGARD THE WORD OF THEIR PROGENITOR WITH ALMOST SACRED REVERENCE. IF IT IS AUTHENTIC ENOUGH--
HEY, I CAN COUNTERFEIT ANYTHING!
COUNTER-FEET, DON'T FAIL ME NOW!
GIMME A MOMENT! COVER ME!
PROTECT ROCKET! NOW!
GUARDIANS! YOU HEARD QUILL!
PROTECT THE ANNOYING PROCYONID!

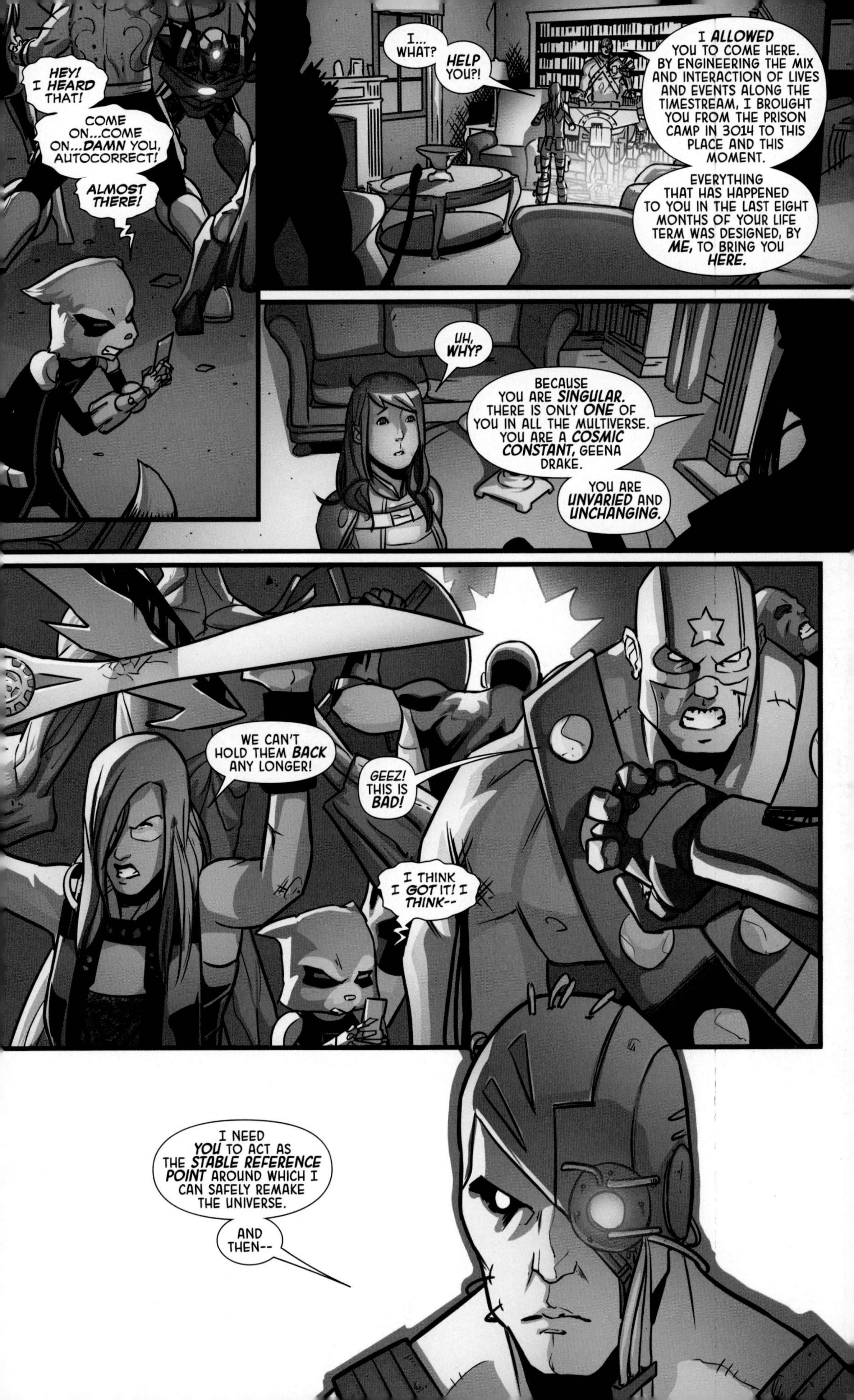
HEY! I HEARD THAT!
COME ON...COME ON...DAMN YOU, AUTOCORRECT!
ALMOST THERE!
I... WHAT? HELP YOU?!
I ALLOWED YOU TO COME HERE. BY ENGINEERING THE MIX AND INTERACTION OF LIVES AND EVENTS ALONG THE TIMESTREAM, I BROUGHT YOU FROM THE PRISON CAMP IN 3014 TO THIS PLACE AND THIS MOMENT.
EVERYTHING THAT HAS HAPPENED TO YOU IN THE LAST EIGHT MONTHS OF YOUR LIFE TERM WAS DESIGNED, BY ME, TO BRING YOU HERE.
UH, WHY?
BECAUSE YOU ARE SINGULAR. THERE IS ONLY ONE OF YOU IN ALL THE MULTIVERSE. YOU ARE A COSMIC CONSTANT, GEENA DRAKE.
YOU ARE UNVARIED AND UNCHANGING.
WE CAN'T HOLD THEM BACK ANY LONGER!
GEEZ! THIS IS BAD!
I THINK I GOT IT! I THINK--
I NEED YOU TO ACT AS THE STABLE REFERENCE POINT AROUND WHICH I CAN SAFELY REMAKE THE UNIVERSE.
AND THEN--

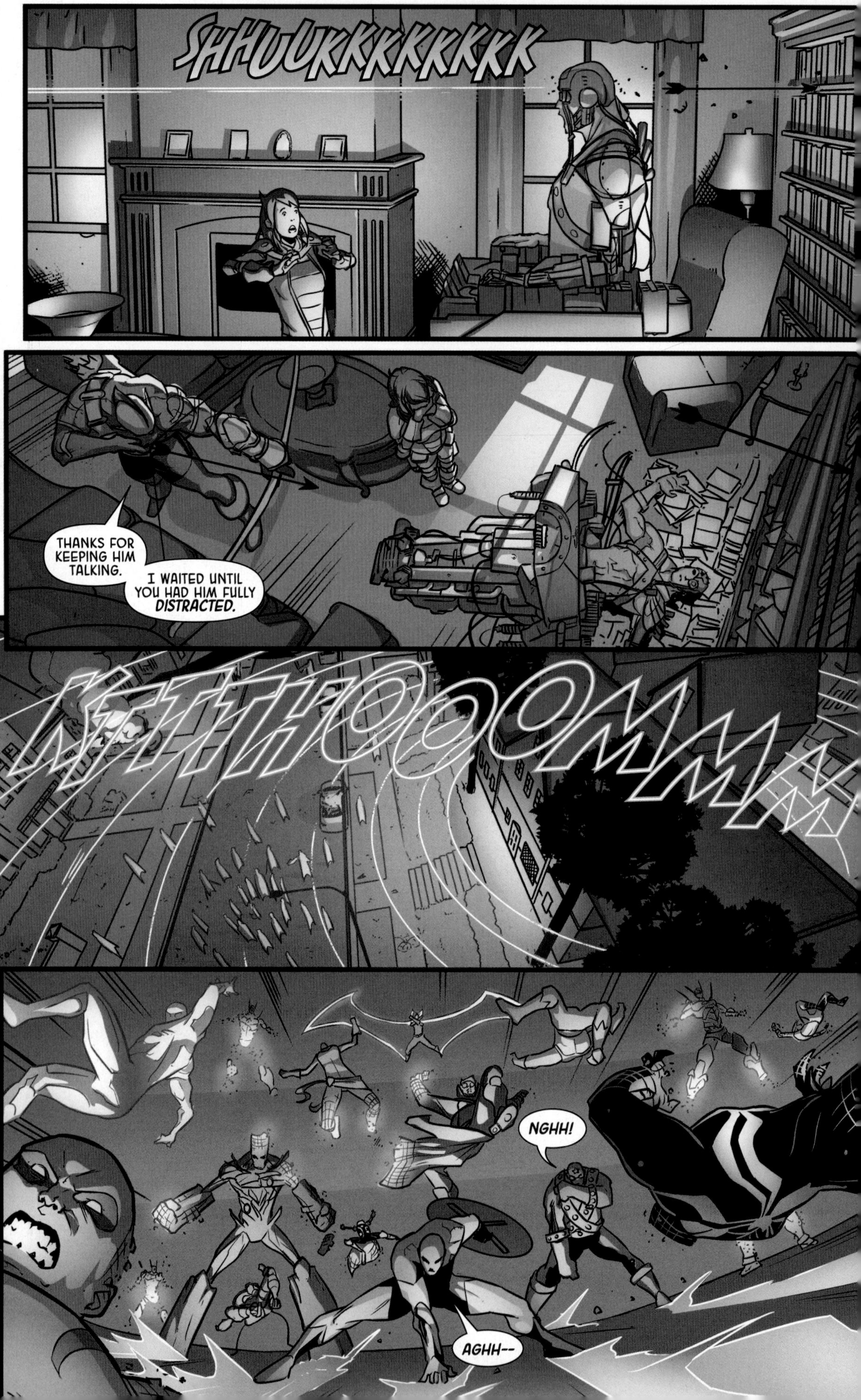
SHUUKKKKKKKK
THANKS FOR KEEPING HIM TALKING.
I WAITED UNTIL YOU HAD HIM FULLY DISTRACTED.
NGHH!
AGHH--

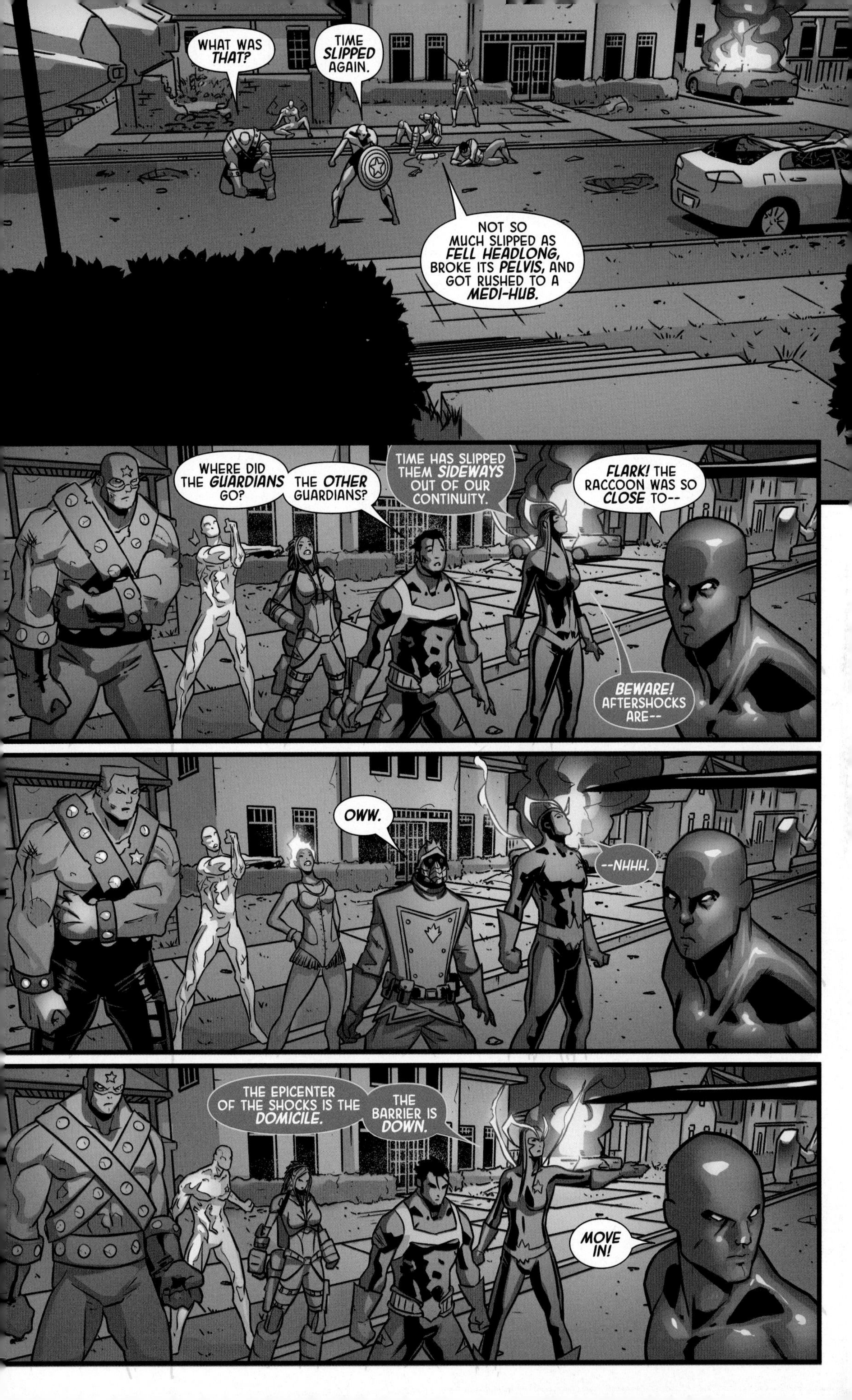
WHAT WAS THAT?
TIME SLIPPED AGAIN.
NOT SO MUCH SLIPPED AS FELL HEADLONG, BROKE ITS PELVIS, AND GOT RUSHED TO A MEDI-HUB.
WHERE DID THE GUARDIANS GO?
THE OTHER GUARDIANS?
TIME HAS SLIPPED THEM SIDEWAYS OUT OF OUR CONTINUITY.
FLARK! THE RACCOON WAS SO CLOSE TO--
BEWARE! AFTERSHOCKS ARE--
OWW.
--NHHH.
THE EPICENTER OF THE SHOCKS IS THE DOMICILE.
THE BARRIER IS DOWN.
MOVE IN!

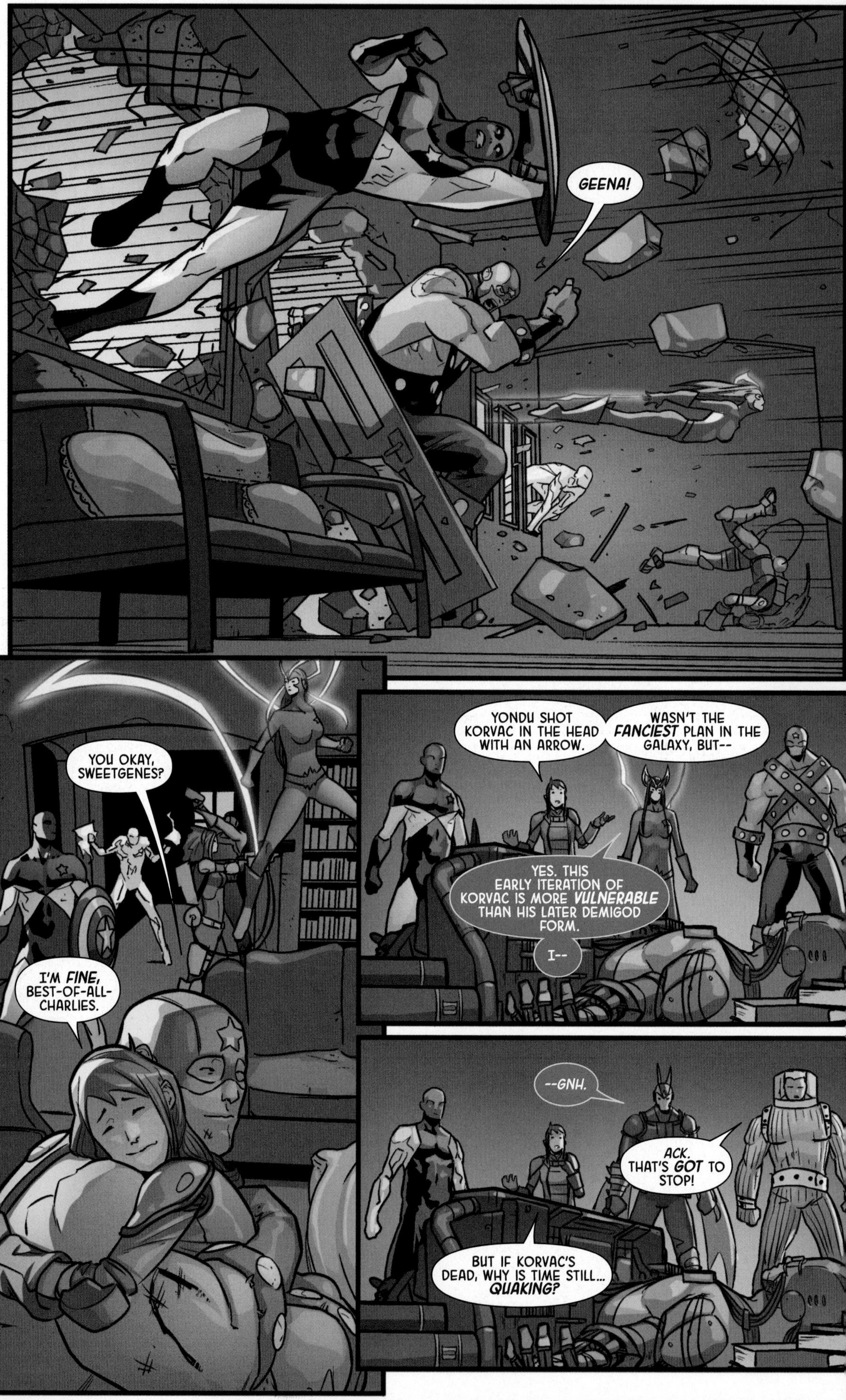
GEENA!
YOU OKAY, SWEETGENES?
I'M FINE, BEST-OF-ALL-CHARLIES.
YONDU SHOT KORVAC IN THE HEAD WITH AN ARROW.
WASN'T THE FANCIEST PLAN IN THE GALAXY, BUT--
YES. THIS EARLY ITERATION OF KORVAC IS MORE VULNERABLE THAN HIS LATER DEMIGOD FORM.
I--
--GNH.
ACK. THAT'S GOT TO STOP!
BUT IF KORVAC'S DEAD, WHY IS TIME STILL... QUAKING?

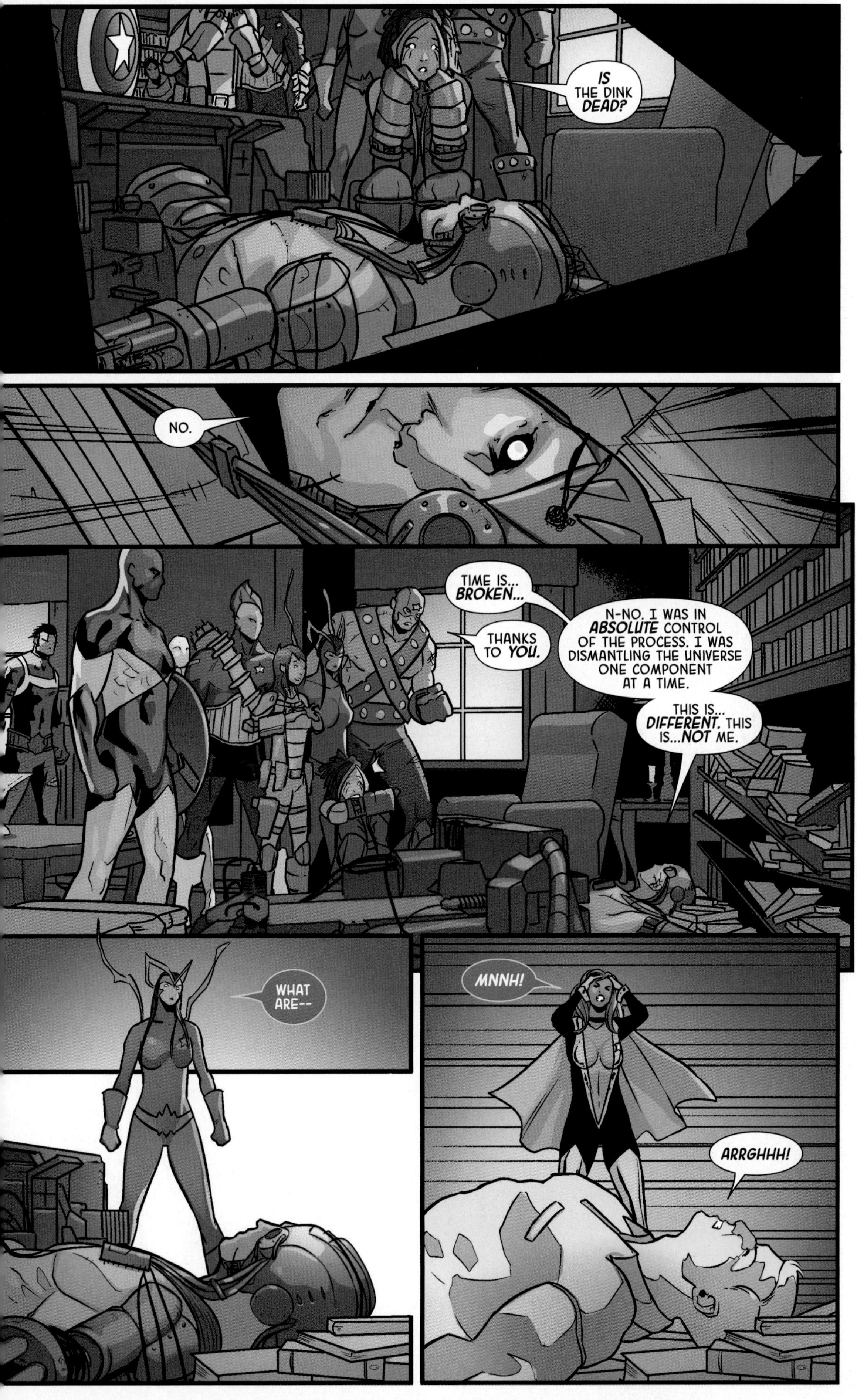
IS THE DINK DEAD?
NO.
TIME IS... BROKEN...
THANKS TO YOU.
N-NO. I WAS IN ABSOLUTE CONTROL OF THE PROCESS. I WAS DISMANTLING THE UNIVERSE ONE COMPONENT AT A TIME.
THIS IS... DIFFERENT. THIS IS...NOT ME.
WHAT ARE--
MNNH!
ARRGHHH!

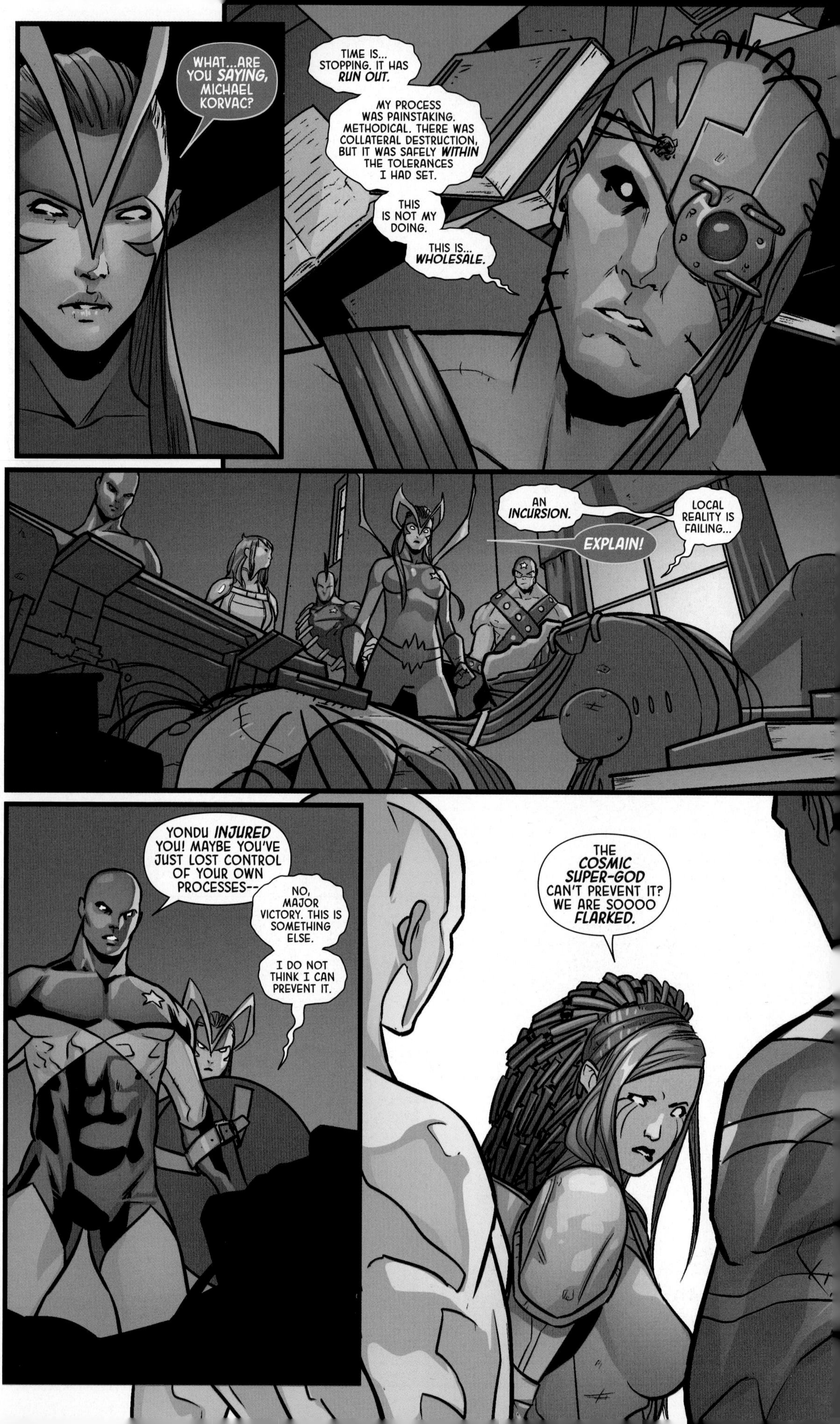
WHAT...ARE YOU SAYING, MICHAEL KORVAC?
TIME IS... STOPPING. IT HAS RUN OUT.
MY PROCESS WAS PAINSTAKING. METHODICAL. THERE WAS COLLATERAL DESTRUCTION, BUT IT WAS SAFELY WITHIN THE TOLERANCES I HAD SET.
THIS IS NOT MY DOING.
THIS IS... WHOLESALE.
AN INCURSION.
LOCAL REALITY IS FAILING...
EXPLAIN!
YONDU INJURED YOU! MAYBE YOU'VE JUST LOST CONTROL OF YOUR OWN PROCESSES--
NO, MAJOR VICTORY. THIS IS SOMETHING ELSE.
I DO NOT THINK I CAN PREVENT IT.
THE COSMIC SUPER-GOD CAN'T PREVENT IT? WE ARE SOOOO FLARKED.

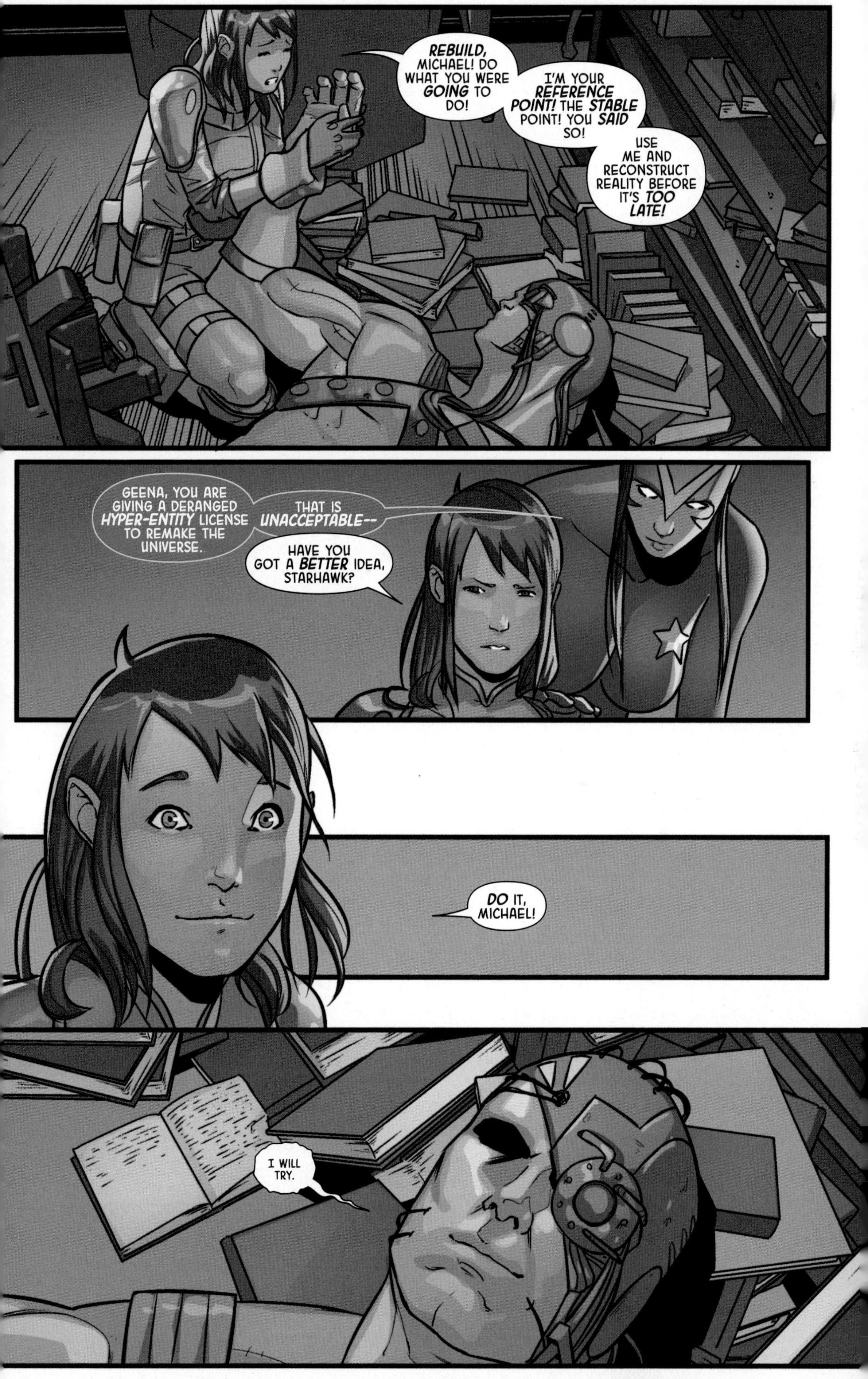
REBUILD, MICHAEL! DO WHAT YOU WERE GOING TO DO!
I'M YOUR REFERENCE POINT! THE STABLE POINT! YOU SAID SO!
USE ME AND RECONSTRUCT REALITY BEFORE IT'S TOO LATE!
GEENA, YOU ARE GIVING A DERANGED HYPER-ENTITY LICENSE TO REMAKE THE UNIVERSE.
THAT IS UNACCEPTABLE--
HAVE YOU GOT A BETTER IDEA, STARHAWK?
DO IT, MICHAEL!
I WILL TRY.

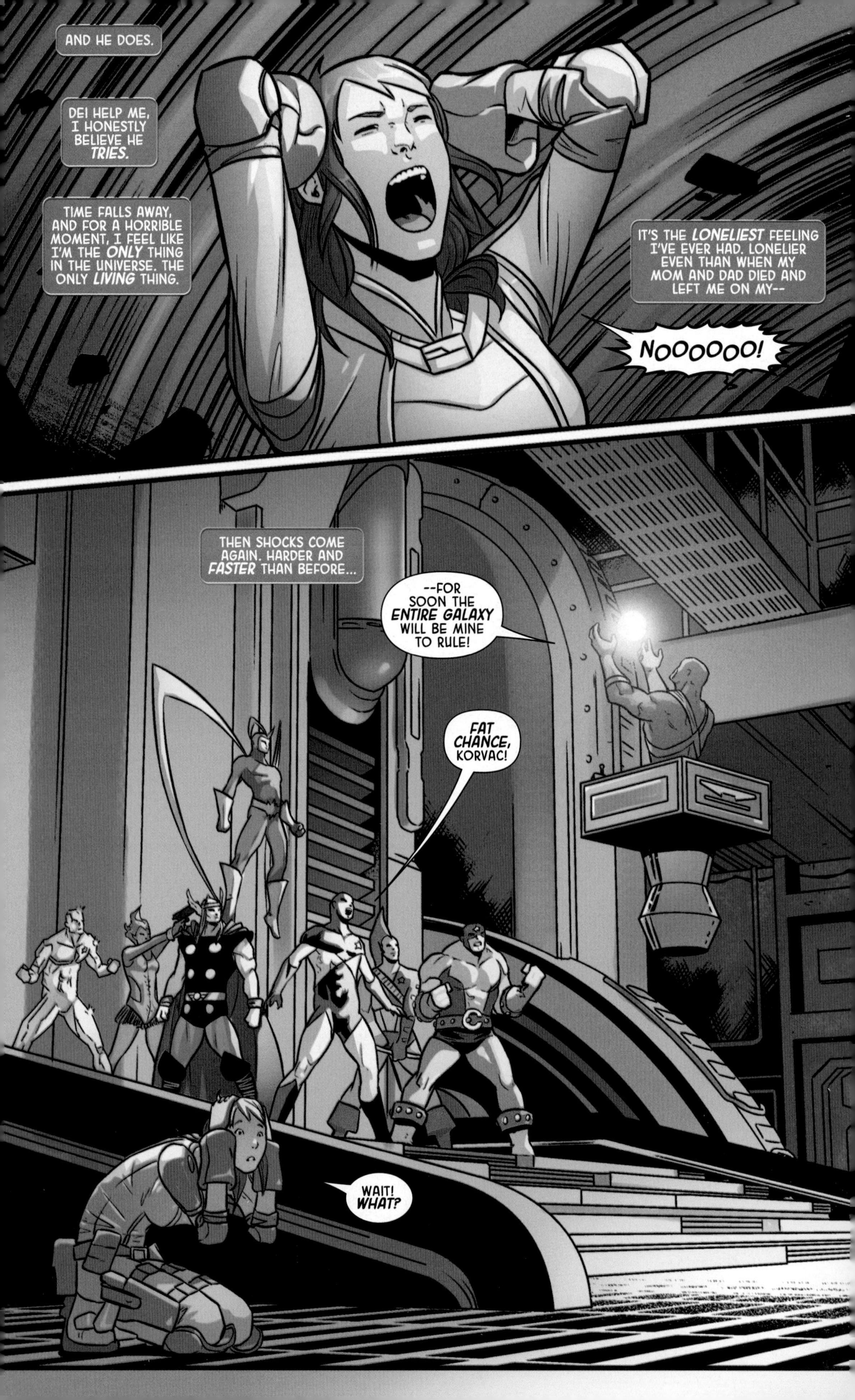

AND HE DOES.
DEI HELP ME, I HONESTLY BELIEVE HE *TRIES.*
TIME FALLS AWAY, AND FOR A HORRIBLE MOMENT, I FEEL LIKE I'M THE *ONLY* THING IN THE UNIVERSE. THE ONLY *LIVING* THING.
IT'S THE *LONELIEST* FEELING I'VE EVER HAD. LONELIER EVEN THAN WHEN MY MOM AND DAD DIED AND LEFT ME ON MY--
NOOOOOO!
THEN SHOCKS COME AGAIN. HARDER AND *FASTER* THAN BEFORE...
--FOR SOON THE *ENTIRE GALAXY* WILL BE MINE TO RULE!
FAT CHANCE, KORVAC!
WAIT! *WHAT?*

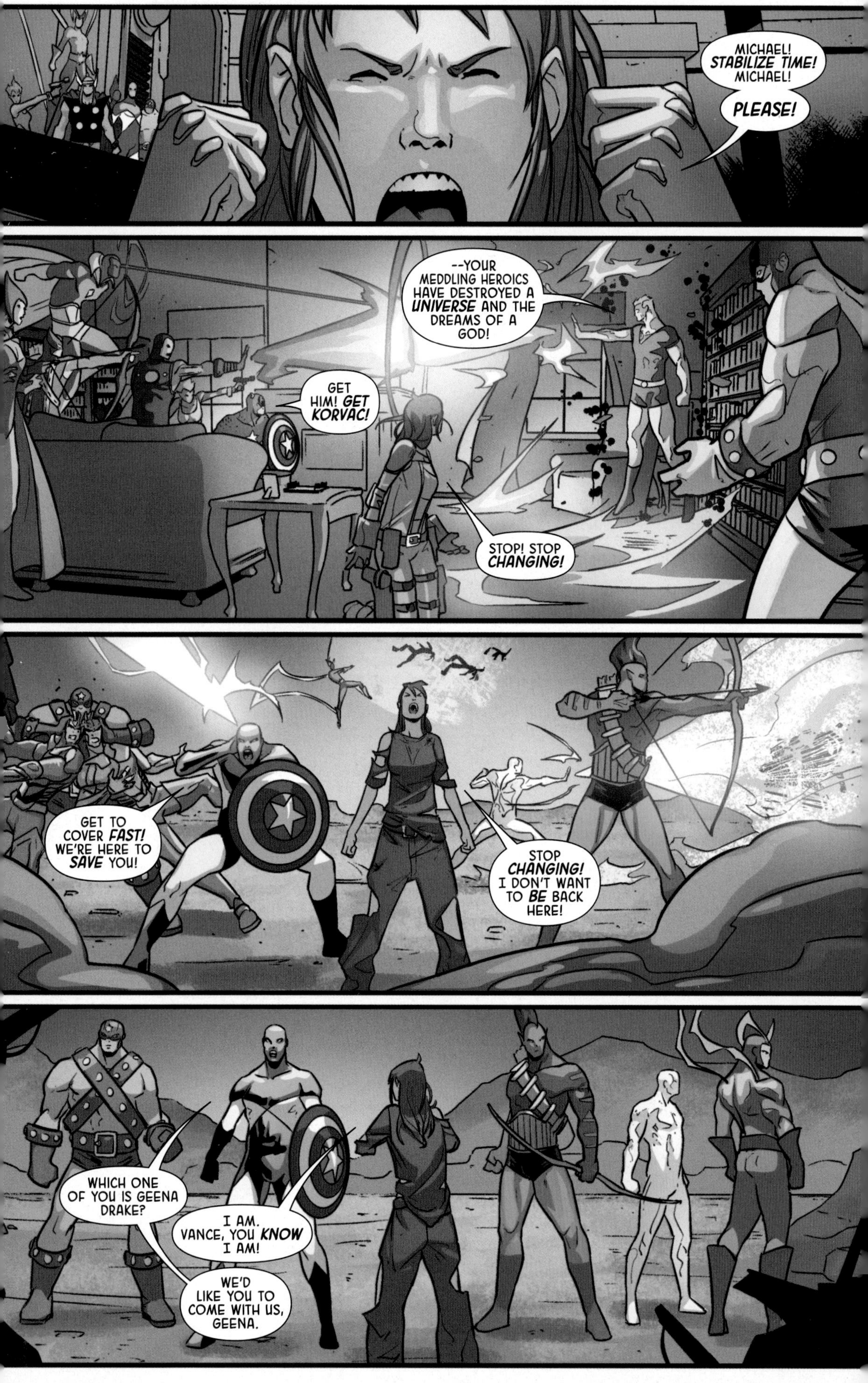
MICHAEL! STABILIZE TIME! MICHAEL!
PLEASE!
--YOUR MEDDLING HEROICS HAVE DESTROYED A UNIVERSE AND THE DREAMS OF A GOD!
GET HIM! GET KORVAC!
STOP! STOP CHANGING!
GET TO COVER FAST! WE'RE HERE TO SAVE YOU!
STOP CHANGING! I DON'T WANT TO BE BACK HERE!
WHICH ONE OF YOU IS GEENA DRAKE?
I AM. VANCE, YOU KNOW I AM!
WE'D LIKE YOU TO COME WITH US, GEENA.

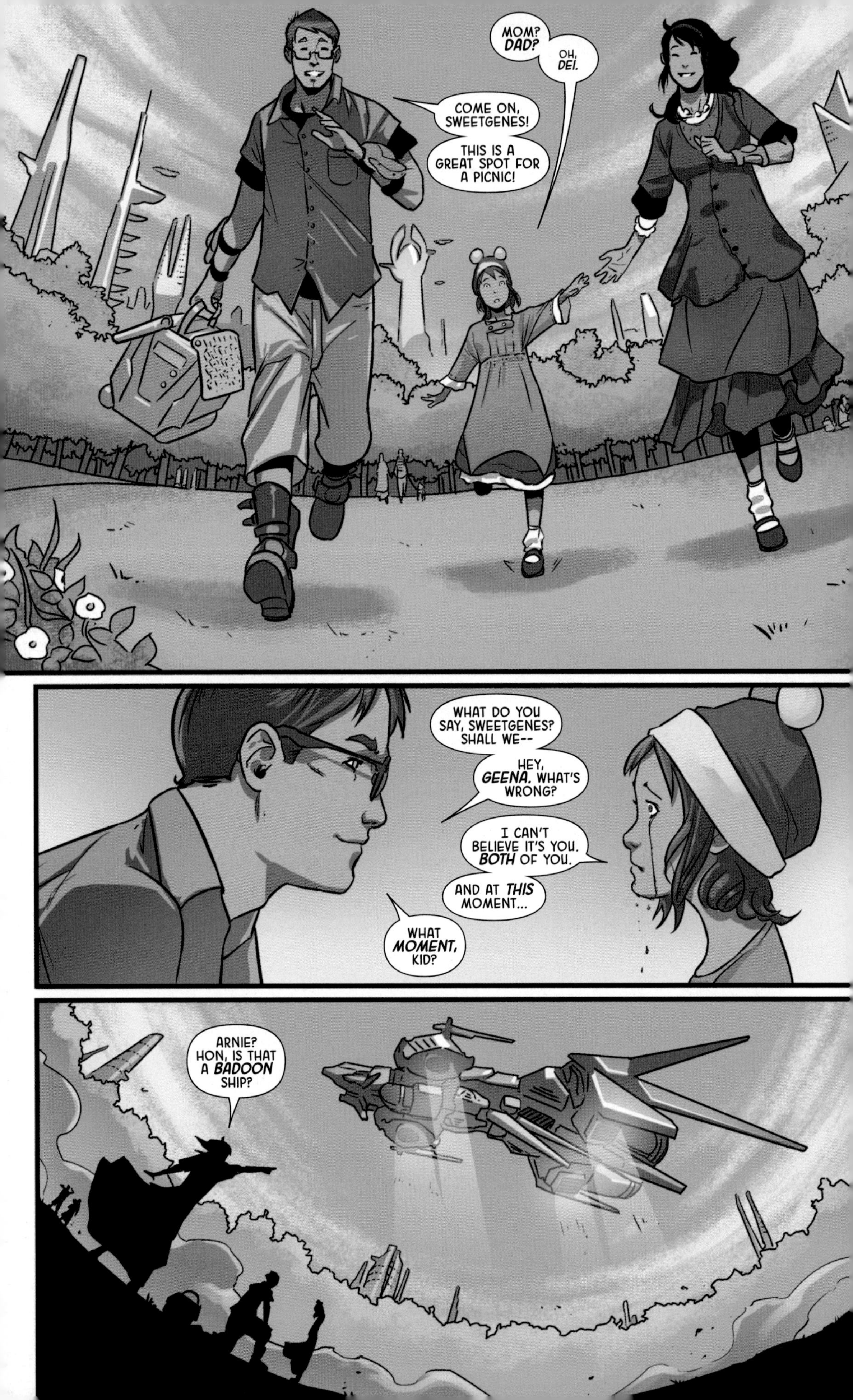
MOM? DAD?
OH, DEI.
COME ON, SWEETGENES!
THIS IS A GREAT SPOT FOR A PICNIC!
WHAT DO YOU SAY, SWEETGENES? SHALL WE--
HEY, GEENA. WHAT'S WRONG?
I CAN'T BELIEVE IT'S YOU. BOTH OF YOU.
AND AT THIS MOMENT...
WHAT MOMENT, KID?
ARNIE? HON, IS THAT A BADOON SHIP?

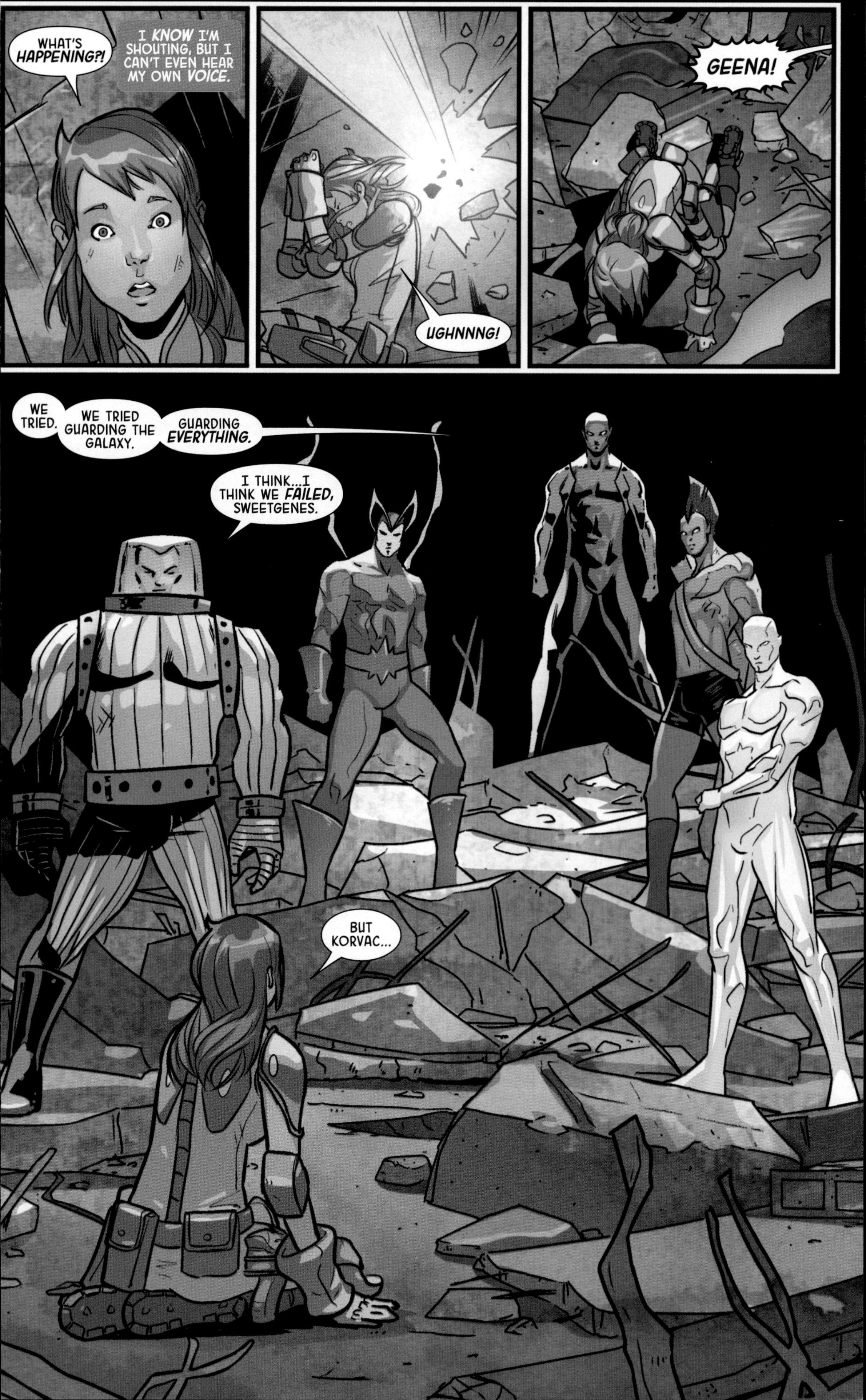
WHAT'S HAPPENING?!
I KNOW I'M SHOUTING, BUT I CAN'T EVEN HEAR MY OWN VOICE.
UGHNNNG!
GEENA!
WE TRIED.
WE TRIED GUARDING THE GALAXY.
GUARDING EVERYTHING.
I THINK...I THINK WE FAILED, SWEETGENES.
BUT KORVAC...

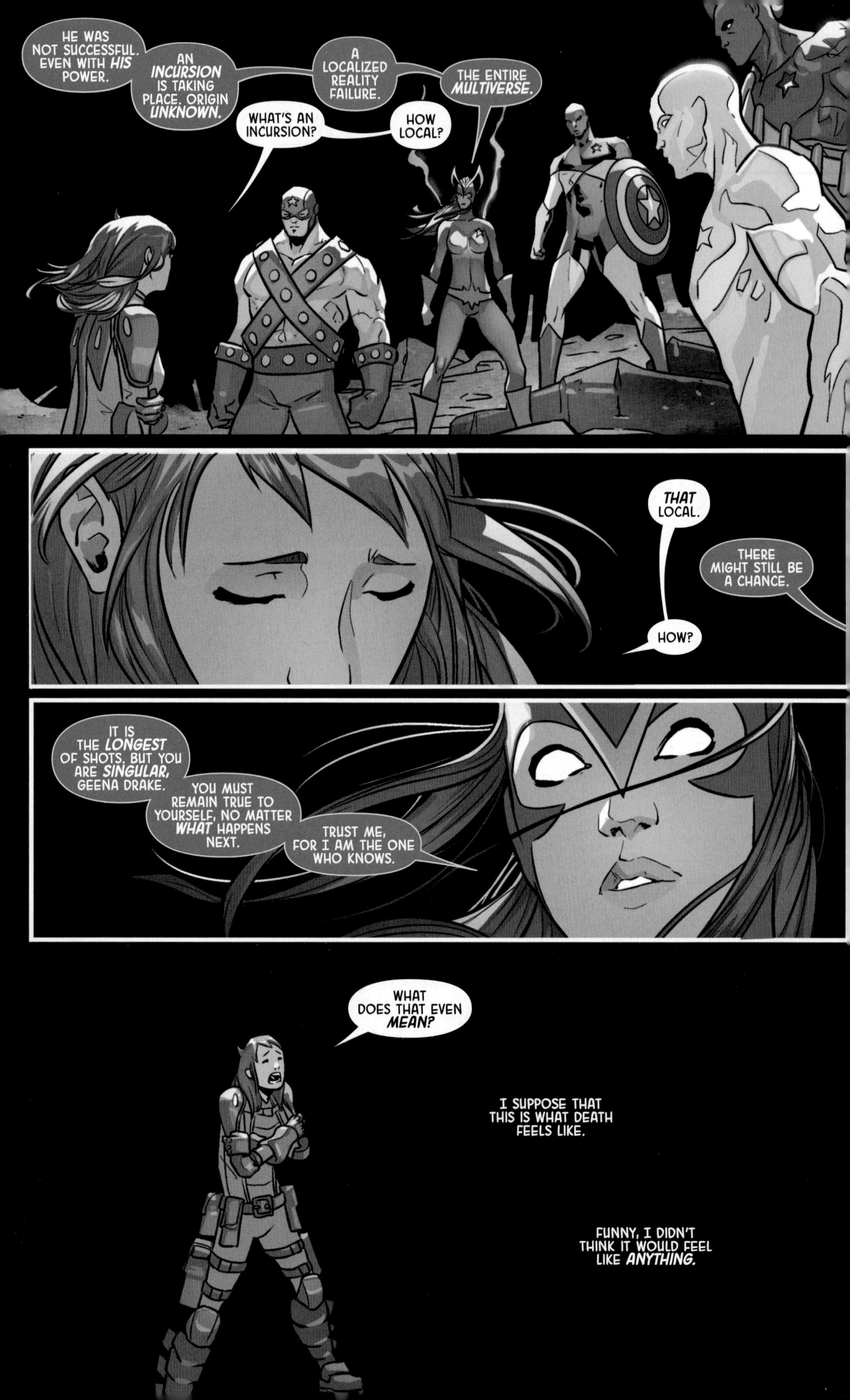
HE WAS NOT SUCCESSFUL. EVEN WITH *HIS* POWER.
AN *INCURSION* IS TAKING PLACE. ORIGIN *UNKNOWN.*
A LOCALIZED REALITY FAILURE.
THE ENTIRE *MULTIVERSE.*
WHAT'S AN INCURSION?
HOW LOCAL?
THAT LOCAL.
THERE MIGHT STILL BE A CHANCE.
HOW?
IT IS THE *LONGEST* OF SHOTS, BUT YOU ARE *SINGULAR,* GEENA DRAKE.
YOU MUST REMAIN TRUE TO YOURSELF, NO MATTER *WHAT* HAPPENS NEXT.
TRUST ME, FOR I AM THE ONE WHO KNOWS.
WHAT DOES THAT EVEN *MEAN?*
I SUPPOSE THAT THIS IS WHAT DEATH FEELS LIKE.
FUNNY, I DIDN'T THINK IT WOULD FEEL LIKE *ANYTHING.*

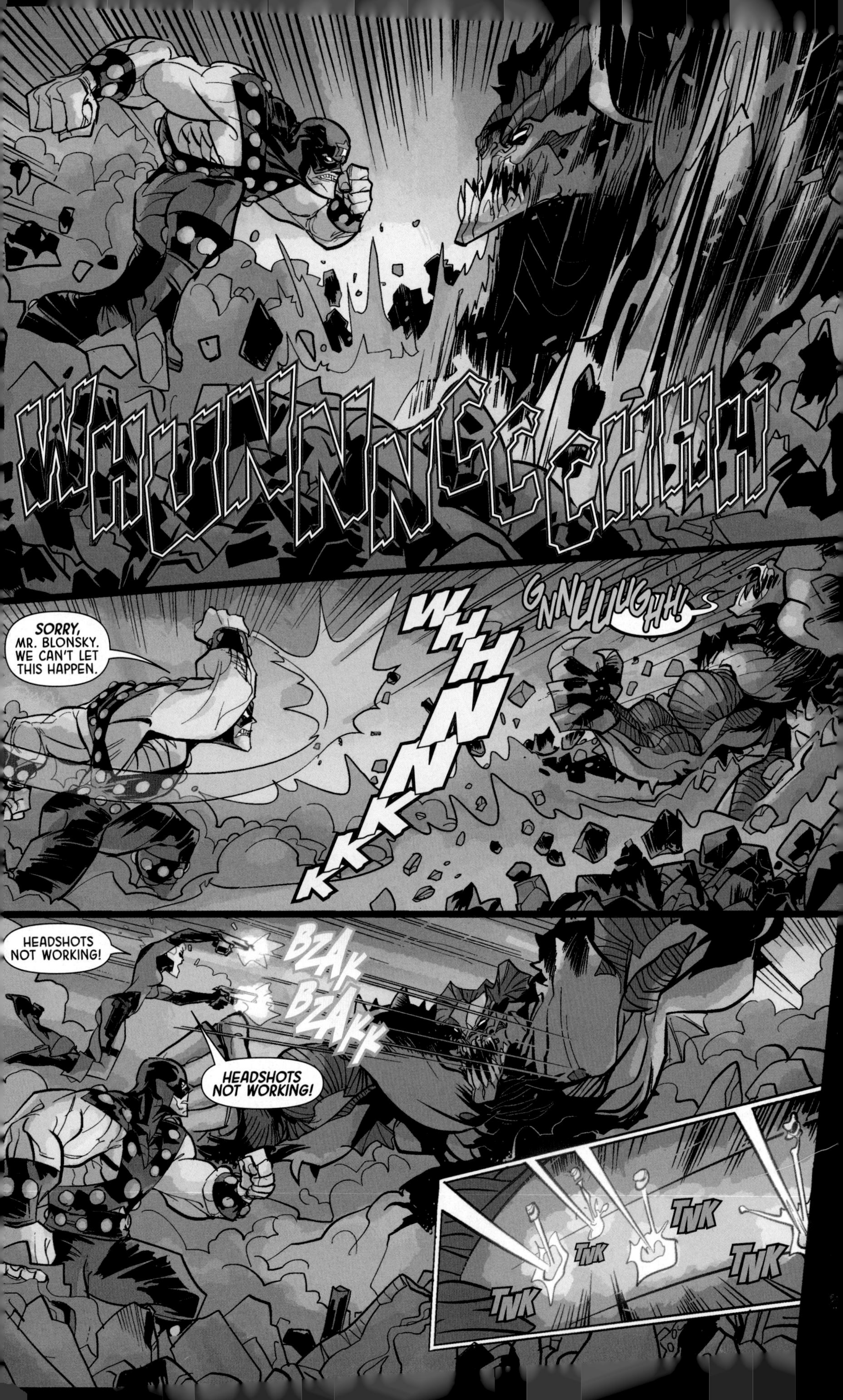
WHUNNGCCHHH
SORRY, MR. BLONSKY. WE CAN'T LET THIS HAPPEN.
WHHNNKKK
GNNUUUGHH!
HEADSHOTS NOT WORKING!
BZAK BZAKK
HEADSHOTS NOT WORKING!
TNK
TNK
TNK
TNK

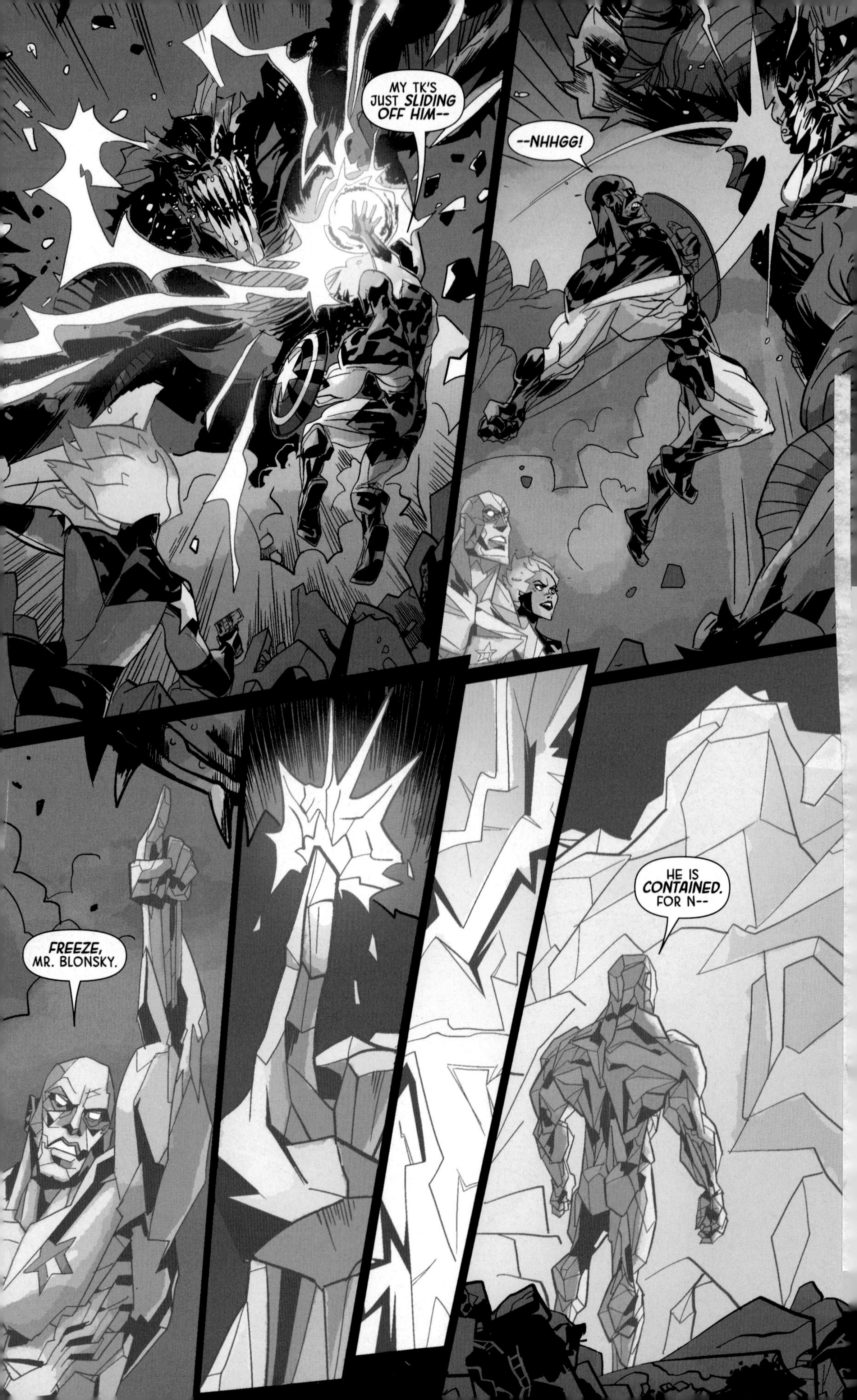
MY TK'S JUST SLIDING OFF HIM--
--NHHGG!
FREEZE, MR. BLONSKY.
HE IS CONTAINED. FOR N--

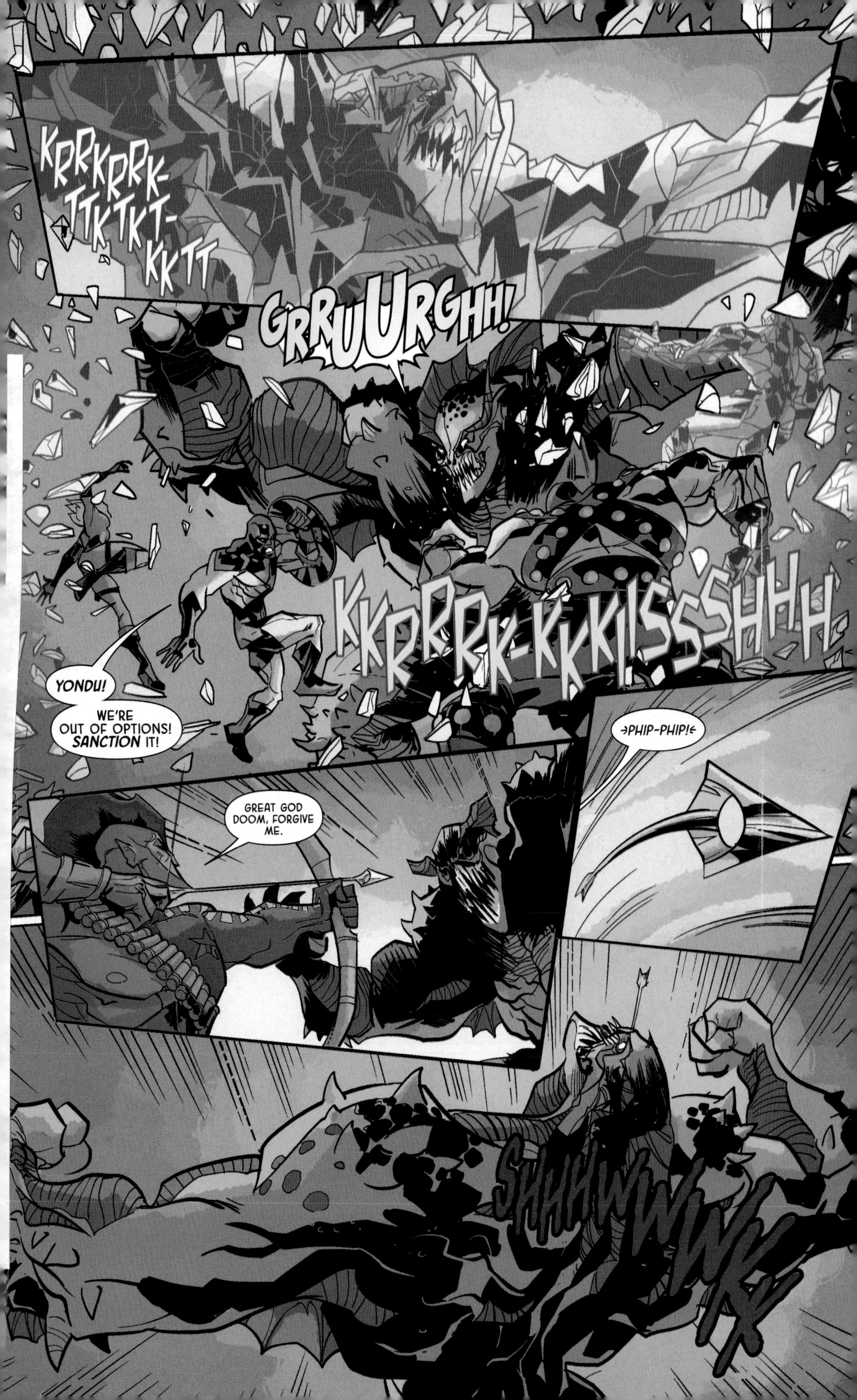
KRRKRRK-TTKTKT-KKTT
GRRUURGHH!
KKRRRK-KKKISSSHHH
YONDU!
WE'RE OUT OF OPTIONS! SANCTION IT!
GREAT GOD DOOM, FORGIVE ME.
PHIP-PHIP!
SHHHWWWK

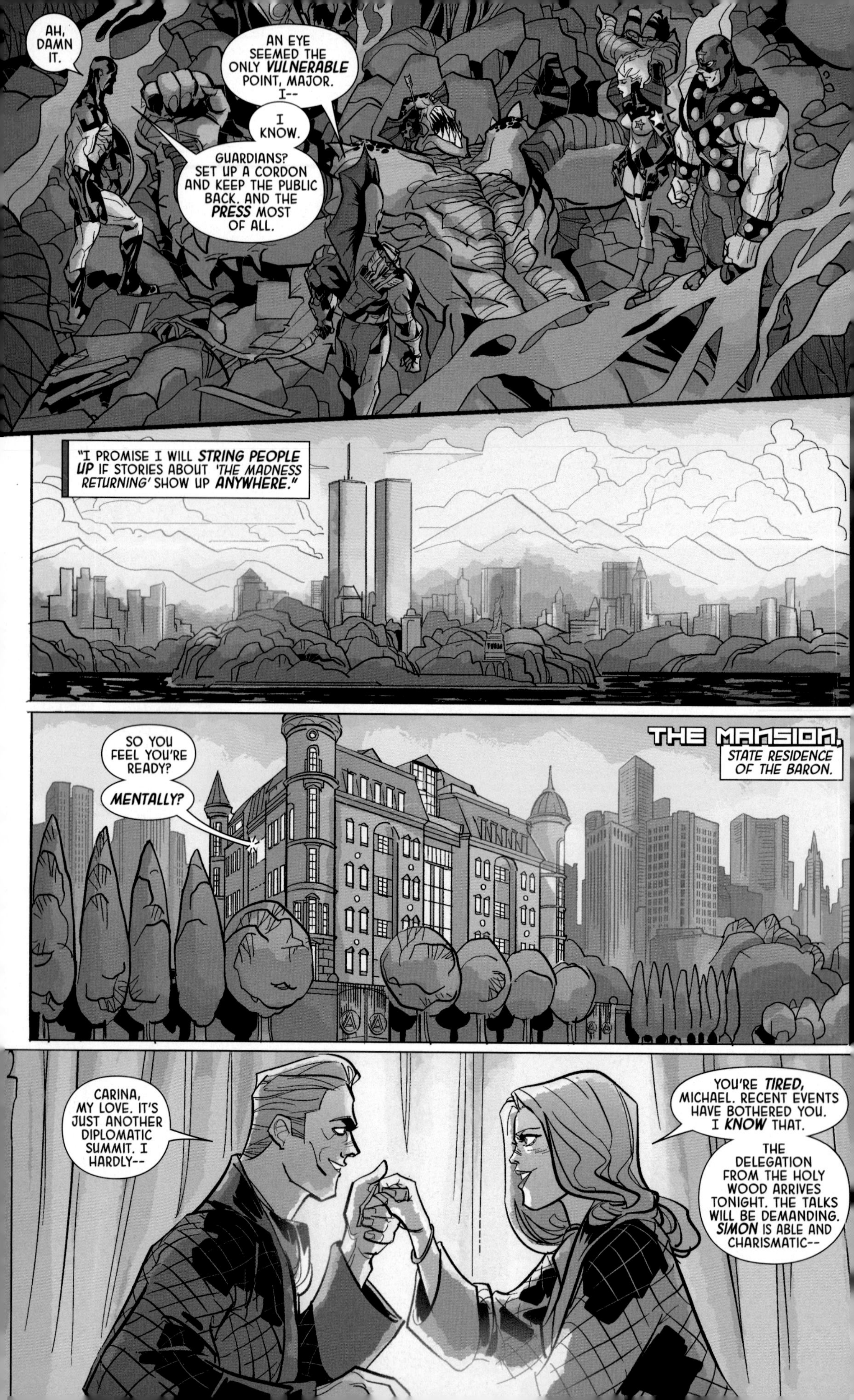
AH, DAMN IT.
AN EYE SEEMED THE ONLY VULNERABLE POINT, MAJOR. I--
I KNOW.
GUARDIANS? SET UP A CORDON AND KEEP THE PUBLIC BACK. AND THE PRESS MOST OF ALL.
"I PROMISE I WILL STRING PEOPLE UP IF STORIES ABOUT 'THE MADNESS RETURNING' SHOW UP ANYWHERE."
THE MANSION,
STATE RESIDENCE OF THE BARON.
SO YOU FEEL YOU'RE READY?
MENTALLY?
CARINA, MY LOVE. IT'S JUST ANOTHER DIPLOMATIC SUMMIT. I HARDLY--
YOU'RE TIRED, MICHAEL. RECENT EVENTS HAVE BOTHERED YOU. I KNOW THAT.
THE DELEGATION FROM THE HOLY WOOD ARRIVES TONIGHT. THE TALKS WILL BE DEMANDING. SIMON IS ABLE AND CHARISMATIC--

WORLD ENOUGH AND TIME

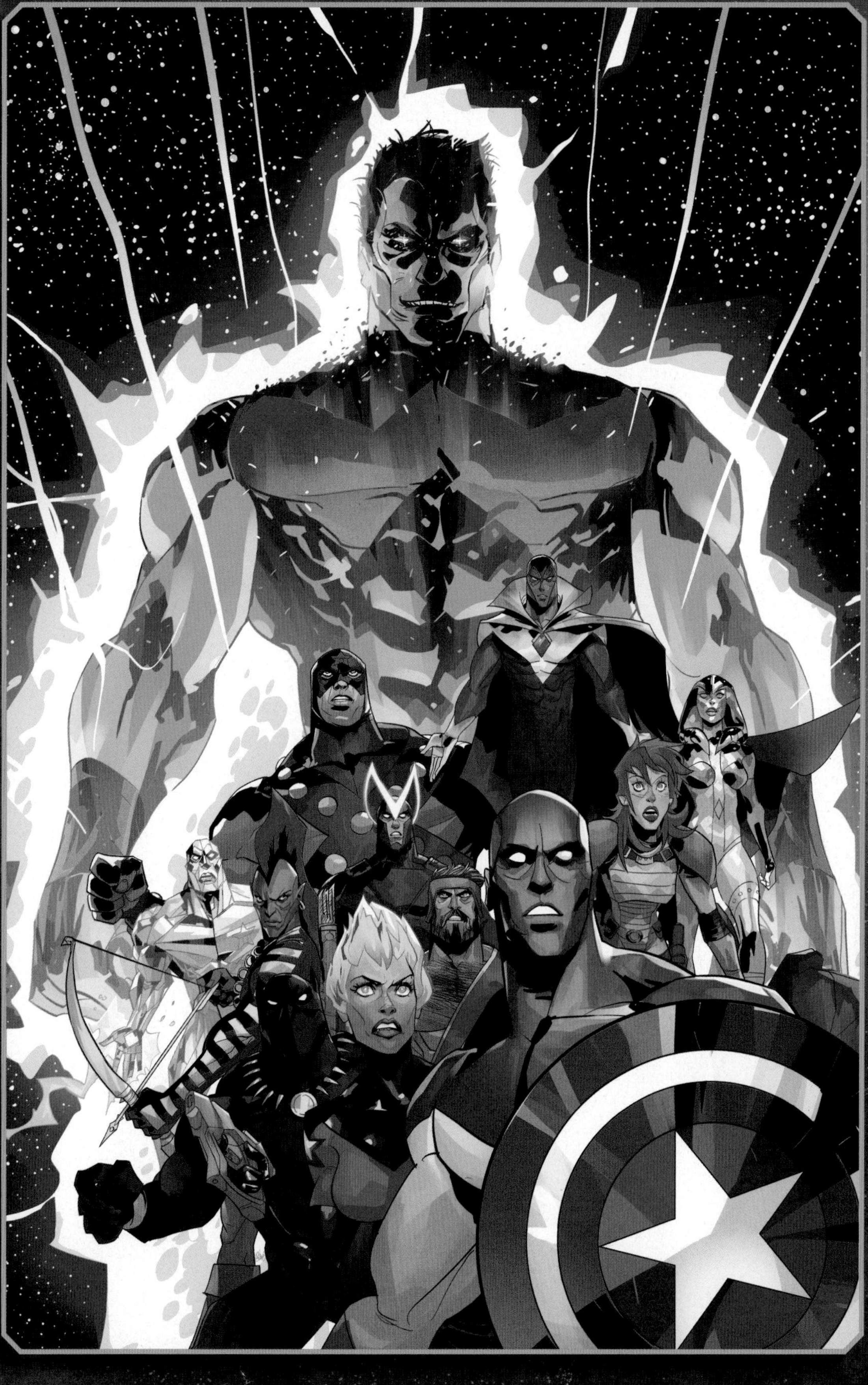

KORVAC SAGA #1

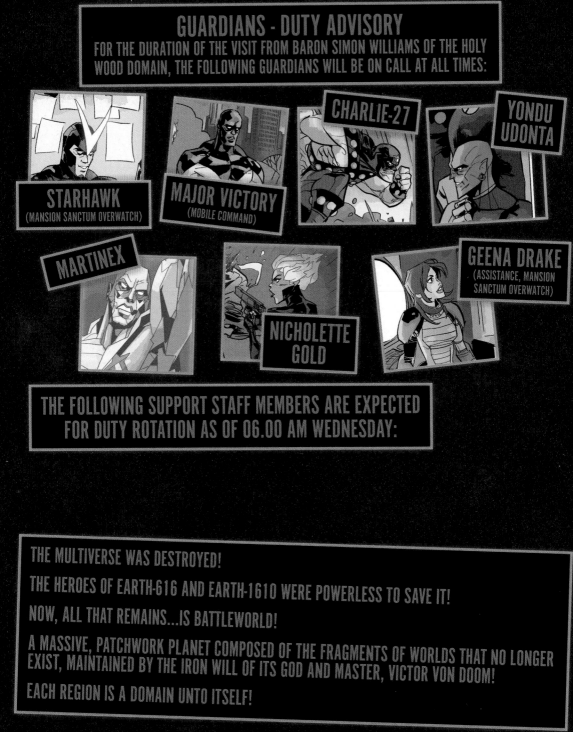

GUARDIANS - DUTY ADVISORY

FOR THE DURATION OF THE VISIT FROM BARON SIMON WILLIAMS OF THE HOLY WOOD DOMAIN, THE FOLLOWING GUARDIANS WILL BE ON CALL AT ALL TIMES:

STARHAWK
(MANSION SANCTUM OVERWATCH)

MAJOR VICTORY
(MOBILE COMMAND)

CHARLIE-27

YONDU UDONTA

MARTINEX

NICHOLETTE GOLD

GEENA DRAKE
(ASSISTANCE, MANSION SANCTUM OVERWATCH)

THE FOLLOWING SUPPORT STAFF MEMBERS ARE EXPECTED FOR DUTY ROTATION AS OF 06.00 AM WEDNESDAY:

THE MULTIVERSE WAS DESTROYED!

THE HEROES OF EARTH-616 AND EARTH-1610 WERE POWERLESS TO SAVE IT!

NOW, ALL THAT REMAINS...IS BATTLEWORLD!

A MASSIVE, PATCHWORK PLANET COMPOSED OF THE FRAGMENTS OF WORLDS THAT NO LONGER EXIST, MAINTAINED BY THE IRON WILL OF ITS GOD AND MASTER, VICTOR VON DOOM!

EACH REGION IS A DOMAIN UNTO ITSELF!

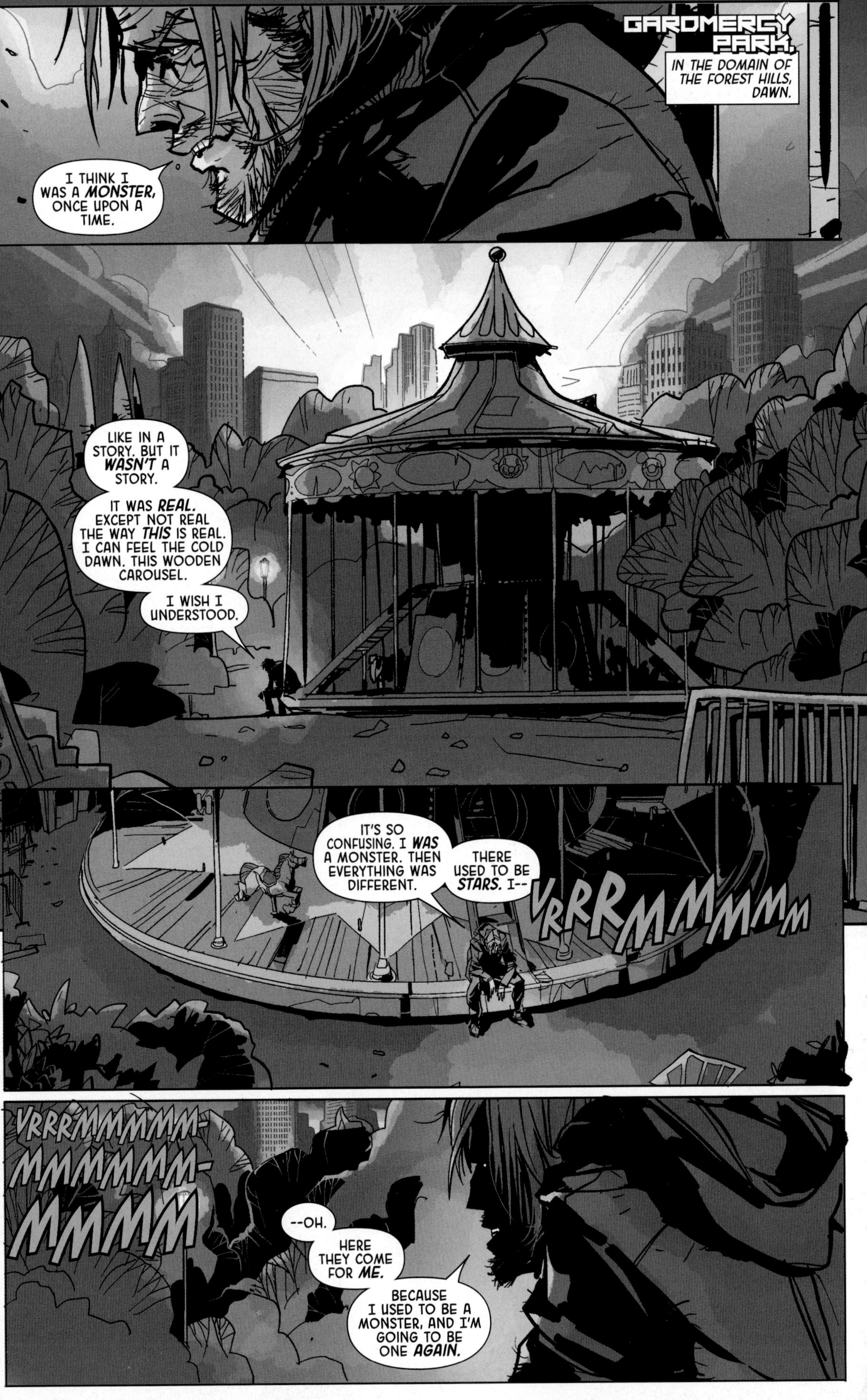
GARDMERCY PARK.
IN THE DOMAIN OF THE FOREST HILLS, DAWN.
I THINK I WAS A MONSTER, ONCE UPON A TIME.
LIKE IN A STORY. BUT IT WASN'T A STORY.
IT WAS REAL. EXCEPT NOT REAL THE WAY THIS IS REAL. I CAN FEEL THE COLD DAWN. THIS WOODEN CAROUSEL.
I WISH I UNDERSTOOD.
IT'S SO CONFUSING. I WAS A MONSTER. THEN EVERYTHING WAS DIFFERENT.
THERE USED TO BE STARS. I--
VRRRMMMMMM
VRRRMMMMMM-MMMMMM-MMMM
--OH.
HERE THEY COME FOR ME.
BECAUSE I USED TO BE A MONSTER, AND I'M GOING TO BE ONE AGAIN.

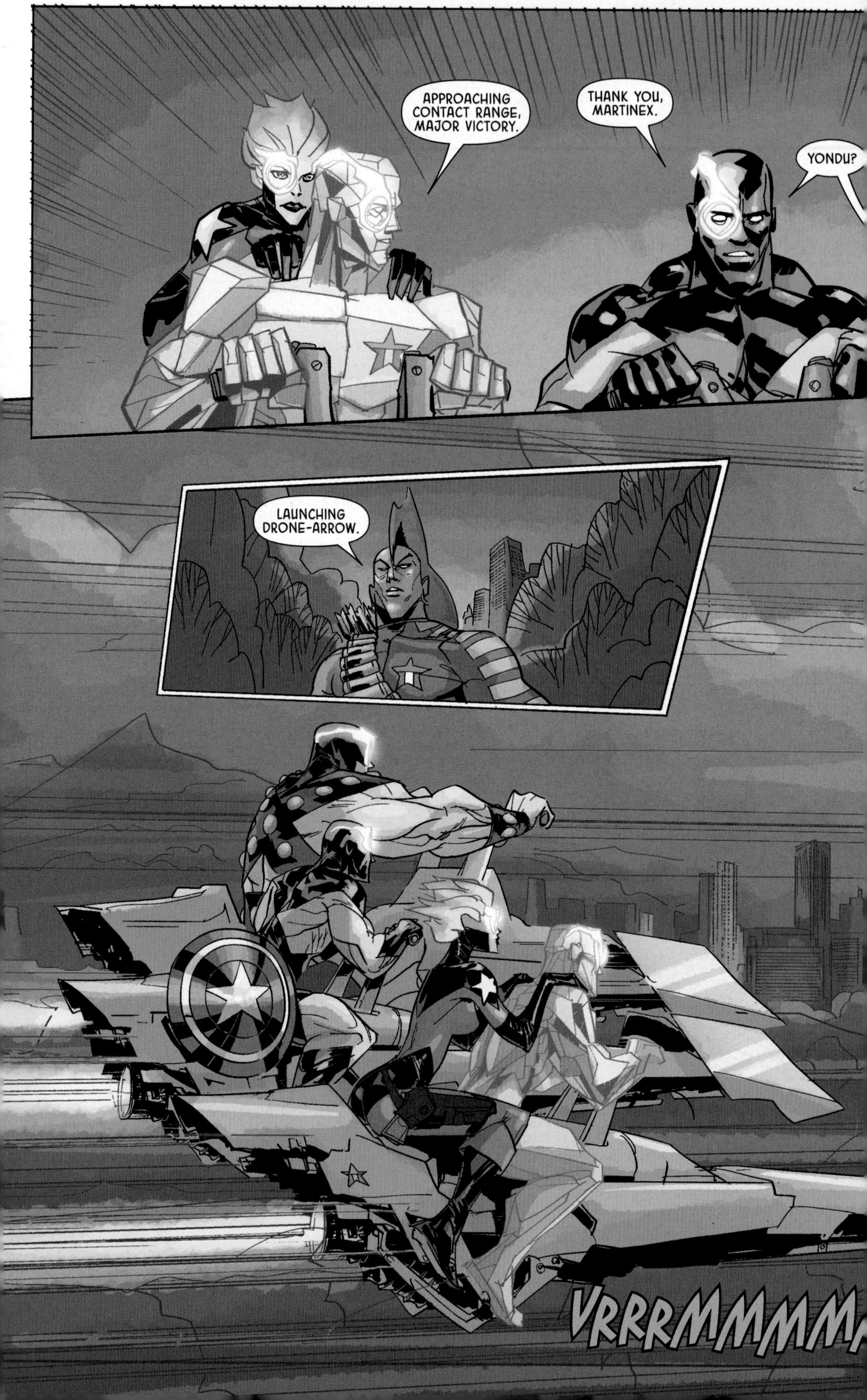
APPROACHING CONTACT RANGE, MAJOR VICTORY.
THANK YOU, MARTINEX.
YONDU?
LAUNCHING DRONE-ARROW.
VRRRMMMMM

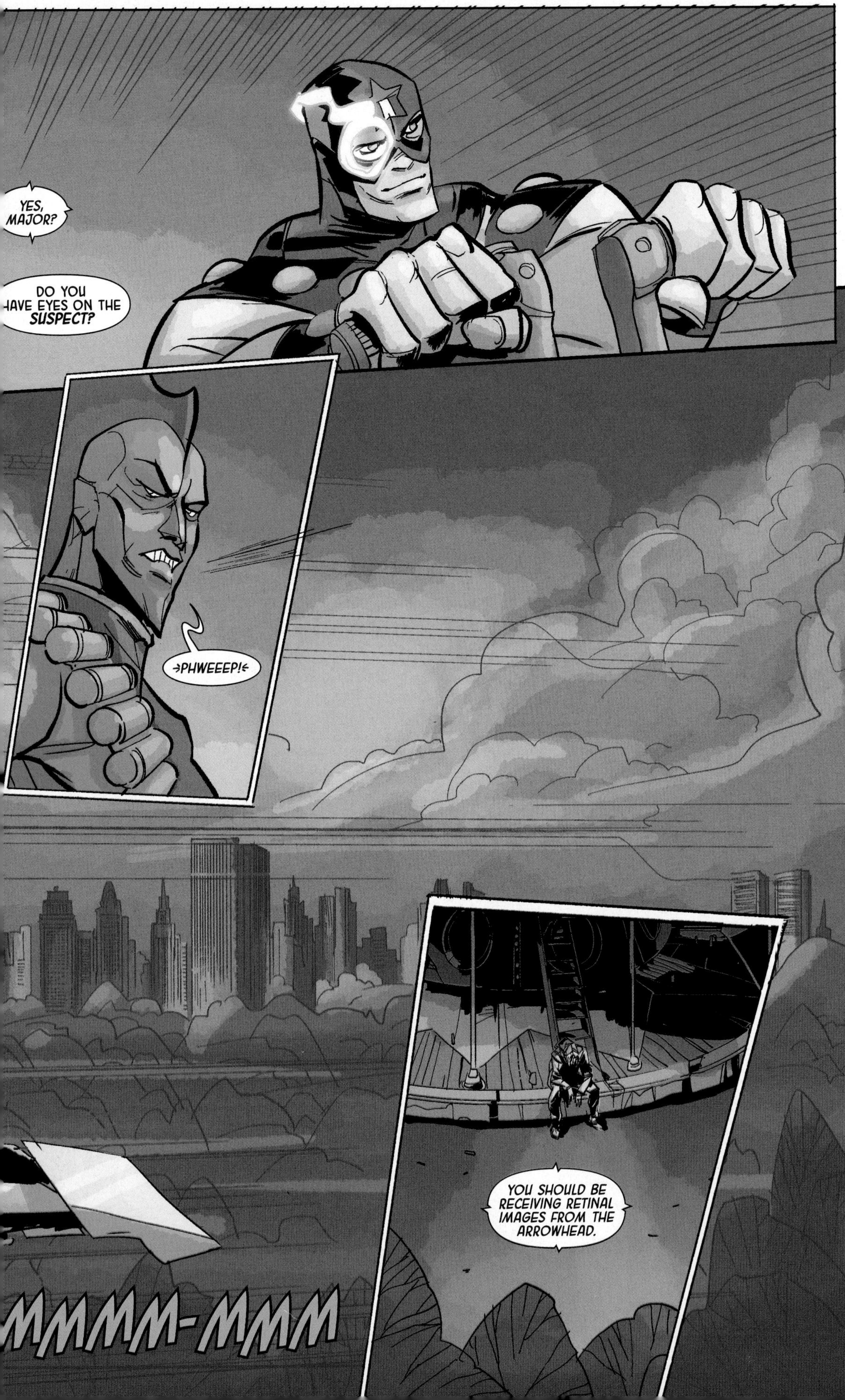
YES, MAJOR?
DO YOU HAVE EYES ON THE SUSPECT?
PHWEEEP!
YOU SHOULD BE RECEIVING RETINAL IMAGES FROM THE ARROWHEAD.
MMMM-MMM

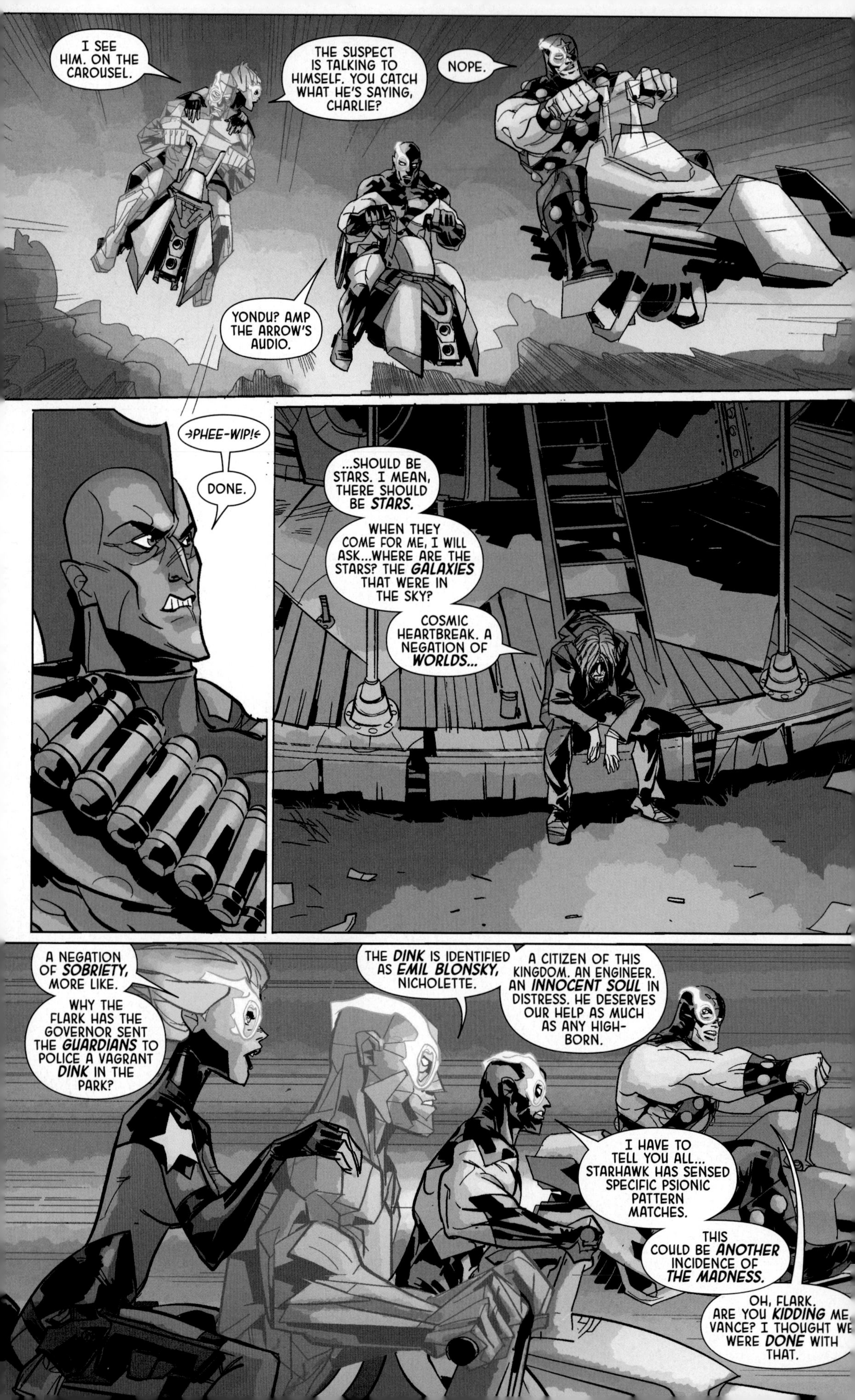

I SEE HIM. ON THE CAROUSEL.
THE SUSPECT IS TALKING TO HIMSELF. YOU CATCH WHAT HE'S SAYING, CHARLIE?
NOPE.
YONDU? AMP THE ARROW'S AUDIO.
PHEE-WIP!
DONE.
...SHOULD BE STARS. I MEAN, THERE SHOULD BE STARS.
WHEN THEY COME FOR ME, I WILL ASK...WHERE ARE THE STARS? THE GALAXIES THAT WERE IN THE SKY?
COSMIC HEARTBREAK. A NEGATION OF WORLDS...
A NEGATION OF SOBRIETY, MORE LIKE.
WHY THE FLARK HAS THE GOVERNOR SENT THE GUARDIANS TO POLICE A VAGRANT DINK IN THE PARK?
THE DINK IS IDENTIFIED AS EMIL BLONSKY, NICHOLETTE.
A CITIZEN OF THIS KINGDOM. AN ENGINEER. AN INNOCENT SOUL IN DISTRESS. HE DESERVES OUR HELP AS MUCH AS ANY HIGH-BORN.
I HAVE TO TELL YOU ALL... STARHAWK HAS SENSED SPECIFIC PSIONIC PATTERN MATCHES.
THIS COULD BE ANOTHER INCIDENCE OF THE MADNESS.
OH, FLARK. ARE YOU KIDDING ME, VANCE? I THOUGHT WE WERE DONE WITH THAT.

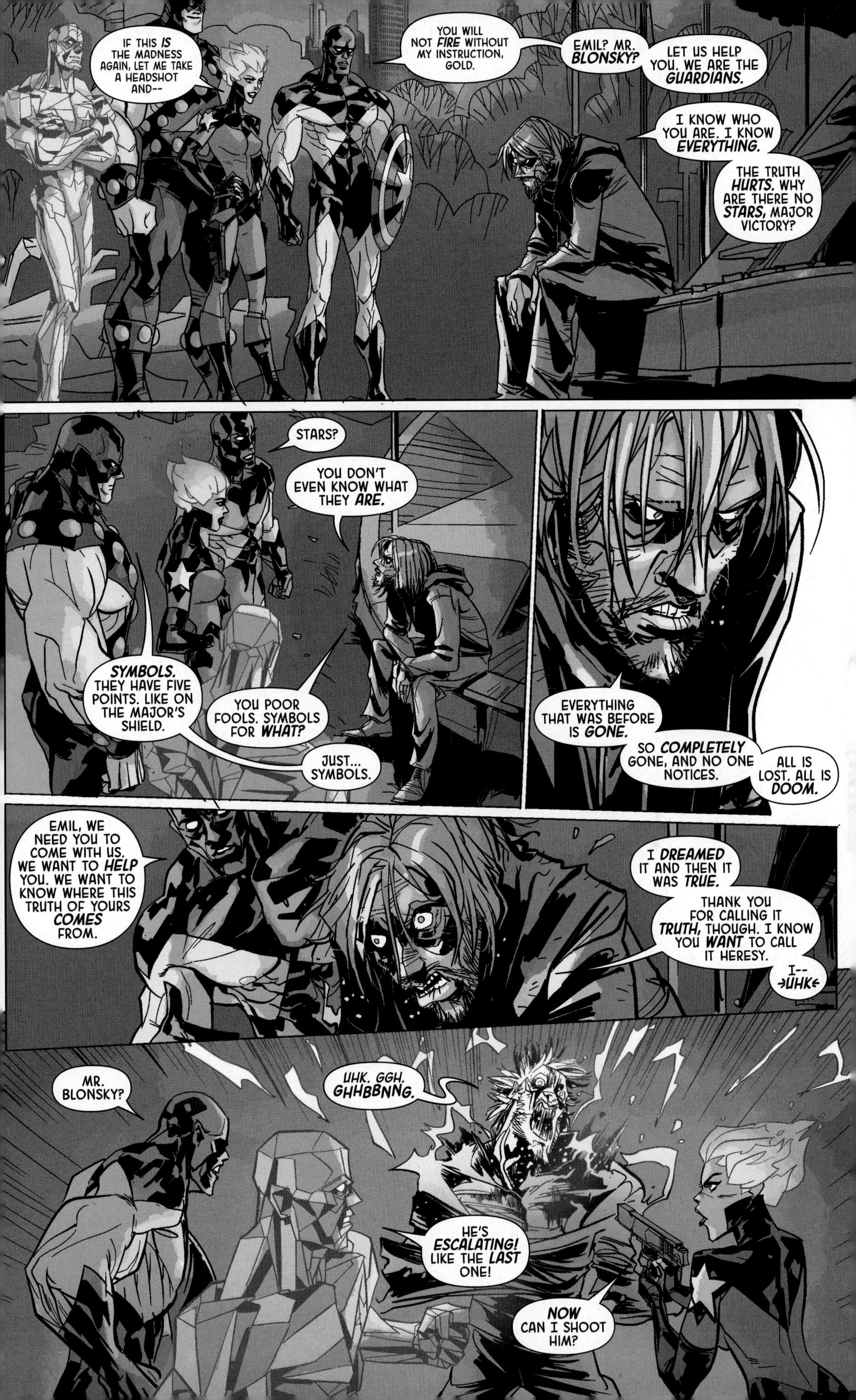
IF THIS IS THE MADNESS AGAIN, LET ME TAKE A HEADSHOT AND--
YOU WILL NOT FIRE WITHOUT MY INSTRUCTION, GOLD.
EMIL? MR. BLONSKY?
LET US HELP YOU. WE ARE THE GUARDIANS.
I KNOW WHO YOU ARE. I KNOW EVERYTHING.
THE TRUTH HURTS. WHY ARE THERE NO STARS, MAJOR VICTORY?
STARS?
YOU DON'T EVEN KNOW WHAT THEY ARE.
SYMBOLS. THEY HAVE FIVE POINTS. LIKE ON THE MAJOR'S SHIELD.
YOU POOR FOOLS. SYMBOLS FOR WHAT?
JUST... SYMBOLS.
EVERYTHING THAT WAS BEFORE IS GONE.
SO COMPLETELY GONE, AND NO ONE NOTICES.
ALL IS LOST. ALL IS DOOM.
EMIL, WE NEED YOU TO COME WITH US. WE WANT TO HELP YOU. WE WANT TO KNOW WHERE THIS TRUTH OF YOURS COMES FROM.
I DREAMED IT AND THEN IT WAS TRUE.
THANK YOU FOR CALLING IT TRUTH, THOUGH. I KNOW YOU WANT TO CALL IT HERESY.
I--
UHK
MR. BLONSKY?
UHK. GGH. GHHBBNNG.
HE'S ESCALATING! LIKE THE LAST ONE!
NOW CAN I SHOOT HIM?

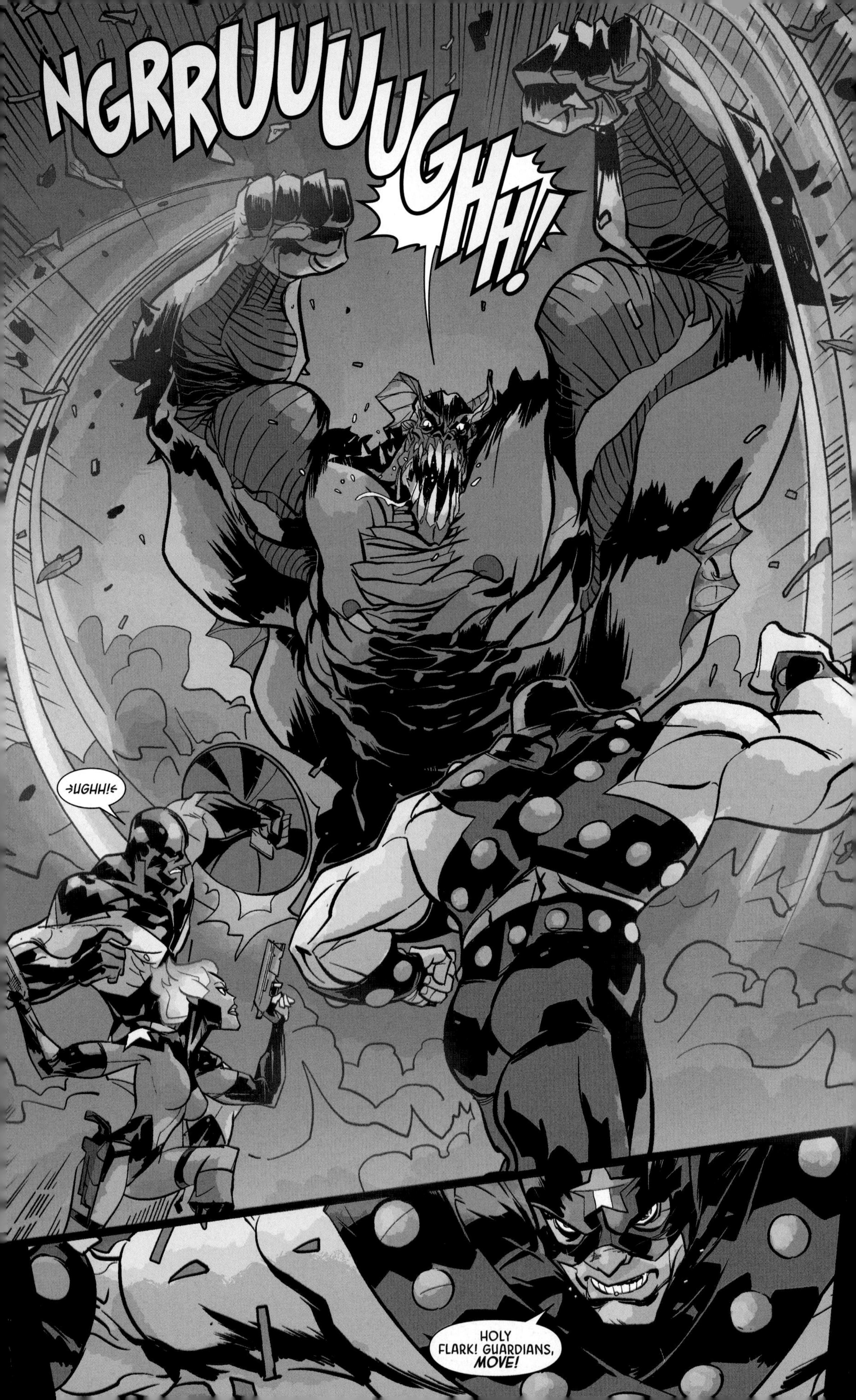
NGRRUUUUUGHH!
UGHH!
HOLY FLARK! GUARDIANS, *MOVE!*

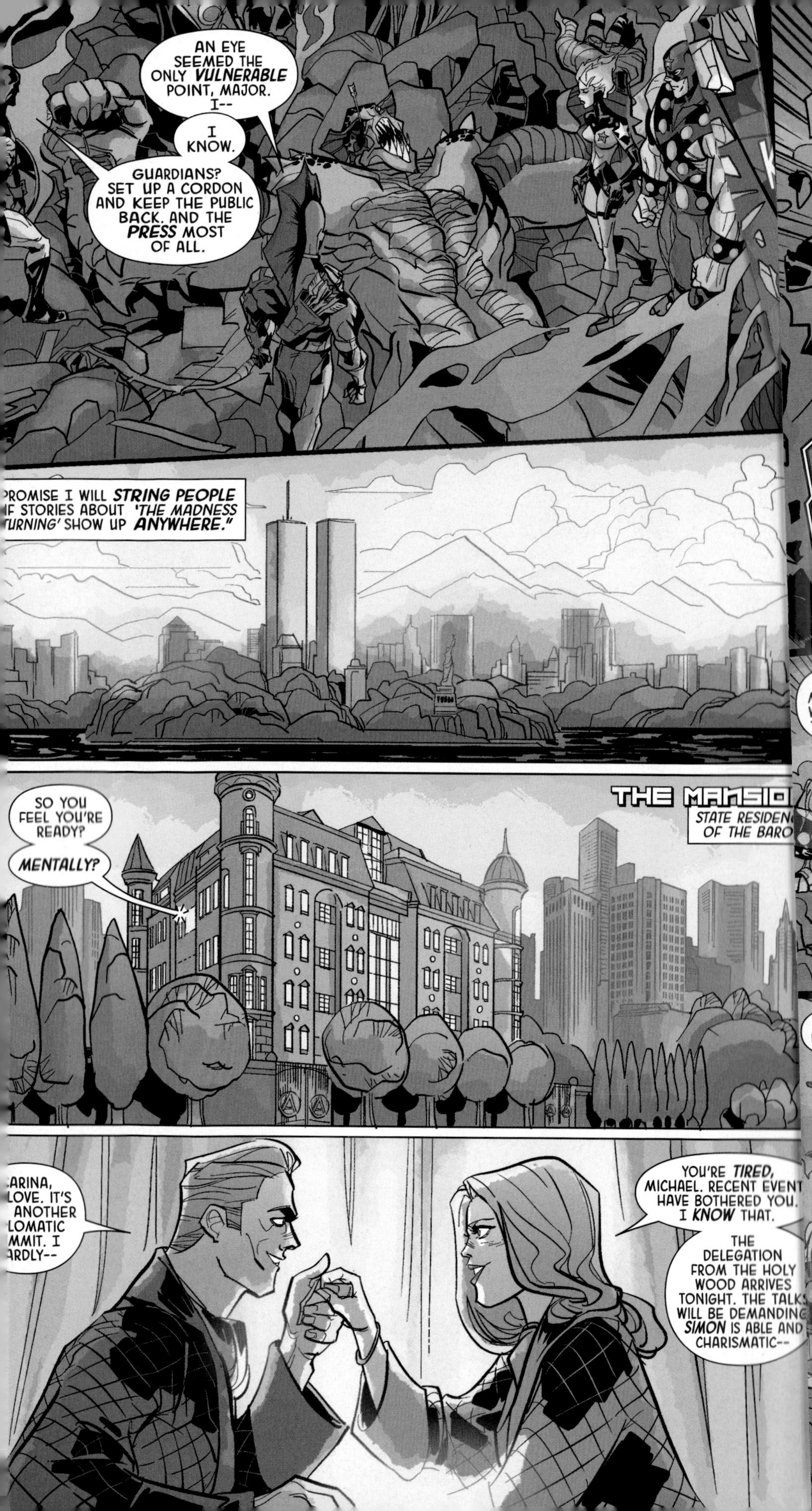
AN EYE SEEMED THE ONLY VULNERABLE POINT, MAJOR. I--
I KNOW.
GUARDIANS? SET UP A CORDON AND KEEP THE PUBLIC BACK. AND THE PRESS MOST OF ALL.
PROMISE I WILL STRING PEOPLE
F STORIES ABOUT 'THE MADNESS
TURNING' SHOW UP ANYWHERE."
THE MANSIO
STATE RESIDEN
OF THE BARO
SO YOU FEEL YOU'RE READY?
MENTALLY?
ARINA, LOVE. IT'S ANOTHER LOMATIC MMIT. I ARDLY--
YOU'RE TIRED, MICHAEL. RECENT EVENT HAVE BOTHERED YOU. I KNOW THAT.
THE DELEGATION FROM THE HOLY WOOD ARRIVES TONIGHT. THE TALKS WILL BE DEMANDING. SIMON IS ABLE AND CHARISMATIC--

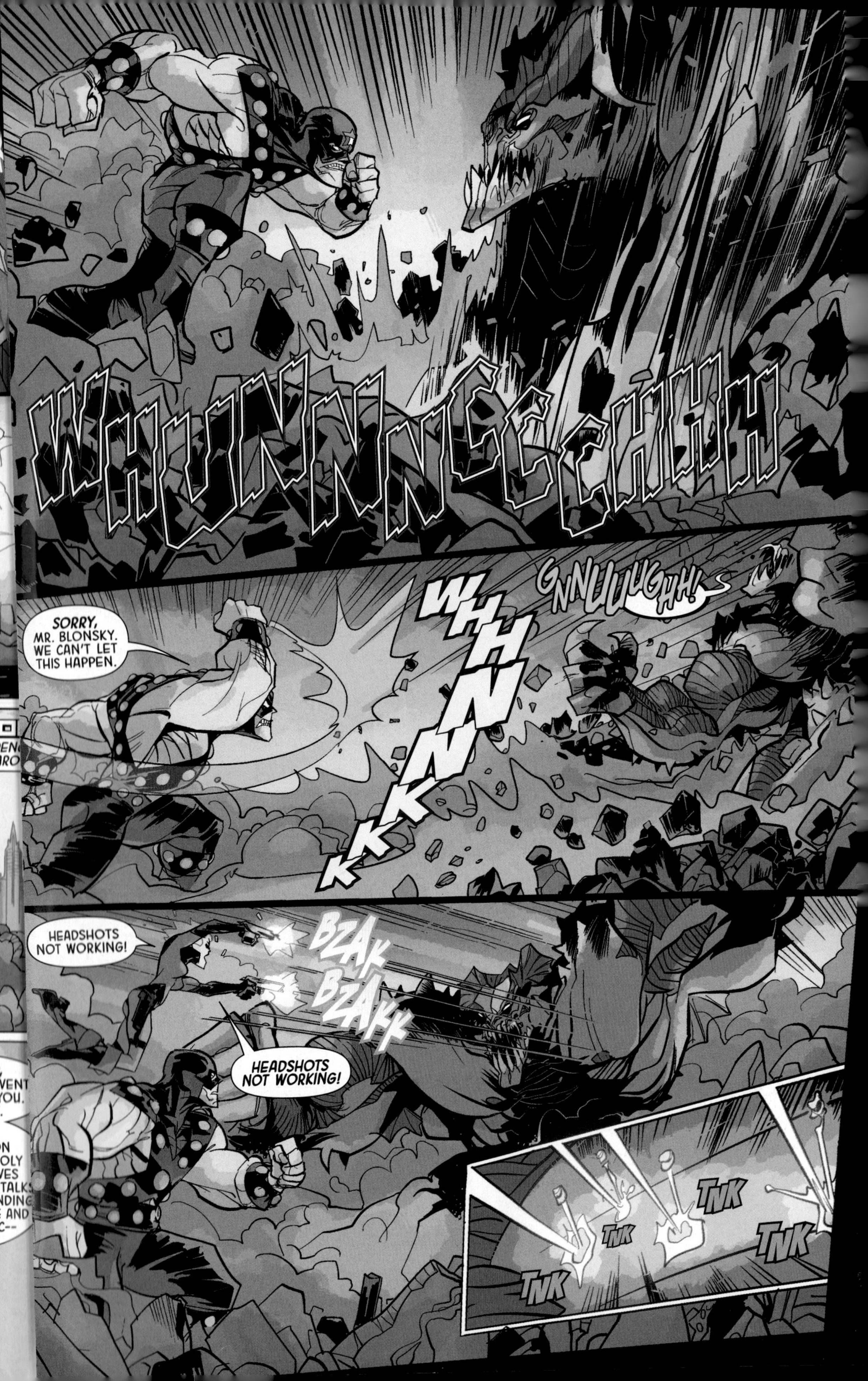
WHUNNNGCCHHH
SORRY, MR. BLONSKY. WE CAN'T LET THIS HAPPEN.
WHHNNNKKK
GNNUUUGHH!
HEADSHOTS NOT WORKING!
BZAK
BZAKK
HEADSHOTS NOT WORKING!
TNK
TNK
TNK
TNK
TNK

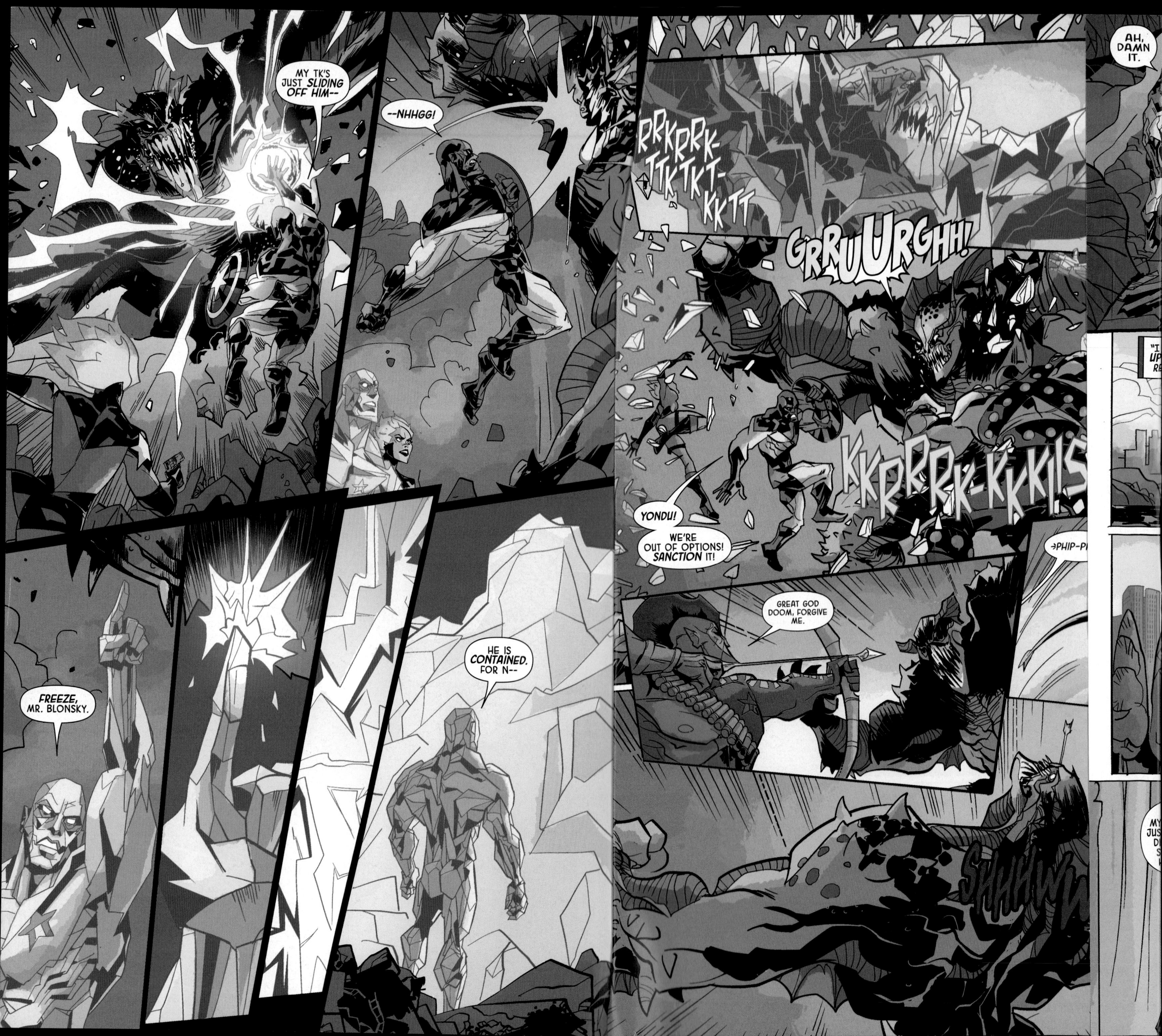
MY TK'S JUST SLIDING OFF HIM--
--NHHGG!
FREEZE, MR. BLONSKY.
HE IS CONTAINED. FOR N--
RRKRRK-TTKTKT-KKTT
GRRUURGHH!
YONDU!
WE'RE OUT OF OPTIONS! SANCTION IT!
GREAT GOD DOOM, FORGIVE ME.
AH, DAMN IT.

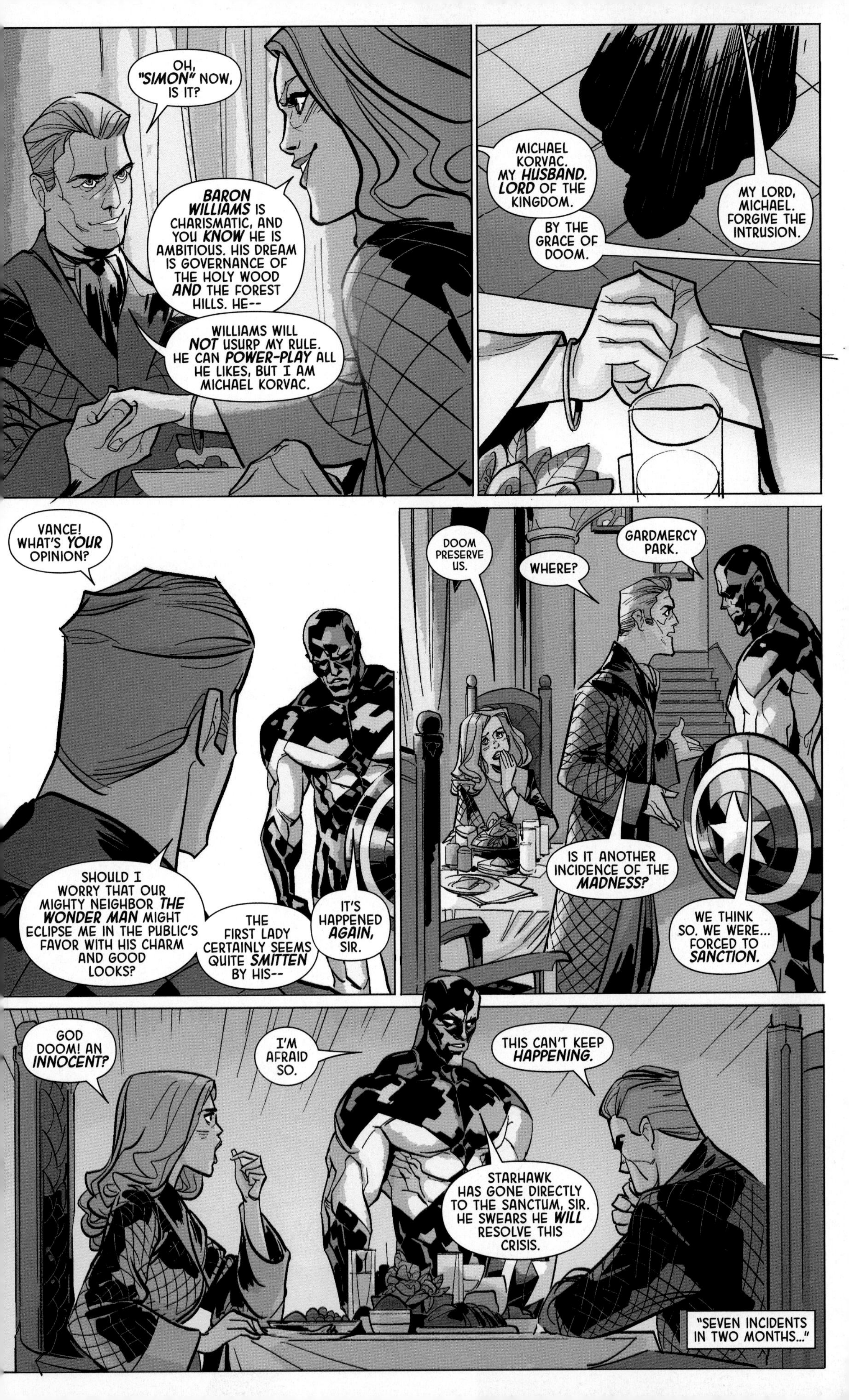
OH, "SIMON" NOW, IS IT?
BARON WILLIAMS IS CHARISMATIC, AND YOU KNOW HE IS AMBITIOUS. HIS DREAM IS GOVERNANCE OF THE HOLY WOOD AND THE FOREST HILLS. HE--
WILLIAMS WILL NOT USURP MY RULE. HE CAN POWER-PLAY ALL HE LIKES, BUT I AM MICHAEL KORVAC.
MICHAEL KORVAC. MY HUSBAND. LORD OF THE KINGDOM.
BY THE GRACE OF DOOM.
MY LORD, MICHAEL. FORGIVE THE INTRUSION.
VANCE! WHAT'S YOUR OPINION?
SHOULD I WORRY THAT OUR MIGHTY NEIGHBOR THE WONDER MAN MIGHT ECLIPSE ME IN THE PUBLIC'S FAVOR WITH HIS CHARM AND GOOD LOOKS?
THE FIRST LADY CERTAINLY SEEMS QUITE SMITTEN BY HIS--
IT'S HAPPENED AGAIN, SIR.
DOOM PRESERVE US.
WHERE?
GARDMERCY PARK.
IS IT ANOTHER INCIDENCE OF THE MADNESS?
WE THINK SO. WE WERE... FORCED TO SANCTION.
GOD DOOM! AN INNOCENT?
I'M AFRAID SO.
THIS CAN'T KEEP HAPPENING.
STARHAWK HAS GONE DIRECTLY TO THE SANCTUM, SIR. HE SWEARS HE WILL RESOLVE THIS CRISIS.
"SEVEN INCIDENTS IN TWO MONTHS..."

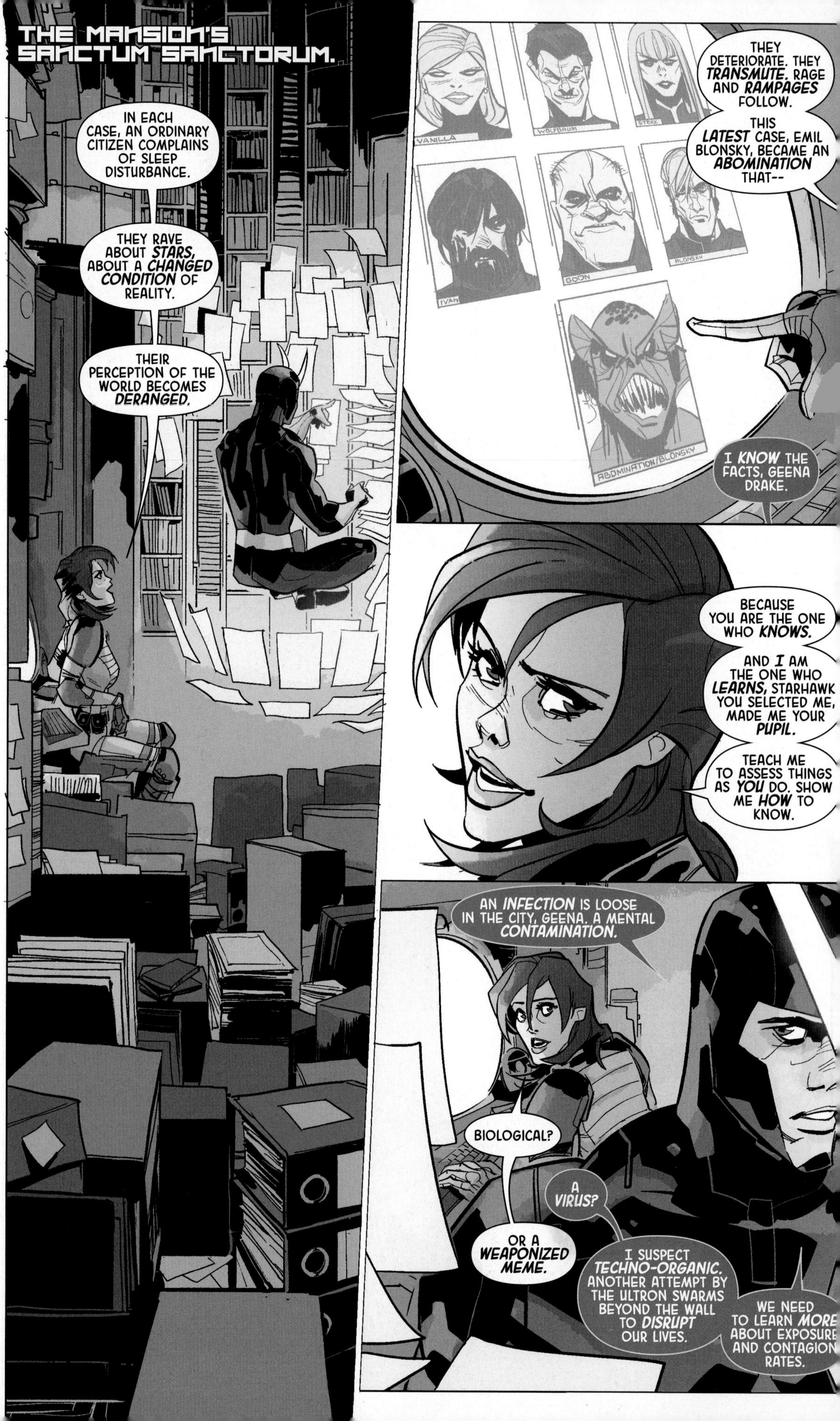
THE MANSION'S SANCTUM SANCTORUM.
IN EACH CASE, AN ORDINARY CITIZEN COMPLAINS OF SLEEP DISTURBANCE.
THEY RAVE ABOUT STARS, ABOUT A CHANGED CONDITION OF REALITY.
THEIR PERCEPTION OF THE WORLD BECOMES DERANGED.
VANILLA
WOLFBAUM
STEKK
IVAN
GOON
BLONSKY
ABOMINATION/BLONSKY
THEY DETERIORATE. THEY TRANSMUTE. RAGE AND RAMPAGES FOLLOW.
THIS LATEST CASE, EMIL BLONSKY, BECAME AN ABOMINATION THAT--
I KNOW THE FACTS, GEENA DRAKE.
BECAUSE YOU ARE THE ONE WHO KNOWS.
AND I AM THE ONE WHO LEARNS, STARHAWK. YOU SELECTED ME, MADE ME YOUR PUPIL.
TEACH ME TO ASSESS THINGS AS YOU DO. SHOW ME HOW TO KNOW.
AN INFECTION IS LOOSE IN THE CITY, GEENA. A MENTAL CONTAMINATION.
BIOLOGICAL?
A VIRUS?
OR A WEAPONIZED MEME.
I SUSPECT TECHNO-ORGANIC. ANOTHER ATTEMPT BY THE ULTRON SWARMS BEYOND THE WALL TO DISRUPT OUR LIVES.
WE NEED TO LEARN MORE ABOUT EXPOSURE AND CONTAGION RATES.

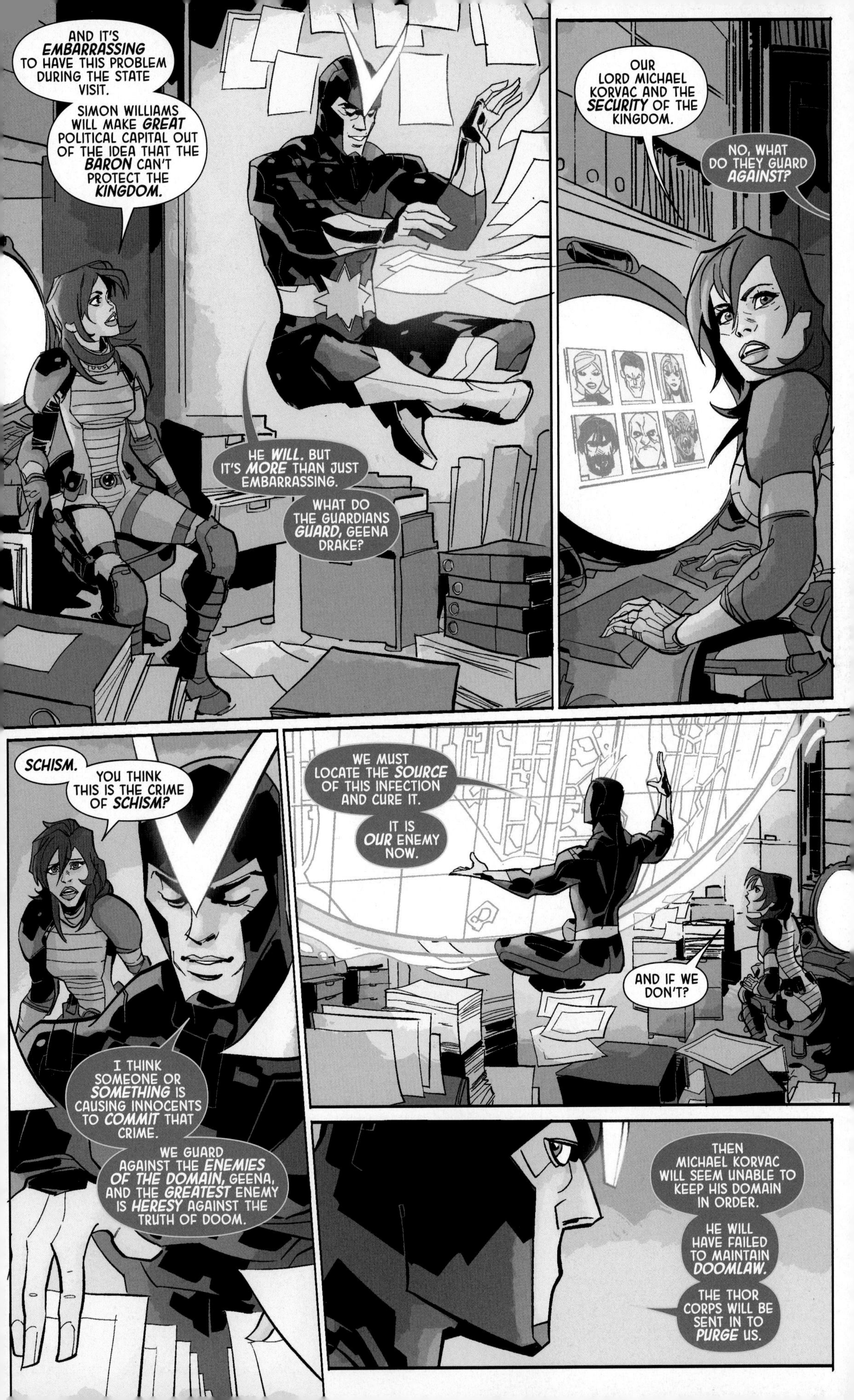
AND IT'S EMBARRASSING TO HAVE THIS PROBLEM DURING THE STATE VISIT.
SIMON WILLIAMS WILL MAKE GREAT POLITICAL CAPITAL OUT OF THE IDEA THAT THE BARON CAN'T PROTECT THE KINGDOM.
HE WILL. BUT IT'S MORE THAN JUST EMBARRASSING.
WHAT DO THE GUARDIANS GUARD, GEENA DRAKE?
OUR LORD MICHAEL KORVAC AND THE SECURITY OF THE KINGDOM.
NO, WHAT DO THEY GUARD AGAINST?
SCHISM.
YOU THINK THIS IS THE CRIME OF SCHISM?
I THINK SOMEONE OR SOMETHING IS CAUSING INNOCENTS TO COMMIT THAT CRIME.
WE GUARD AGAINST THE ENEMIES OF THE DOMAIN, GEENA, AND THE GREATEST ENEMY IS HERESY AGAINST THE TRUTH OF DOOM.
WE MUST LOCATE THE SOURCE OF THIS INFECTION AND CURE IT.
IT IS OUR ENEMY NOW.
AND IF WE DON'T?
THEN MICHAEL KORVAC WILL SEEM UNABLE TO KEEP HIS DOMAIN IN ORDER.
HE WILL HAVE FAILED TO MAINTAIN DOOMLAW.
THE THOR CORPS WILL BE SENT IN TO PURGE US.

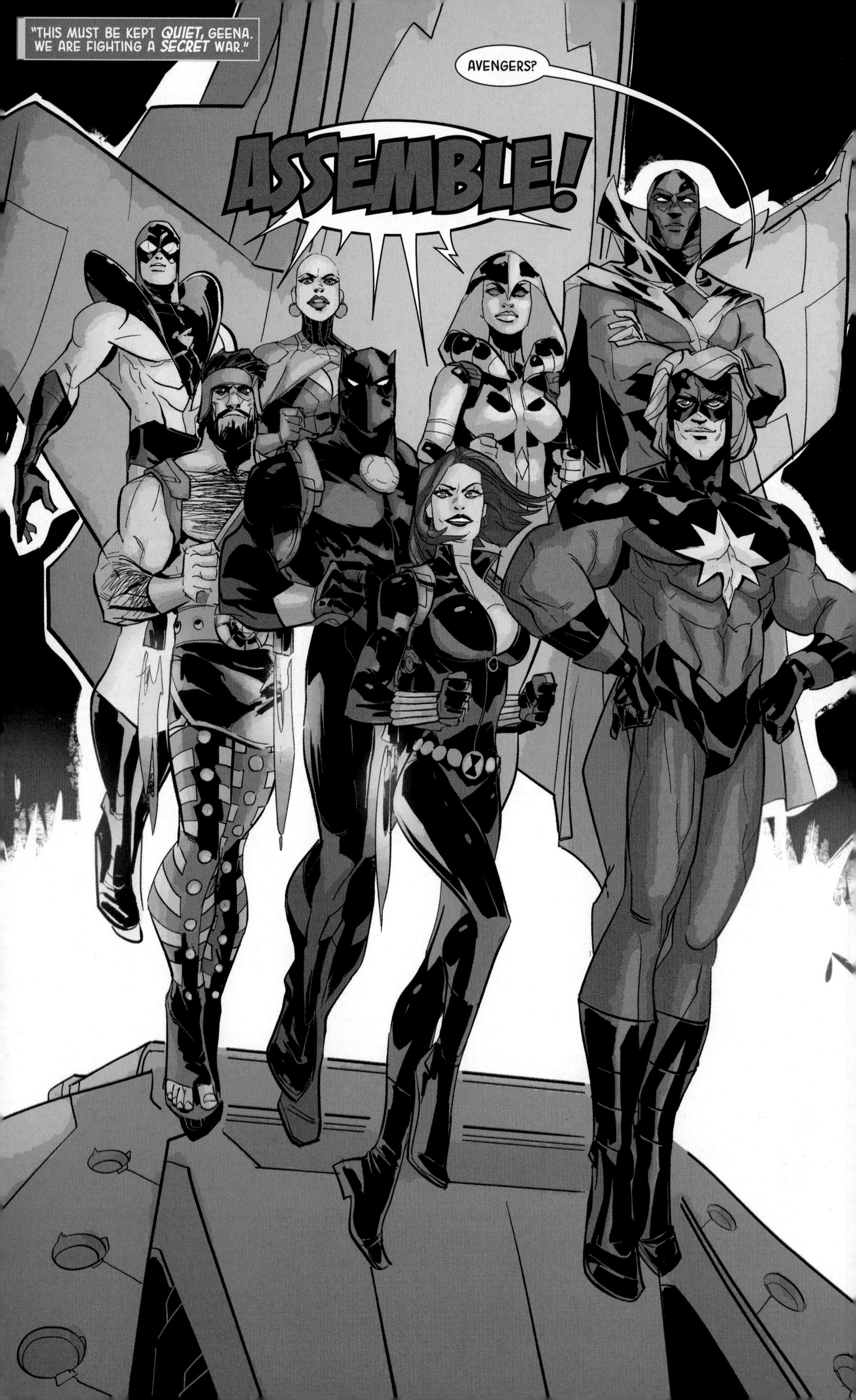
"THIS MUST BE KEPT QUIET, GEENA. WE ARE FIGHTING A SECRET WAR."
AVENGERS?
ASSEMBLE!

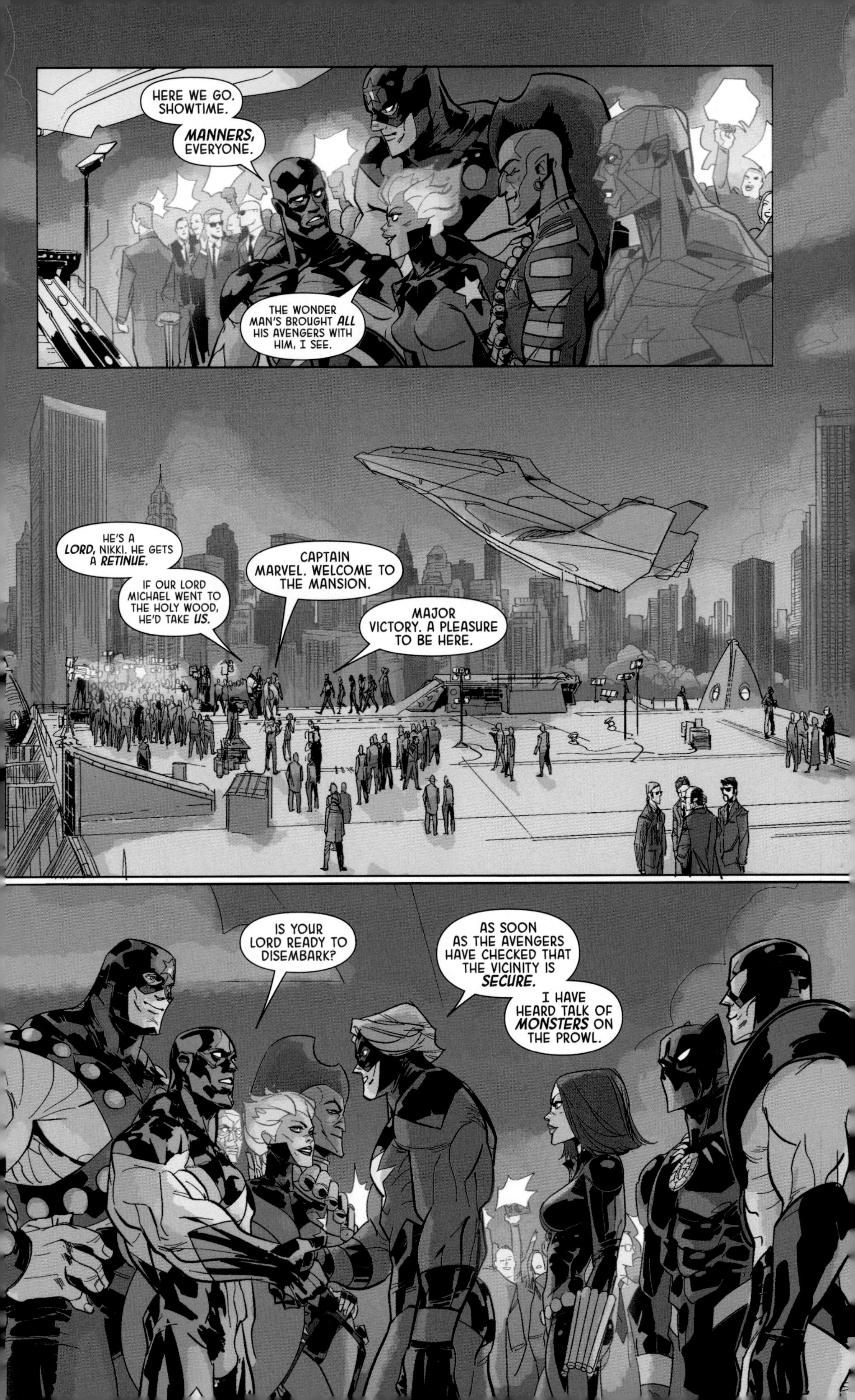
HERE WE GO. SHOWTIME.
MANNERS, EVERYONE.
THE WONDER MAN'S BROUGHT ALL HIS AVENGERS WITH HIM, I SEE.
HE'S A LORD, NIKKI. HE GETS A RETINUE.
IF OUR LORD MICHAEL WENT TO THE HOLY WOOD, HE'D TAKE US.
CAPTAIN MARVEL. WELCOME TO THE MANSION.
MAJOR VICTORY. A PLEASURE TO BE HERE.
IS YOUR LORD READY TO DISEMBARK?
AS SOON AS THE AVENGERS HAVE CHECKED THAT THE VICINITY IS SECURE.
I HAVE HEARD TALK OF MONSTERS ON THE PROWL.

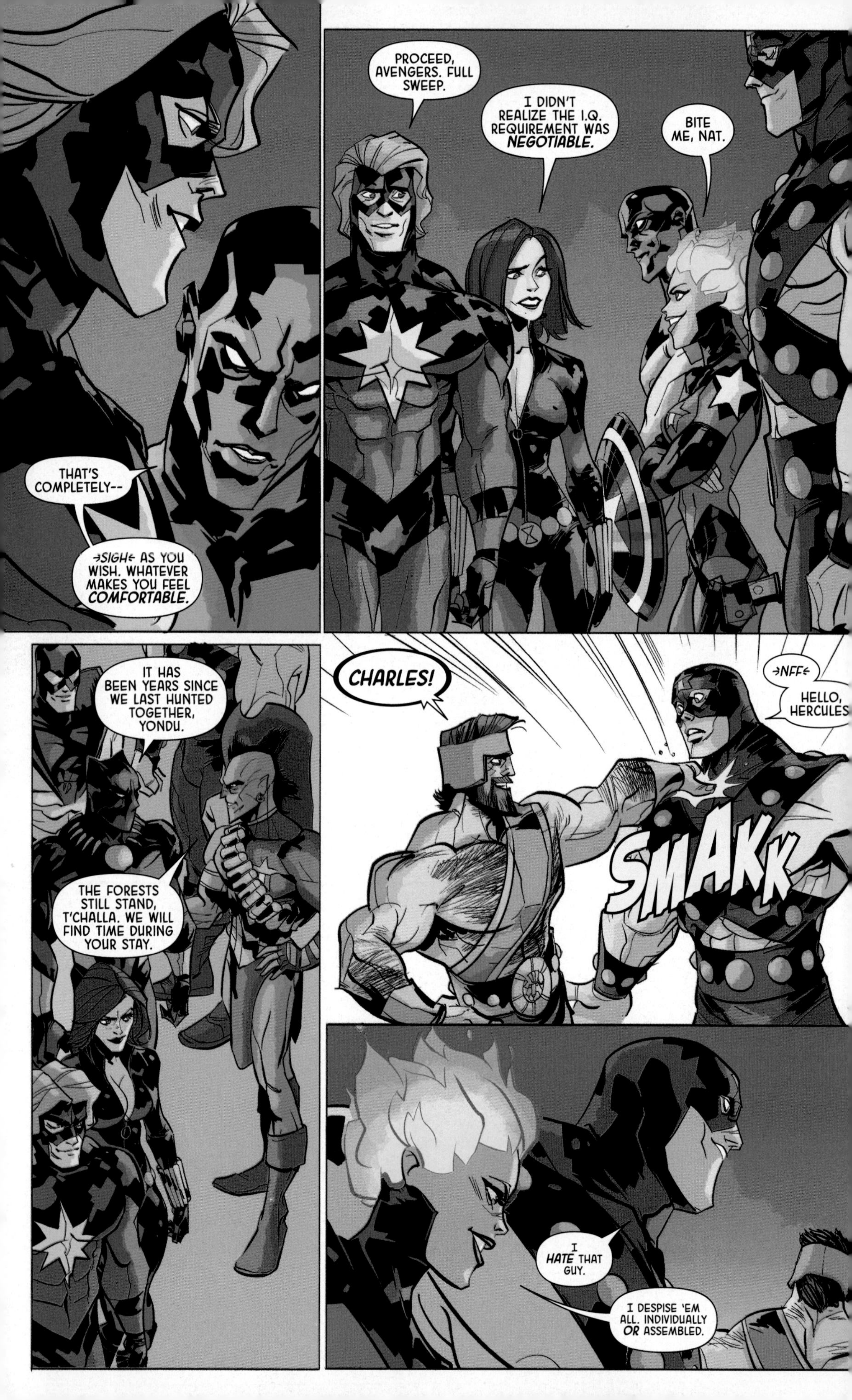
THAT'S COMPLETELY--
⇝SIGH⇜ AS YOU WISH. WHATEVER MAKES YOU FEEL COMFORTABLE.
PROCEED, AVENGERS. FULL SWEEP.
I DIDN'T REALIZE THE I.Q. REQUIREMENT WAS NEGOTIABLE.
BITE ME, NAT.
IT HAS BEEN YEARS SINCE WE LAST HUNTED TOGETHER, YONDU.
THE FORESTS STILL STAND, T'CHALLA. WE WILL FIND TIME DURING YOUR STAY.
CHARLES!
⇝NFF⇜
HELLO, HERCULES
SMAKK
I HATE THAT GUY.
I DESPISE 'EM ALL. INDIVIDUALLY OR ASSEMBLED.

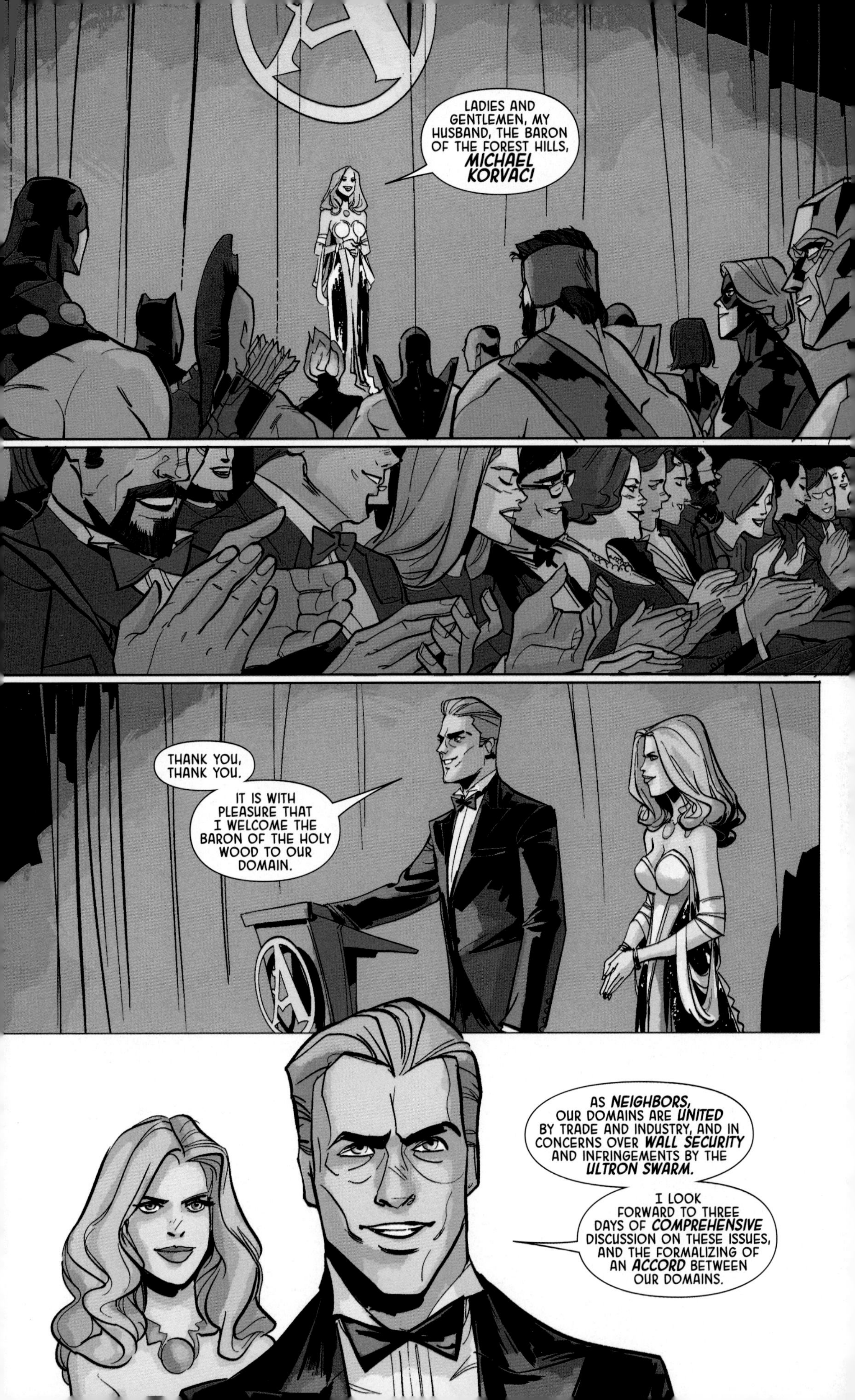
LADIES AND GENTLEMEN, MY HUSBAND, THE BARON OF THE FOREST HILLS, MICHAEL KORVAC!
THANK YOU, THANK YOU.
IT IS WITH PLEASURE THAT I WELCOME THE BARON OF THE HOLY WOOD TO OUR DOMAIN.
AS NEIGHBORS, OUR DOMAINS ARE UNITED BY TRADE AND INDUSTRY, AND IN CONCERNS OVER WALL SECURITY AND INFRINGEMENTS BY THE ULTRON SWARM.
I LOOK FORWARD TO THREE DAYS OF COMPREHENSIVE DISCUSSION ON THESE ISSUES, AND THE FORMALIZING OF AN ACCORD BETWEEN OUR DOMAINS.

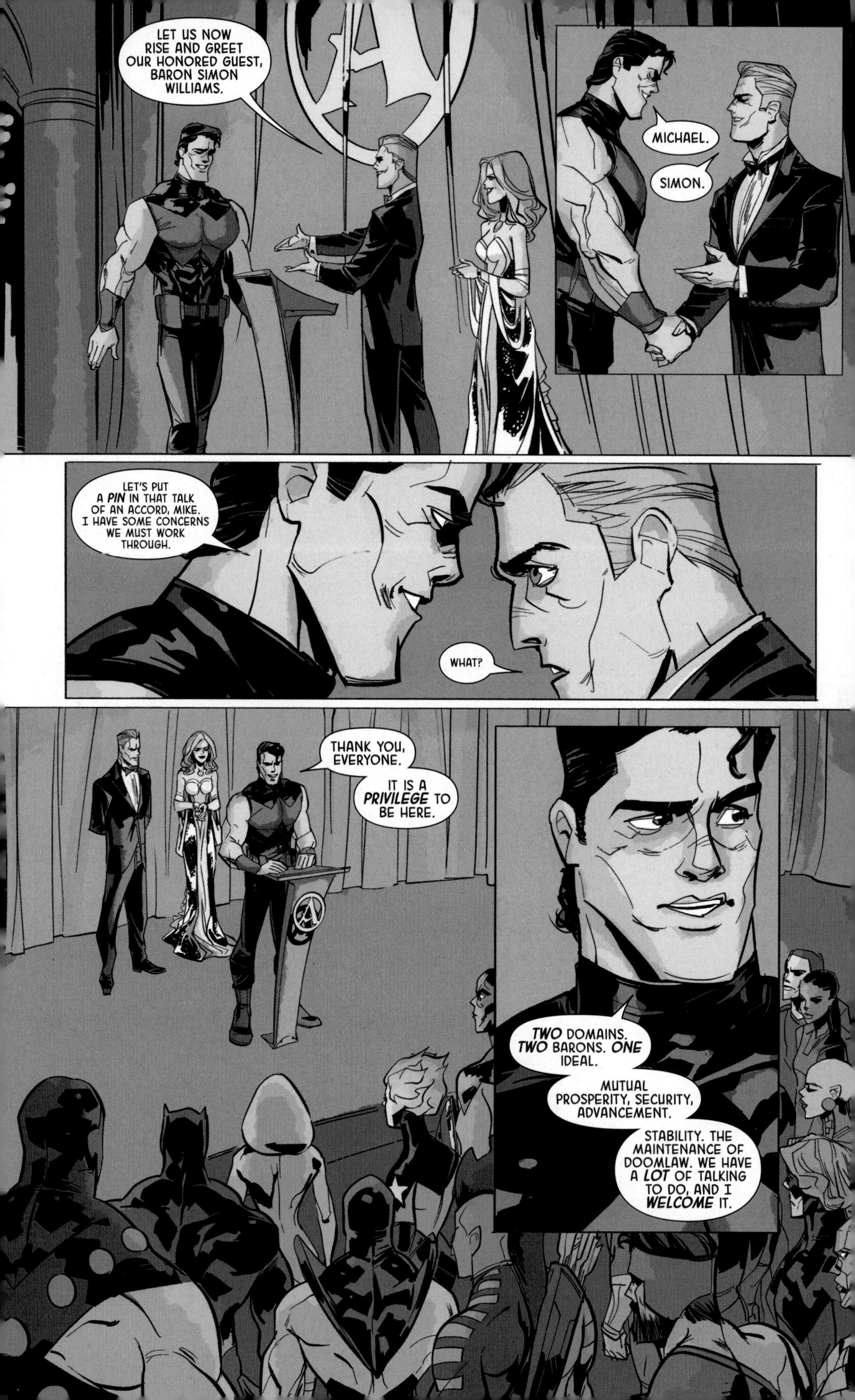
LET US NOW RISE AND GREET OUR HONORED GUEST, BARON SIMON WILLIAMS.
MICHAEL.
SIMON.
LET'S PUT A PIN IN THAT TALK OF AN ACCORD, MIKE. I HAVE SOME CONCERNS WE MUST WORK THROUGH.
WHAT?
THANK YOU, EVERYONE.
IT IS A PRIVILEGE TO BE HERE.
TWO DOMAINS. TWO BARONS. ONE IDEAL.
MUTUAL PROSPERITY, SECURITY, ADVANCEMENT.
STABILITY. THE MAINTENANCE OF DOOMLAW. WE HAVE A LOT OF TALKING TO DO, AND I WELCOME IT.

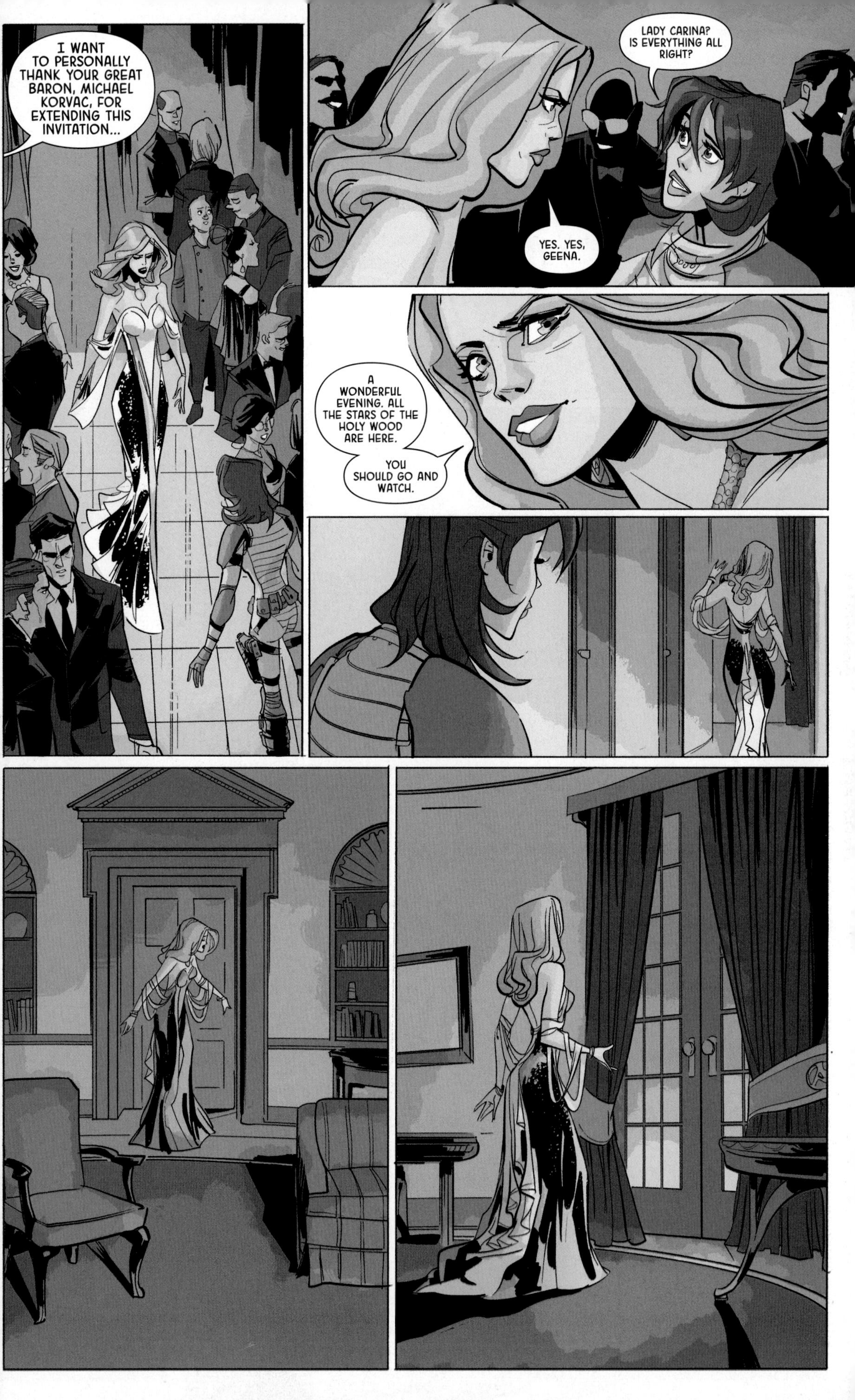
I WANT TO PERSONALLY THANK YOUR GREAT BARON, MICHAEL KORVAC, FOR EXTENDING THIS INVITATION...
LADY CARINA? IS EVERYTHING ALL RIGHT?
YES. YES, GEENA.
A WONDERFUL EVENING. ALL THE STARS OF THE HOLY WOOD ARE HERE.
YOU SHOULD GO AND WATCH.

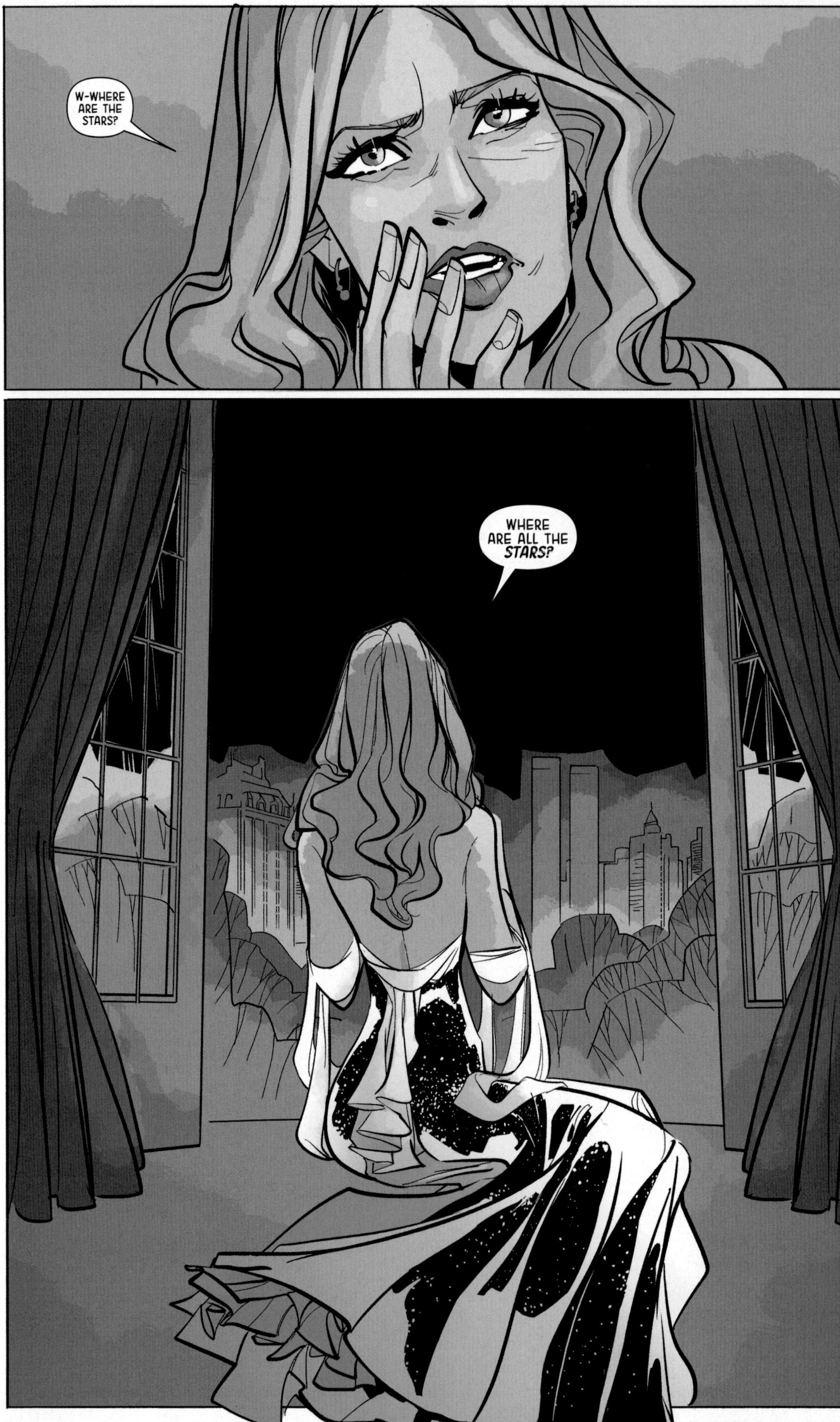
W-WHERE ARE THE STARS?
WHERE ARE ALL THE STARS?

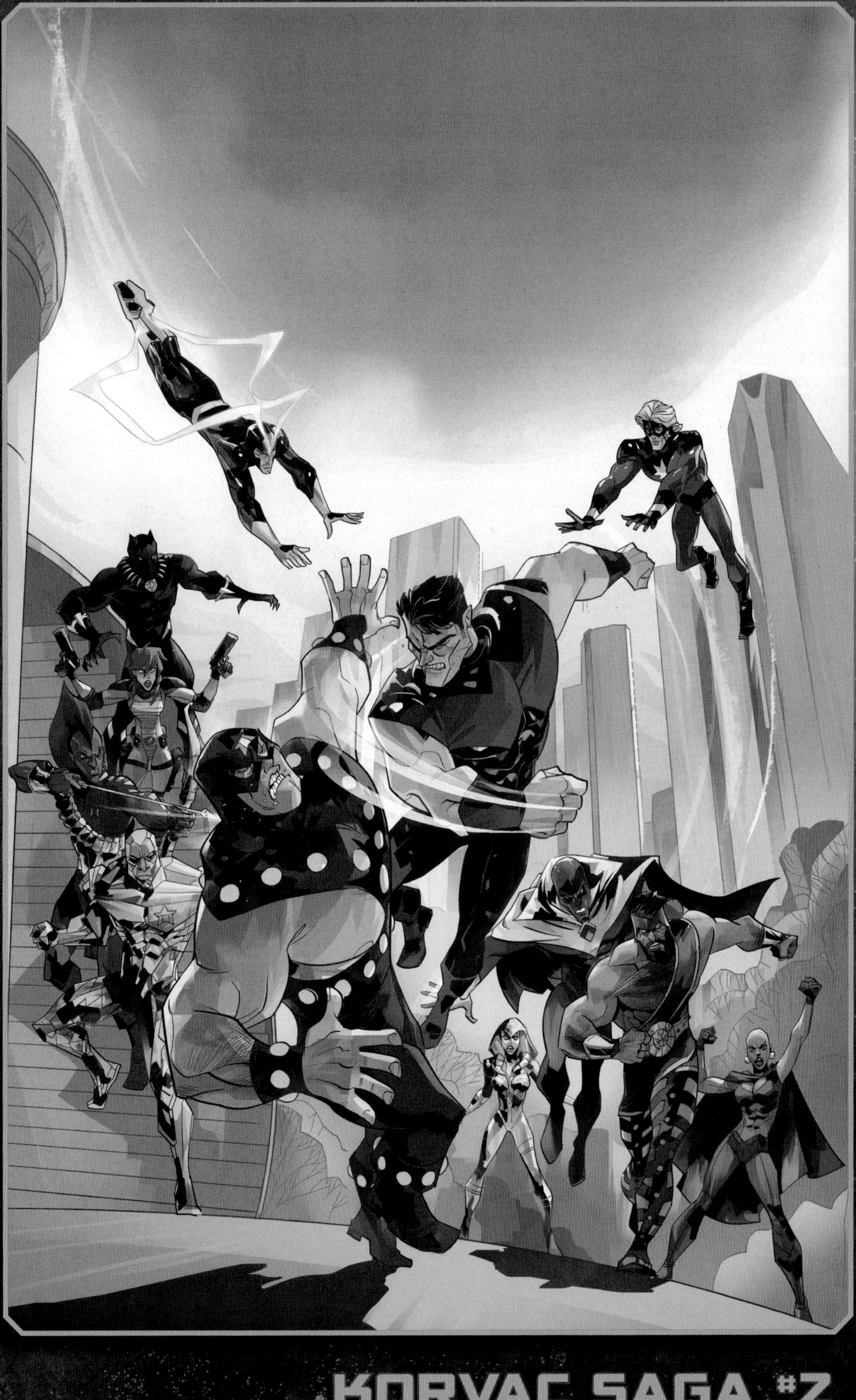

KORVAC SAGA #2

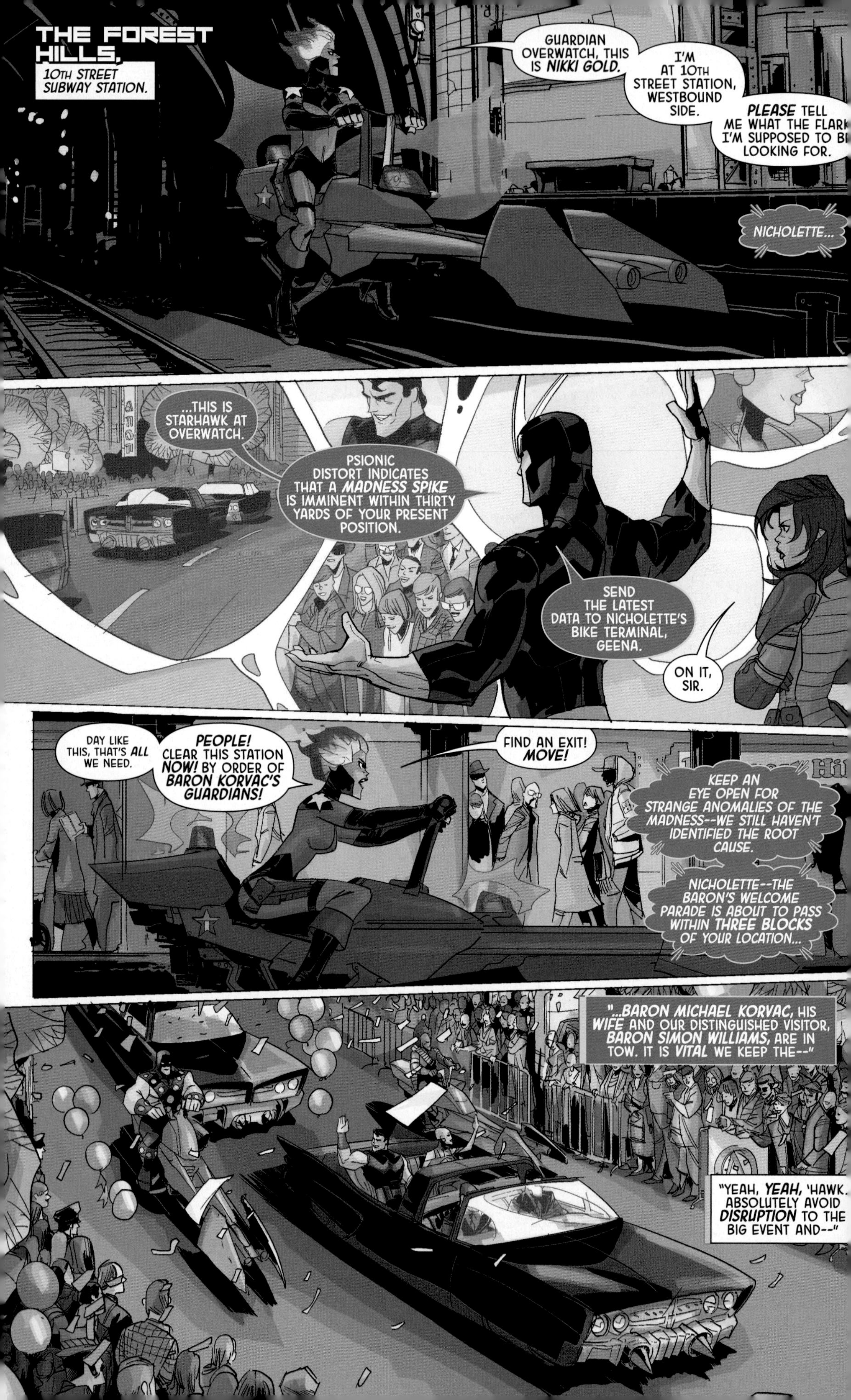
THE FOREST HILLS,
10TH STREET SUBWAY STATION.
GUARDIAN OVERWATCH, THIS IS NIKKI GOLD.
I'M AT 10TH STREET STATION, WESTBOUND SIDE.
PLEASE TELL ME WHAT THE FLARK I'M SUPPOSED TO BE LOOKING FOR.
NICHOLETTE...
...THIS IS STARHAWK AT OVERWATCH.
PSIONIC DISTORT INDICATES THAT A MADNESS SPIKE IS IMMINENT WITHIN THIRTY YARDS OF YOUR PRESENT POSITION.
SEND THE LATEST DATA TO NICHOLETTE'S BIKE TERMINAL, GEENA.
ON IT, SIR.
DAY LIKE THIS, THAT'S ALL WE NEED.
PEOPLE! CLEAR THIS STATION NOW! BY ORDER OF BARON KORVAC'S GUARDIANS!
FIND AN EXIT! MOVE!
KEEP AN EYE OPEN FOR STRANGE ANOMALIES OF THE MADNESS--WE STILL HAVEN'T IDENTIFIED THE ROOT CAUSE.
NICHOLETTE--THE BARON'S WELCOME PARADE IS ABOUT TO PASS WITHIN THREE BLOCKS OF YOUR LOCATION...
"...BARON MICHAEL KORVAC, HIS WIFE AND OUR DISTINGUISHED VISITOR, BARON SIMON WILLIAMS, ARE IN TOW. IT IS VITAL WE KEEP THE--"
"YEAH, YEAH, 'HAWK. ABSOLUTELY AVOID DISRUPTION TO THE BIG EVENT AND--"

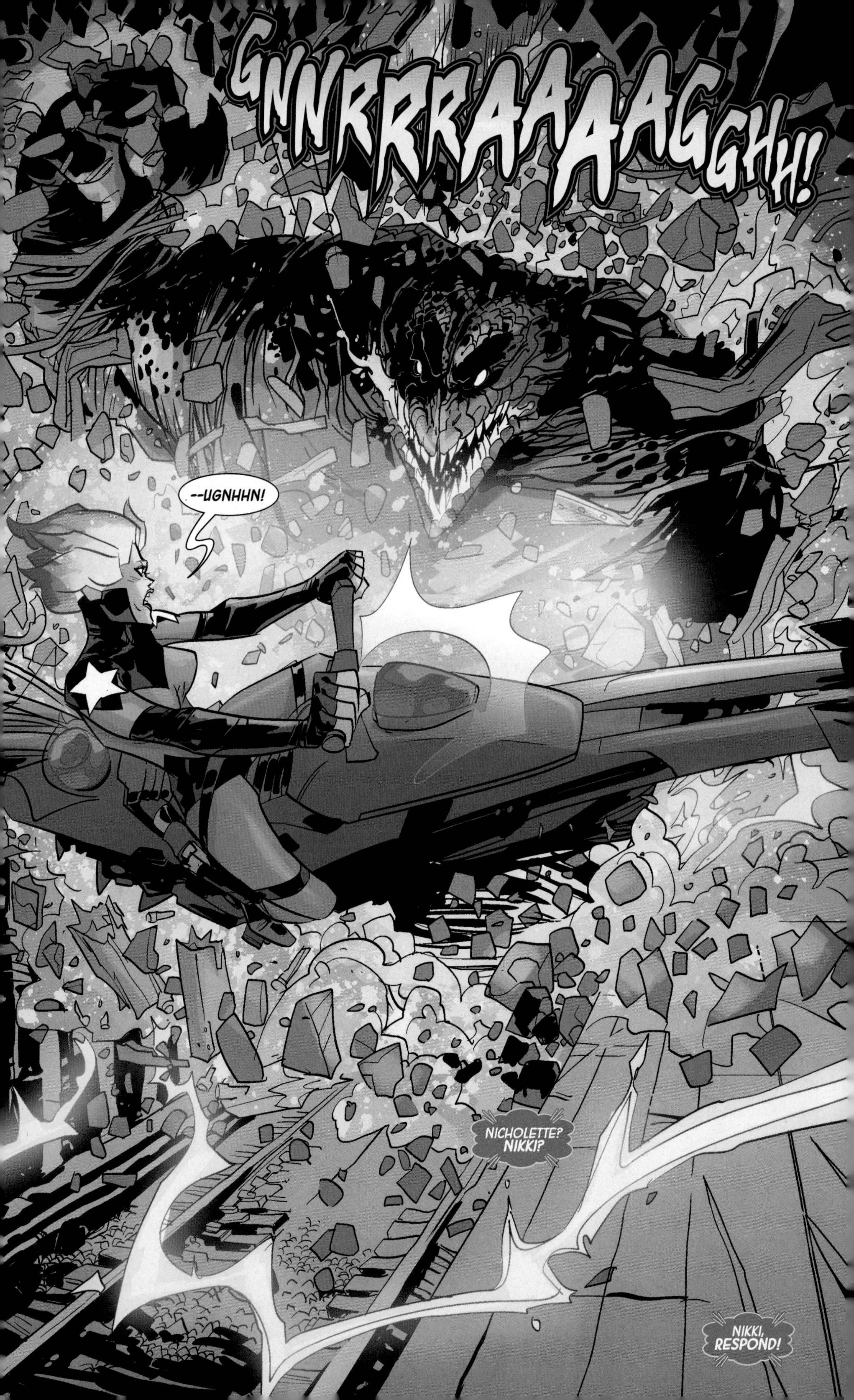
GNNRRRAAAAGGHH!
--UGNHHN!
NICHOLETTE? NIKKI?
NIKKI, RESPOND!

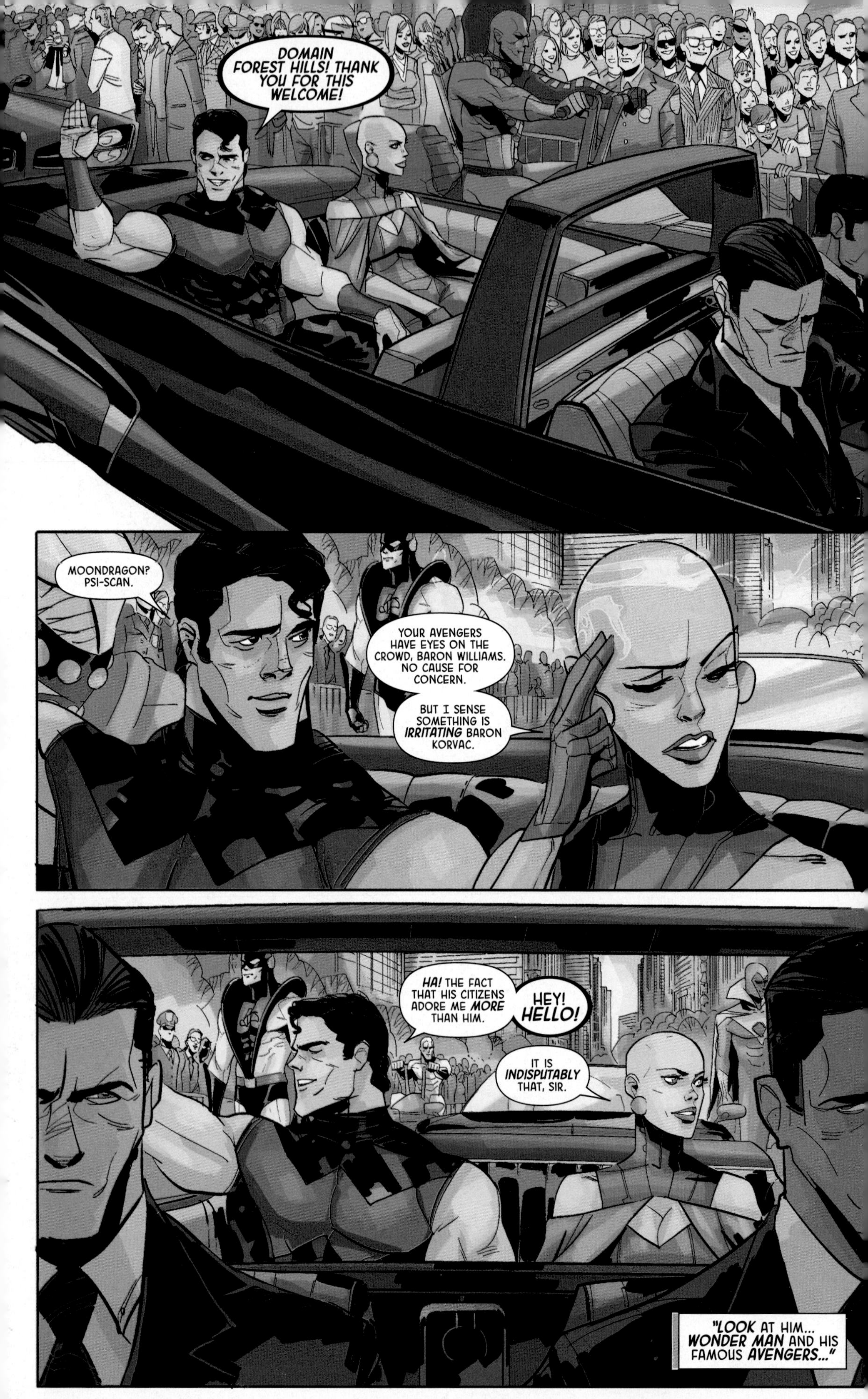
DOMAIN FOREST HILLS! THANK YOU FOR THIS WELCOME!
MOONDRAGON? PSI-SCAN.
YOUR AVENGERS HAVE EYES ON THE CROWD, BARON WILLIAMS. NO CAUSE FOR CONCERN.
BUT I SENSE SOMETHING IS IRRITATING BARON KORVAC.
HA! THE FACT THAT HIS CITIZENS ADORE ME MORE THAN HIM.
HEY! HELLO!
IT IS INDISPUTABLY THAT, SIR.
"LOOK AT HIM... WONDER MAN AND HIS FAMOUS AVENGERS..."

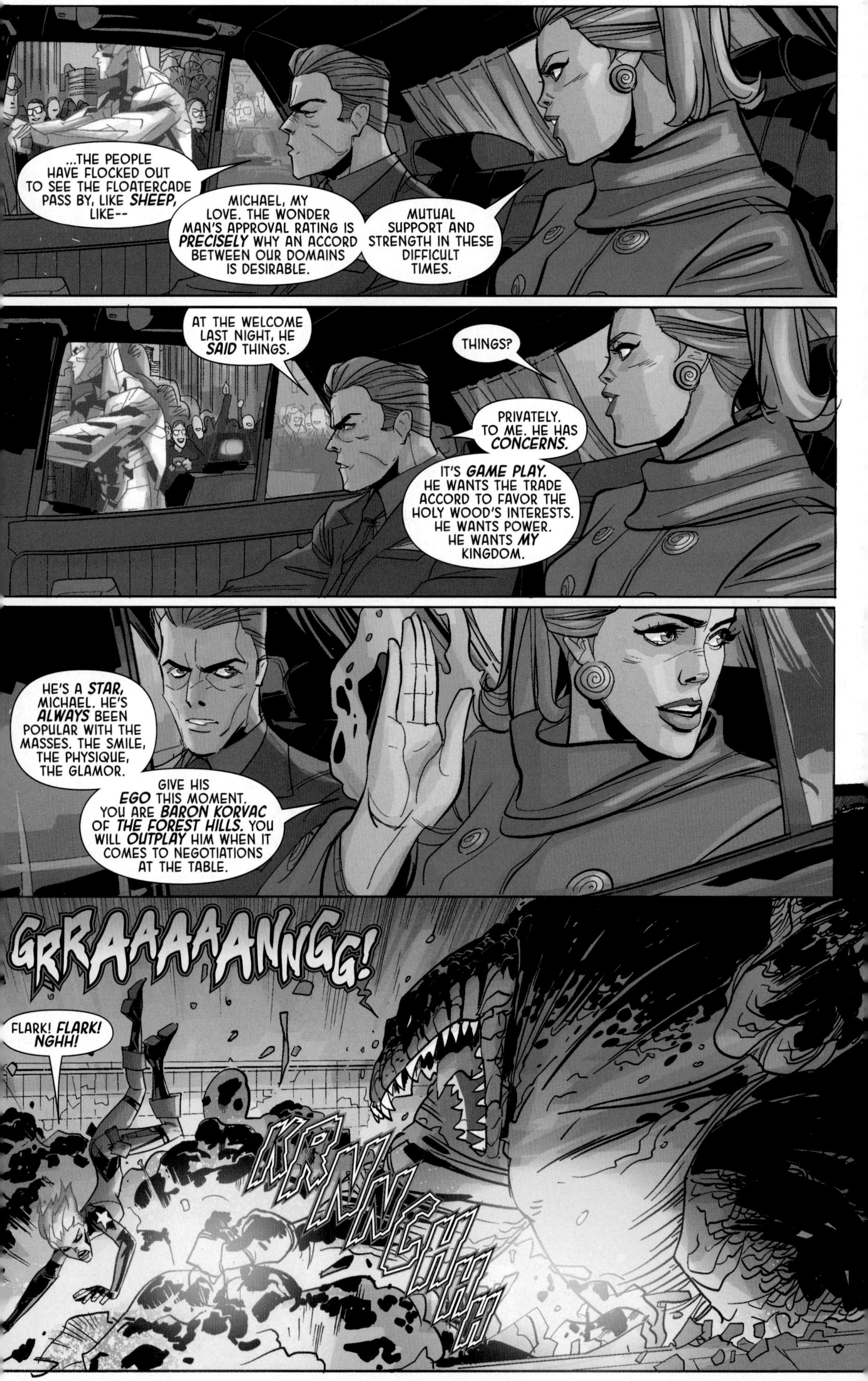
...THE PEOPLE HAVE FLOCKED OUT TO SEE THE FLOATERCADE PASS BY, LIKE SHEEP, LIKE--
MICHAEL, MY LOVE. THE WONDER MAN'S APPROVAL RATING IS PRECISELY WHY AN ACCORD BETWEEN OUR DOMAINS IS DESIRABLE.
MUTUAL SUPPORT AND STRENGTH IN THESE DIFFICULT TIMES.
AT THE WELCOME LAST NIGHT, HE SAID THINGS.
THINGS?
PRIVATELY. TO ME. HE HAS CONCERNS.
IT'S GAME PLAY. HE WANTS THE TRADE ACCORD TO FAVOR THE HOLY WOOD'S INTERESTS. HE WANTS POWER. HE WANTS MY KINGDOM.
HE'S A STAR, MICHAEL. HE'S ALWAYS BEEN POPULAR WITH THE MASSES. THE SMILE, THE PHYSIQUE, THE GLAMOR.
GIVE HIS EGO THIS MOMENT. YOU ARE BARON KORVAC OF THE FOREST HILLS. YOU WILL OUTPLAY HIM WHEN IT COMES TO NEGOTIATIONS AT THE TABLE.
GRRAAAAAANNGG!
FLARK! FLARK! NGHH!
KRNNGHHH

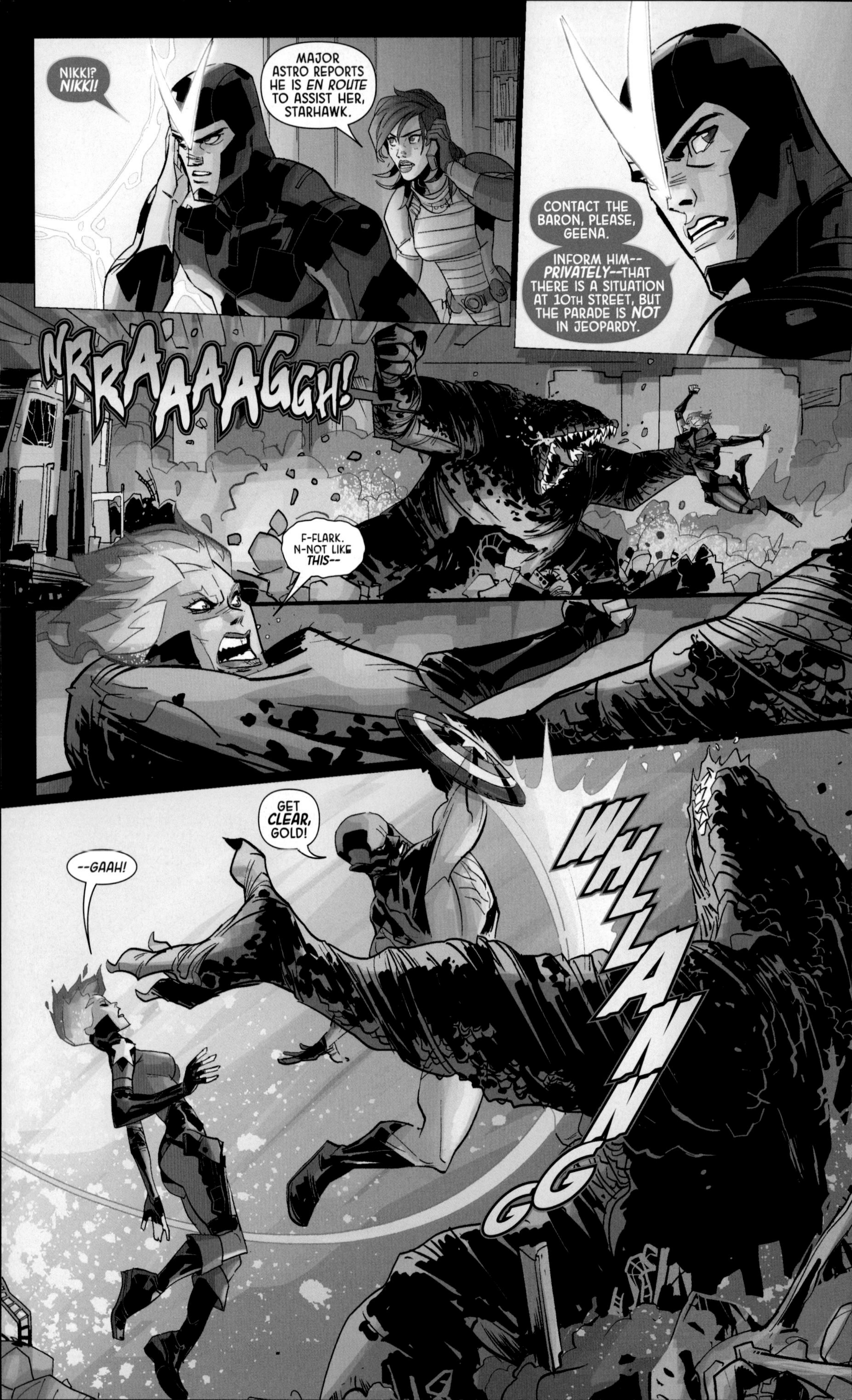
NIKKI? NIKKI!
MAJOR ASTRO REPORTS HE IS EN ROUTE TO ASSIST HER, STARHAWK.
CONTACT THE BARON, PLEASE, GEENA.
INFORM HIM-- PRIVATELY--THAT THERE IS A SITUATION AT 10TH STREET, BUT THE PARADE IS NOT IN JEOPARDY.
NRRAAAAAGGH!
F-FLARK. N-NOT LIKE THIS--
GET CLEAR, GOLD!
--GAAH!
WHHAANNGG

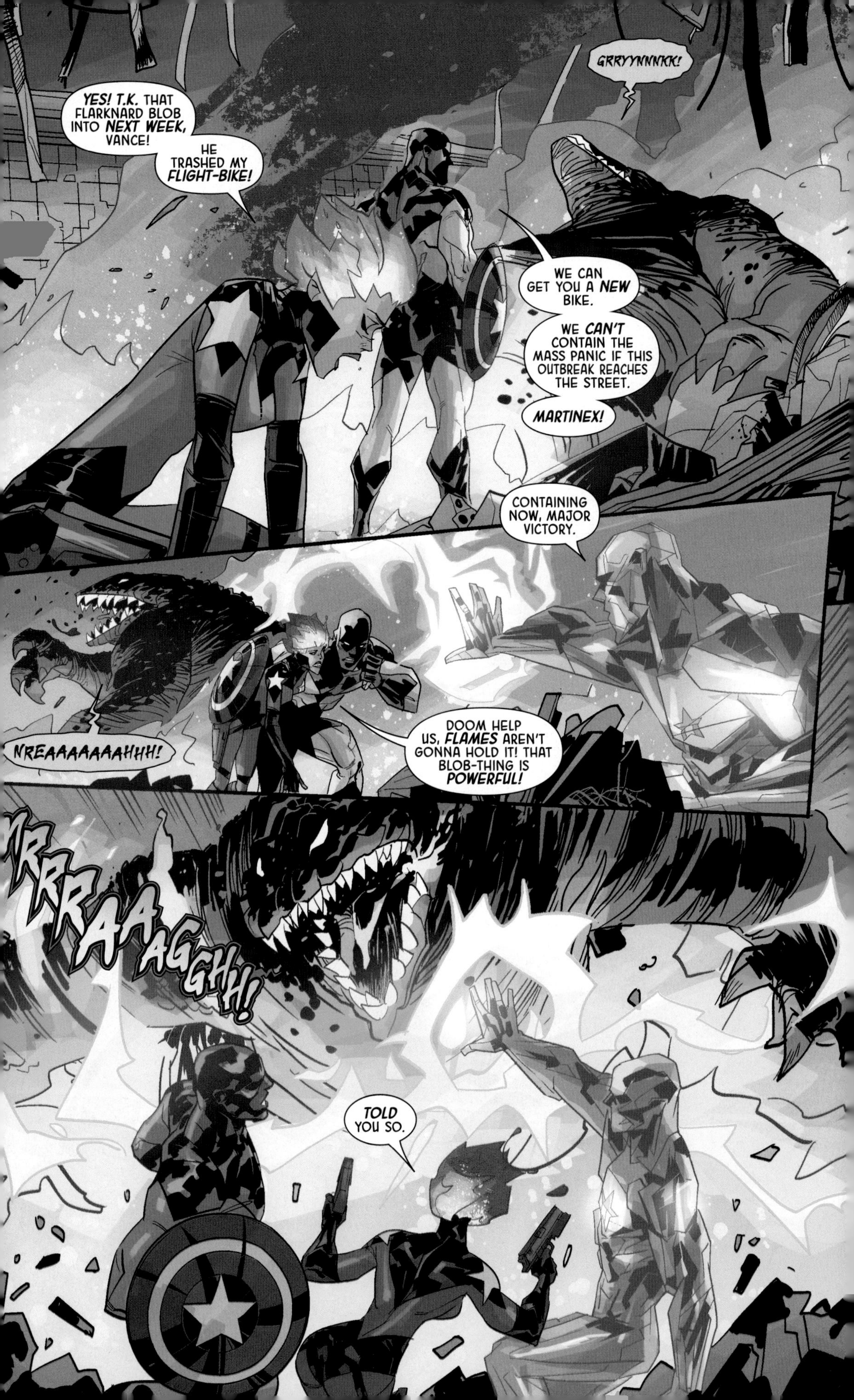
YES! T.K. THAT FLARKNARD BLOB INTO NEXT WEEK, VANCE!
HE TRASHED MY FLIGHT-BIKE!
GRRYYNNNKK!
WE CAN GET YOU A NEW BIKE.
WE CAN'T CONTAIN THE MASS PANIC IF THIS OUTBREAK REACHES THE STREET.
MARTINEX!
CONTAINING NOW, MAJOR VICTORY.
NREAAAAAAAHHH!
DOOM HELP US, FLAMES AREN'T GONNA HOLD IT! THAT BLOB-THING IS POWERFUL!
RRRRAAAAGGHH!
TOLD YOU SO.

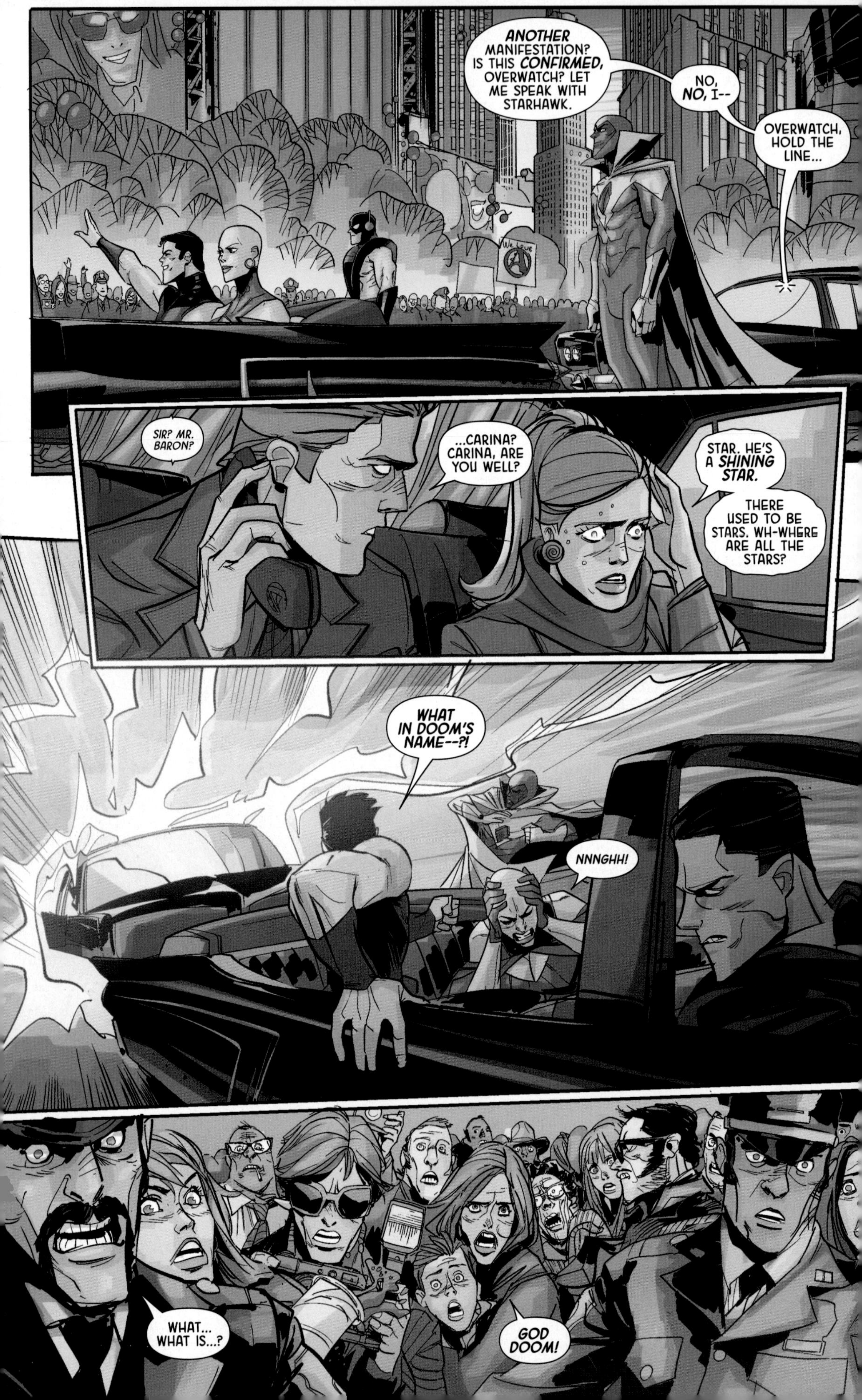
ANOTHER MANIFESTATION? IS THIS CONFIRMED, OVERWATCH? LET ME SPEAK WITH STARHAWK.
NO, NO, I--
OVERWATCH, HOLD THE LINE...
We Love
SIR? MR. BARON?
...CARINA? CARINA, ARE YOU WELL?
STAR. HE'S A SHINING STAR.
THERE USED TO BE STARS. WH-WHERE ARE ALL THE STARS?
WHAT IN DOOM'S NAME--?!
NNNGHH!
WHAT... WHAT IS...?
GOD DOOM!

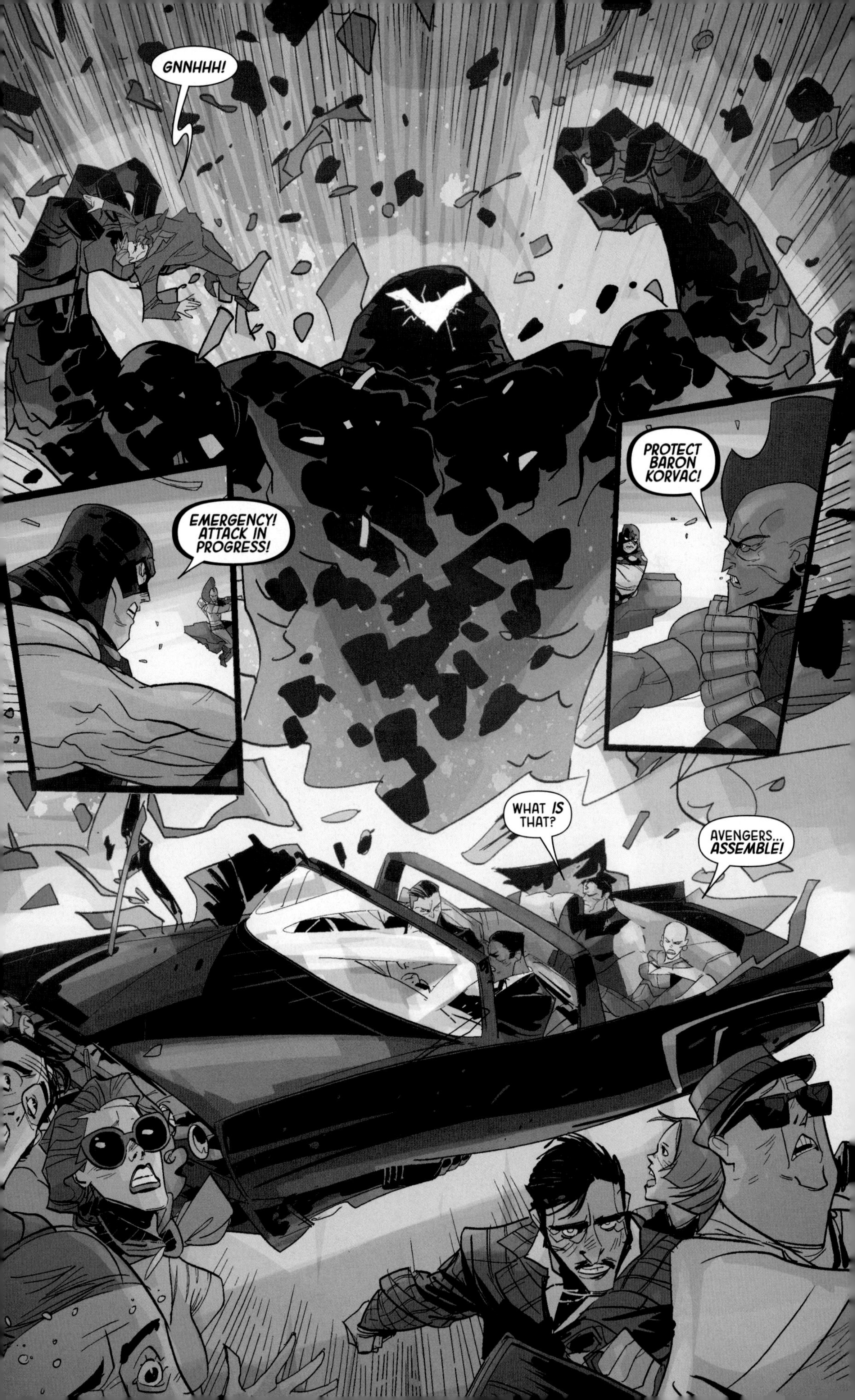
GNNHHH!
EMERGENCY! ATTACK IN PROGRESS!
PROTECT BARON KORVAC!
WHAT *IS* THAT?
AVENGERS... **ASSEMBLE!**

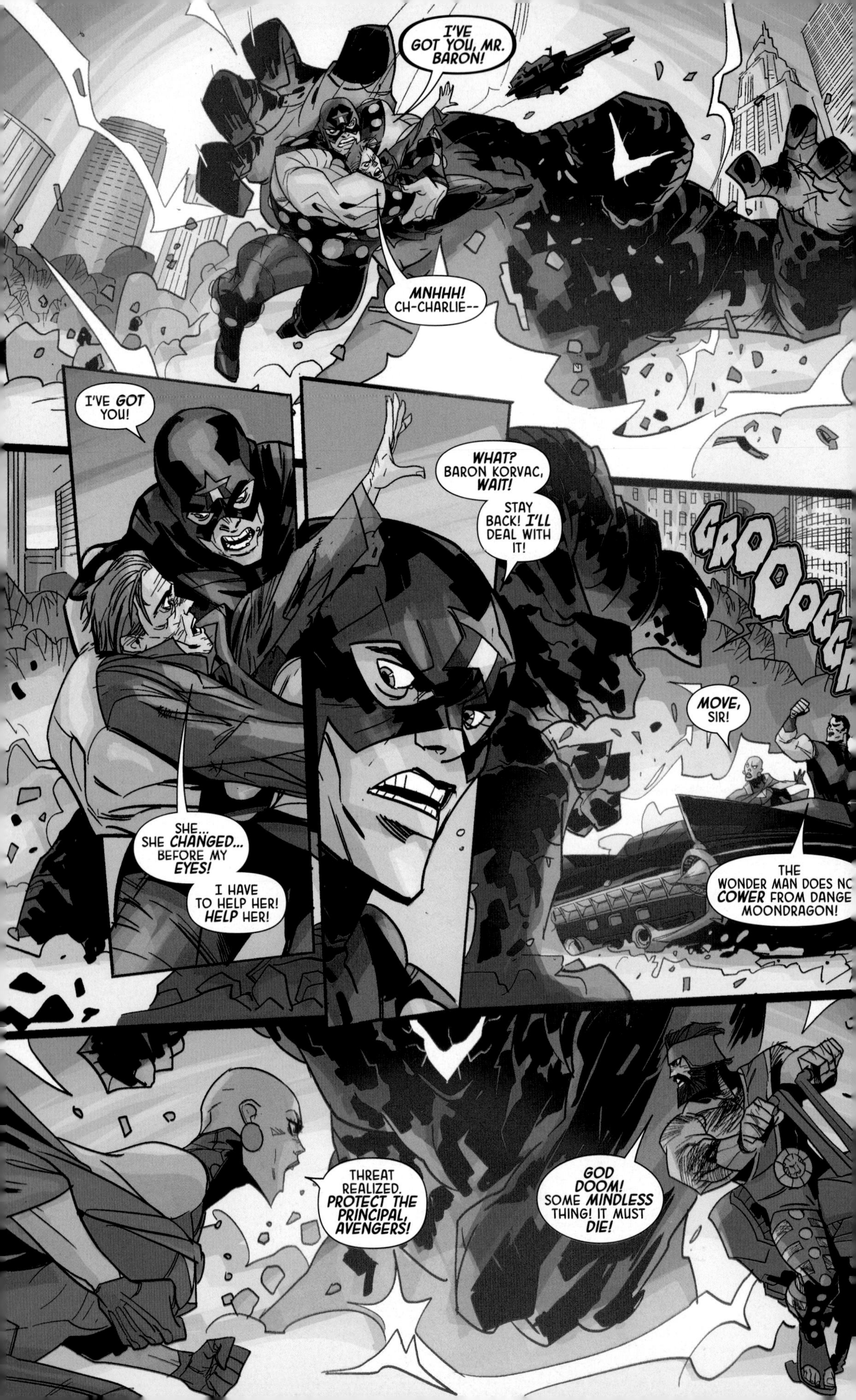
I'VE GOT YOU, MR. BARON!
MNHHH! CH-CHARLIE--
I'VE GOT YOU!
WHAT? BARON KORVAC, WAIT!
STAY BACK! I'LL DEAL WITH IT!
GROOOOGG
SHE... SHE CHANGED... BEFORE MY EYES!
I HAVE TO HELP HER! HELP HER!
MOVE, SIR!
THE WONDER MAN DOES NO
COWER FROM DANGE
MOONDRAGON!
THREAT REALIZED. PROTECT THE PRINCIPAL, AVENGERS!
GOD DOOM! SOME MINDLESS THING! IT MUST DIE!

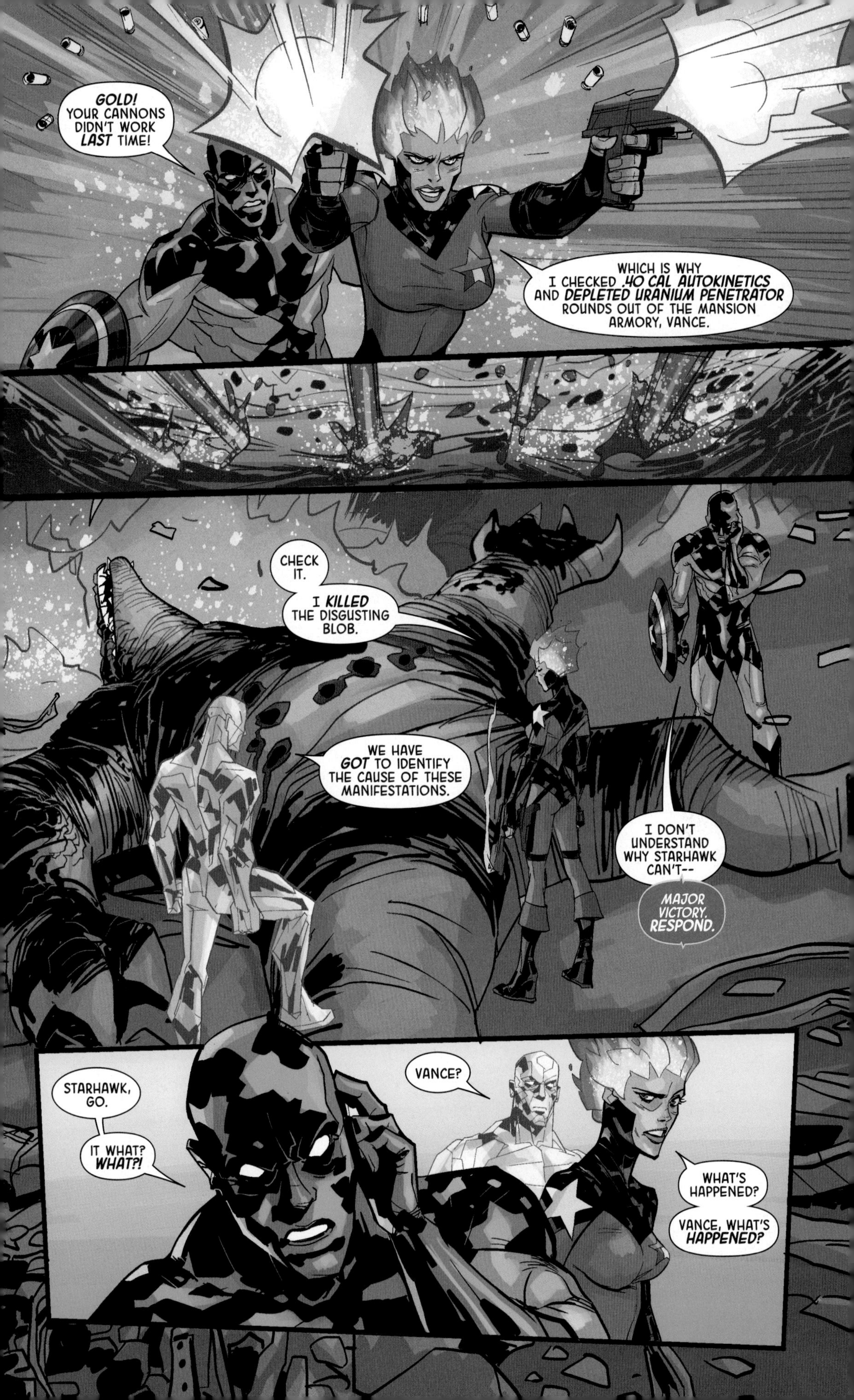
GOLD! YOUR CANNONS DIDN'T WORK LAST TIME!
WHICH IS WHY I CHECKED .40 CAL AUTOKINETICS AND DEPLETED URANIUM PENETRATOR ROUNDS OUT OF THE MANSION ARMORY, VANCE.
CHECK IT.
I KILLED THE DISGUSTING BLOB.
WE HAVE GOT TO IDENTIFY THE CAUSE OF THESE MANIFESTATIONS.
I DON'T UNDERSTAND WHY STARHAWK CAN'T--
MAJOR VICTORY. RESPOND.
STARHAWK, GO.
IT WHAT? WHAT?!
VANCE?
WHAT'S HAPPENED?
VANCE, WHAT'S HAPPENED?

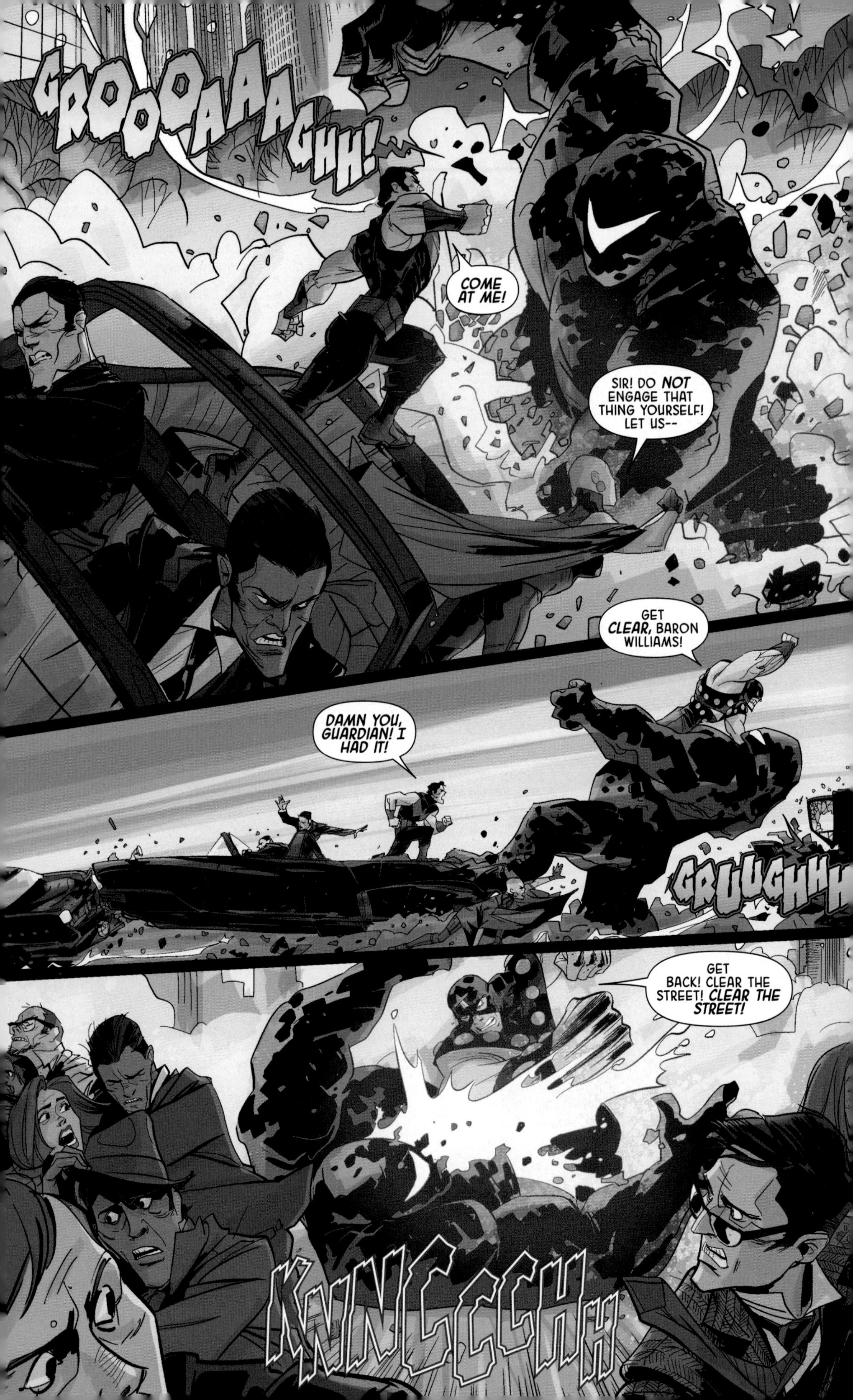
GROOOAAAGHH!
COME AT ME!
SIR! DO NOT ENGAGE THAT THING YOURSELF! LET US--
GET CLEAR, BARON WILLIAMS!
DAMN YOU, GUARDIAN! I HAD IT!
GRUUGHHH
GET BACK! CLEAR THE STREET! CLEAR THE STREET!
KNNCCCHH

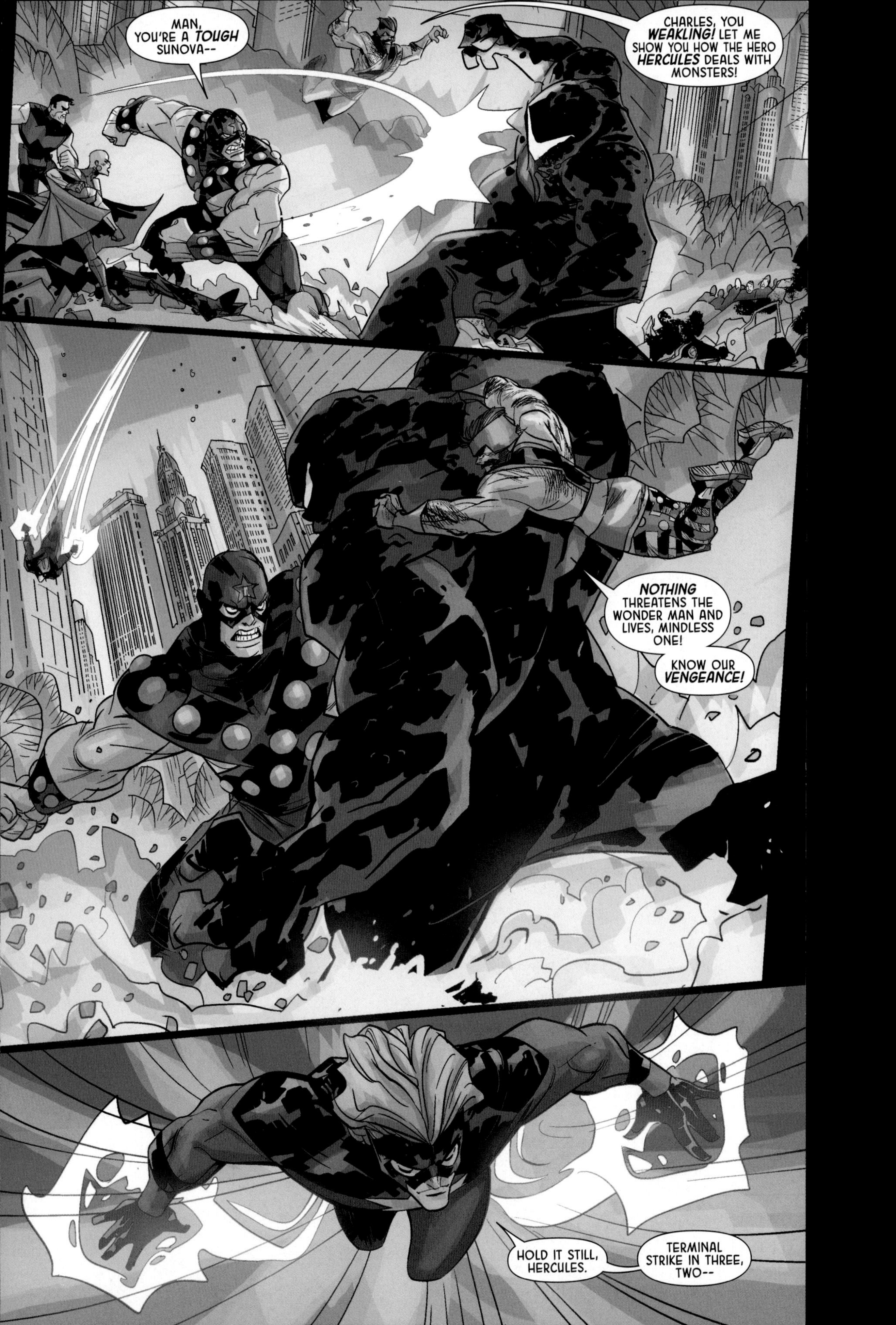

MAN, YOU'RE A TOUGH SUNOVA--
CHARLES, YOU WEAKLING! LET ME SHOW YOU HOW THE HERO HERCULES DEALS WITH MONSTERS!
NOTHING THREATENS THE WONDER MAN AND LIVES, MINDLESS ONE!
KNOW OUR VENGEANCE!
HOLD IT STILL, HERCULES.
TERMINAL STRIKE IN THREE, TWO--

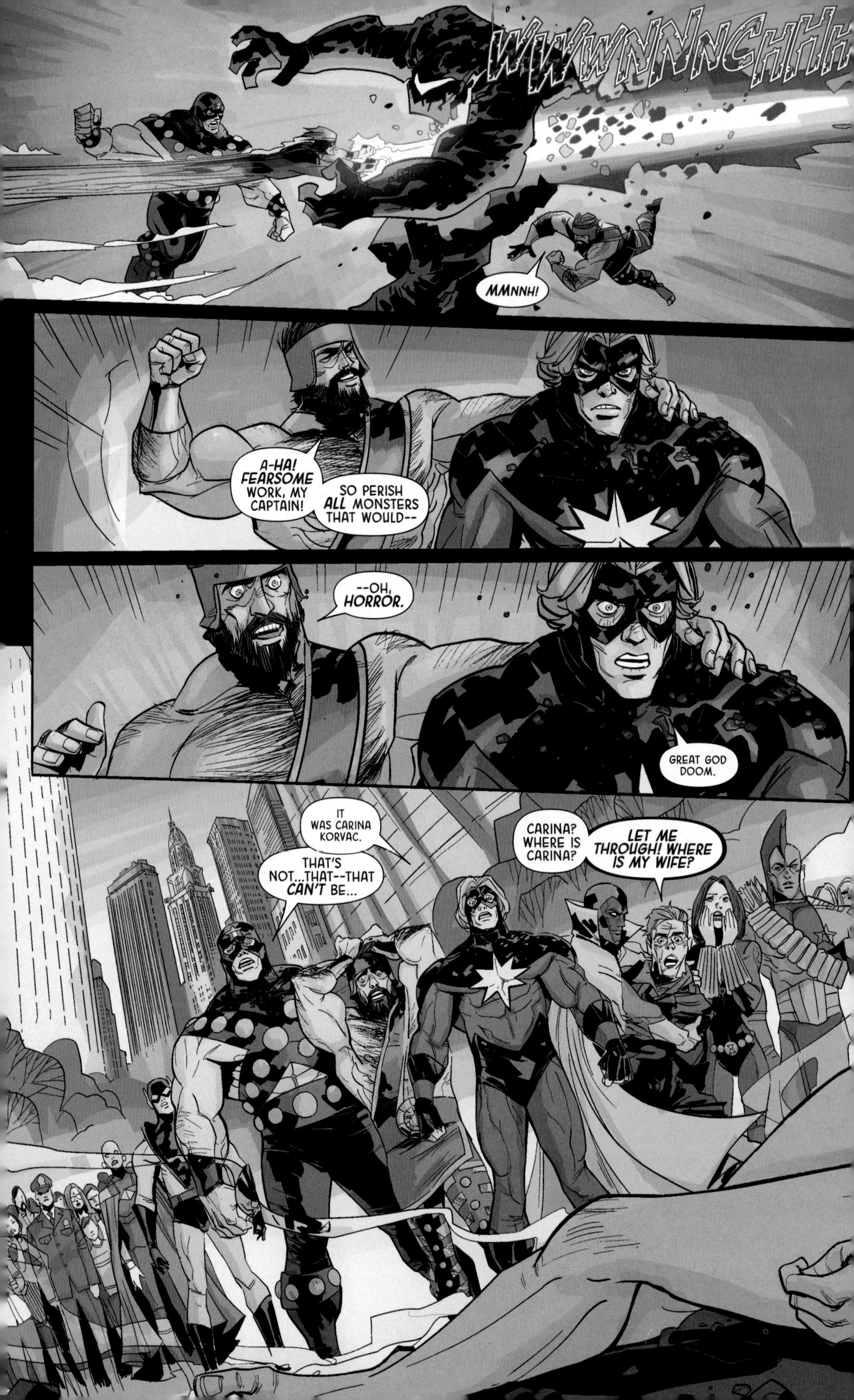
WWWNNNCHHH
MMNNH!
A-HA! FEARSOME WORK, MY CAPTAIN!
SO PERISH ALL MONSTERS THAT WOULD--
--OH, HORROR.
GREAT GOD DOOM.
IT WAS CARINA KORVAC.
THAT'S NOT...THAT--THAT CAN'T BE...
CARINA? WHERE IS CARINA?
LET ME THROUGH! WHERE IS MY WIFE?

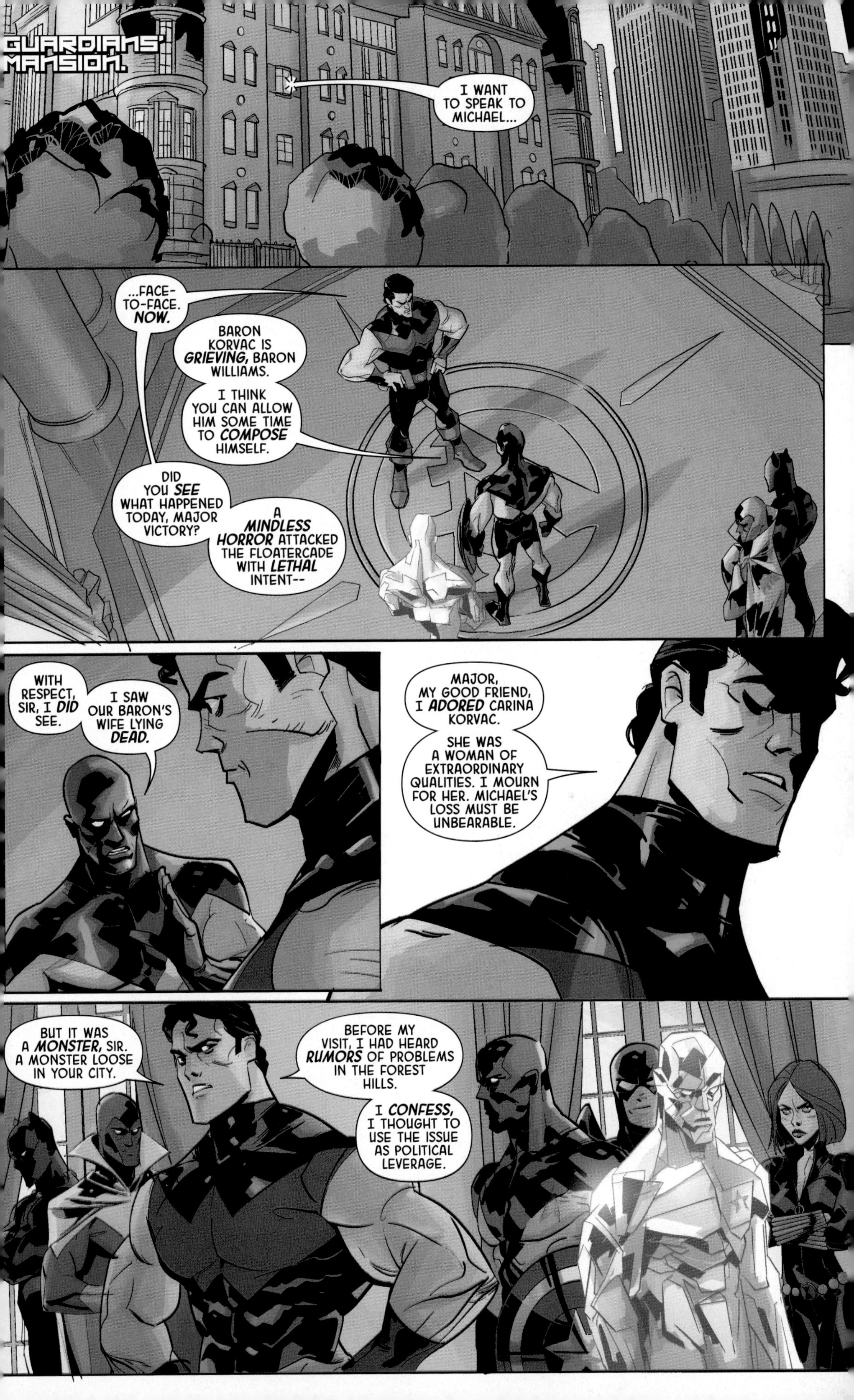
GUARDIANS' MANSION.
I WANT TO SPEAK TO MICHAEL...
...FACE-TO-FACE. NOW.
BARON KORVAC IS GRIEVING, BARON WILLIAMS.
I THINK YOU CAN ALLOW HIM SOME TIME TO COMPOSE HIMSELF.
DID YOU SEE WHAT HAPPENED TODAY, MAJOR VICTORY?
A MINDLESS HORROR ATTACKED THE FLOATERCADE WITH LETHAL INTENT--
WITH RESPECT, SIR, I DID SEE.
I SAW OUR BARON'S WIFE LYING DEAD.
MAJOR, MY GOOD FRIEND, I ADORED CARINA KORVAC.
SHE WAS A WOMAN OF EXTRAORDINARY QUALITIES. I MOURN FOR HER. MICHAEL'S LOSS MUST BE UNBEARABLE.
BUT IT WAS A MONSTER, SIR. A MONSTER LOOSE IN YOUR CITY.
BEFORE MY VISIT, I HAD HEARD RUMORS OF PROBLEMS IN THE FOREST HILLS.
I CONFESS, I THOUGHT TO USE THE ISSUE AS POLITICAL LEVERAGE.

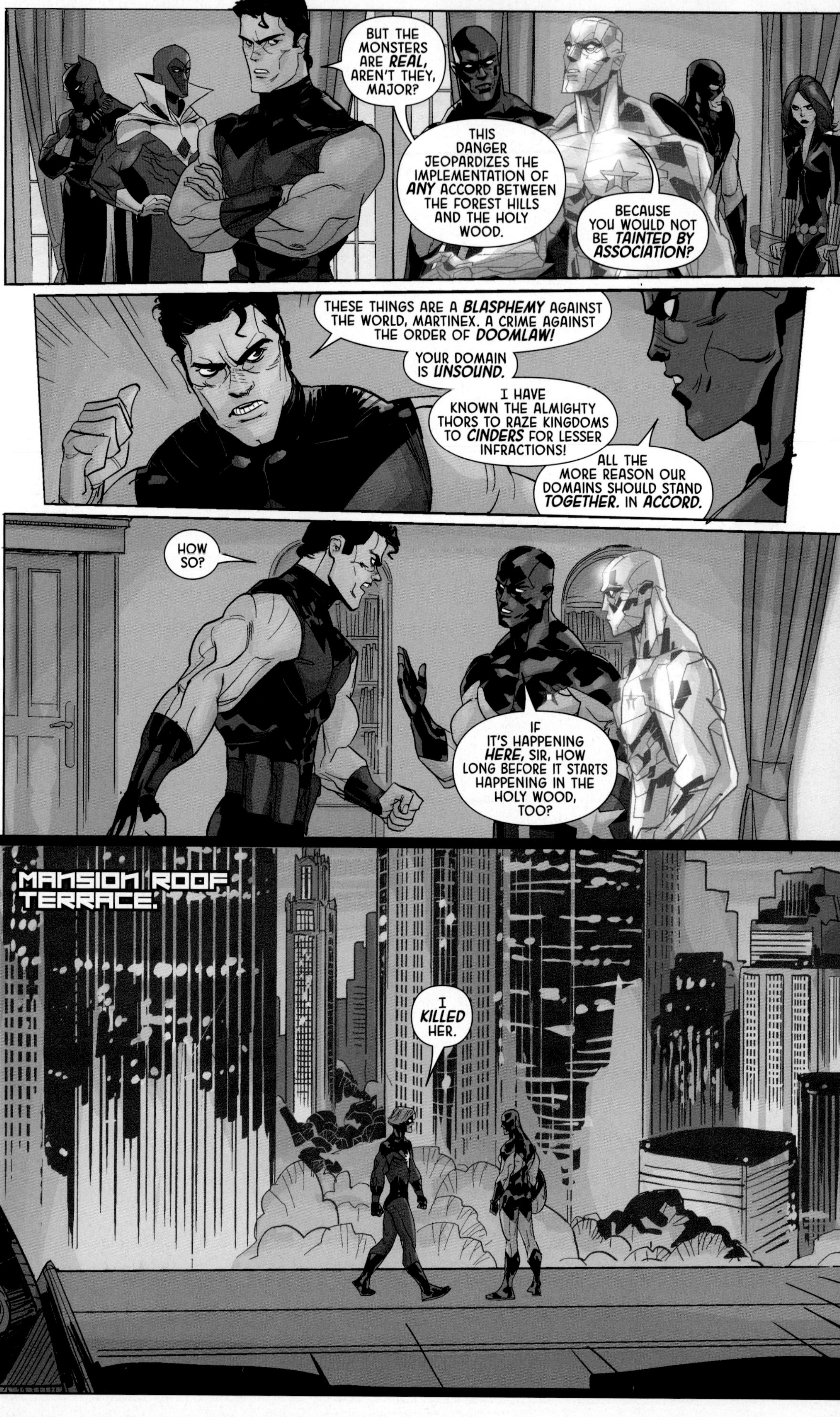
BUT THE MONSTERS ARE REAL, AREN'T THEY, MAJOR?
THIS DANGER JEOPARDIZES THE IMPLEMENTATION OF ANY ACCORD BETWEEN THE FOREST HILLS AND THE HOLY WOOD.
BECAUSE YOU WOULD NOT BE TAINTED BY ASSOCIATION?
THESE THINGS ARE A BLASPHEMY AGAINST THE WORLD, MARTINEX. A CRIME AGAINST THE ORDER OF DOOMLAW!
YOUR DOMAIN IS UNSOUND.
I HAVE KNOWN THE ALMIGHTY THORS TO RAZE KINGDOMS TO CINDERS FOR LESSER INFRACTIONS!
ALL THE MORE REASON OUR DOMAINS SHOULD STAND TOGETHER. IN ACCORD.
HOW SO?
IF IT'S HAPPENING HERE, SIR, HOW LONG BEFORE IT STARTS HAPPENING IN THE HOLY WOOD, TOO?
MANSION ROOF TERRACE.
I KILLED HER.

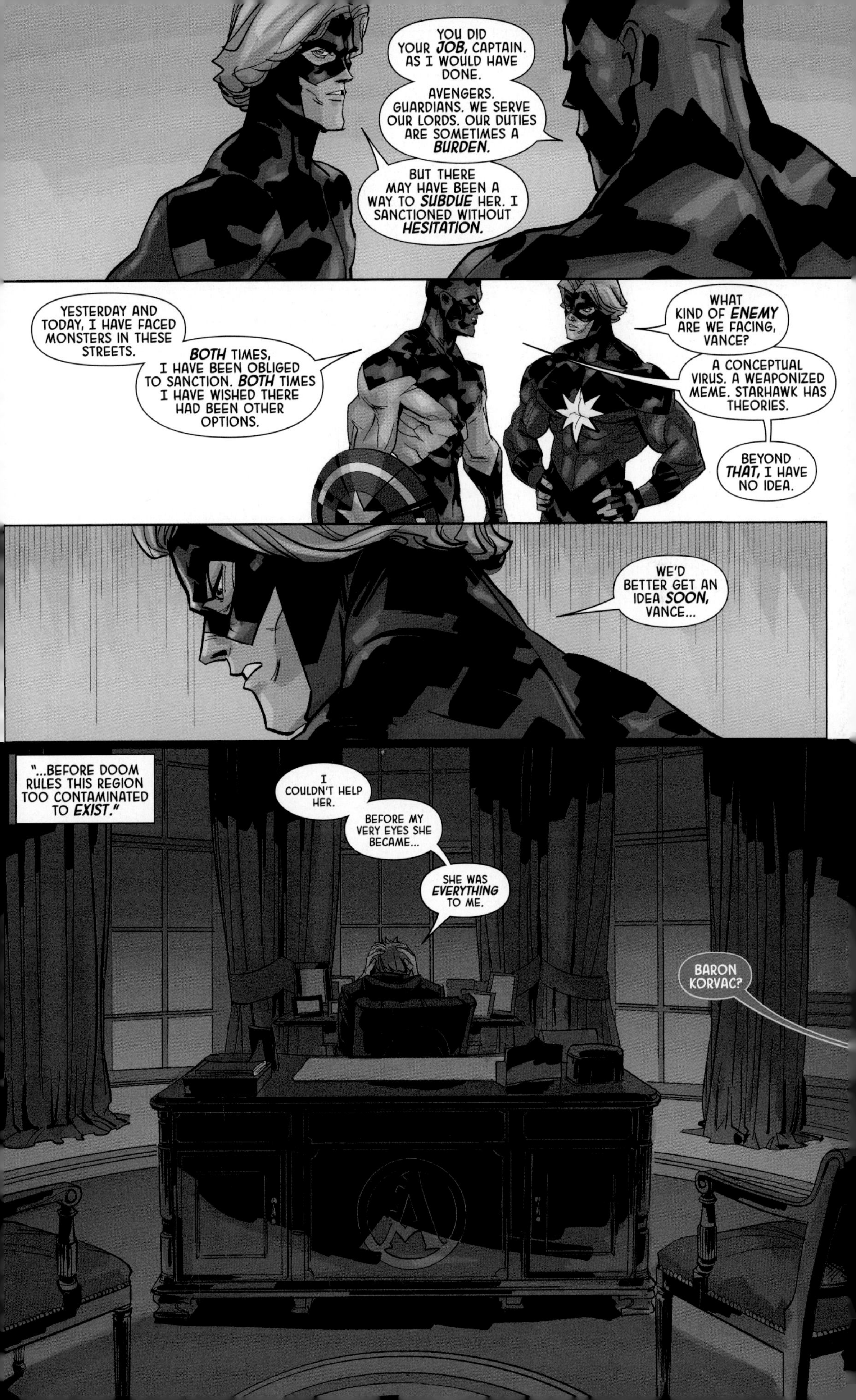
YOU DID YOUR JOB, CAPTAIN. AS I WOULD HAVE DONE.
AVENGERS. GUARDIANS. WE SERVE OUR LORDS. OUR DUTIES ARE SOMETIMES A BURDEN.
BUT THERE MAY HAVE BEEN A WAY TO SUBDUE HER. I SANCTIONED WITHOUT HESITATION.
YESTERDAY AND TODAY, I HAVE FACED MONSTERS IN THESE STREETS.
BOTH TIMES, I HAVE BEEN OBLIGED TO SANCTION. BOTH TIMES I HAVE WISHED THERE HAD BEEN OTHER OPTIONS.
WHAT KIND OF ENEMY ARE WE FACING, VANCE?
A CONCEPTUAL VIRUS. A WEAPONIZED MEME. STARHAWK HAS THEORIES.
BEYOND THAT, I HAVE NO IDEA.
WE'D BETTER GET AN IDEA SOON, VANCE...
"...BEFORE DOOM RULES THIS REGION TOO CONTAMINATED TO EXIST."
I COULDN'T HELP HER.
BEFORE MY VERY EYES SHE BECAME...
SHE WAS EVERYTHING TO ME.
BARON KORVAC?

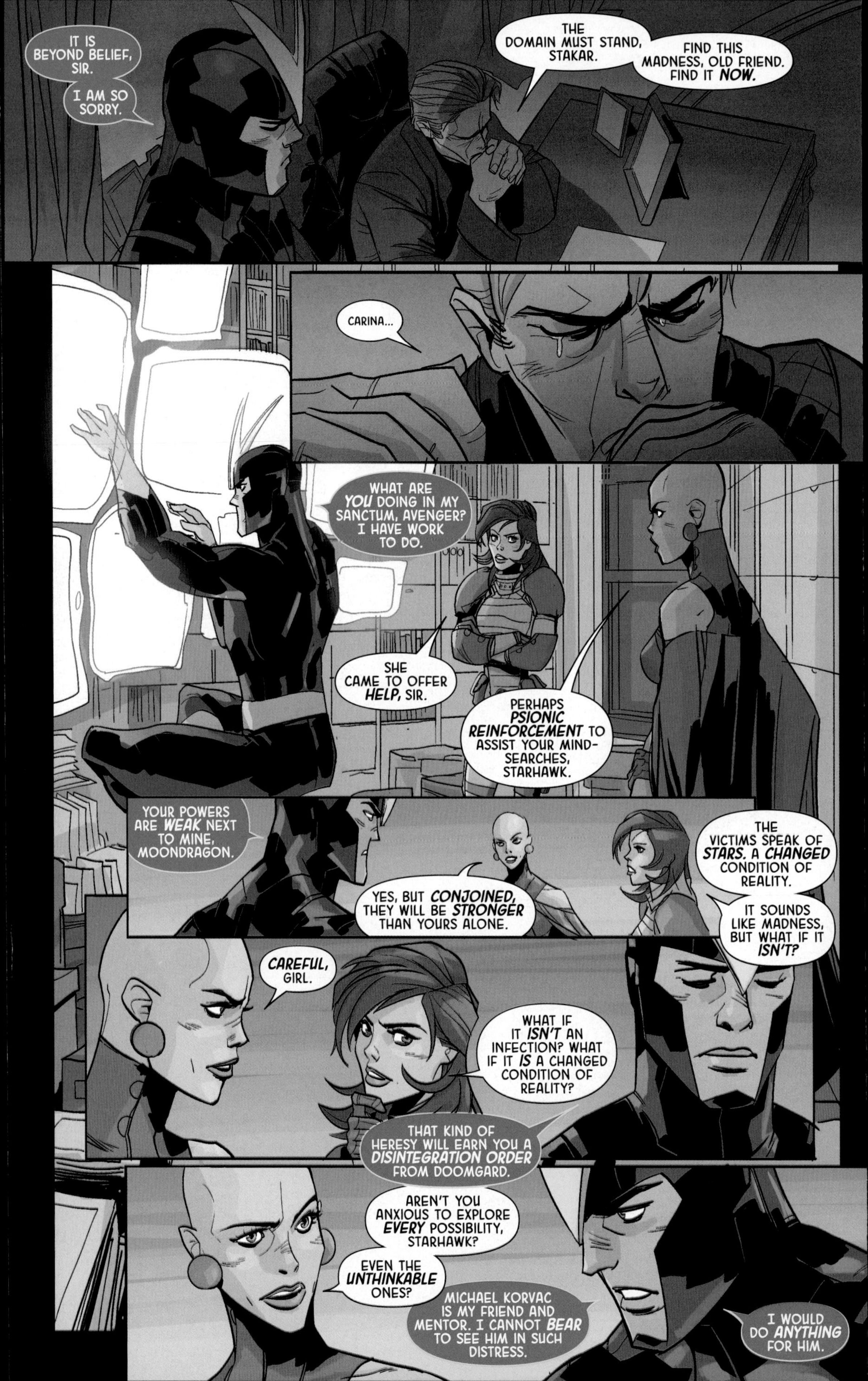
IT IS BEYOND BELIEF, SIR.
I AM SO SORRY.
THE DOMAIN MUST STAND, STAKAR.
FIND THIS MADNESS, OLD FRIEND. FIND IT NOW.
CARINA...
WHAT ARE YOU DOING IN MY SANCTUM, AVENGER? I HAVE WORK TO DO.
SHE CAME TO OFFER HELP, SIR.
PERHAPS PSIONIC REINFORCEMENT TO ASSIST YOUR MIND-SEARCHES, STARHAWK.
YOUR POWERS ARE WEAK NEXT TO MINE, MOONDRAGON.
YES, BUT CONJOINED, THEY WILL BE STRONGER THAN YOURS ALONE.
THE VICTIMS SPEAK OF STARS. A CHANGED CONDITION OF REALITY.
IT SOUNDS LIKE MADNESS, BUT WHAT IF IT ISN'T?
CAREFUL, GIRL.
WHAT IF IT ISN'T AN INFECTION? WHAT IF IT IS A CHANGED CONDITION OF REALITY?
THAT KIND OF HERESY WILL EARN YOU A DISINTEGRATION ORDER FROM DOOMGARD.
AREN'T YOU ANXIOUS TO EXPLORE EVERY POSSIBILITY, STARHAWK?
EVEN THE UNTHINKABLE ONES?
MICHAEL KORVAC IS MY FRIEND AND MENTOR. I CANNOT BEAR TO SEE HIM IN SUCH DISTRESS.
I WOULD DO ANYTHING FOR HIM.

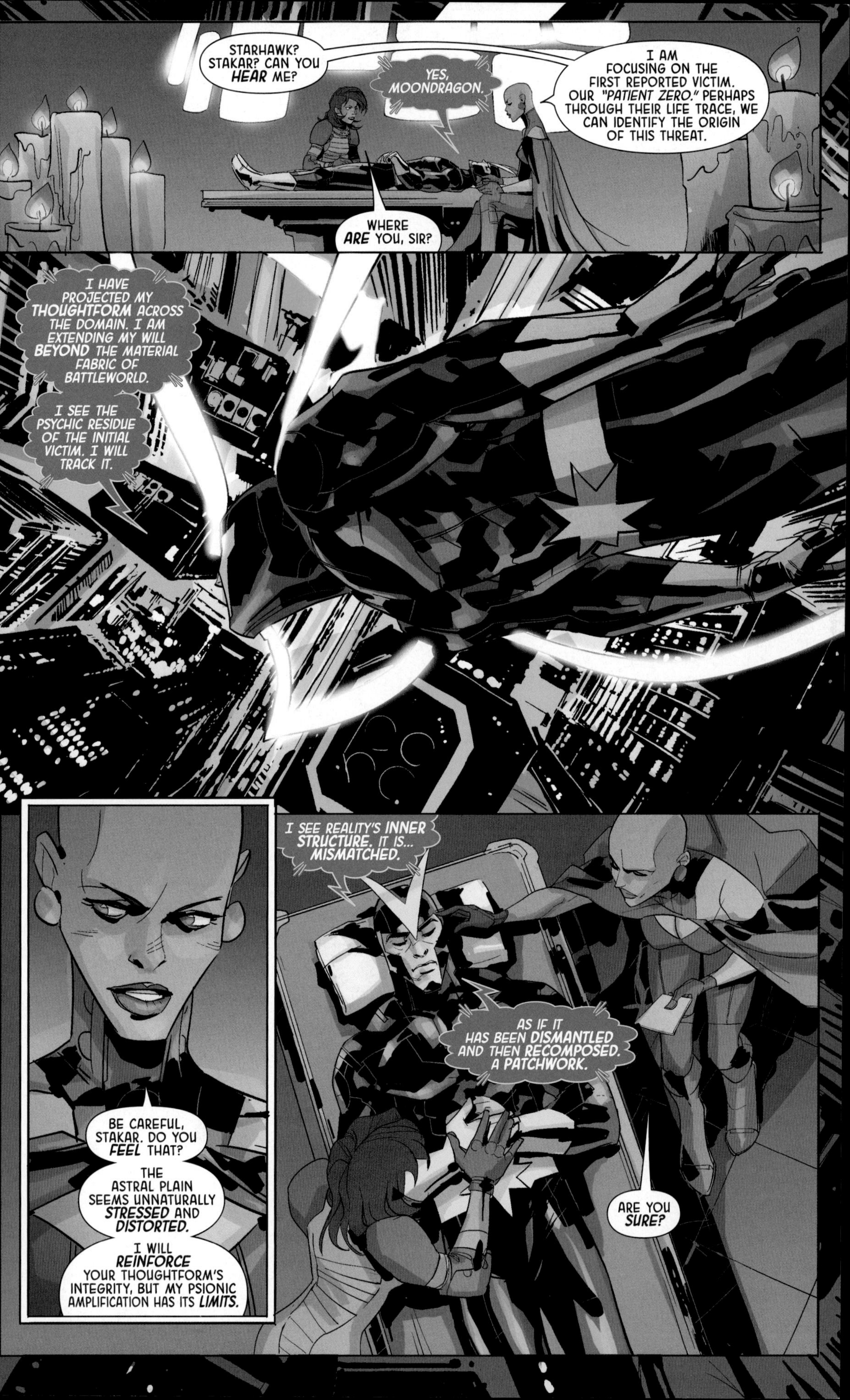
STARHAWK? STAKAR? CAN YOU HEAR ME?
YES, MOONDRAGON.
I AM FOCUSING ON THE FIRST REPORTED VICTIM. OUR "PATIENT ZERO." PERHAPS THROUGH THEIR LIFE TRACE, WE CAN IDENTIFY THE ORIGIN OF THIS THREAT.
WHERE ARE YOU, SIR?
I HAVE PROJECTED MY THOUGHTFORM ACROSS THE DOMAIN. I AM EXTENDING MY WILL BEYOND THE MATERIAL FABRIC OF BATTLEWORLD.
I SEE THE PSYCHIC RESIDUE OF THE INITIAL VICTIM. I WILL TRACK IT.
BE CAREFUL, STAKAR. DO YOU FEEL THAT?
THE ASTRAL PLAIN SEEMS UNNATURALLY STRESSED AND DISTORTED.
I WILL REINFORCE YOUR THOUGHTFORM'S INTEGRITY, BUT MY PSIONIC AMPLIFICATION HAS ITS LIMITS.
I SEE REALITY'S INNER STRUCTURE. IT IS... MISMATCHED.
AS IF IT HAS BEEN DISMANTLED AND THEN RECOMPOSED. A PATCHWORK.
ARE YOU SURE?

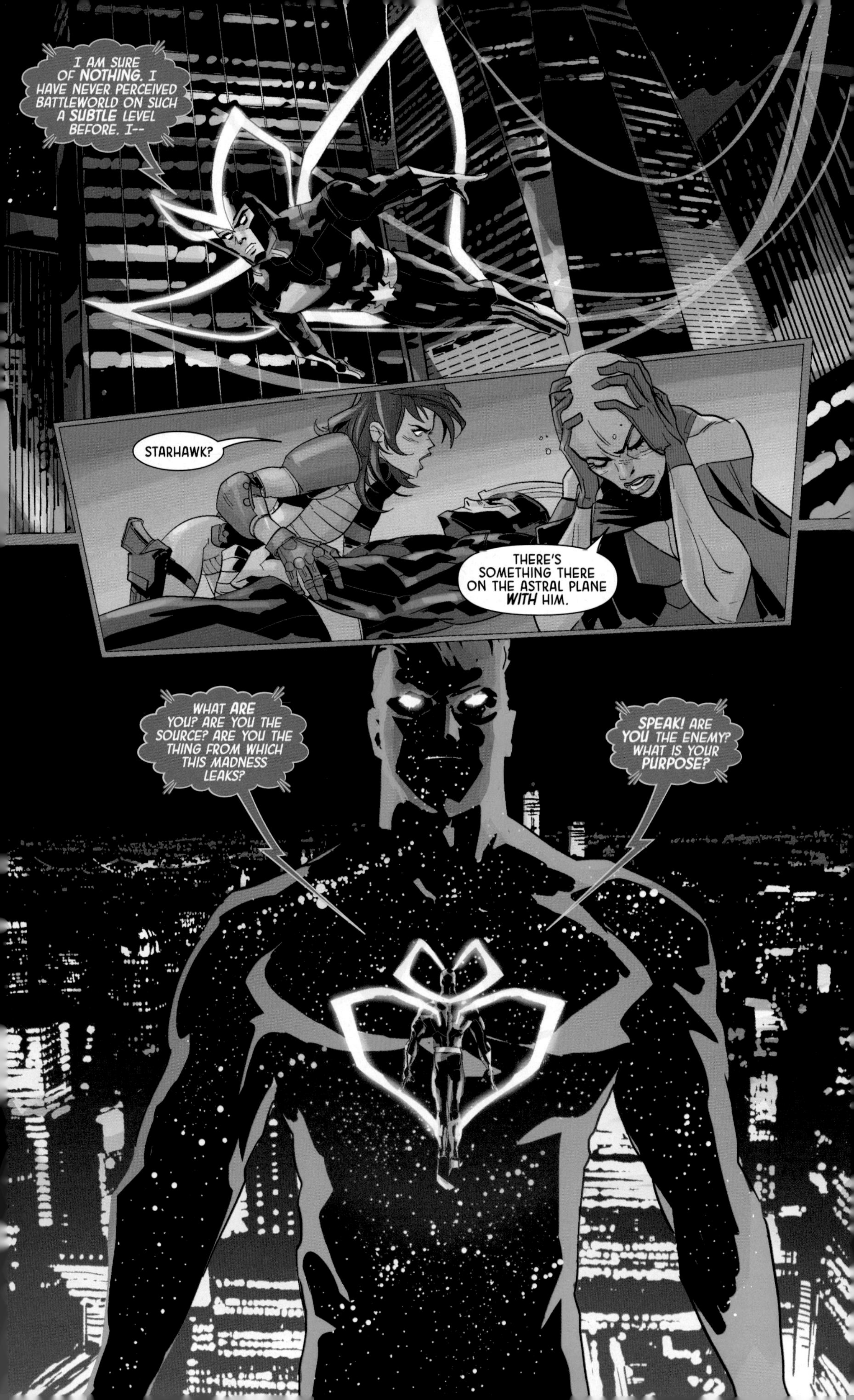

I AM SURE OF NOTHING. I HAVE NEVER PERCEIVED BATTLEWORLD ON SUCH A SUBTLE LEVEL BEFORE. I--
STARHAWK?
THERE'S SOMETHING THERE ON THE ASTRAL PLANE WITH HIM.
WHAT ARE YOU? ARE YOU THE SOURCE? ARE YOU THE THING FROM WHICH THIS MADNESS LEAKS?
SPEAK! ARE YOU THE ENEMY? WHAT IS YOUR PURPOSE?

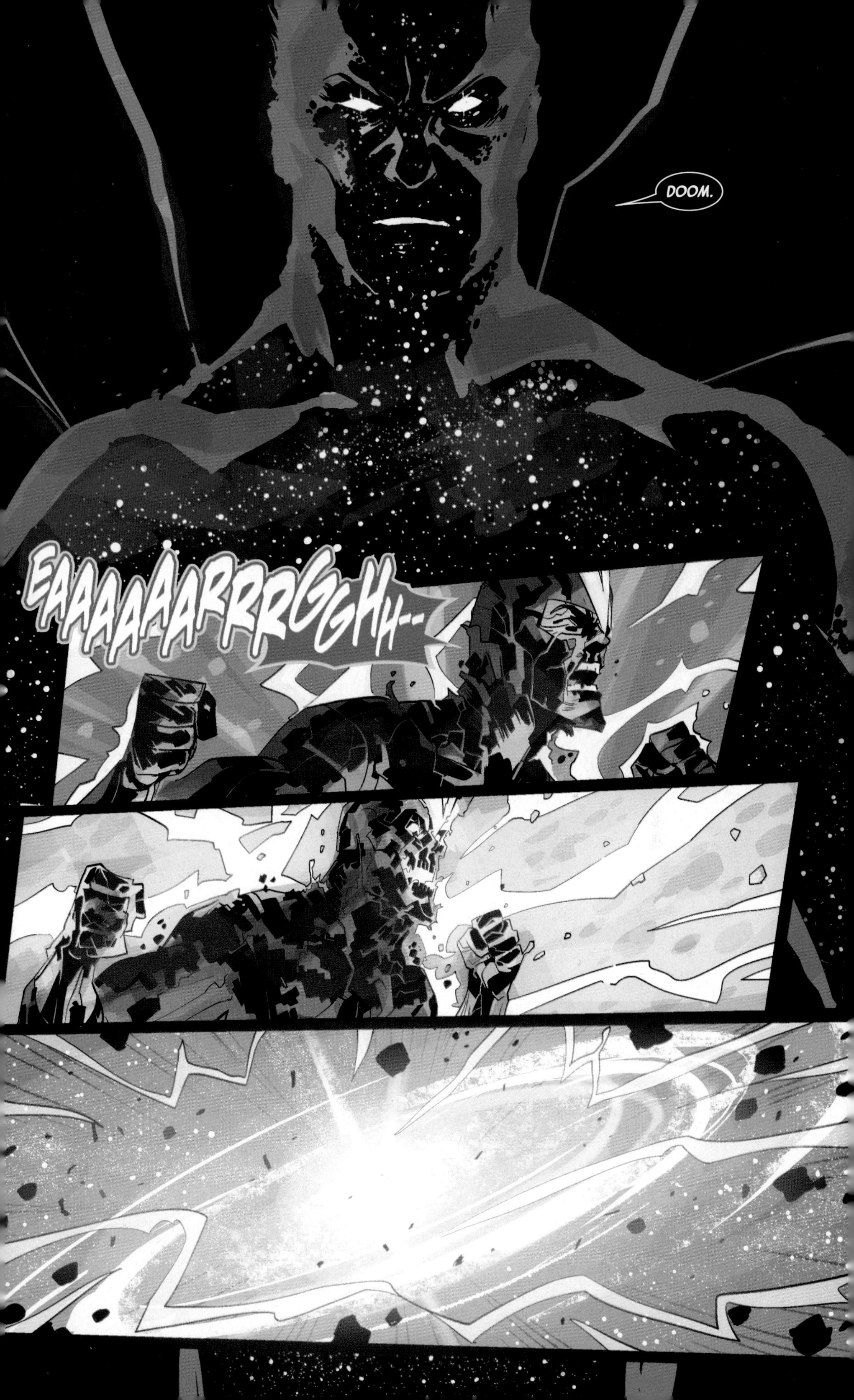
DOOM.
EAAAAAARRRGGHH--

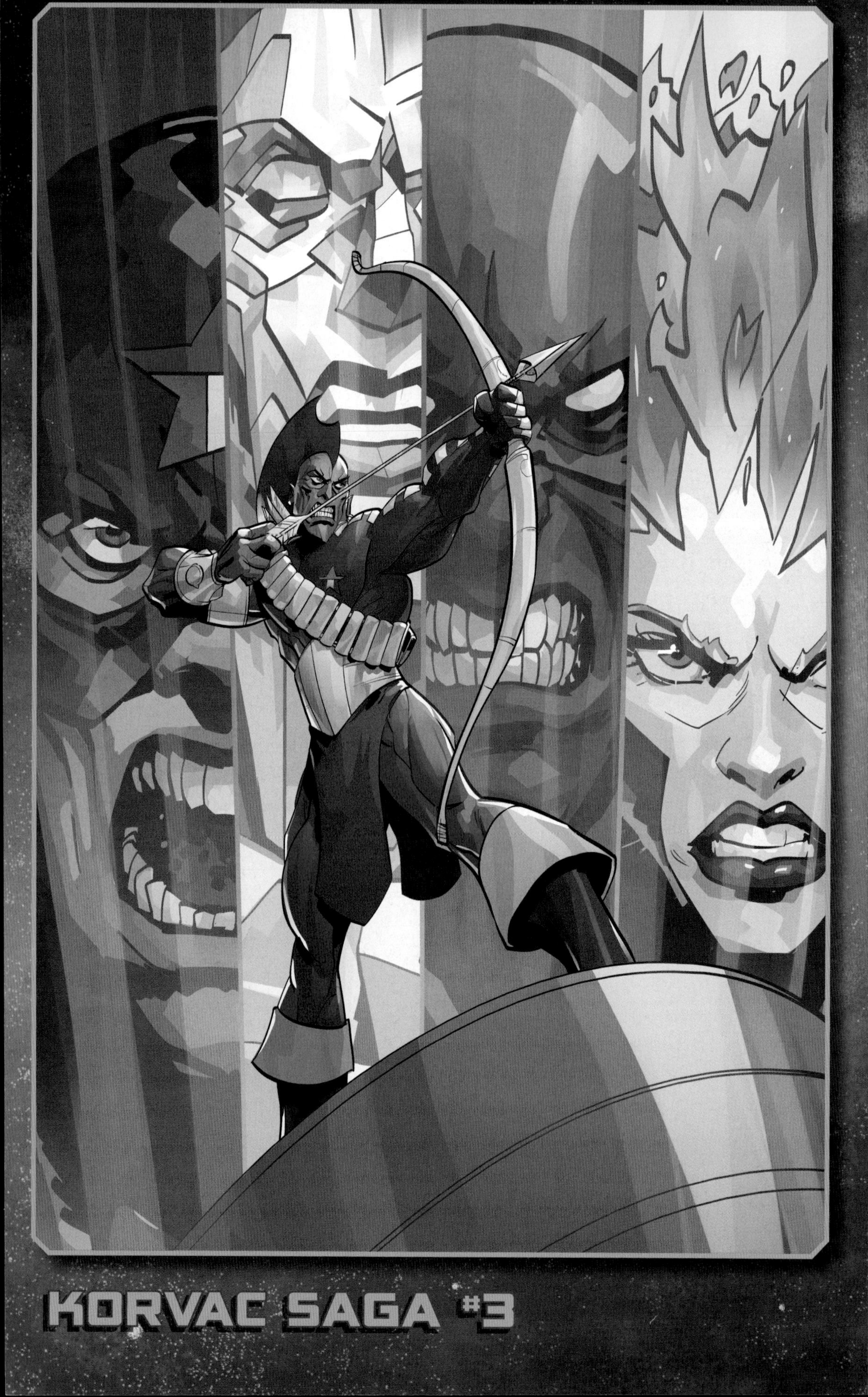

KORVAC SAGA #3

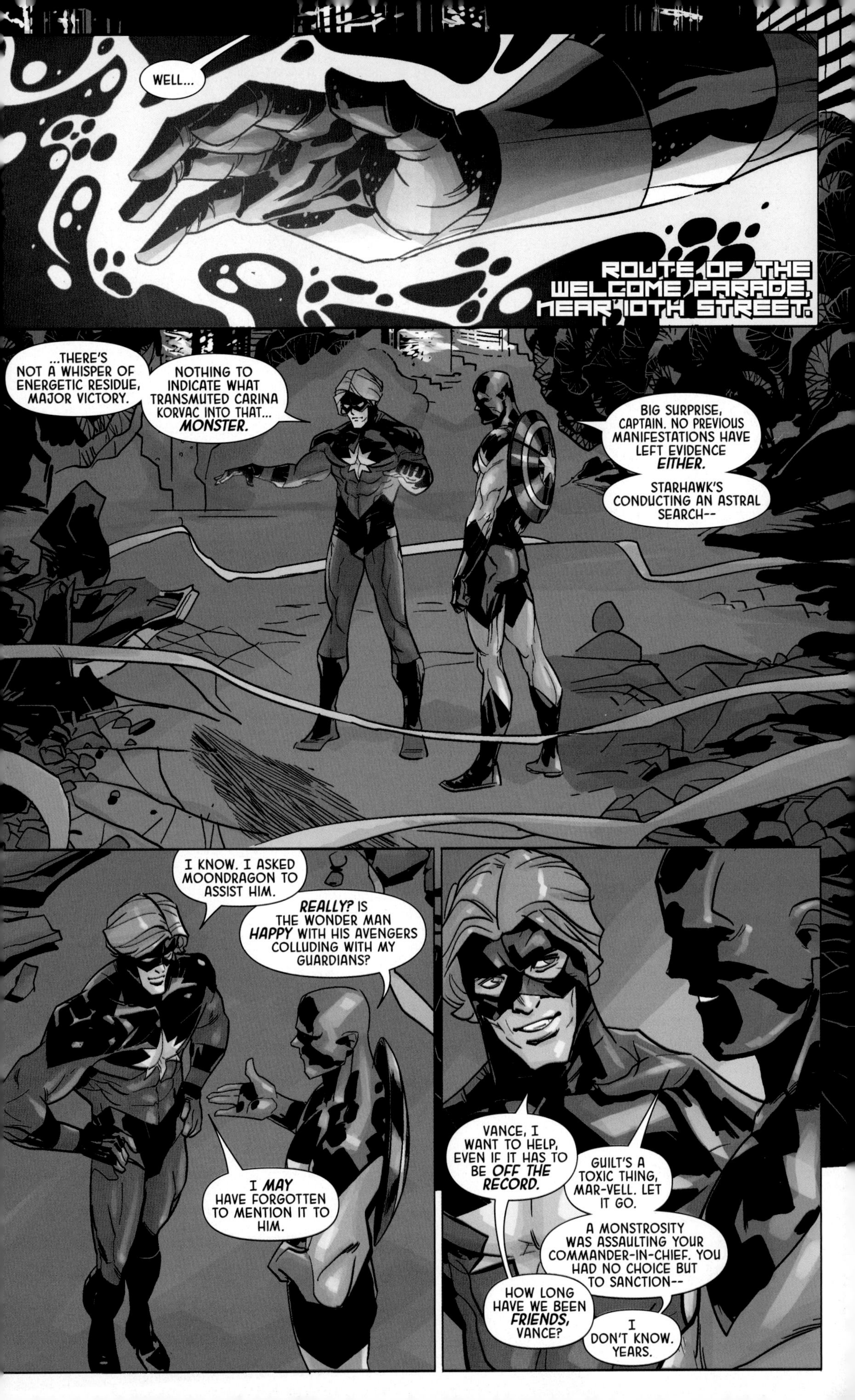
WELL...
ROUTE OF THE WELCOME PARADE, NEAR 10TH STREET.
...THERE'S NOT A WHISPER OF ENERGETIC RESIDUE, MAJOR VICTORY.
NOTHING TO INDICATE WHAT TRANSMUTED CARINA KORVAC INTO THAT... MONSTER.
BIG SURPRISE, CAPTAIN. NO PREVIOUS MANIFESTATIONS HAVE LEFT EVIDENCE EITHER.
STARHAWK'S CONDUCTING AN ASTRAL SEARCH--
I KNOW. I ASKED MOONDRAGON TO ASSIST HIM.
REALLY? IS THE WONDER MAN HAPPY WITH HIS AVENGERS COLLUDING WITH MY GUARDIANS?
I MAY HAVE FORGOTTEN TO MENTION IT TO HIM.
VANCE, I WANT TO HELP, EVEN IF IT HAS TO BE OFF THE RECORD.
GUILT'S A TOXIC THING, MAR-VELL. LET IT GO.
A MONSTROSITY WAS ASSAULTING YOUR COMMANDER-IN-CHIEF. YOU HAD NO CHOICE BUT TO SANCTION--
HOW LONG HAVE WE BEEN FRIENDS, VANCE?
I DON'T KNOW. YEARS.

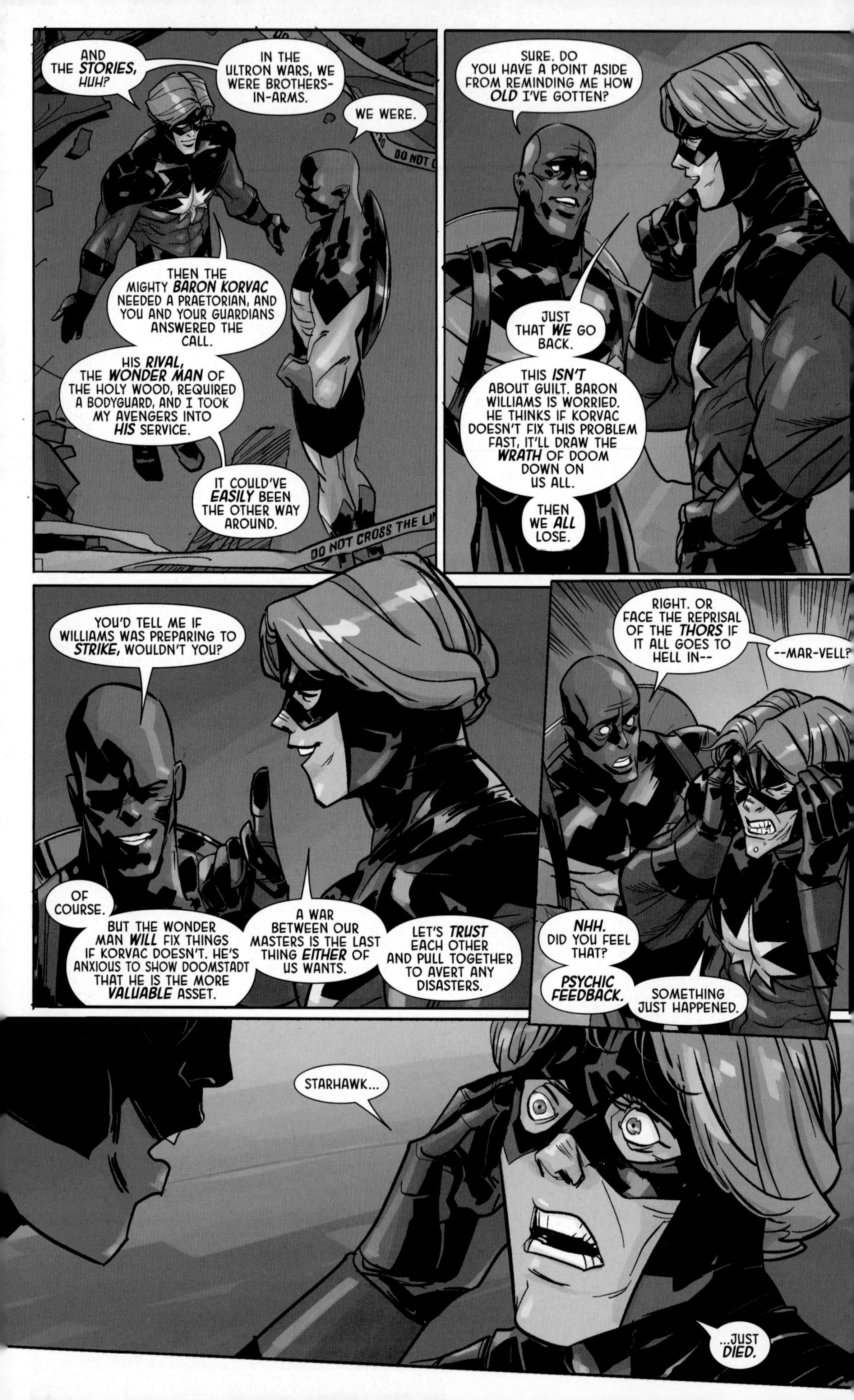
AND THE STORIES, HUH?
IN THE ULTRON WARS, WE WERE BROTHERS-IN-ARMS.
WE WERE.
DO NOT C
THEN THE MIGHTY BARON KORVAC NEEDED A PRAETORIAN, AND YOU AND YOUR GUARDIANS ANSWERED THE CALL.
HIS RIVAL, THE WONDER MAN OF THE HOLY WOOD, REQUIRED A BODYGUARD, AND I TOOK MY AVENGERS INTO HIS SERVICE.
IT COULD'VE EASILY BEEN THE OTHER WAY AROUND.
DO NOT CROSS THE LI
SURE. DO YOU HAVE A POINT ASIDE FROM REMINDING ME HOW OLD I'VE GOTTEN?
JUST THAT WE GO BACK.
THIS ISN'T ABOUT GUILT. BARON WILLIAMS IS WORRIED. HE THINKS IF KORVAC DOESN'T FIX THIS PROBLEM FAST, IT'LL DRAW THE WRATH OF DOOM DOWN ON US ALL.
THEN WE ALL LOSE.
YOU'D TELL ME IF WILLIAMS WAS PREPARING TO STRIKE, WOULDN'T YOU?
OF COURSE.
BUT THE WONDER MAN WILL FIX THINGS IF KORVAC DOESN'T. HE'S ANXIOUS TO SHOW DOOMSTADT THAT HE IS THE MORE VALUABLE ASSET.
A WAR BETWEEN OUR MASTERS IS THE LAST THING EITHER OF US WANTS.
LET'S TRUST EACH OTHER AND PULL TOGETHER TO AVERT ANY DISASTERS.
RIGHT. OR FACE THE REPRISAL OF THE THORS IF IT ALL GOES TO HELL IN--
--MAR-VELL?
NHH. DID YOU FEEL THAT?
PSYCHIC FEEDBACK.
SOMETHING JUST HAPPENED.
STARHAWK...
...JUST DIED.

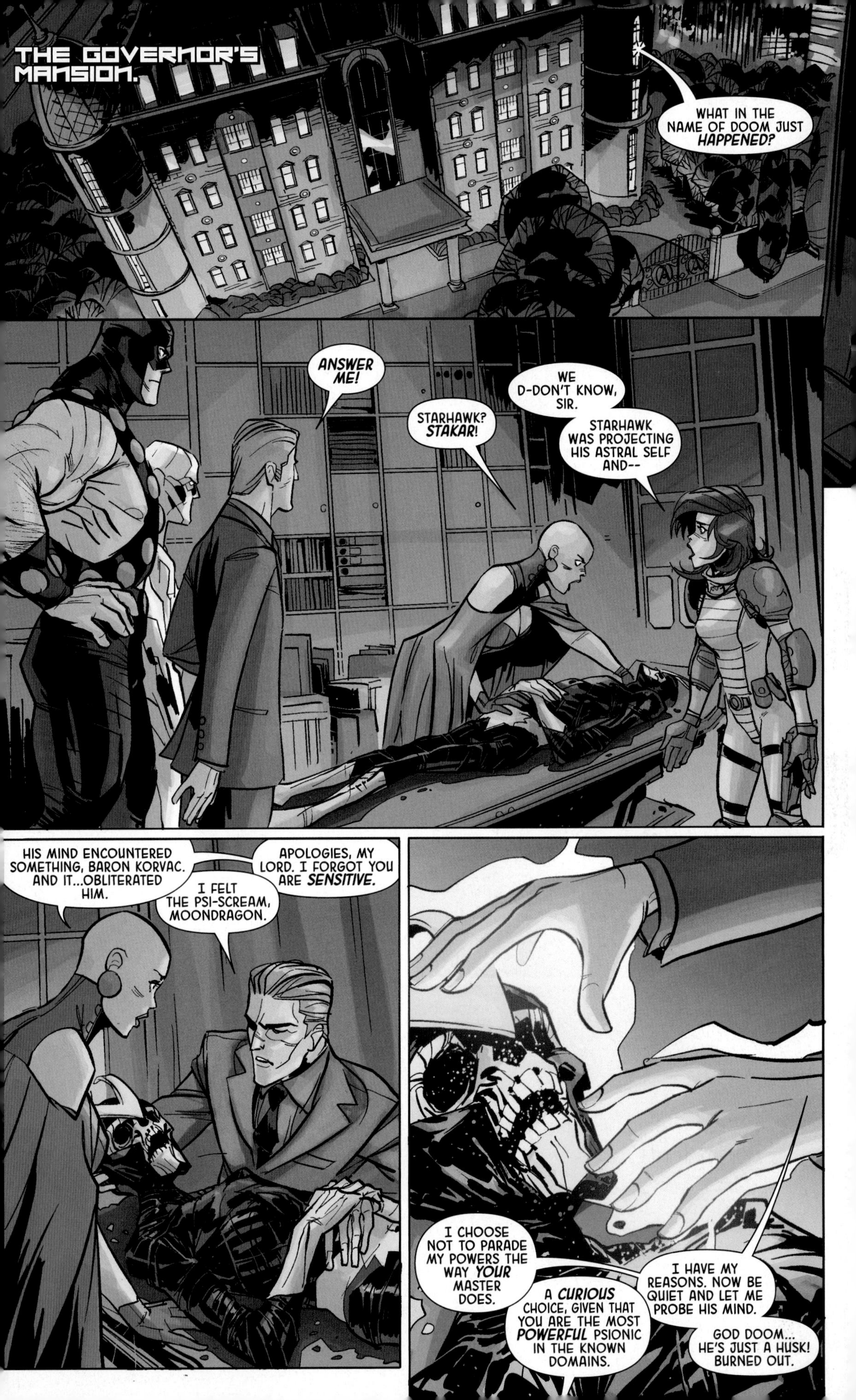
THE GOVERNOR'S MANSION.
WHAT IN THE NAME OF DOOM JUST HAPPENED?
ANSWER ME!
STARHAWK? STAKAR!
WE D-DON'T KNOW, SIR.
STARHAWK WAS PROJECTING HIS ASTRAL SELF AND--
HIS MIND ENCOUNTERED SOMETHING, BARON KORVAC. AND IT...OBLITERATED HIM.
I FELT THE PSI-SCREAM, MOONDRAGON.
APOLOGIES, MY LORD. I FORGOT YOU ARE SENSITIVE.
I CHOOSE NOT TO PARADE MY POWERS THE WAY YOUR MASTER DOES.
A CURIOUS CHOICE, GIVEN THAT YOU ARE THE MOST POWERFUL PSIONIC IN THE KNOWN DOMAINS.
I HAVE MY REASONS. NOW BE QUIET AND LET ME PROBE HIS MIND.
GOD DOOM... HE'S JUST A HUSK! BURNED OUT.

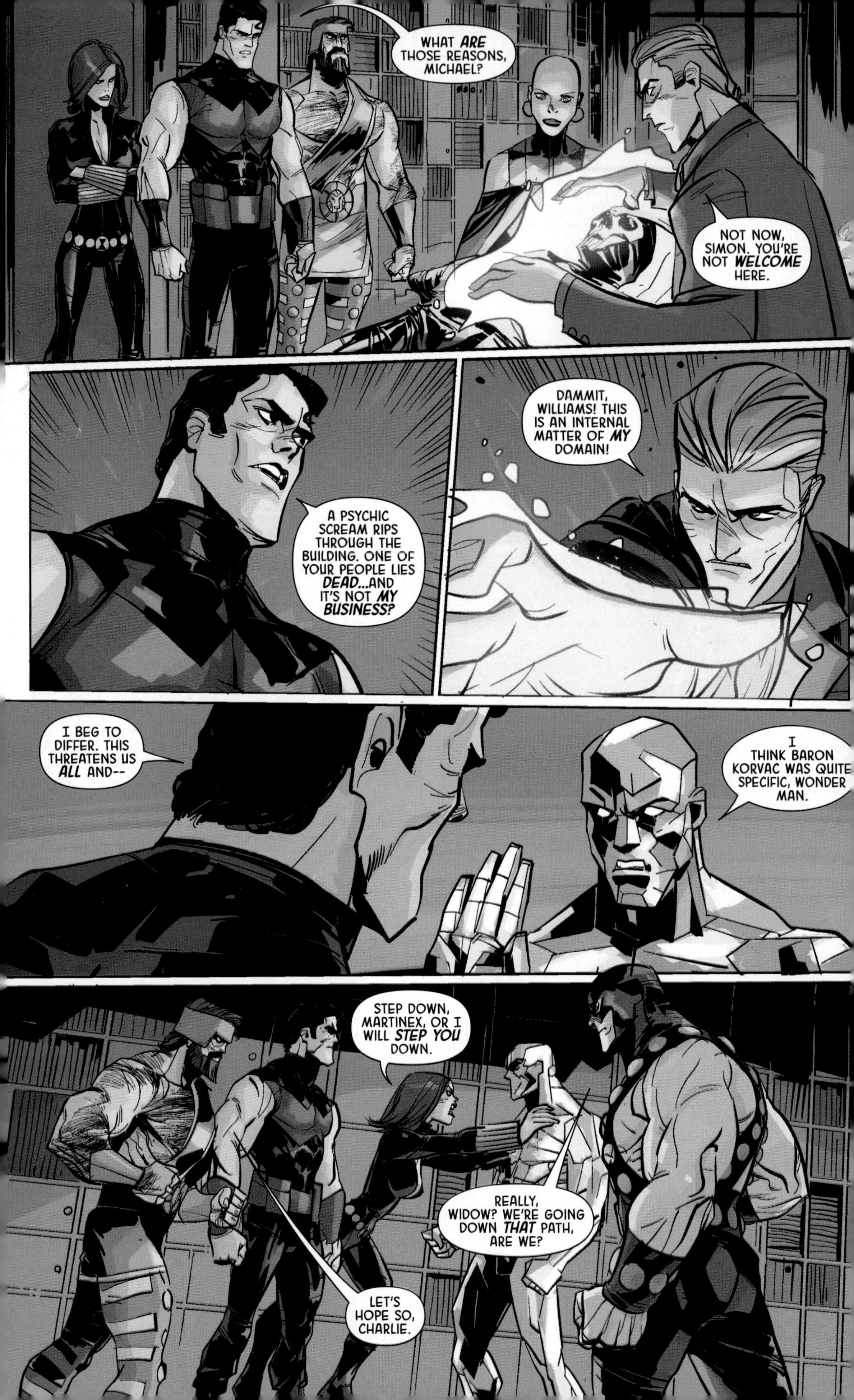
WHAT ARE THOSE REASONS, MICHAEL?
NOT NOW, SIMON. YOU'RE NOT WELCOME HERE.
A PSYCHIC SCREAM RIPS THROUGH THE BUILDING. ONE OF YOUR PEOPLE LIES DEAD...AND IT'S NOT MY BUSINESS?
DAMMIT, WILLIAMS! THIS IS AN INTERNAL MATTER OF MY DOMAIN!
I BEG TO DIFFER. THIS THREATENS US ALL AND--
I THINK BARON KORVAC WAS QUITE SPECIFIC, WONDER MAN.
STEP DOWN, MARTINEX, OR I WILL STEP YOU DOWN.
REALLY, WIDOW? WE'RE GOING DOWN THAT PATH, ARE WE?
LET'S HOPE SO, CHARLIE.

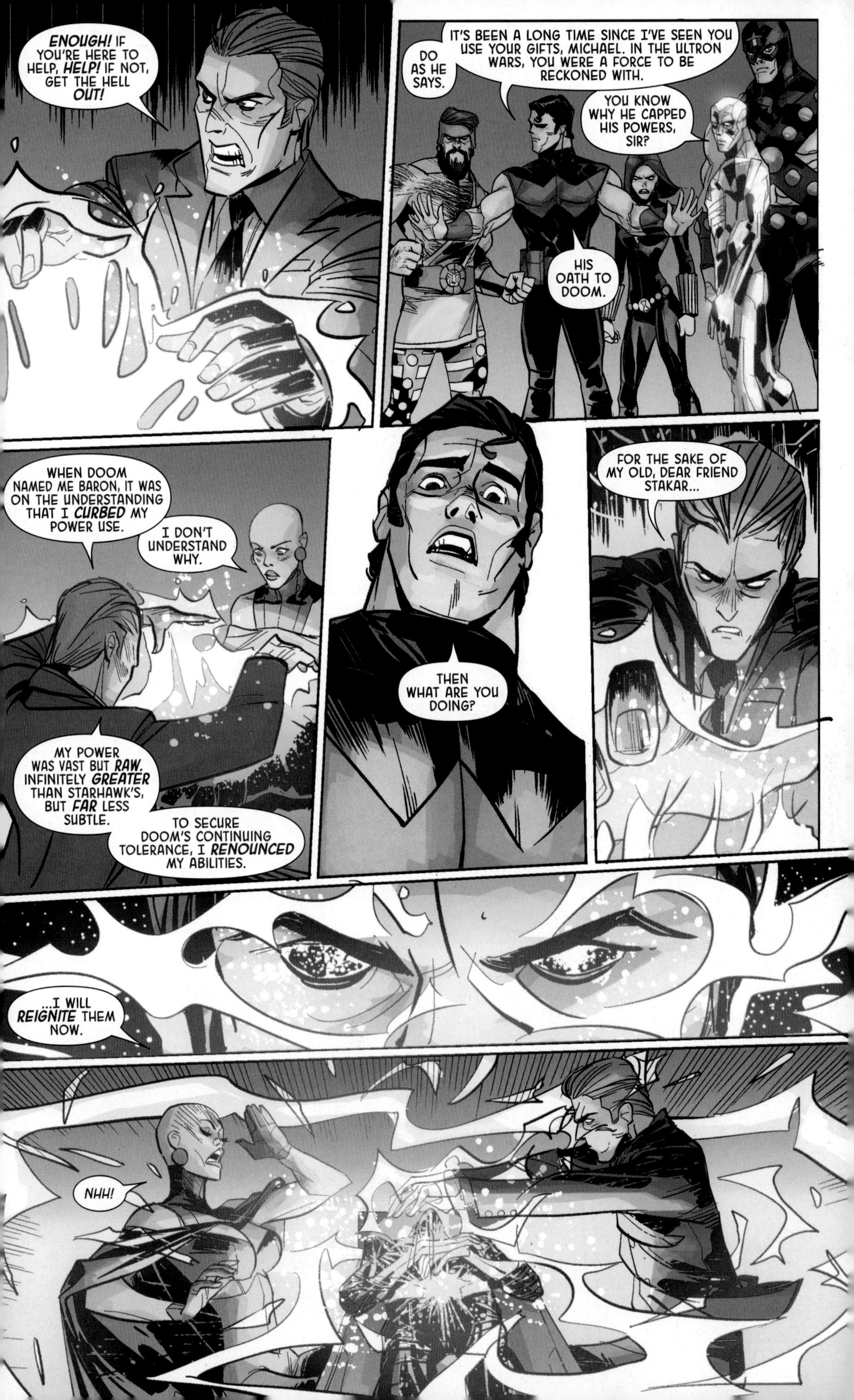
ENOUGH! IF YOU'RE HERE TO HELP, HELP! IF NOT, GET THE HELL OUT!
DO AS HE SAYS.
IT'S BEEN A LONG TIME SINCE I'VE SEEN YOU USE YOUR GIFTS, MICHAEL. IN THE ULTRON WARS, YOU WERE A FORCE TO BE RECKONED WITH.
YOU KNOW WHY HE CAPPED HIS POWERS, SIR?
HIS OATH TO DOOM.
WHEN DOOM NAMED ME BARON, IT WAS ON THE UNDERSTANDING THAT I CURBED MY POWER USE.
I DON'T UNDERSTAND WHY.
MY POWER WAS VAST BUT RAW. INFINITELY GREATER THAN STARHAWK'S, BUT FAR LESS SUBTLE.
TO SECURE DOOM'S CONTINUING TOLERANCE, I RENOUNCED MY ABILITIES.
THEN WHAT ARE YOU DOING?
FOR THE SAKE OF MY OLD, DEAR FRIEND STAKAR...
...I WILL REIGNITE THEM NOW.
NHH!

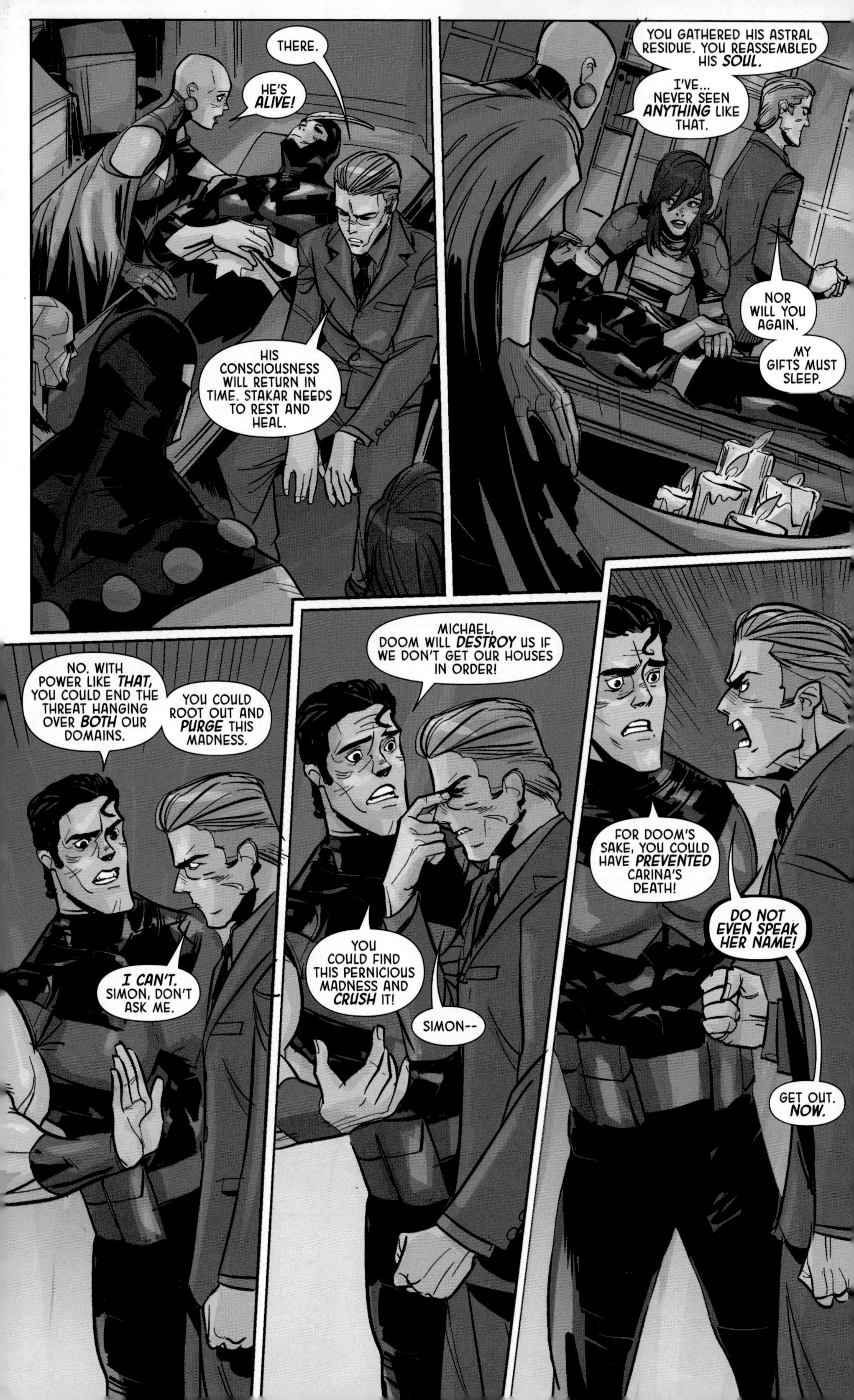
THERE.
HE'S ALIVE!
HIS CONSCIOUSNESS WILL RETURN IN TIME. STAKAR NEEDS TO REST AND HEAL.
YOU GATHERED HIS ASTRAL RESIDUE. YOU REASSEMBLED HIS SOUL.
I'VE... NEVER SEEN ANYTHING LIKE THAT.
NOR WILL YOU AGAIN.
MY GIFTS MUST SLEEP.
NO. WITH POWER LIKE THAT, YOU COULD END THE THREAT HANGING OVER BOTH OUR DOMAINS.
YOU COULD ROOT OUT AND PURGE THIS MADNESS.
I CAN'T. SIMON, DON'T ASK ME.
MICHAEL, DOOM WILL DESTROY US IF WE DON'T GET OUR HOUSES IN ORDER!
YOU COULD FIND THIS PERNICIOUS MADNESS AND CRUSH IT!
SIMON--
FOR DOOM'S SAKE, YOU COULD HAVE PREVENTED CARINA'S DEATH!
DO NOT EVEN SPEAK HER NAME!
GET OUT. NOW.

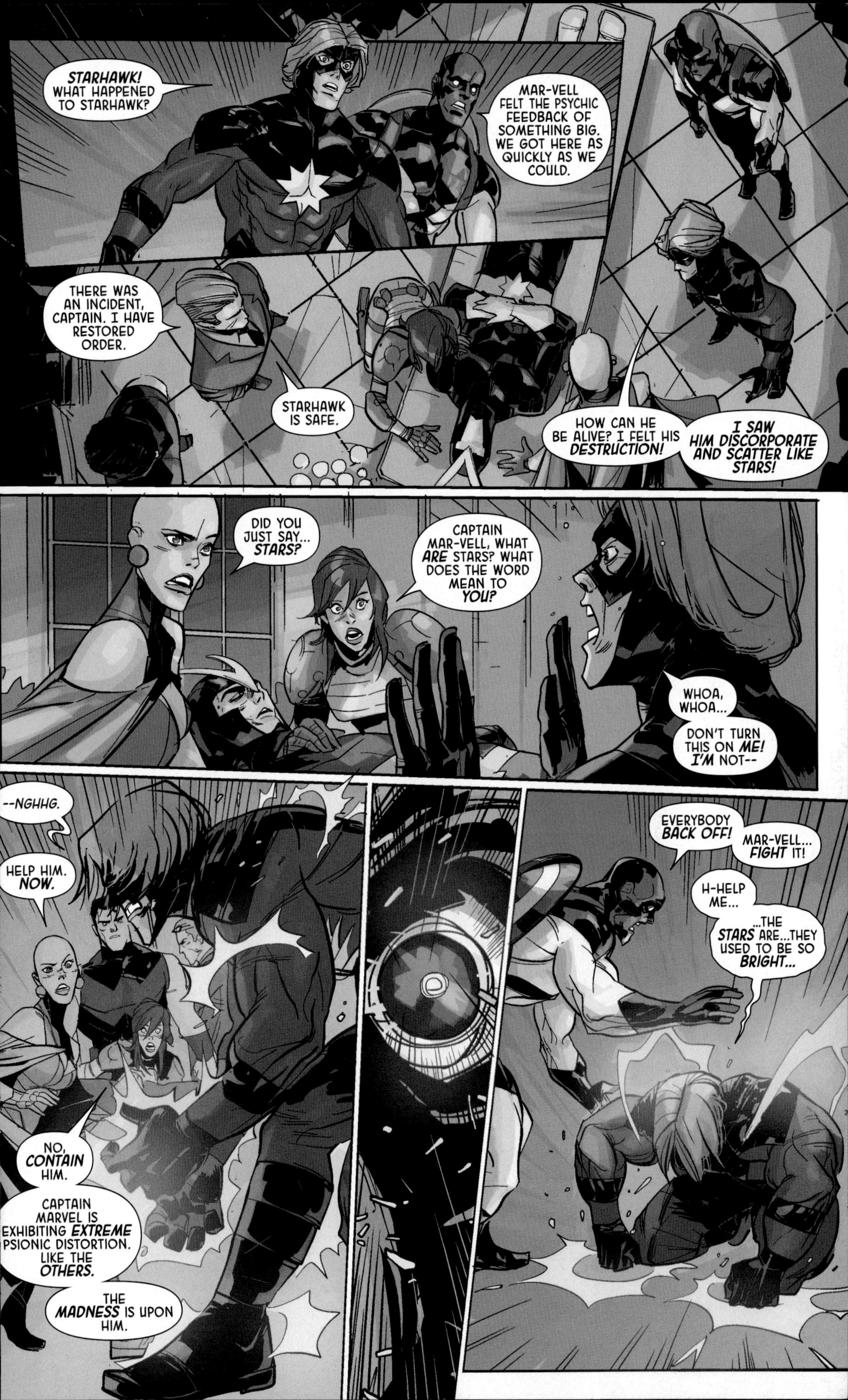
STARHAWK! WHAT HAPPENED TO STARHAWK?
MAR-VELL FELT THE PSYCHIC FEEDBACK OF SOMETHING BIG. WE GOT HERE AS QUICKLY AS WE COULD.
THERE WAS AN INCIDENT, CAPTAIN. I HAVE RESTORED ORDER.
STARHAWK IS SAFE.
HOW CAN HE BE ALIVE? I FELT HIS DESTRUCTION!
I SAW HIM DISCORPORATE AND SCATTER LIKE STARS!
DID YOU JUST SAY... STARS?
CAPTAIN MAR-VELL, WHAT ARE STARS? WHAT DOES THE WORD MEAN TO YOU?
WHOA, WHOA...
DON'T TURN THIS ON ME! I'M NOT--
--NGHHG.
HELP HIM. NOW.
NO, CONTAIN HIM.
CAPTAIN MARVEL IS EXHIBITING EXTREME PSIONIC DISTORTION. LIKE THE OTHERS.
THE MADNESS IS UPON HIM.
EVERYBODY BACK OFF!
MAR-VELL... FIGHT IT!
H-HELP ME...
...THE STARS ARE...THEY USED TO BE SO BRIGHT...

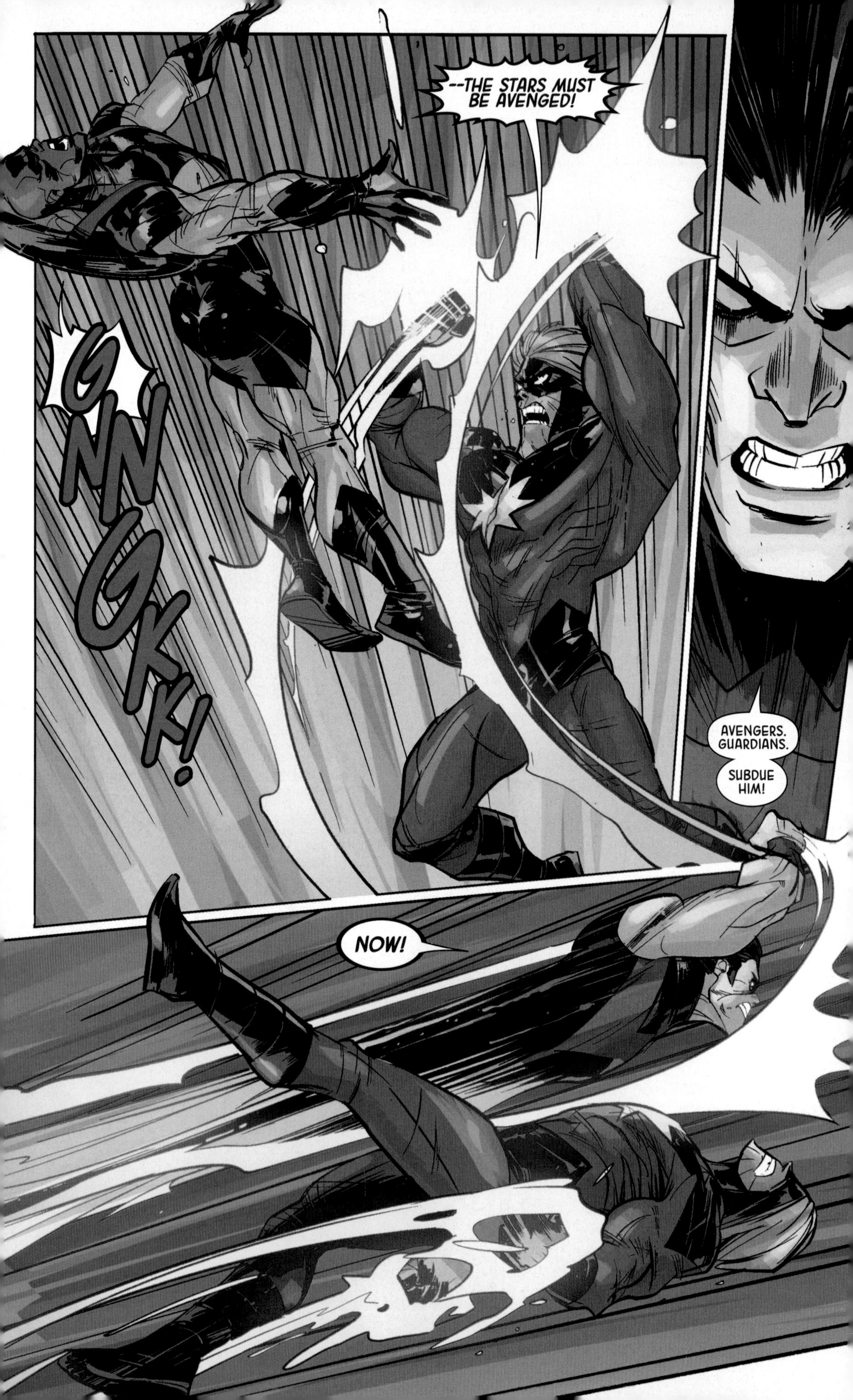
--THE STARS MUST BE AVENGED!
GNNGKK!
AVENGERS. GUARDIANS.
SUBDUE HIM!
NOW!

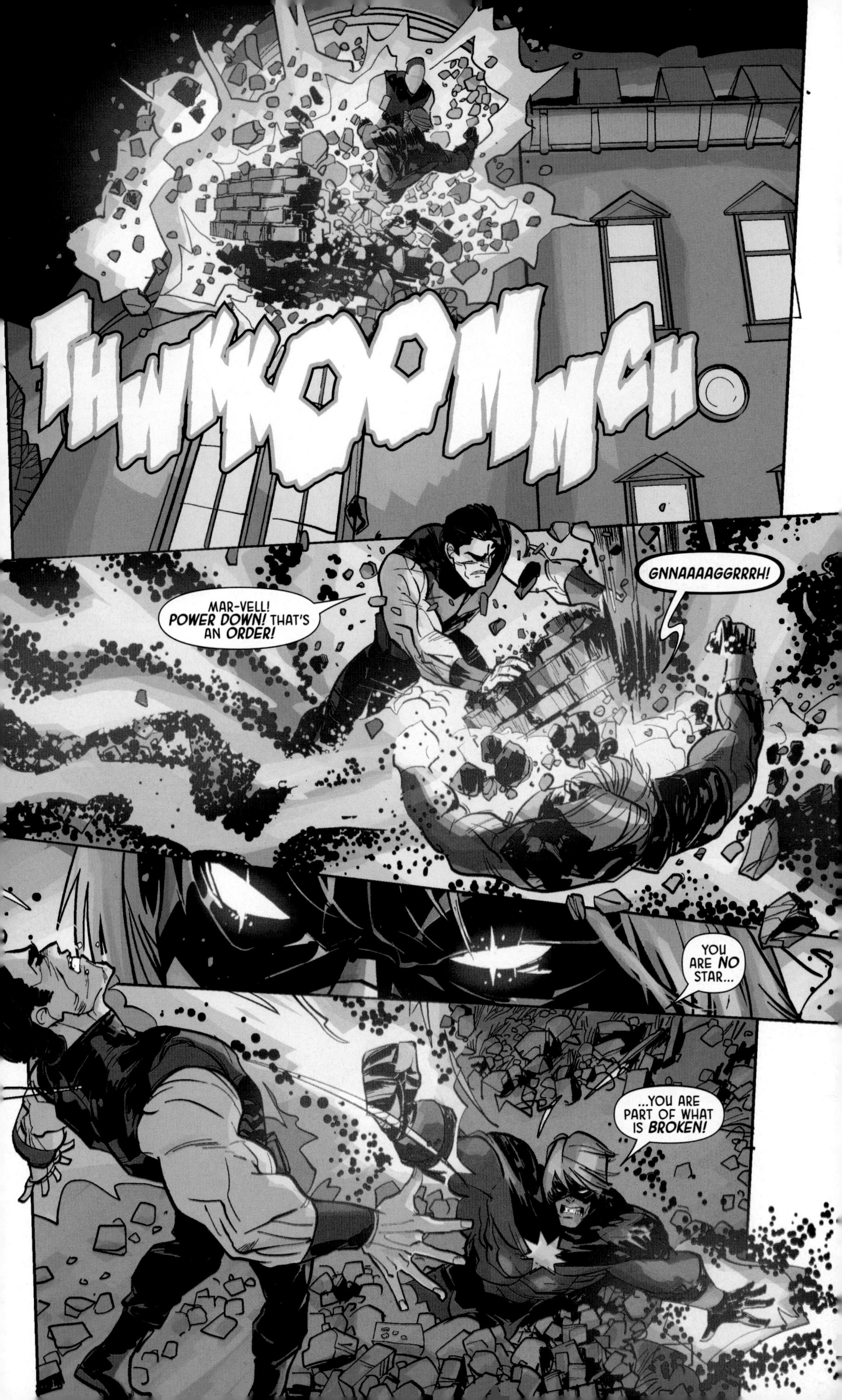
THWKOOMMCH
MAR-VELL! POWER DOWN! THAT'S AN ORDER!
GNNAAAAAGGRRRH!
YOU ARE NO STAR...
...YOU ARE PART OF WHAT IS BROKEN!

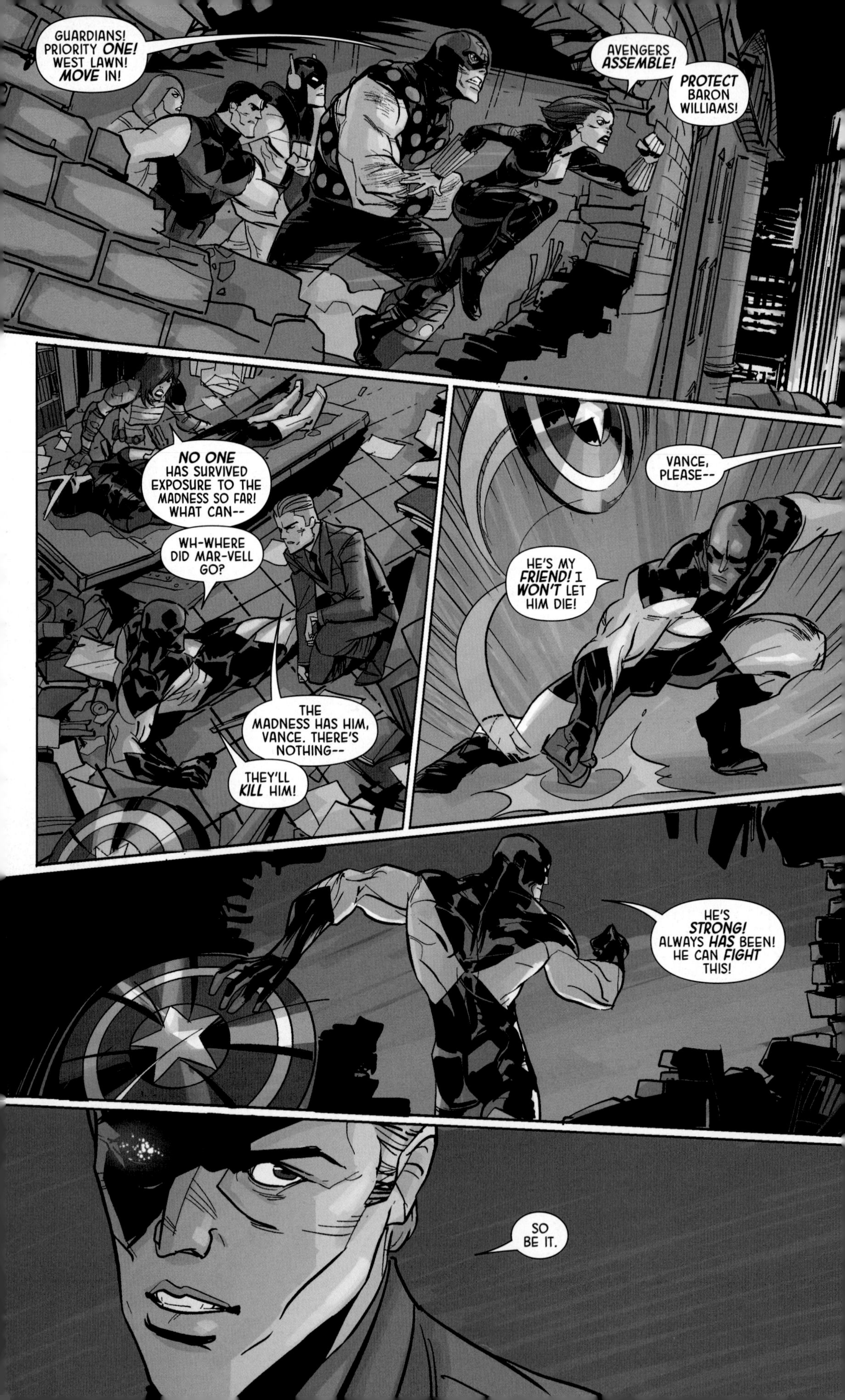
GUARDIANS! PRIORITY ONE! WEST LAWN! MOVE IN!
AVENGERS ASSEMBLE!
PROTECT BARON WILLIAMS!
NO ONE HAS SURVIVED EXPOSURE TO THE MADNESS SO FAR! WHAT CAN--
WH-WHERE DID MAR-VELL GO?
THE MADNESS HAS HIM, VANCE. THERE'S NOTHING--
THEY'LL KILL HIM!
VANCE, PLEASE--
HE'S MY FRIEND! I WON'T LET HIM DIE!
HE'S STRONG! ALWAYS HAS BEEN! HE CAN FIGHT THIS!
SO BE IT.

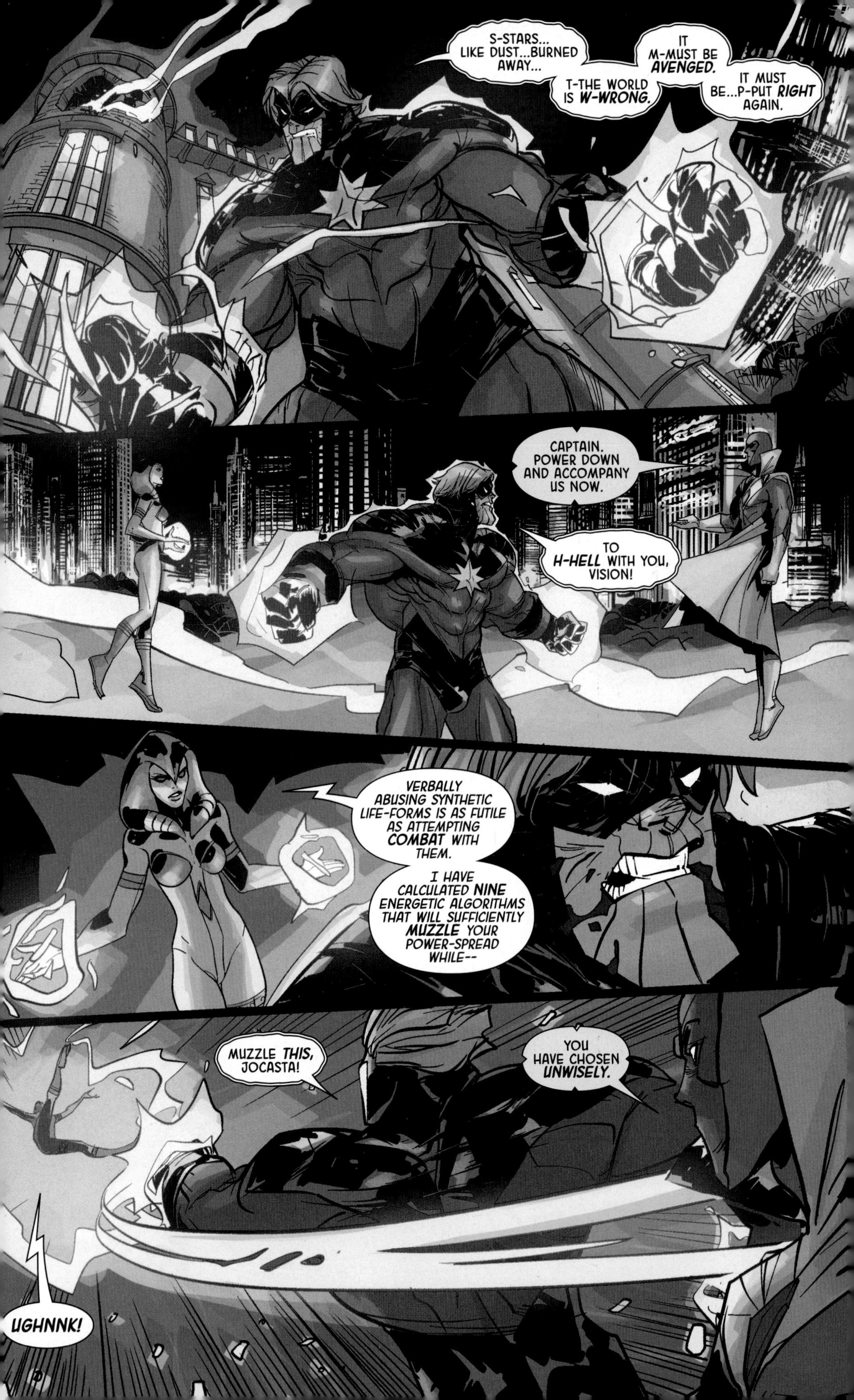

S-STARS... LIKE DUST...BURNED AWAY...
T-THE WORLD IS W-WRONG.
IT M-MUST BE AVENGED.
IT MUST BE...P-PUT RIGHT AGAIN.
CAPTAIN. POWER DOWN AND ACCOMPANY US NOW.
TO H-HELL WITH YOU, VISION!
VERBALLY ABUSING SYNTHETIC LIFE-FORMS IS AS FUTILE AS ATTEMPTING COMBAT WITH THEM.
I HAVE CALCULATED NINE ENERGETIC ALGORITHMS THAT WILL SUFFICIENTLY MUZZLE YOUR POWER-SPREAD WHILE--
MUZZLE THIS, JOCASTA!
YOU HAVE CHOSEN UNWISELY.
UGHNNK!

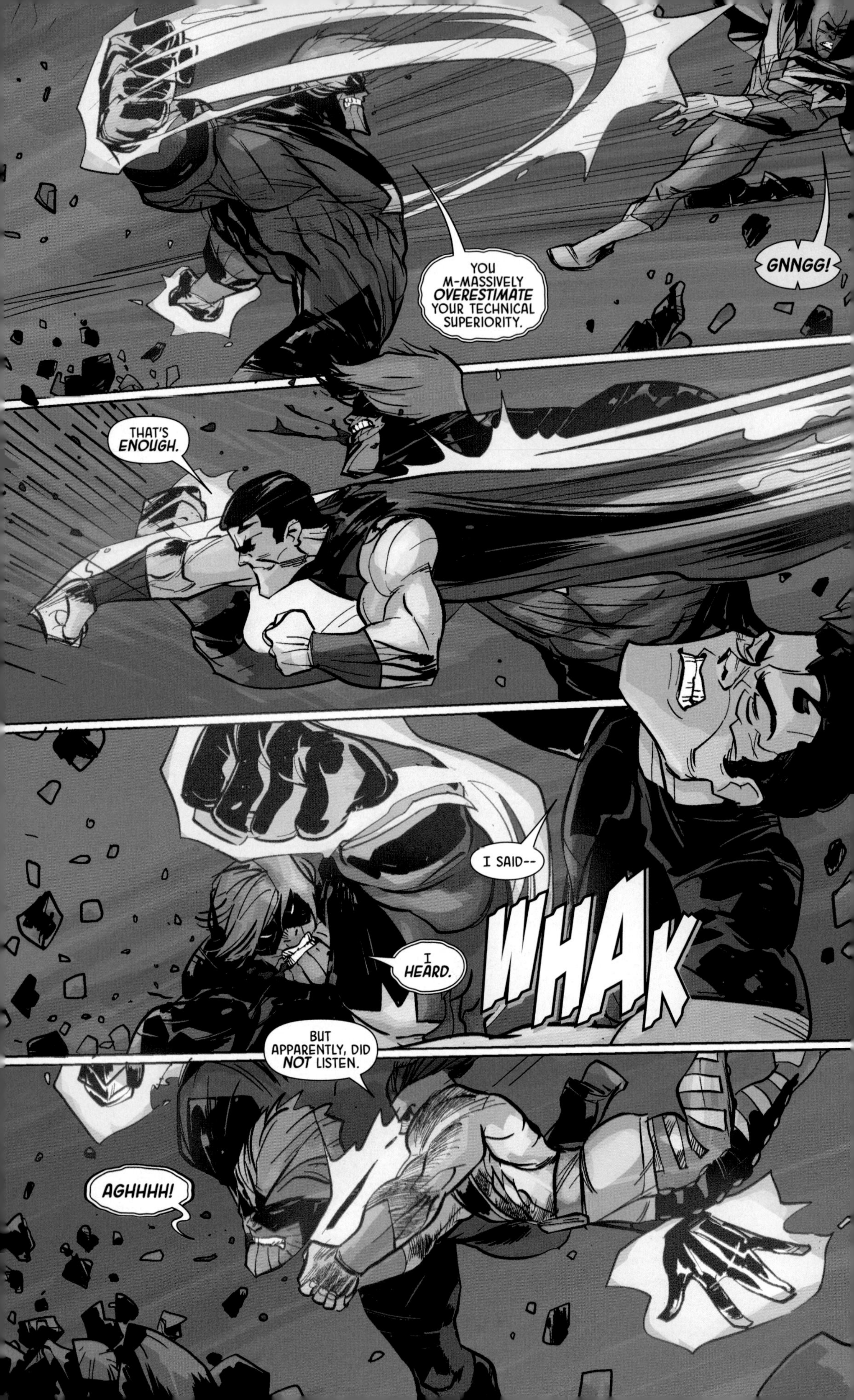
YOU M-MASSIVELY OVERESTIMATE YOUR TECHNICAL SUPERIORITY.
GNNGG!
THAT'S ENOUGH.
I SAID--
WHAK
I HEARD.
BUT APPARENTLY, DID NOT LISTEN.
AGHHHH!

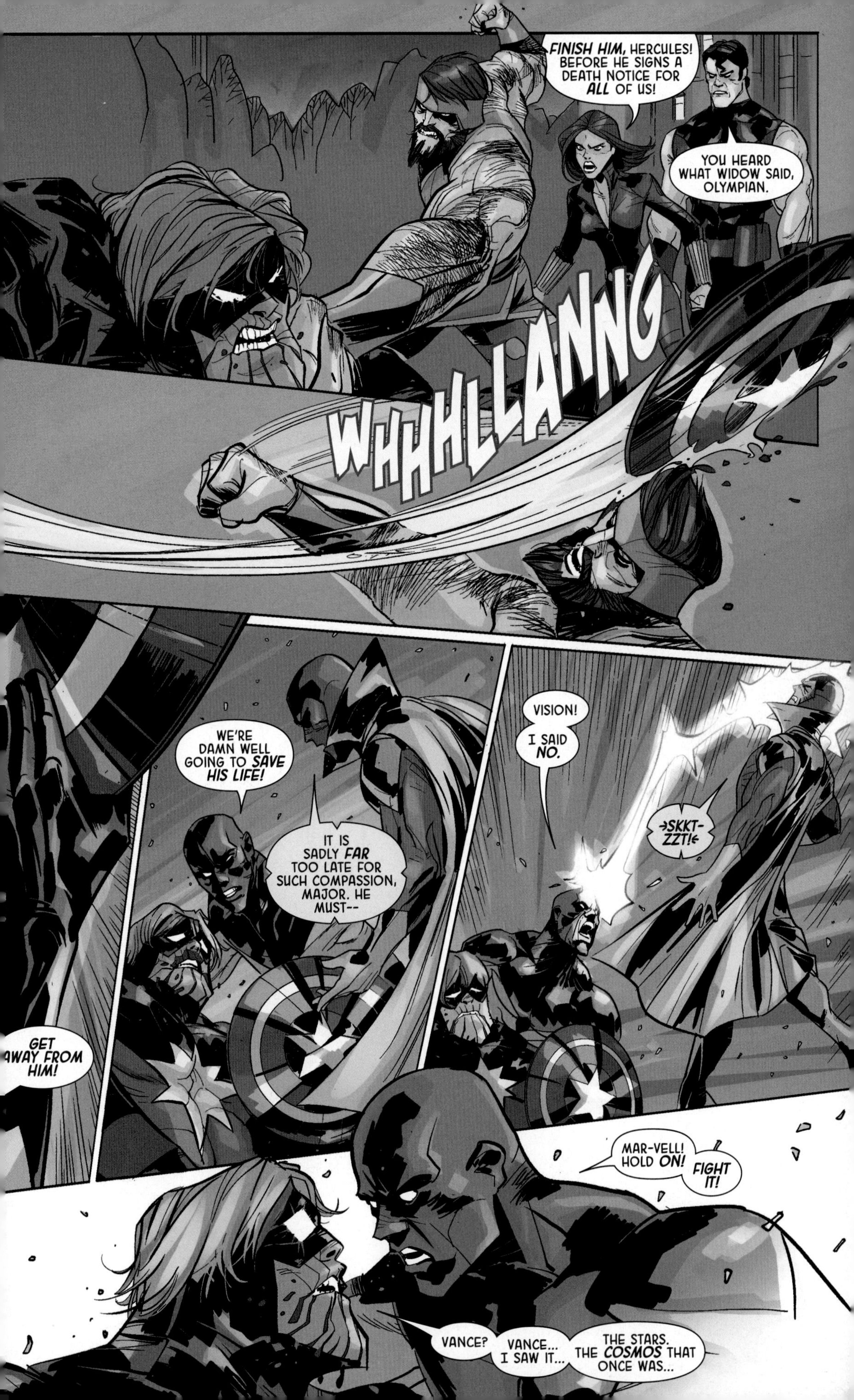
FINISH HIM, HERCULES! BEFORE HE SIGNS A DEATH NOTICE FOR ALL OF US!
YOU HEARD WHAT WIDOW SAID, OLYMPIAN.
WHHHLLANNG
WE'RE DAMN WELL GOING TO SAVE HIS LIFE!
IT IS SADLY FAR TOO LATE FOR SUCH COMPASSION, MAJOR. HE MUST--
GET AWAY FROM HIM!
VISION! I SAID NO.
SKKT-ZZT!
MAR-VELL! HOLD ON! FIGHT IT!
VANCE?
VANCE... I SAW IT...
THE STARS. THE COSMOS THAT ONCE WAS...

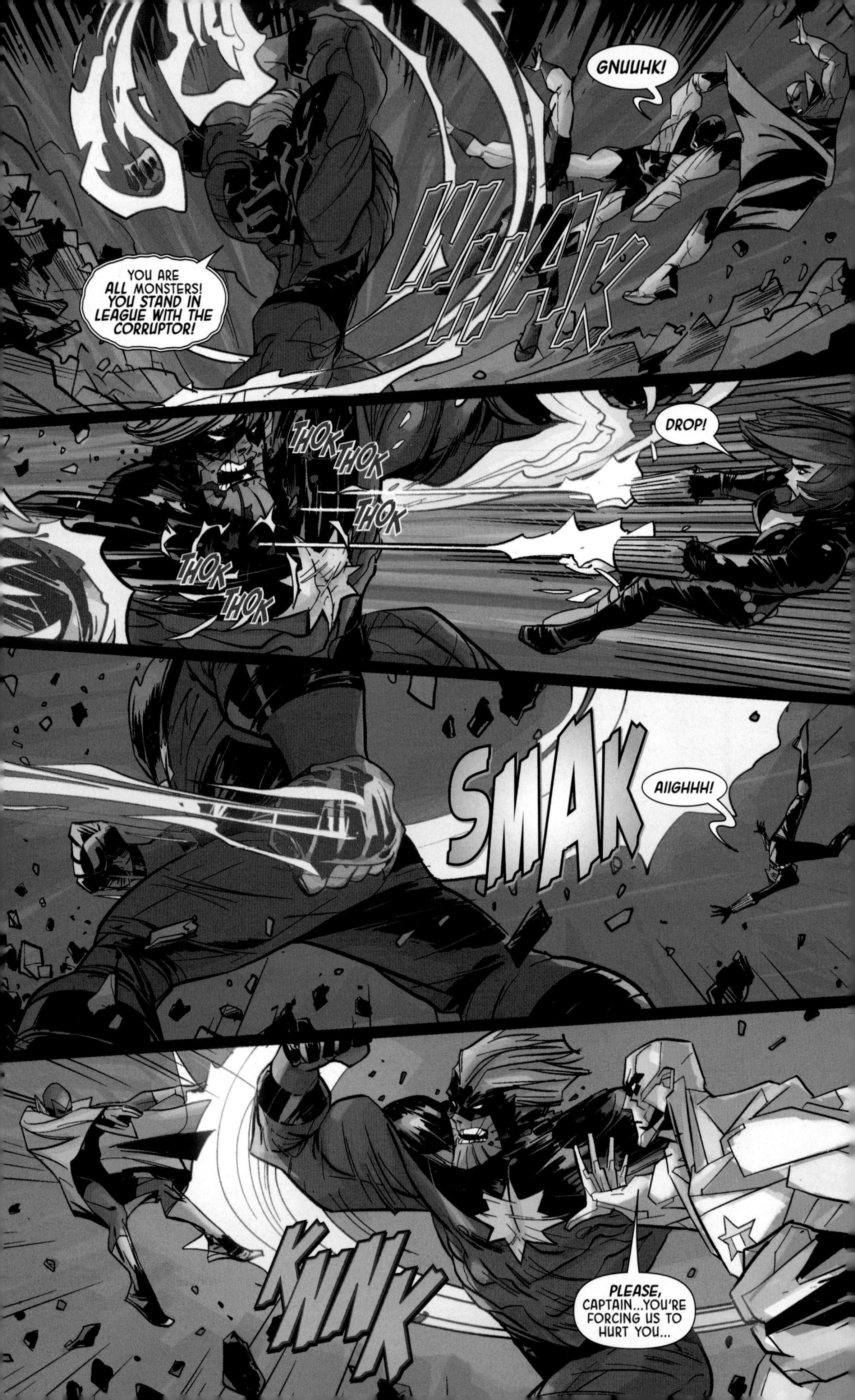
GNUUHK!
WHAK
YOU ARE ALL MONSTERS! YOU STAND IN LEAGUE WITH THE CORRUPTOR!
DROP!
THOK THOK
THOK
THOK
THOK
SMAK
AIIGHHH!
KNINK
PLEASE, CAPTAIN...YOU'RE FORCING US TO HURT YOU...

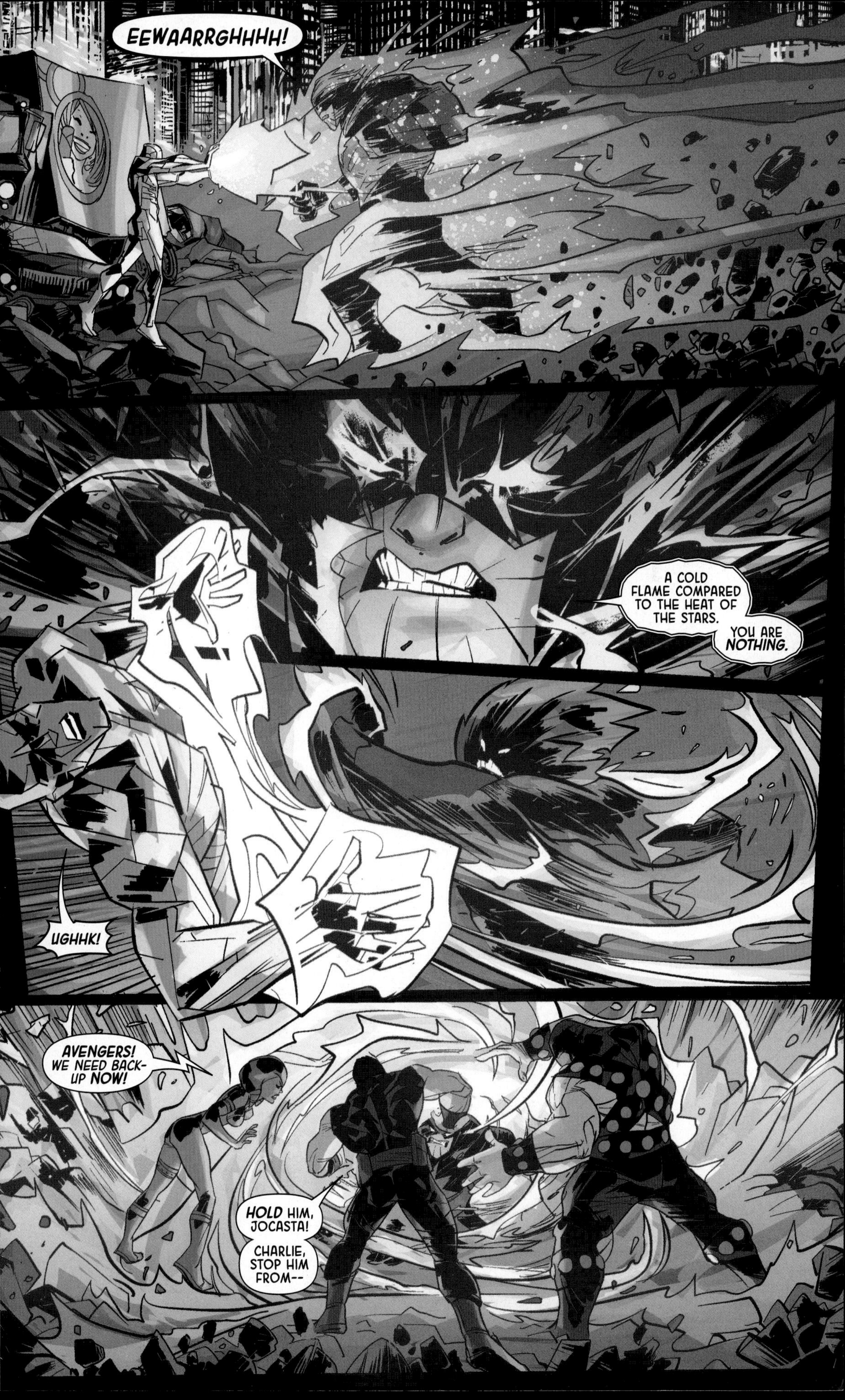
EEWAARRGHHHH!
A COLD FLAME COMPARED TO THE HEAT OF THE STARS.
YOU ARE NOTHING.
UGHHK!
AVENGERS! WE NEED BACK-UP NOW!
HOLD HIM, JOCASTA!
CHARLIE, STOP HIM FROM--

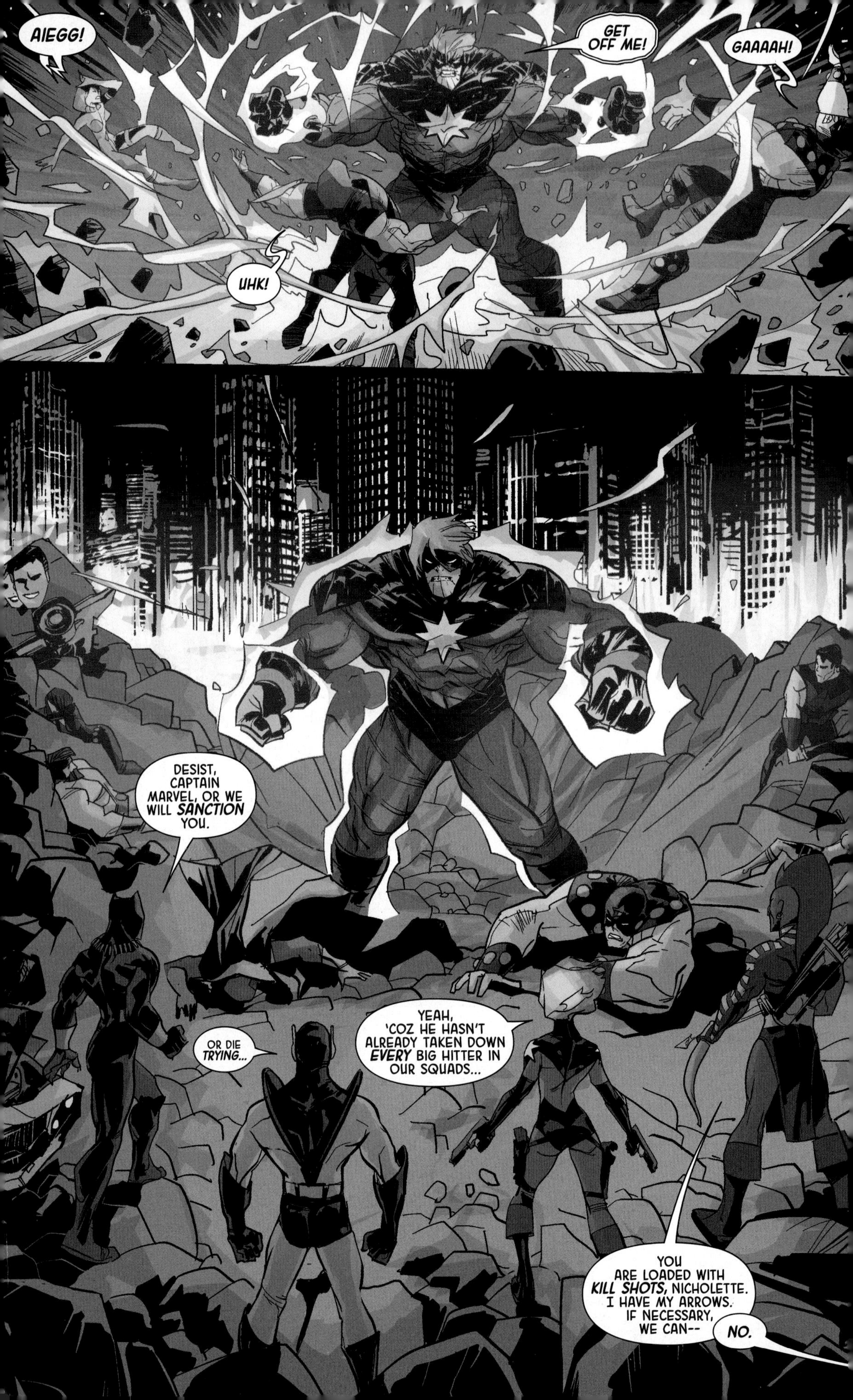
AIEGG!
GET OFF ME!
GAAAAH!
UHK!
DESIST, CAPTAIN MARVEL, OR WE WILL SANCTION YOU.
OR DIE TRYING...
YEAH, 'COZ HE HASN'T ALREADY TAKEN DOWN EVERY BIG HITTER IN OUR SQUADS...
YOU ARE LOADED WITH KILL SHOTS, NICHOLETTE. I HAVE MY ARROWS. IF NECESSARY, WE CAN--
NO.

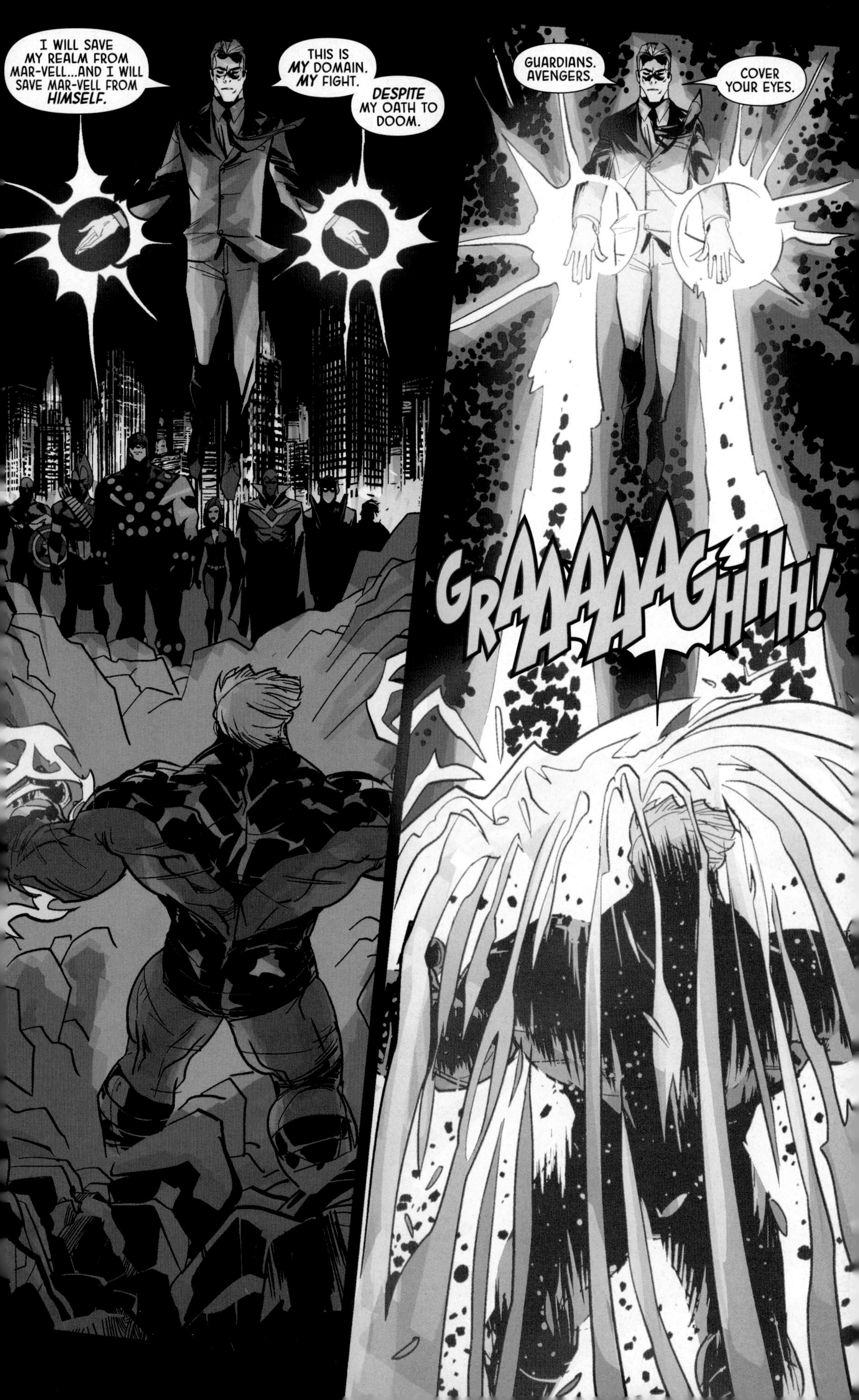
I WILL SAVE MY REALM FROM MAR-VELL...AND I WILL SAVE MAR-VELL FROM *HIMSELF.*
THIS IS *MY* DOMAIN. *MY* FIGHT.
DESPITE MY OATH TO DOOM.
GUARDIANS. AVENGERS.
COVER YOUR EYES.
GRAAAAAGHHH!

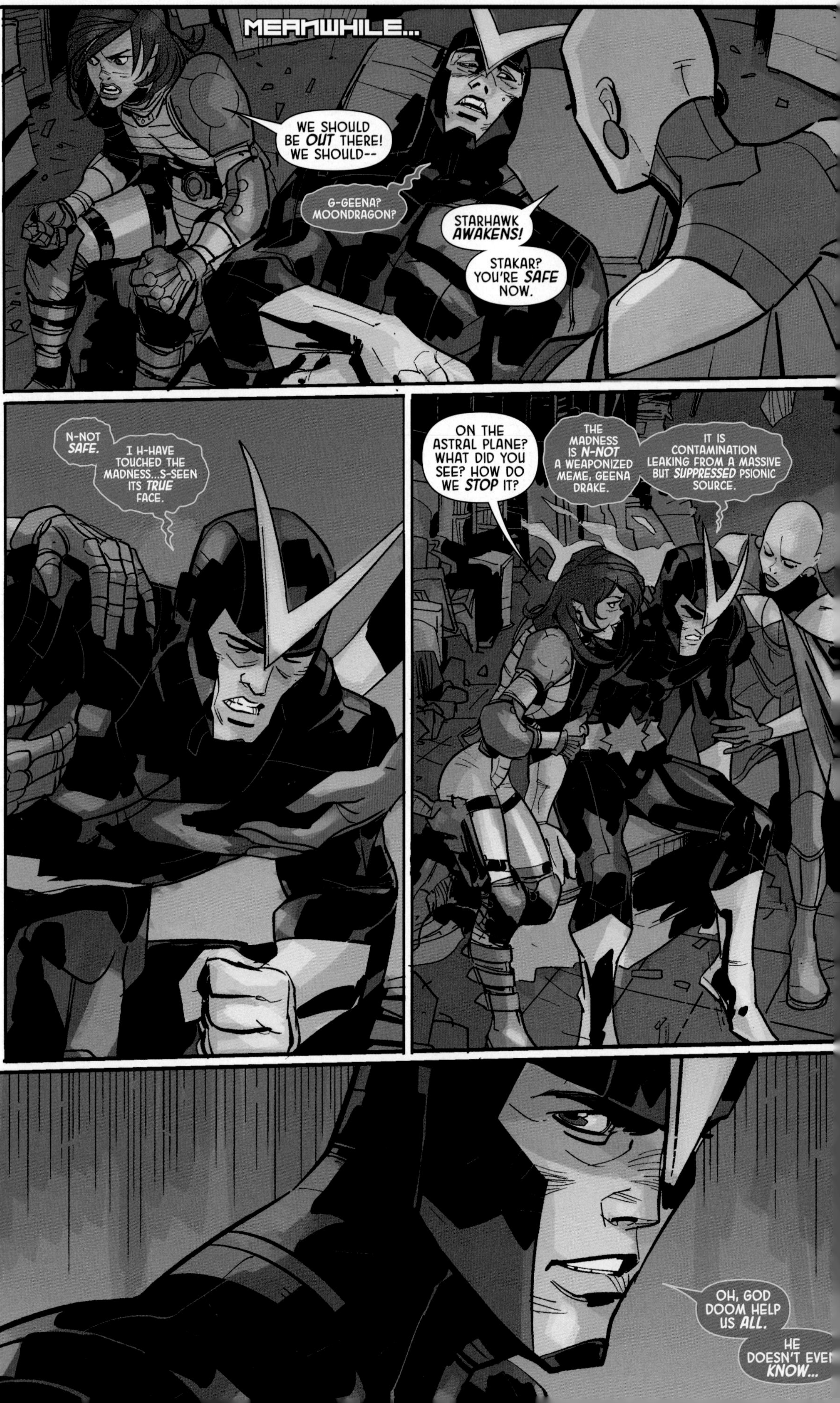
MEANWHILE...
WE SHOULD BE OUT THERE! WE SHOULD--
G-GEENA? MOONDRAGON?
STARHAWK AWAKENS!
STAKAR? YOU'RE SAFE NOW.
N-NOT SAFE.
I H-HAVE TOUCHED THE MADNESS...S-SEEN ITS TRUE FACE.
ON THE ASTRAL PLANE? WHAT DID YOU SEE? HOW DO WE STOP IT?
THE MADNESS IS N-NOT A WEAPONIZED MEME, GEENA DRAKE.
IT IS CONTAMINATION LEAKING FROM A MASSIVE BUT SUPPRESSED PSIONIC SOURCE.
OH, GOD DOOM HELP US ALL.
HE DOESN'T EVEN KNOW...

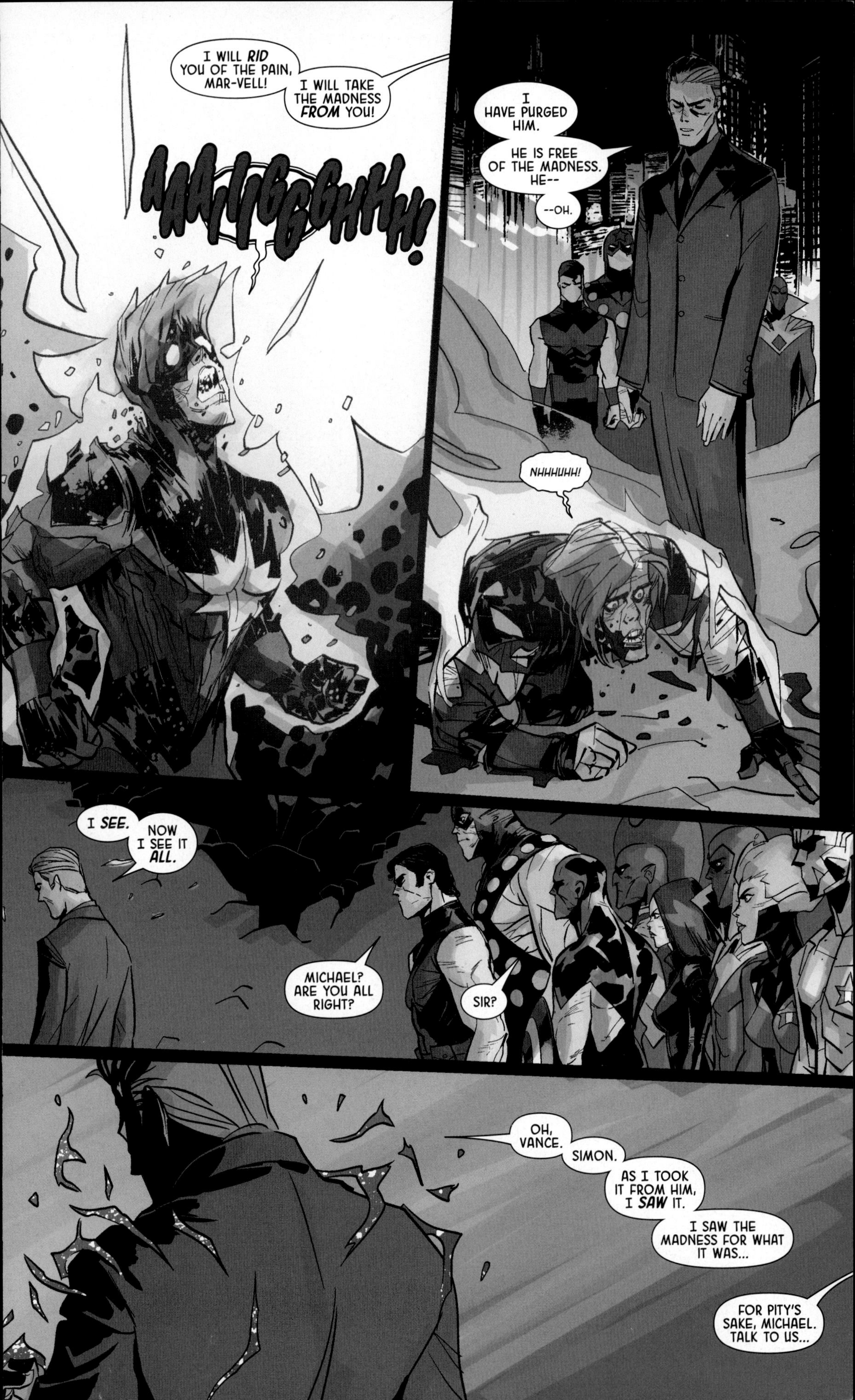

I WILL RID YOU OF THE PAIN, MAR-VELL!
I WILL TAKE THE MADNESS FROM YOU!
AAAAIIGGGHHHH!
I HAVE PURGED HIM.
HE IS FREE OF THE MADNESS. HE--
--OH.
NHHHUHH!
I SEE.
NOW I SEE IT ALL.
MICHAEL? ARE YOU ALL RIGHT?
SIR?
OH, VANCE.
SIMON.
AS I TOOK IT FROM HIM, I SAW IT.
I SAW THE MADNESS FOR WHAT IT WAS...
FOR PITY'S SAKE, MICHAEL. TALK TO US...

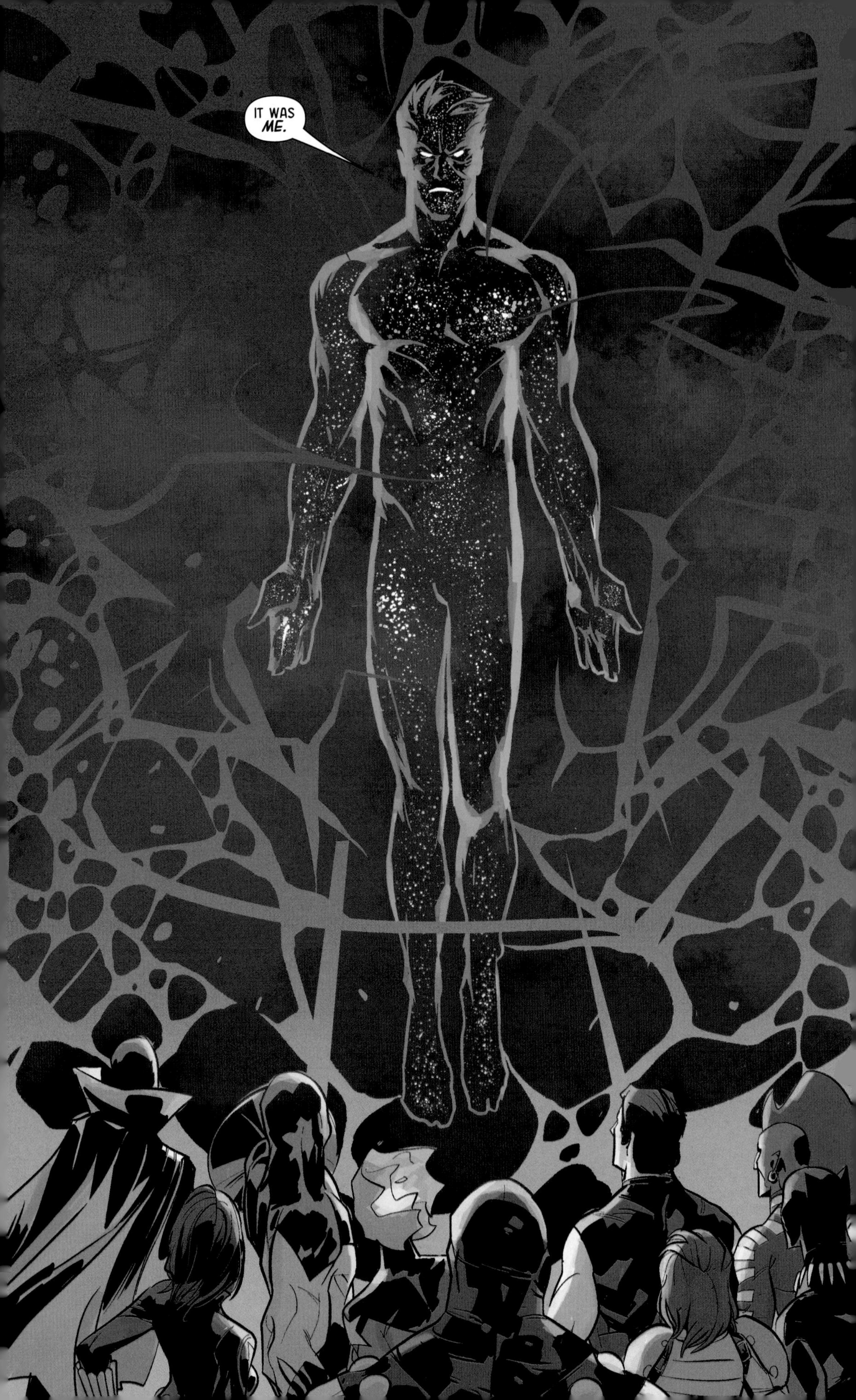
IT WAS ME.

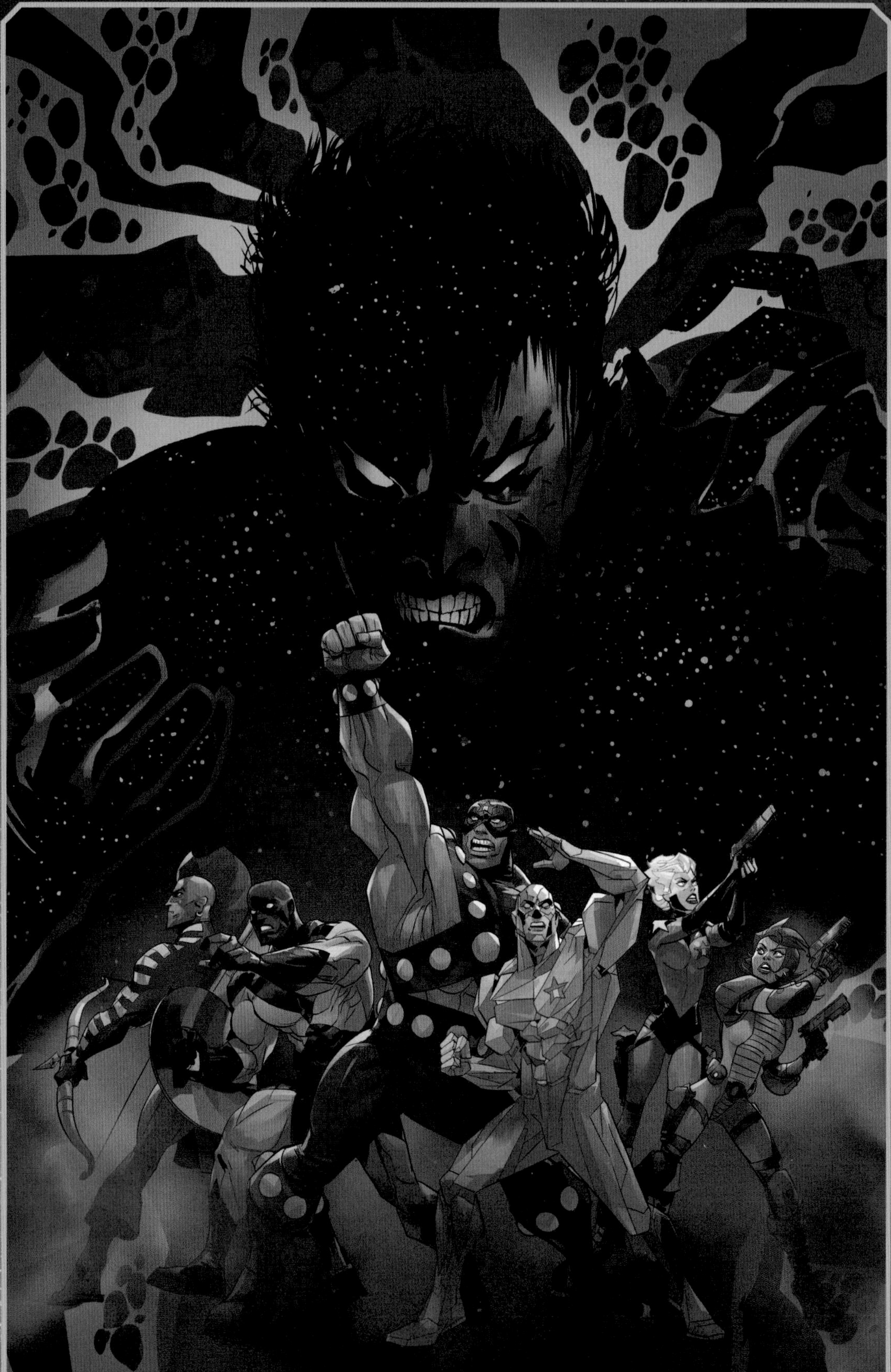

KORVAC SAGA #4

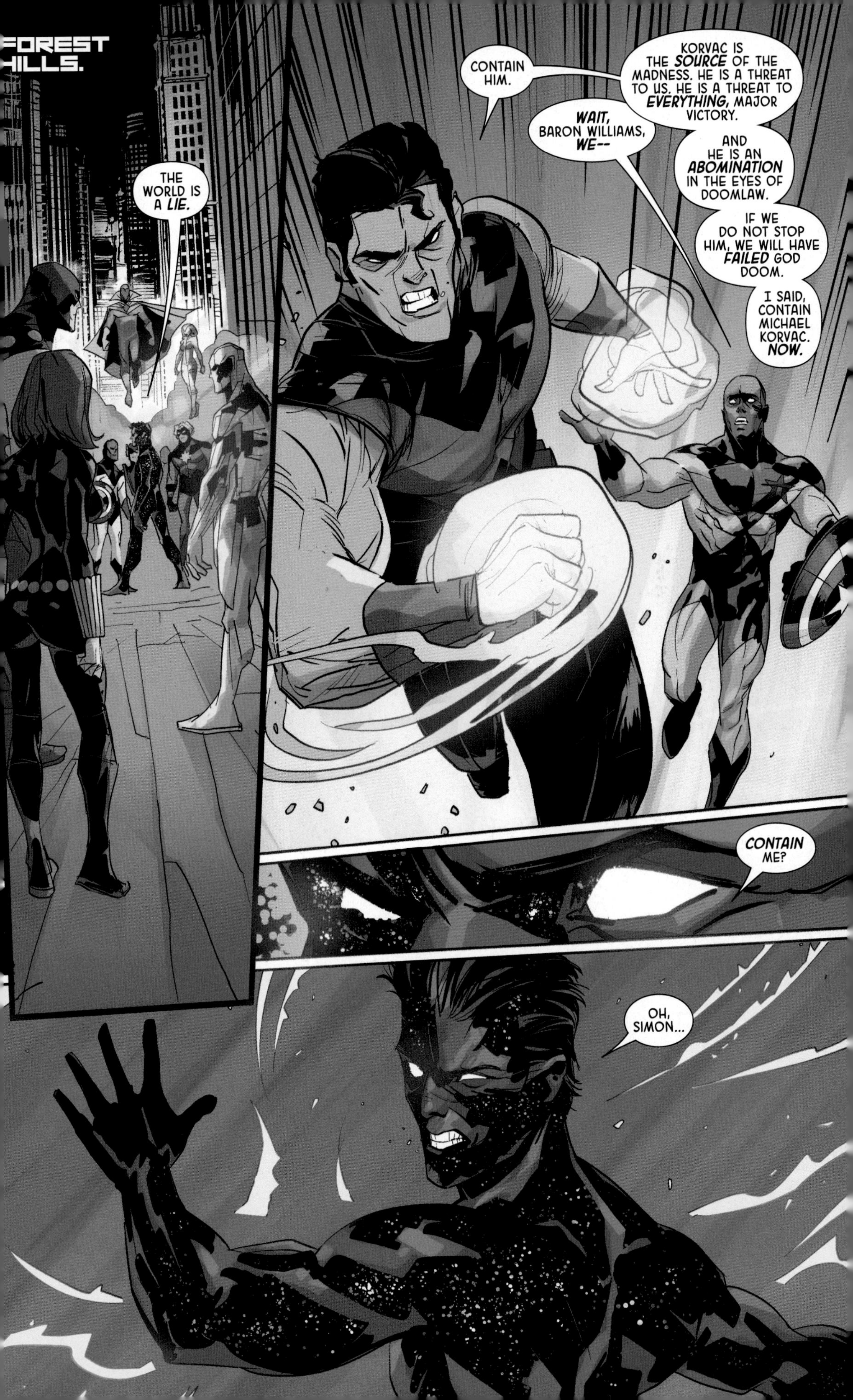
FOREST HILLS.
THE WORLD IS A LIE.
CONTAIN HIM.
KORVAC IS THE SOURCE OF THE MADNESS. HE IS A THREAT TO US. HE IS A THREAT TO EVERYTHING, MAJOR VICTORY.
WAIT, BARON WILLIAMS, WE--
AND HE IS AN ABOMINATION IN THE EYES OF DOOMLAW.
IF WE DO NOT STOP HIM, WE WILL HAVE FAILED GOD DOOM.
I SAID, CONTAIN MICHAEL KORVAC. NOW.
CONTAIN ME?
OH, SIMON...

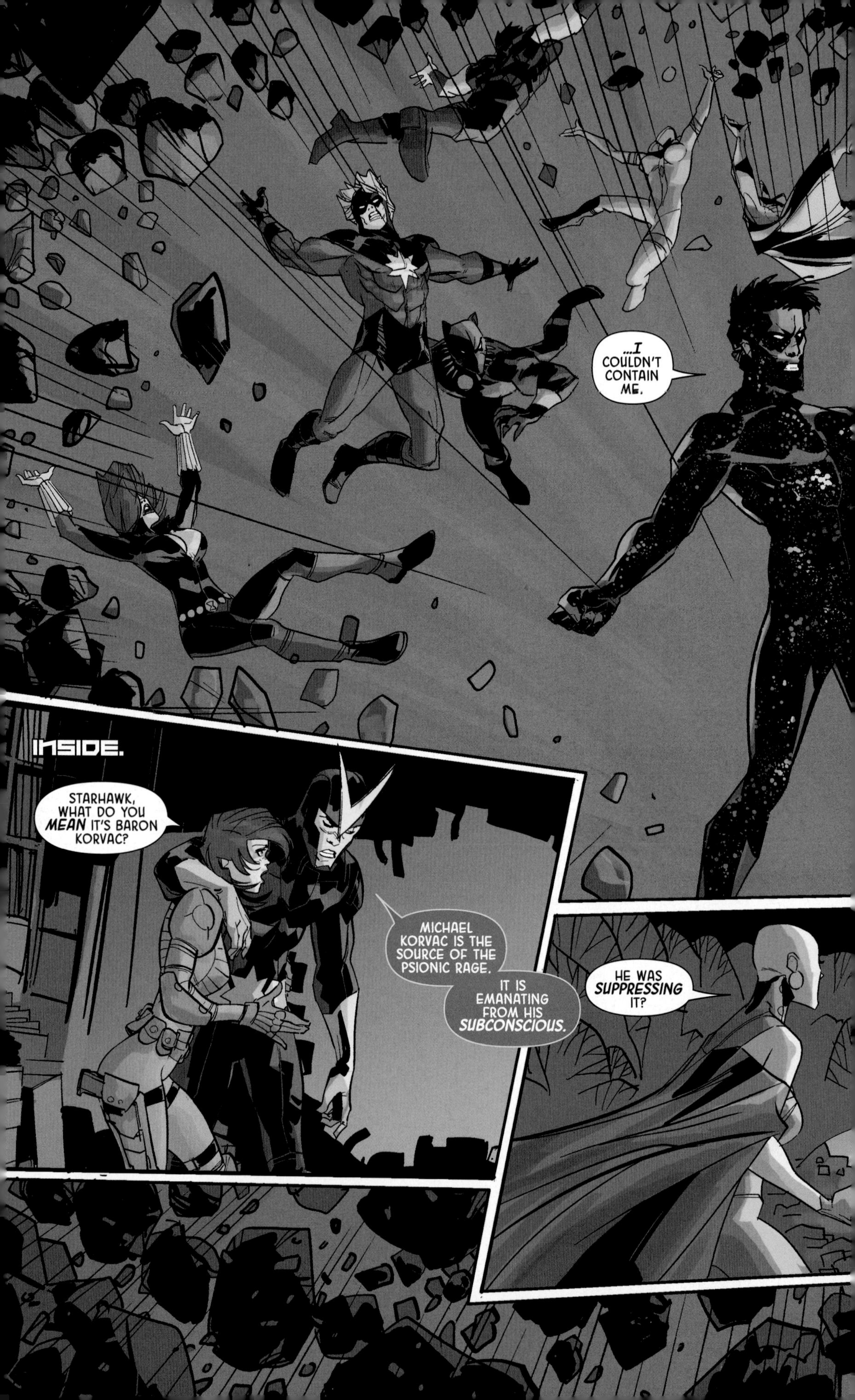

...I COULDN'T CONTAIN ME.
INSIDE.
STARHAWK, WHAT DO YOU MEAN IT'S BARON KORVAC?
MICHAEL KORVAC IS THE SOURCE OF THE PSIONIC RAGE.
IT IS EMANATING FROM HIS SUBCONSCIOUS.
HE WAS SUPPRESSING IT?

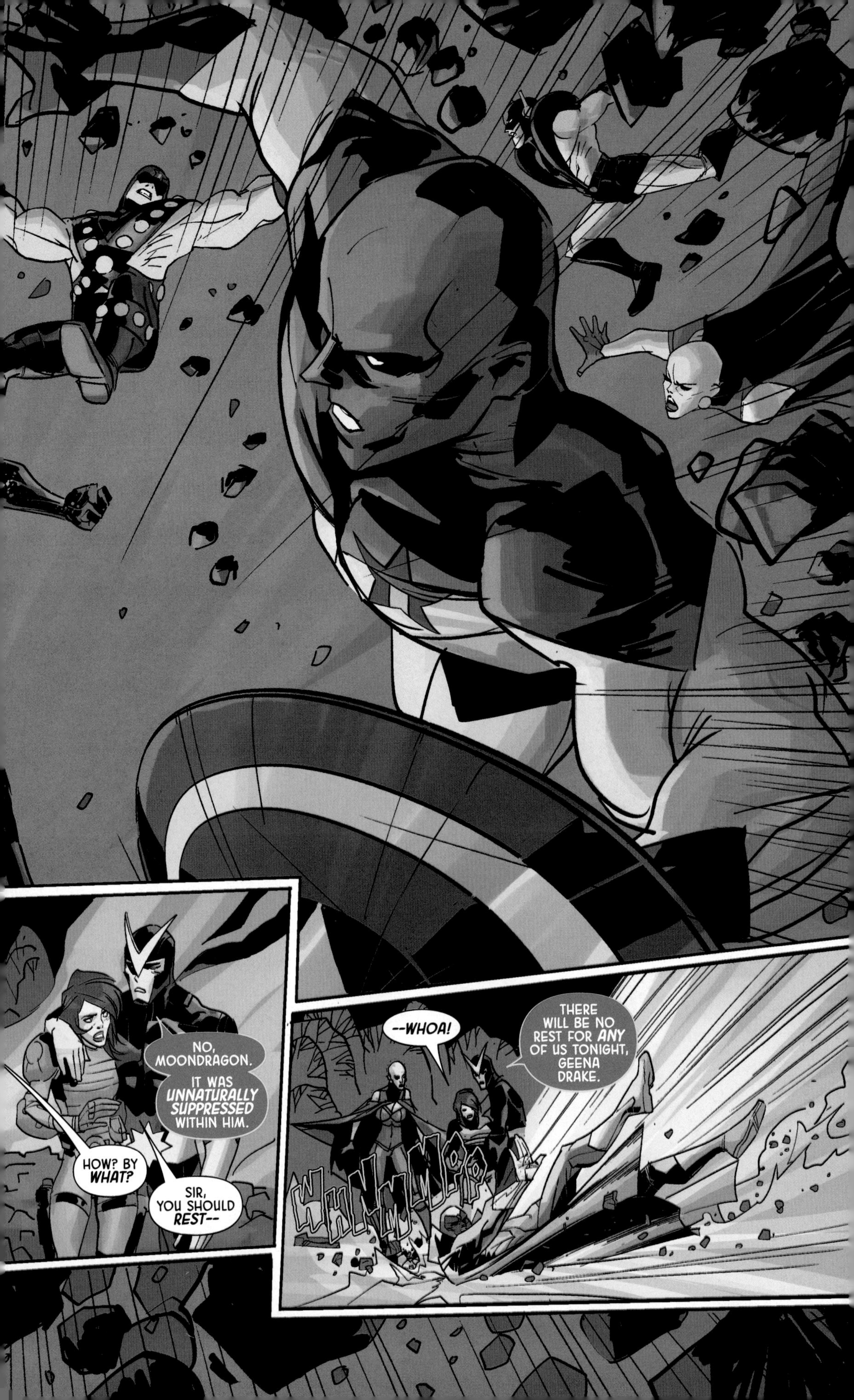
NO, MOONDRAGON.
IT WAS UNNATURALLY SUPPRESSED WITHIN HIM.
HOW? BY WHAT?
SIR, YOU SHOULD REST--
--WHOA!
THERE WILL BE NO REST FOR ANY OF US TONIGHT, GEENA DRAKE.
WHHMMMOOOP

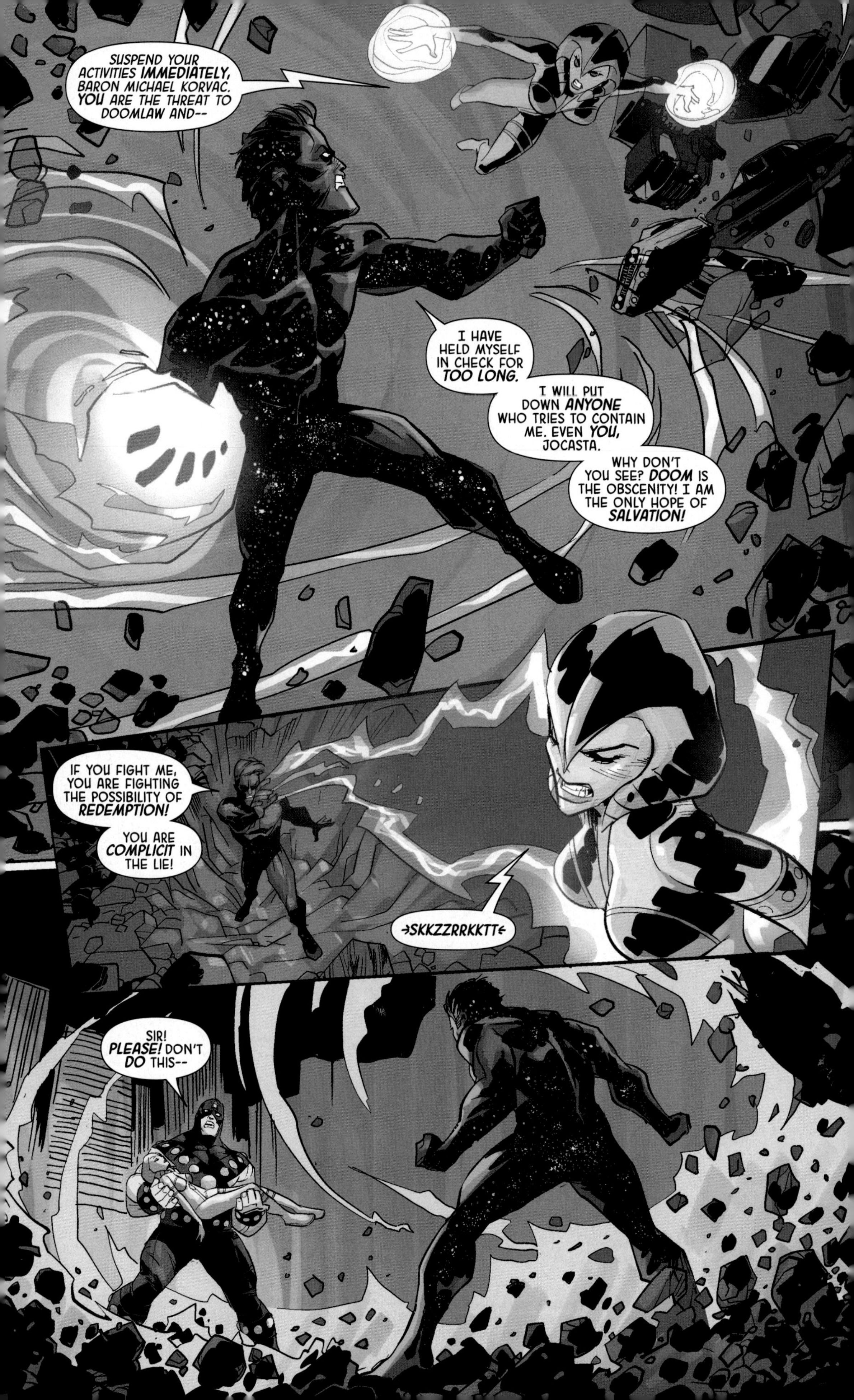
SUSPEND YOUR ACTIVITIES IMMEDIATELY, BARON MICHAEL KORVAC. YOU ARE THE THREAT TO DOOMLAW AND--
I HAVE HELD MYSELF IN CHECK FOR TOO LONG.
I WILL PUT DOWN ANYONE WHO TRIES TO CONTAIN ME. EVEN YOU, JOCASTA.
WHY DON'T YOU SEE? DOOM IS THE OBSCENITY! I AM THE ONLY HOPE OF SALVATION!
IF YOU FIGHT ME, YOU ARE FIGHTING THE POSSIBILITY OF REDEMPTION!
YOU ARE COMPLICIT IN THE LIE!
SKKZZRRKKTT
SIR! PLEASE! DON'T DO THIS--

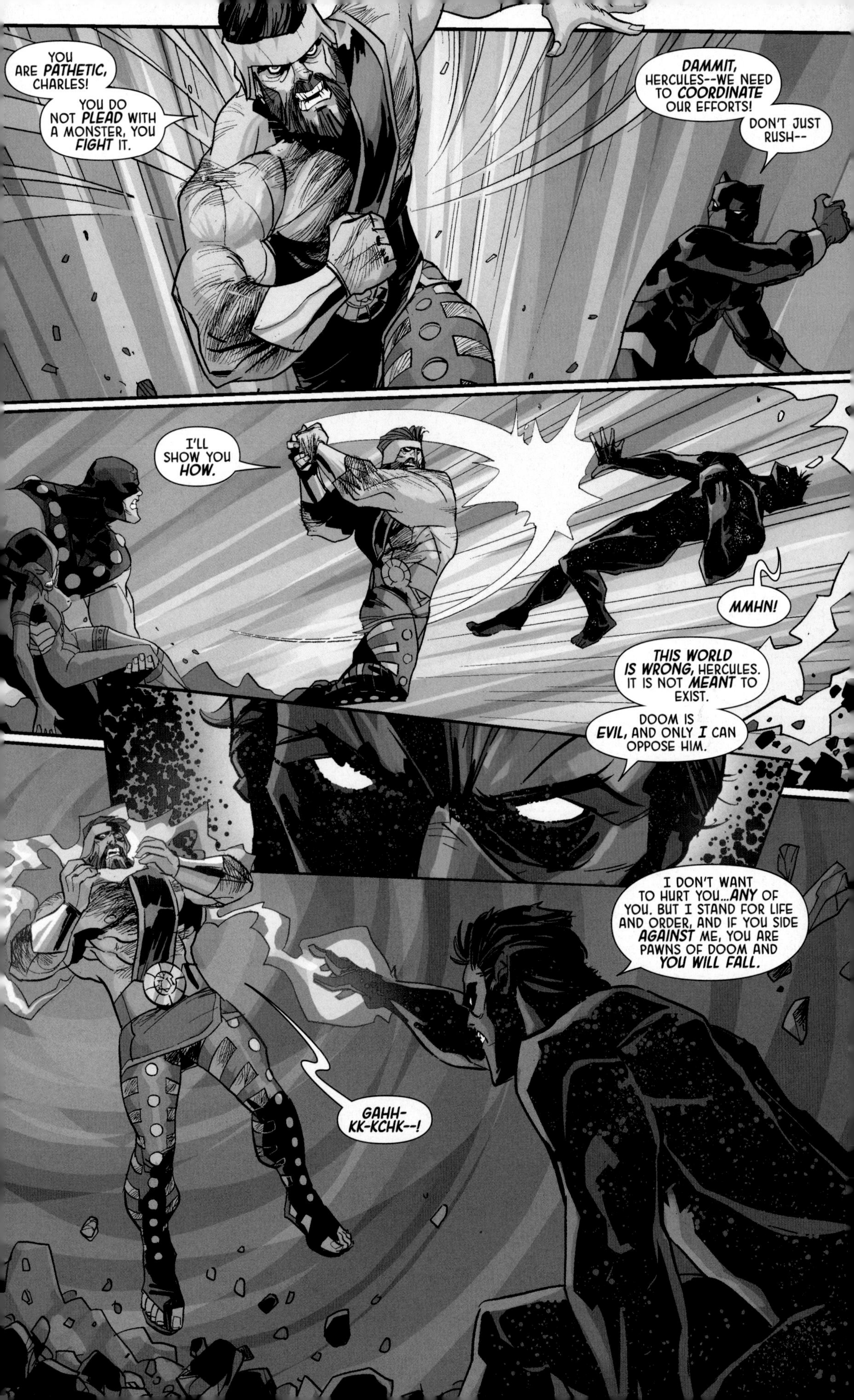
YOU ARE PATHETIC, CHARLES!
YOU DO NOT PLEAD WITH A MONSTER, YOU FIGHT IT.
DAMMIT, HERCULES--WE NEED TO COORDINATE OUR EFFORTS!
DON'T JUST RUSH--
I'LL SHOW YOU HOW.
MMHN!
THIS WORLD IS WRONG, HERCULES. IT IS NOT MEANT TO EXIST.
DOOM IS EVIL, AND ONLY I CAN OPPOSE HIM.
I DON'T WANT TO HURT YOU...ANY OF YOU. BUT I STAND FOR LIFE AND ORDER, AND IF YOU SIDE AGAINST ME, YOU ARE PAWNS OF DOOM AND YOU WILL FALL.
GAHH-KK-KCHK--!

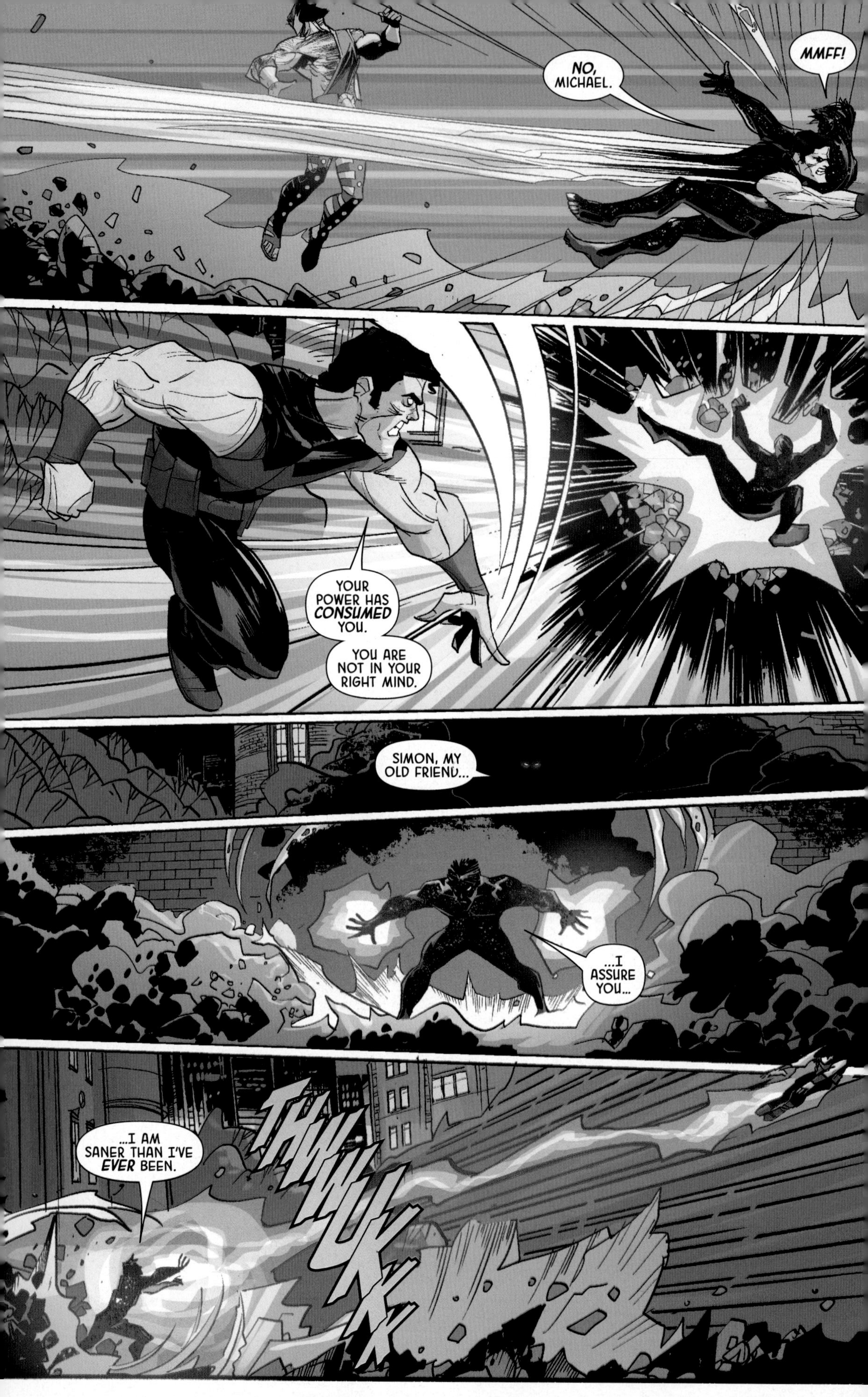
NO, MICHAEL.
MMFF!
YOUR POWER HAS CONSUMED YOU.
YOU ARE NOT IN YOUR RIGHT MIND.
SIMON, MY OLD FRIEND...
...I ASSURE YOU...
...I AM SANER THAN I'VE EVER BEEN.
THWUKK

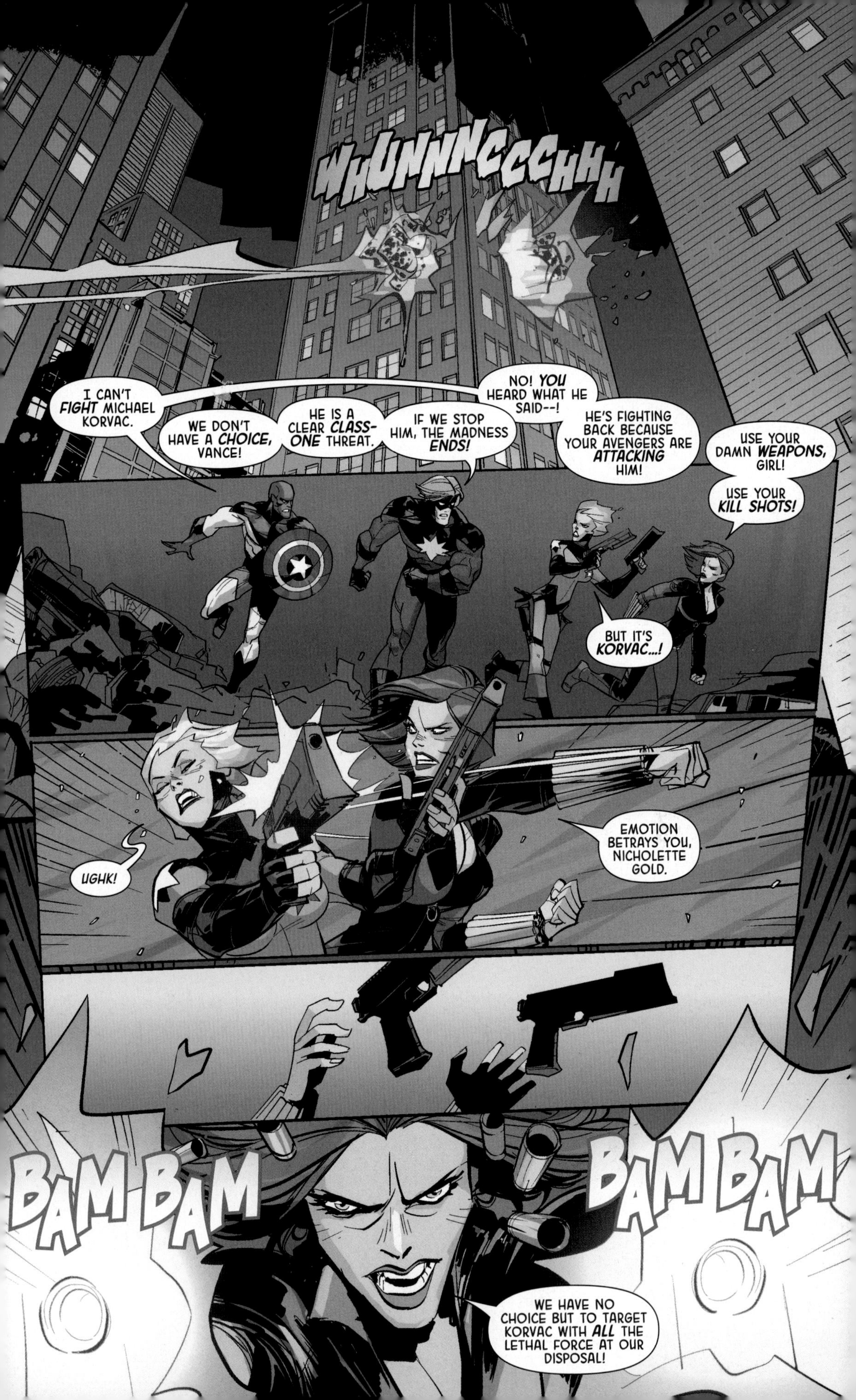
WHUNNNCCCHHH
I CAN'T FIGHT MICHAEL KORVAC.
WE DON'T HAVE A CHOICE, VANCE!
HE IS A CLEAR CLASS-ONE THREAT.
IF WE STOP HIM, THE MADNESS ENDS!
NO! YOU HEARD WHAT HE SAID--!
HE'S FIGHTING BACK BECAUSE YOUR AVENGERS ARE ATTACKING HIM!
USE YOUR DAMN WEAPONS, GIRL!
USE YOUR KILL SHOTS!
BUT IT'S KORVAC...!
UGHK!
EMOTION BETRAYS YOU, NICHOLETTE GOLD.
BAM BAM
BAM BAM
WE HAVE NO CHOICE BUT TO TARGET KORVAC WITH ALL THE LETHAL FORCE AT OUR DISPOSAL!

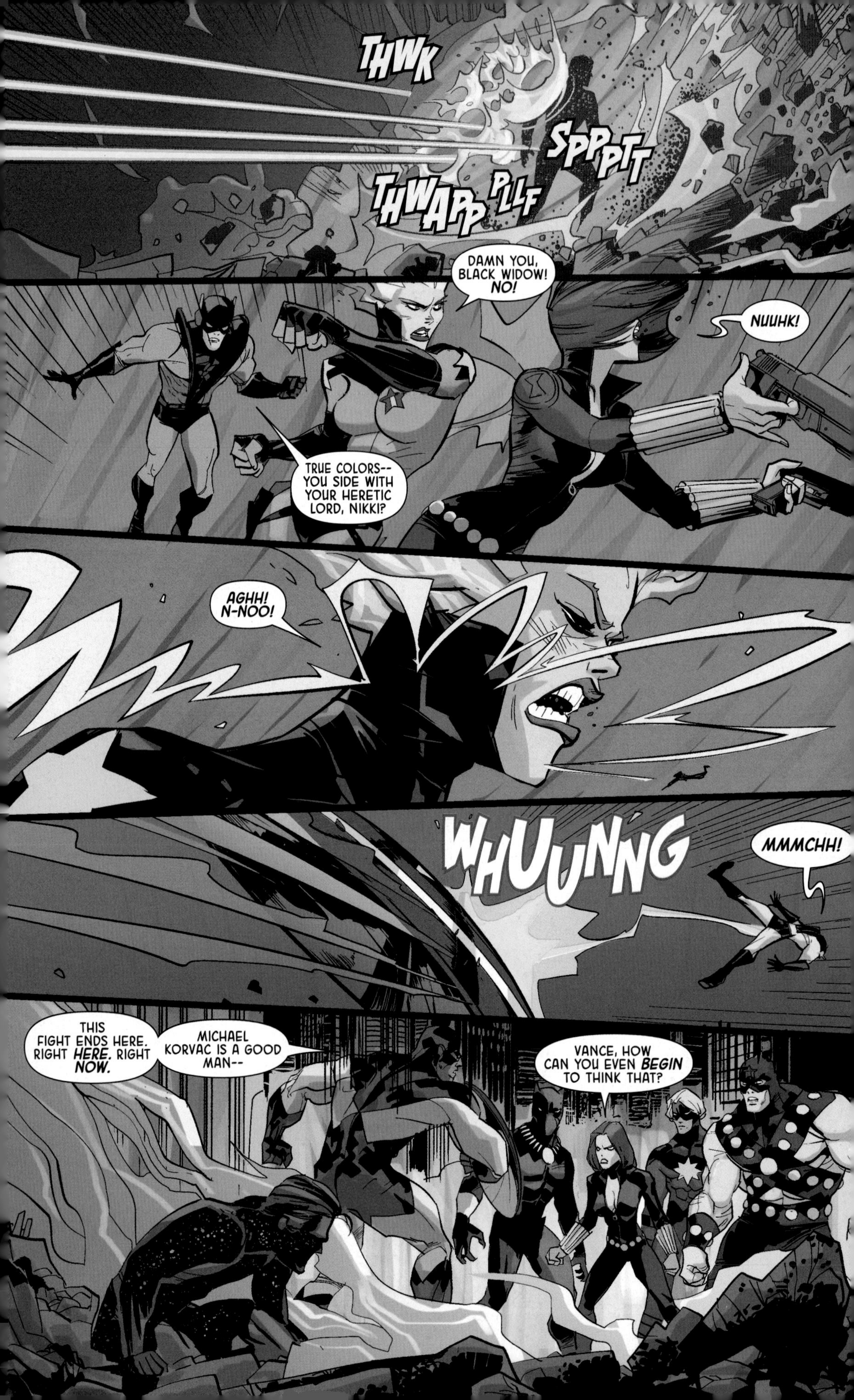
THWK
SPPPTT
THWAPP PLLF
DAMN YOU, BLACK WIDOW! NO!
NUUHK!
TRUE COLORS-- YOU SIDE WITH YOUR HERETIC LORD, NIKKI?
AGHH! N-NOO!
WHUUNNG
MMMCHH!
THIS FIGHT ENDS HERE. RIGHT HERE. RIGHT NOW.
MICHAEL KORVAC IS A GOOD MAN--
VANCE, HOW CAN YOU EVEN BEGIN TO THINK THAT?

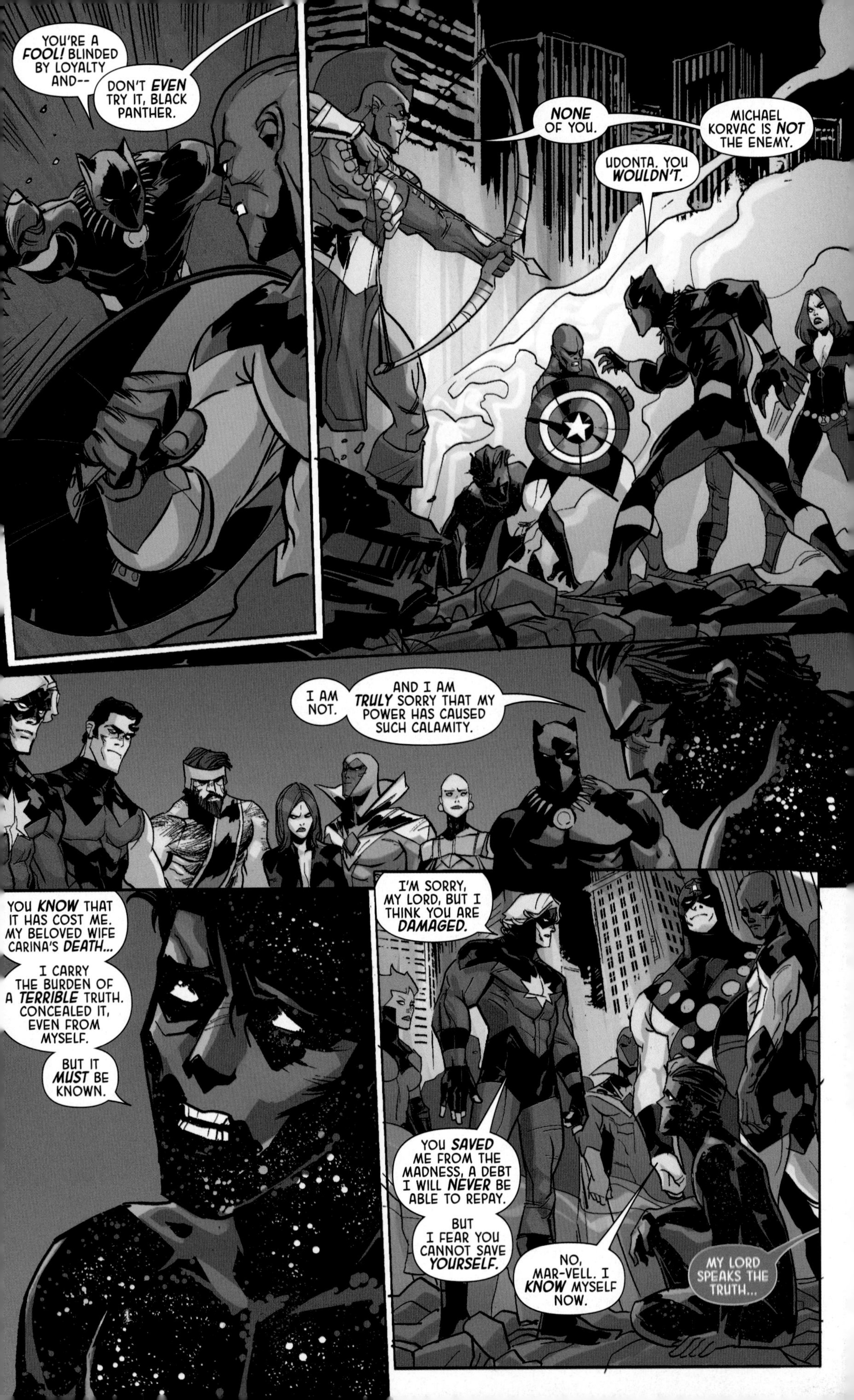

YOU'RE A FOOL! BLINDED BY LOYALTY AND--
DON'T EVEN TRY IT, BLACK PANTHER.
NONE OF YOU.
MICHAEL KORVAC IS NOT THE ENEMY.
UDONTA. YOU WOULDN'T.
I AM NOT.
AND I AM TRULY SORRY THAT MY POWER HAS CAUSED SUCH CALAMITY.
YOU KNOW THAT IT HAS COST ME. MY BELOVED WIFE CARINA'S DEATH...
I CARRY THE BURDEN OF A TERRIBLE TRUTH. CONCEALED IT, EVEN FROM MYSELF.
BUT IT MUST BE KNOWN.
I'M SORRY, MY LORD, BUT I THINK YOU ARE DAMAGED.
YOU SAVED ME FROM THE MADNESS, A DEBT I WILL NEVER BE ABLE TO REPAY.
BUT I FEAR YOU CANNOT SAVE YOURSELF.
NO, MAR-VELL. I KNOW MYSELF NOW.
MY LORD SPEAKS THE TRUTH...

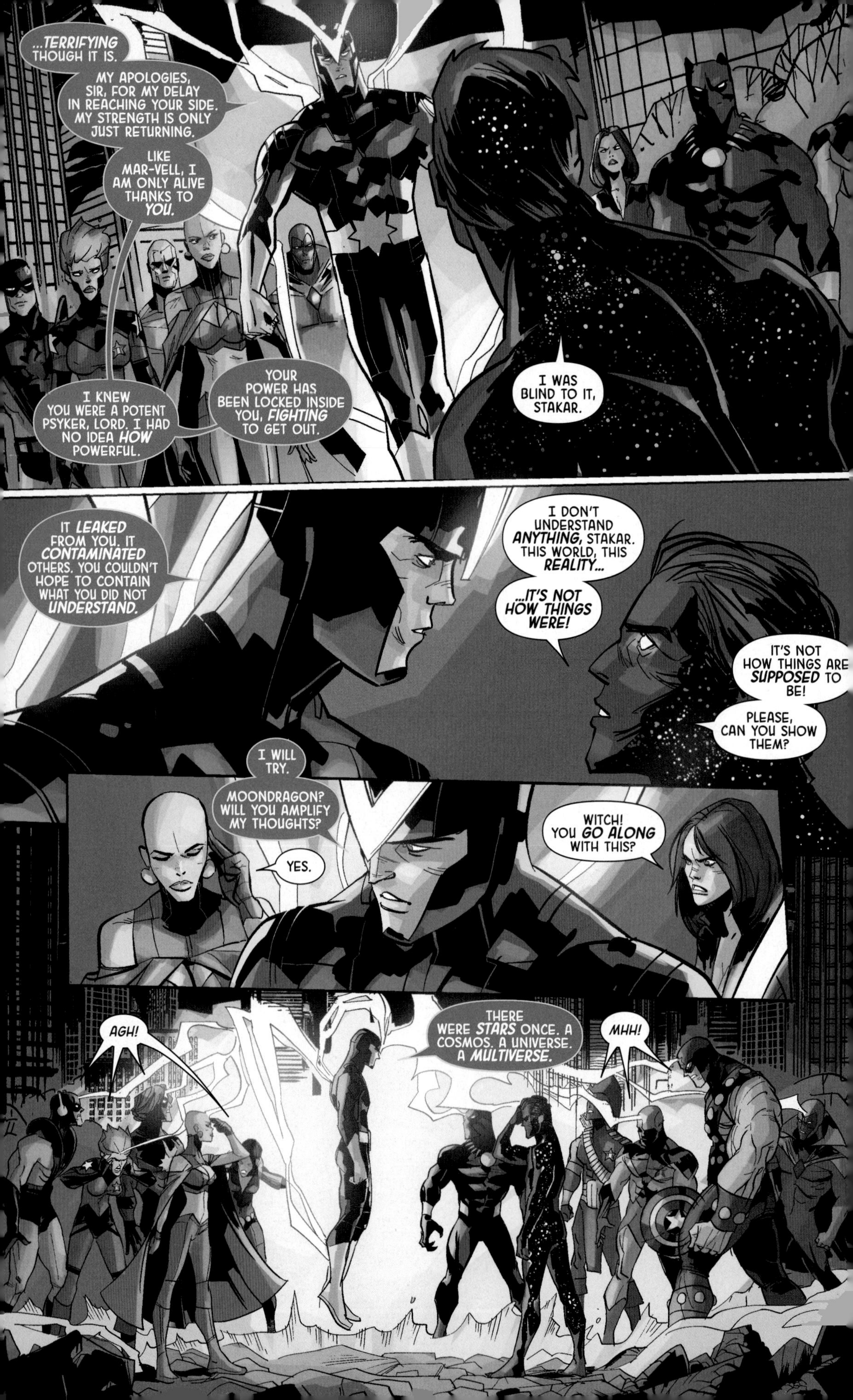
...TERRIFYING THOUGH IT IS.
MY APOLOGIES, SIR, FOR MY DELAY IN REACHING YOUR SIDE. MY STRENGTH IS ONLY JUST RETURNING.
LIKE MAR-VELL, I AM ONLY ALIVE THANKS TO YOU.
I KNEW YOU WERE A POTENT PSYKER, LORD. I HAD NO IDEA HOW POWERFUL.
YOUR POWER HAS BEEN LOCKED INSIDE YOU, FIGHTING TO GET OUT.
I WAS BLIND TO IT, STAKAR.
IT LEAKED FROM YOU. IT CONTAMINATED OTHERS. YOU COULDN'T HOPE TO CONTAIN WHAT YOU DID NOT UNDERSTAND.
I DON'T UNDERSTAND ANYTHING, STAKAR. THIS WORLD, THIS REALITY...
...IT'S NOT HOW THINGS WERE!
IT'S NOT HOW THINGS ARE SUPPOSED TO BE!
PLEASE, CAN YOU SHOW THEM?
I WILL TRY.
MOONDRAGON? WILL YOU AMPLIFY MY THOUGHTS?
YES.
WITCH! YOU GO ALONG WITH THIS?
AGH!
THERE WERE STARS ONCE. A COSMOS. A UNIVERSE. A MULTIVERSE.
MHH!

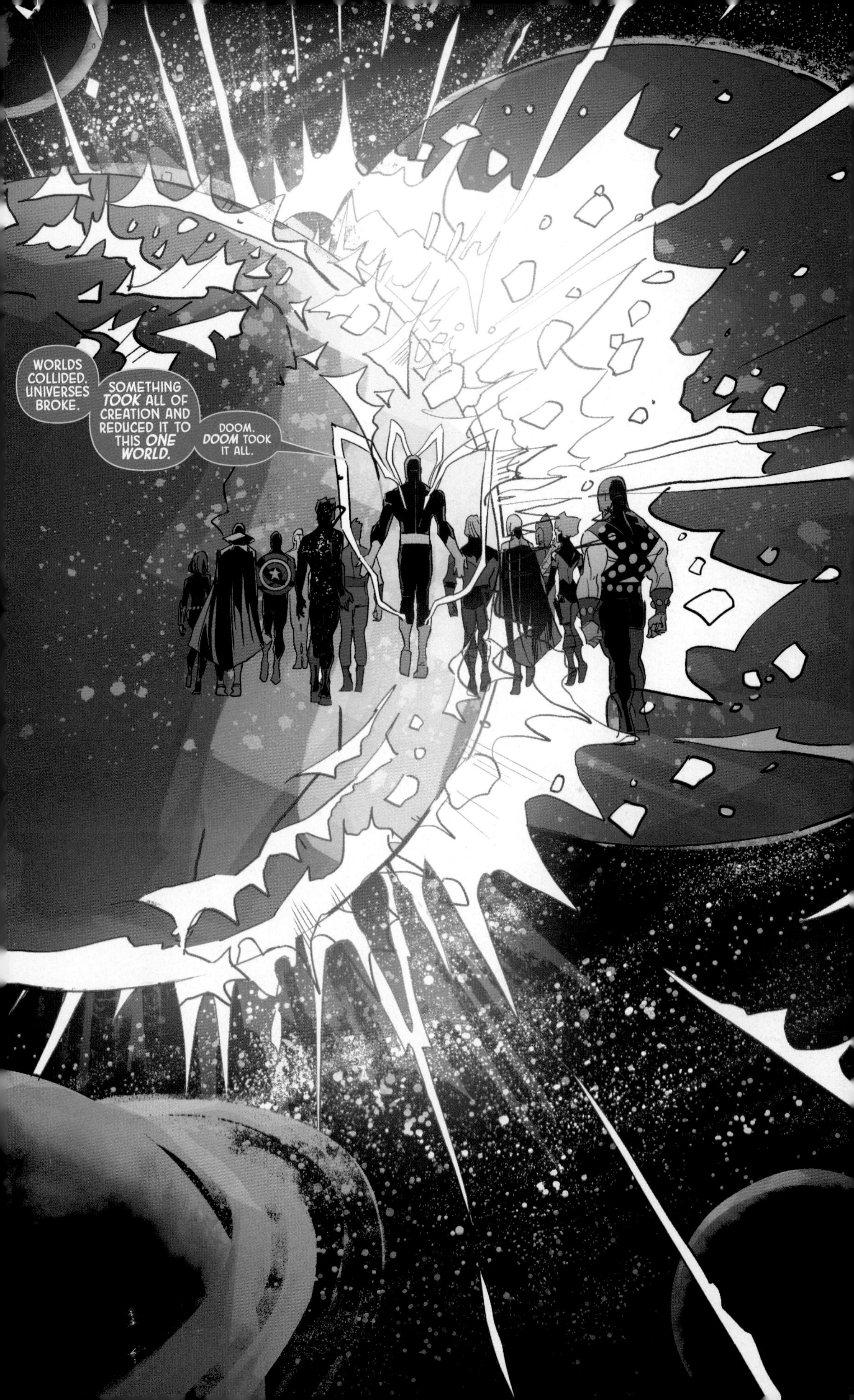
WORLDS COLLIDED. UNIVERSES BROKE.
SOMETHING TOOK ALL OF CREATION AND REDUCED IT TO THIS ONE WORLD.
DOOM. DOOM TOOK IT ALL.

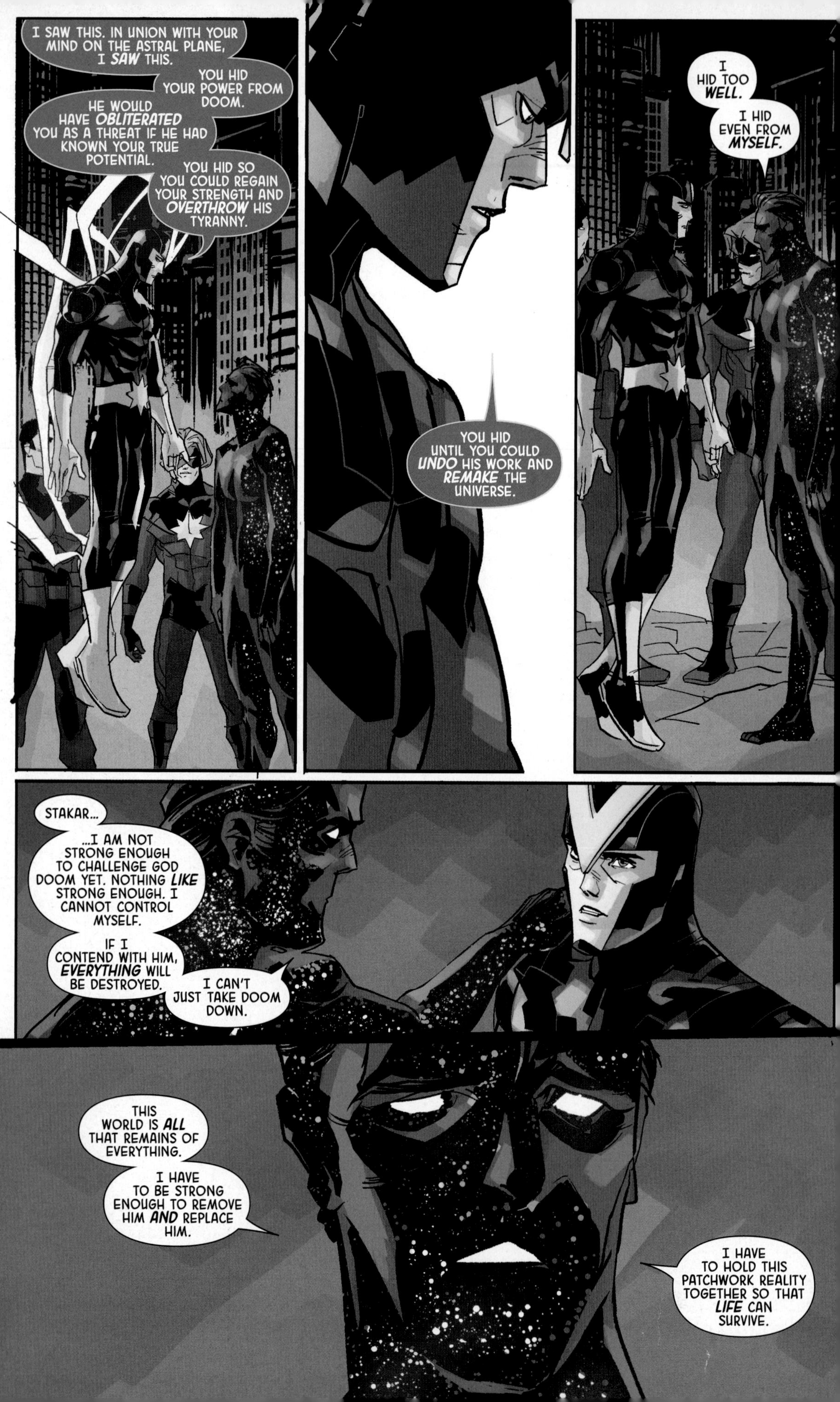
I SAW THIS. IN UNION WITH YOUR MIND ON THE ASTRAL PLANE, I SAW THIS.
YOU HID YOUR POWER FROM DOOM.
HE WOULD HAVE OBLITERATED YOU AS A THREAT IF HE HAD KNOWN YOUR TRUE POTENTIAL.
YOU HID SO YOU COULD REGAIN YOUR STRENGTH AND OVERTHROW HIS TYRANNY.
YOU HID UNTIL YOU COULD UNDO HIS WORK AND REMAKE THE UNIVERSE.
I HID TOO WELL.
I HID EVEN FROM MYSELF.
STAKAR...
...I AM NOT STRONG ENOUGH TO CHALLENGE GOD DOOM YET. NOTHING LIKE STRONG ENOUGH. I CANNOT CONTROL MYSELF.
IF I CONTEND WITH HIM, EVERYTHING WILL BE DESTROYED.
I CAN'T JUST TAKE DOOM DOWN.
THIS WORLD IS ALL THAT REMAINS OF EVERYTHING.
I HAVE TO BE STRONG ENOUGH TO REMOVE HIM AND REPLACE HIM.
I HAVE TO HOLD THIS PATCHWORK REALITY TOGETHER SO THAT LIFE CAN SURVIVE.

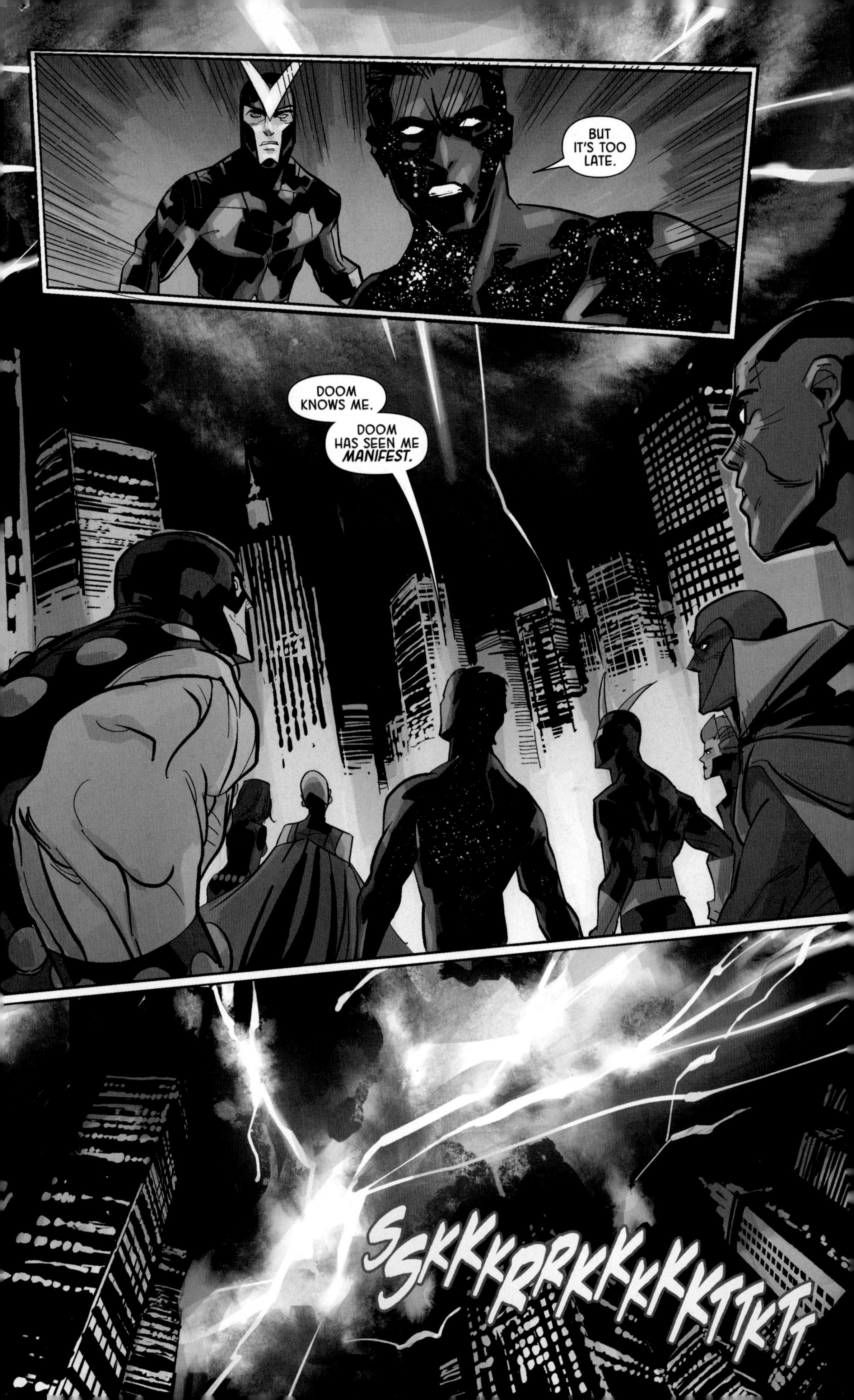
BUT IT'S TOO LATE.
DOOM KNOWS ME.
DOOM HAS SEEN ME *MANIFEST.*
SSKKKRRKKKKKTTKTT

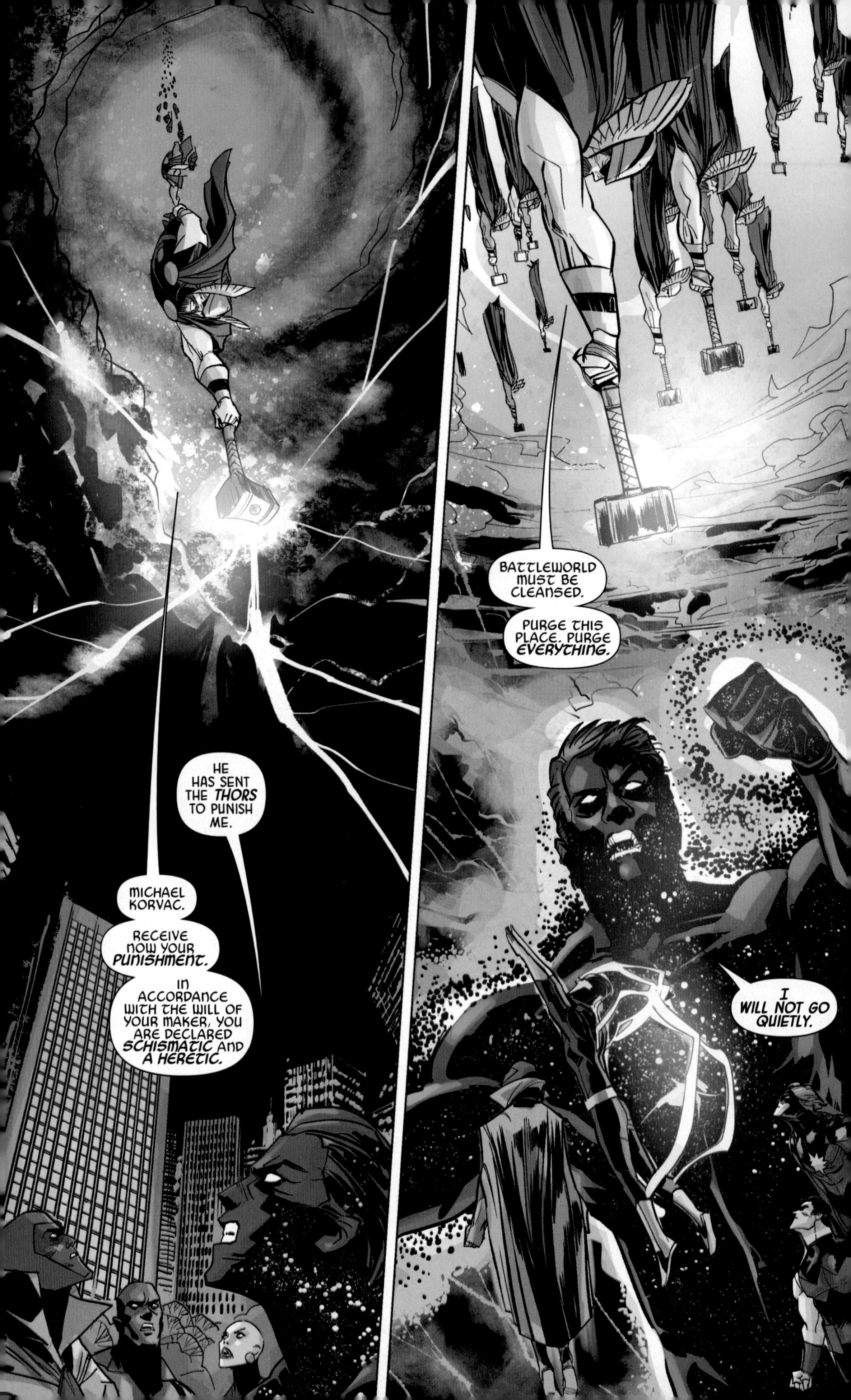
HE HAS SENT THE THORS TO PUNISH ME.
MICHAEL KORVAC.
RECEIVE NOW YOUR PUNISHMENT.
IN ACCORDANCE WITH THE WILL OF YOUR MAKER, YOU ARE DECLARED SCHISMATIC AND A HERETIC.
BATTLEWORLD MUST BE CLEANSED.
PURGE THIS PLACE. PURGE EVERYTHING.
I WILL NOT GO QUIETLY.

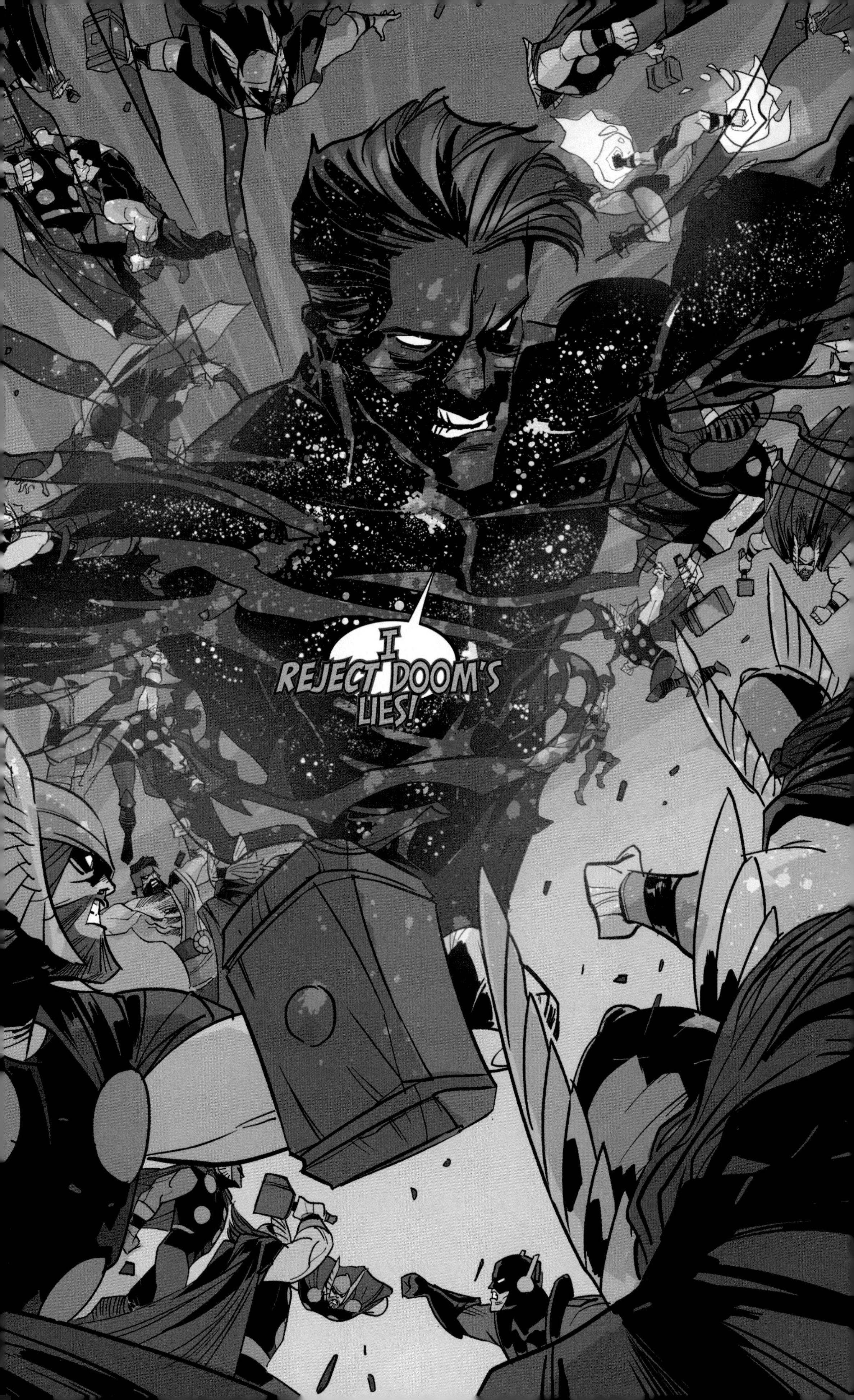
I REJECT DOOM'S LIES!

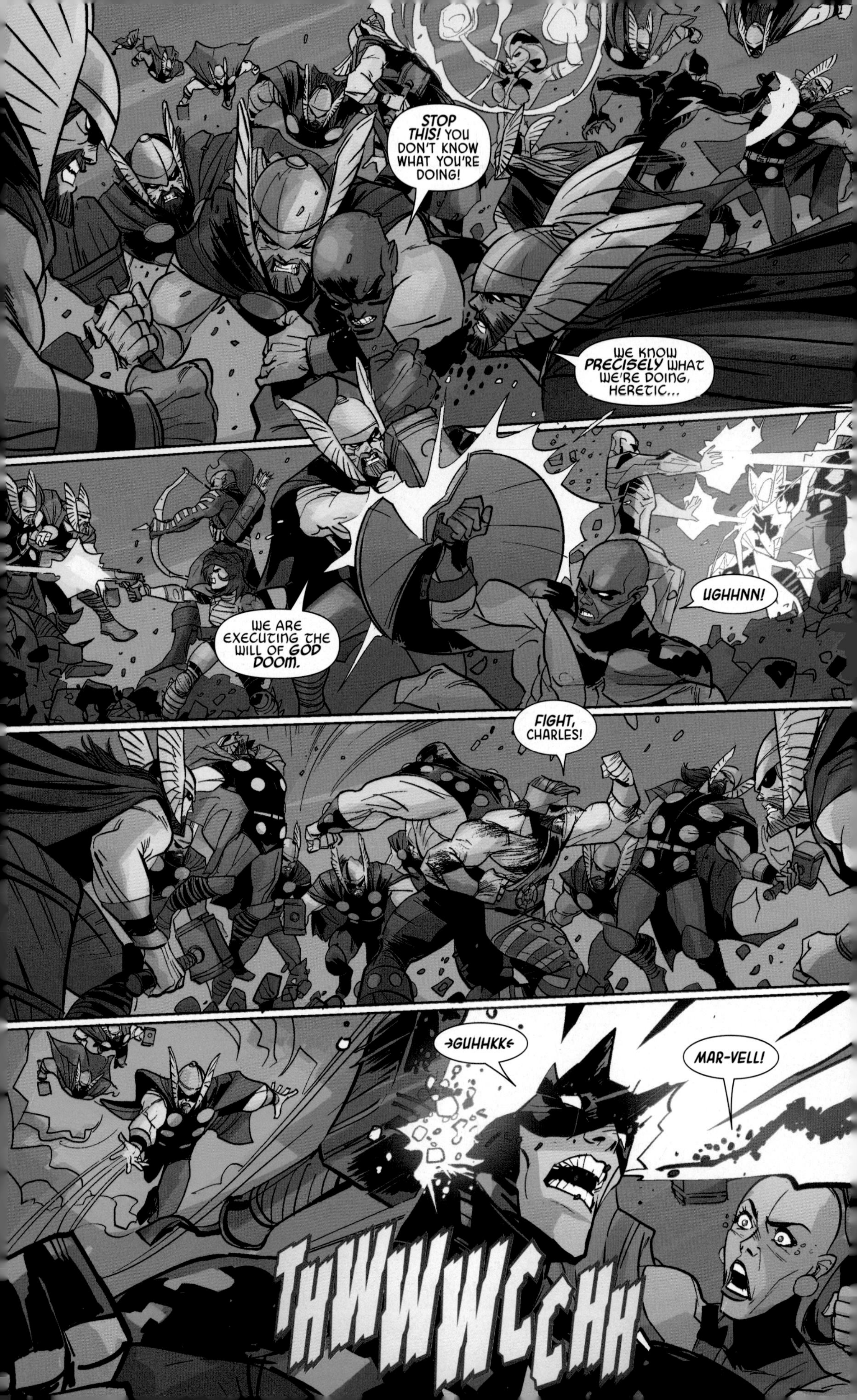
STOP THIS! YOU DON'T KNOW WHAT YOU'RE DOING!
WE KNOW PRECISELY WHAT WE'RE DOING, HERETIC...
WE ARE EXECUTING THE WILL OF GOD DOOM.
UGHHNN!
FIGHT, CHARLES!
›GUHHKK‹
MAR-VELL!
THWWWCCHH

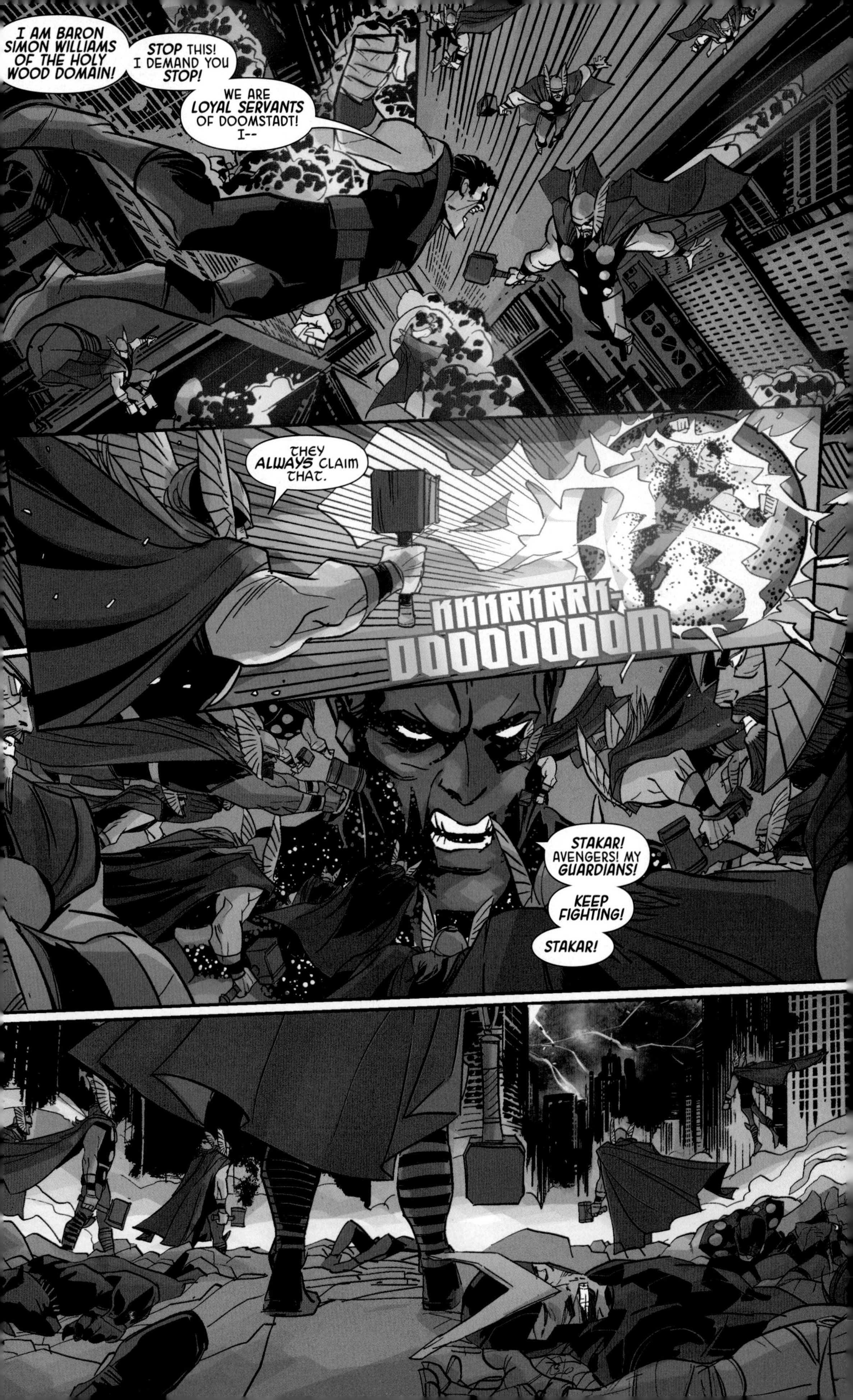

I AM BARON SIMON WILLIAMS OF THE HOLY WOOD DOMAIN!
STOP THIS! I DEMAND YOU STOP!
WE ARE LOYAL SERVANTS OF DOOMSTADT! I--
THEY ALWAYS CLAIM THAT.
KKKRKRRK-DOOOOOOOM
STAKAR! AVENGERS! MY GUARDIANS!
KEEP FIGHTING!
STAKAR!

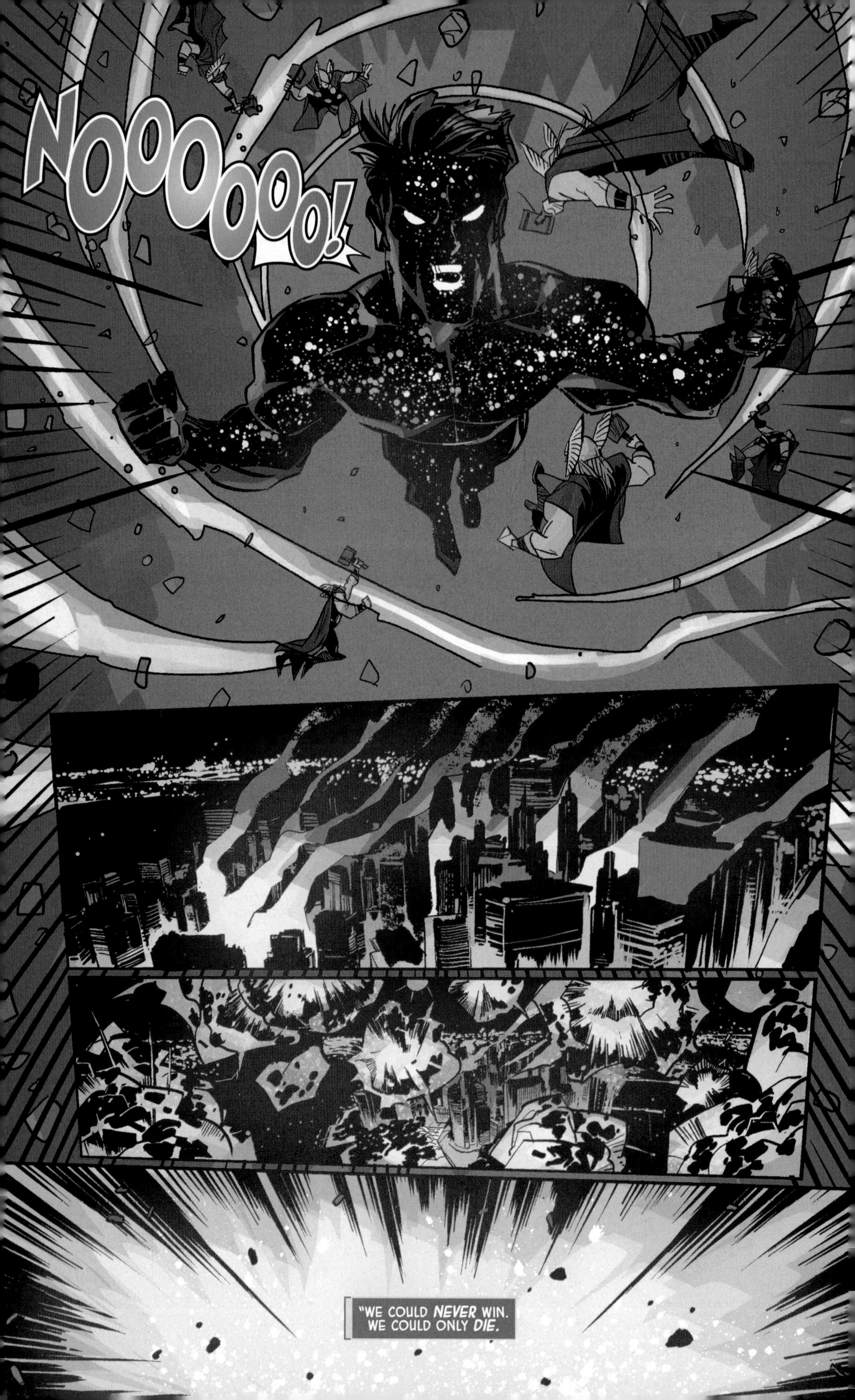
NOOOOOOO!
"WE COULD NEVER WIN. WE COULD ONLY DIE.

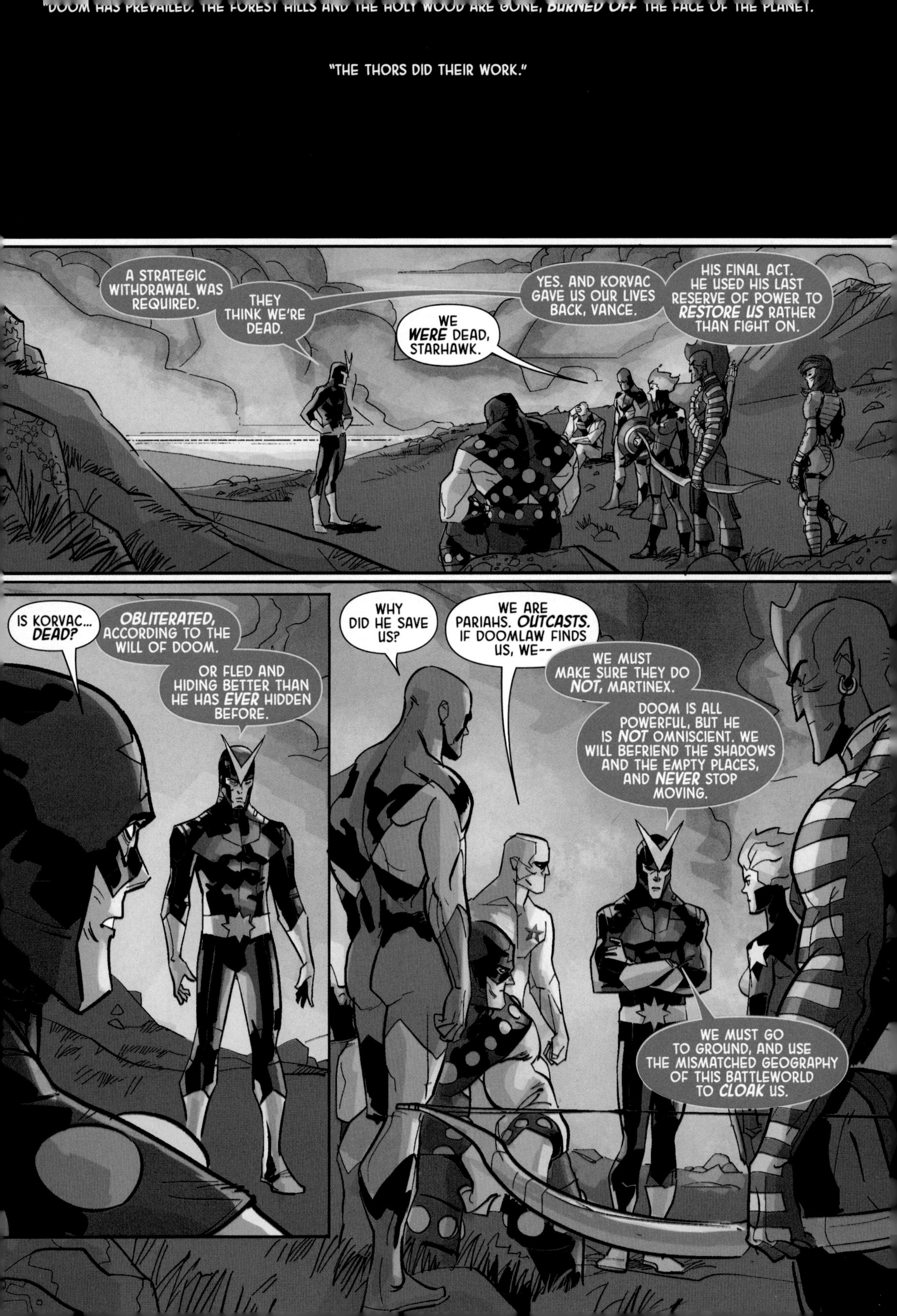
"DOOM HAS PREVAILED. THE FOREST HILLS AND THE HOLY WOOD ARE GONE, BURNED OFF THE FACE OF THE PLANET.
"THE THORS DID THEIR WORK."
A STRATEGIC WITHDRAWAL WAS REQUIRED.
THEY THINK WE'RE DEAD.
WE WERE DEAD, STARHAWK.
YES. AND KORVAC GAVE US OUR LIVES BACK, VANCE.
HIS FINAL ACT. HE USED HIS LAST RESERVE OF POWER TO RESTORE US RATHER THAN FIGHT ON.
IS KORVAC... DEAD?
OBLITERATED, ACCORDING TO THE WILL OF DOOM.
OR FLED AND HIDING BETTER THAN HE HAS EVER HIDDEN BEFORE.
WHY DID HE SAVE US?
WE ARE PARIAHS. OUTCASTS. IF DOOMLAW FINDS US, WE--
WE MUST MAKE SURE THEY DO NOT, MARTINEX.
DOOM IS ALL POWERFUL, BUT HE IS NOT OMNISCIENT. WE WILL BEFRIEND THE SHADOWS AND THE EMPTY PLACES, AND NEVER STOP MOVING.
WE MUST GO TO GROUND, AND USE THE MISMATCHED GEOGRAPHY OF THIS BATTLEWORLD TO CLOAK US.

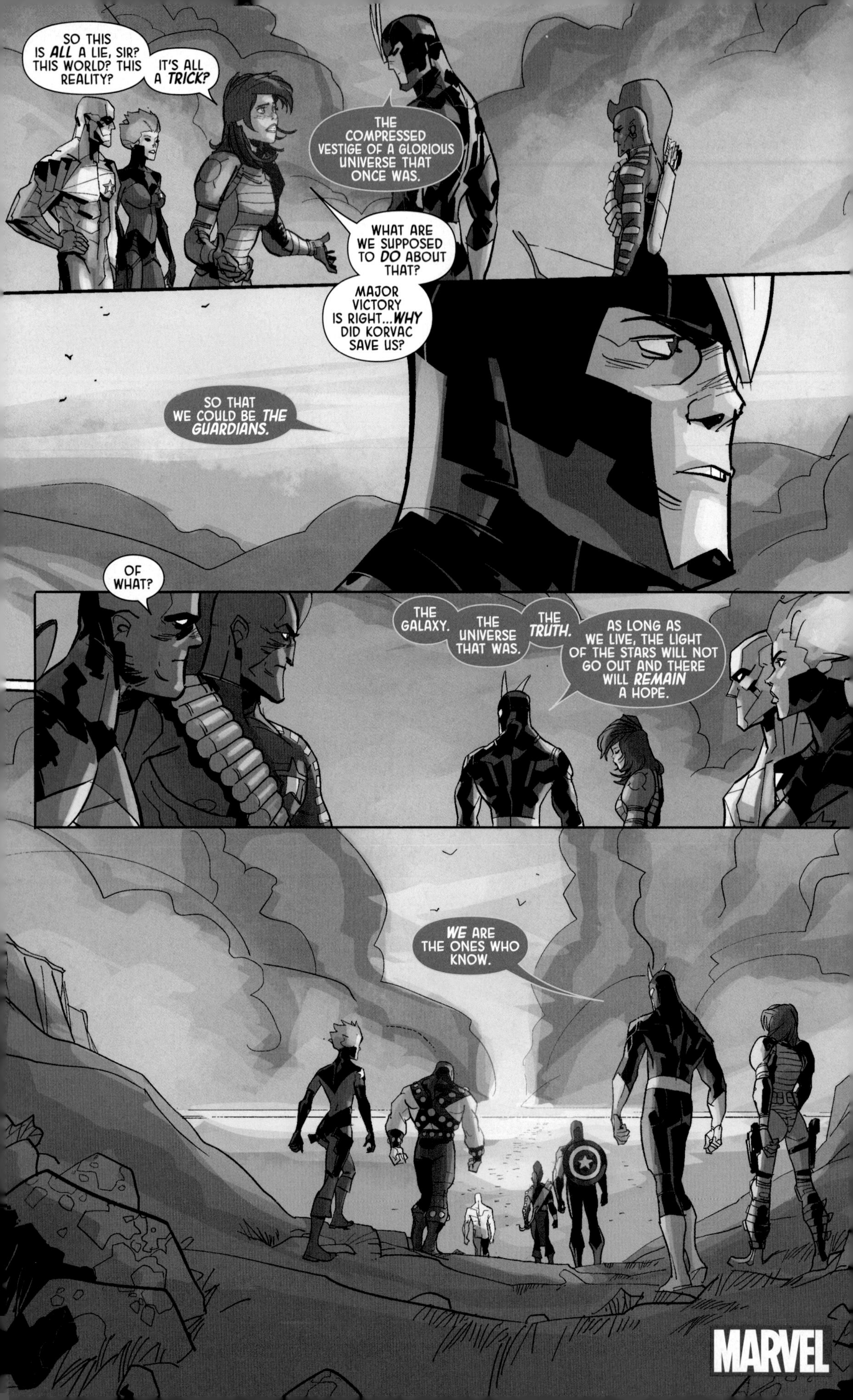
SO THIS IS ALL A LIE, SIR? THIS WORLD? THIS REALITY?
IT'S ALL A TRICK?
THE COMPRESSED VESTIGE OF A GLORIOUS UNIVERSE THAT ONCE WAS.
WHAT ARE WE SUPPOSED TO DO ABOUT THAT?
MAJOR VICTORY IS RIGHT...WHY DID KORVAC SAVE US?
SO THAT WE COULD BE THE GUARDIANS.
OF WHAT?
THE GALAXY.
THE UNIVERSE THAT WAS.
THE TRUTH.
AS LONG AS WE LIVE, THE LIGHT OF THE STARS WILL NOT GO OUT AND THERE WILL REMAIN A HOPE.
WE ARE THE ONES WHO KNOW.
MARVEL

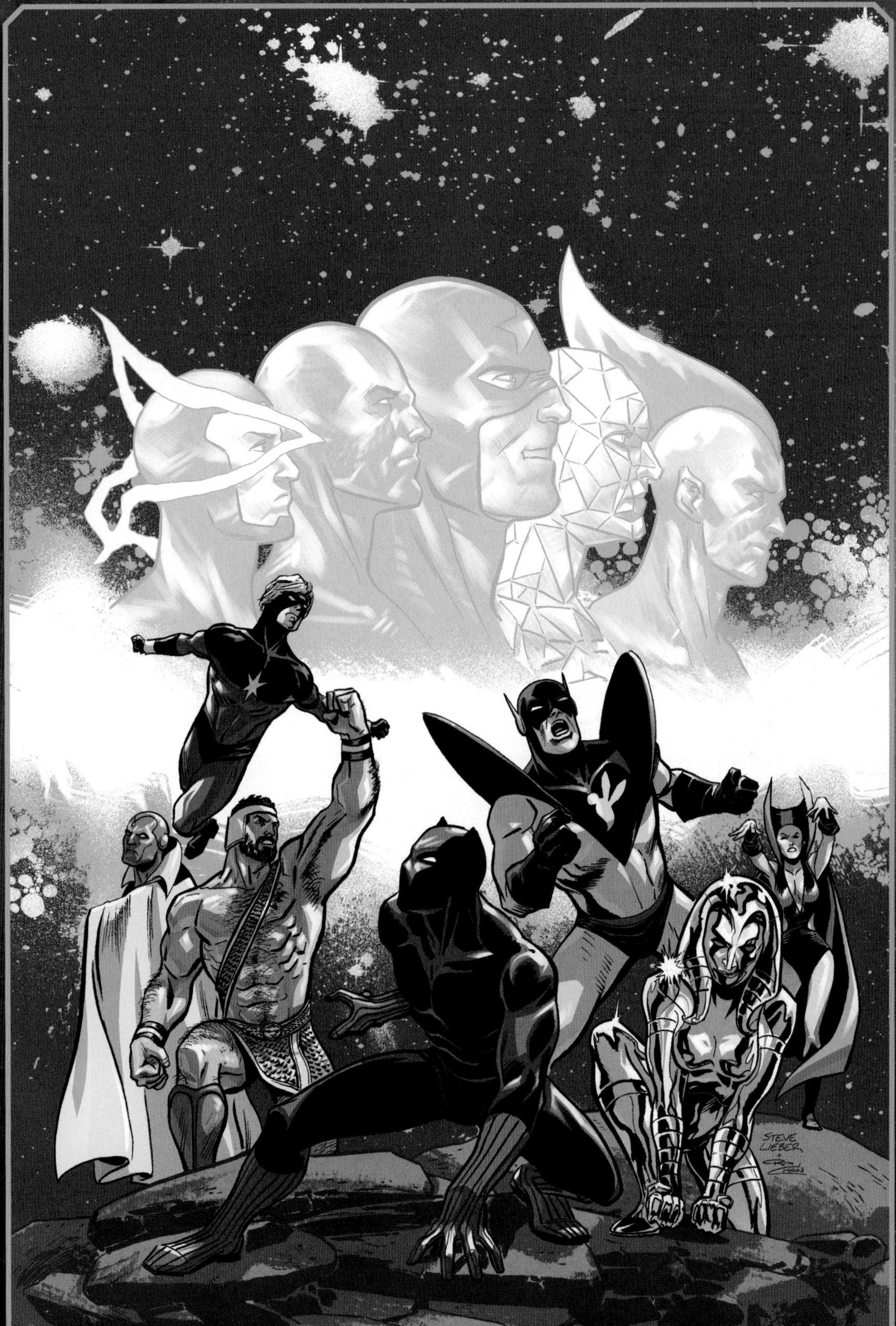
STEVE LIEBER + RON CHAN

KORVAC SAGA #1 VARIANT
BY STEVE LIEBER & RON CHAN

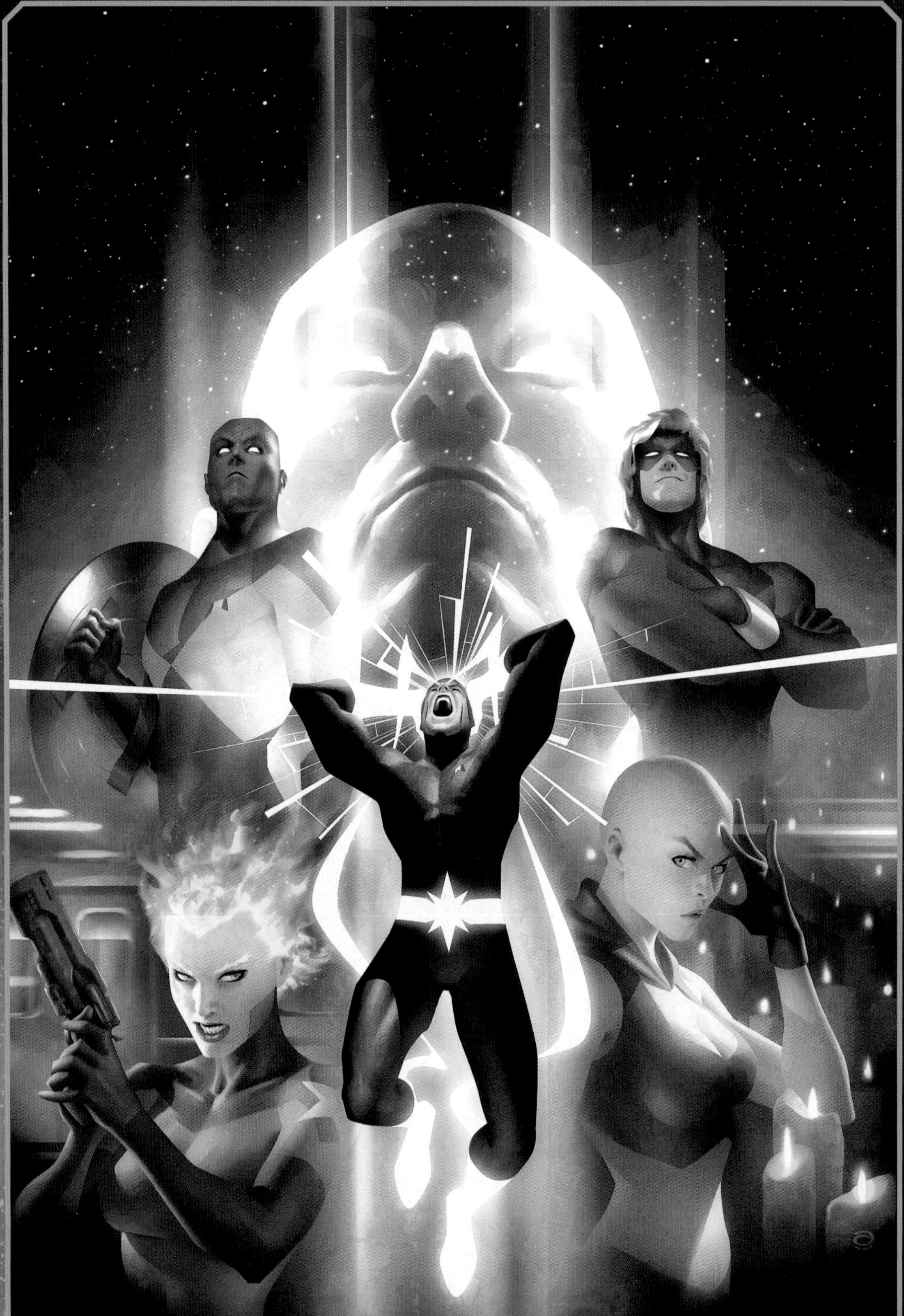

KORVAC SAGA #2 VARIANT
BY ALEX GARNER

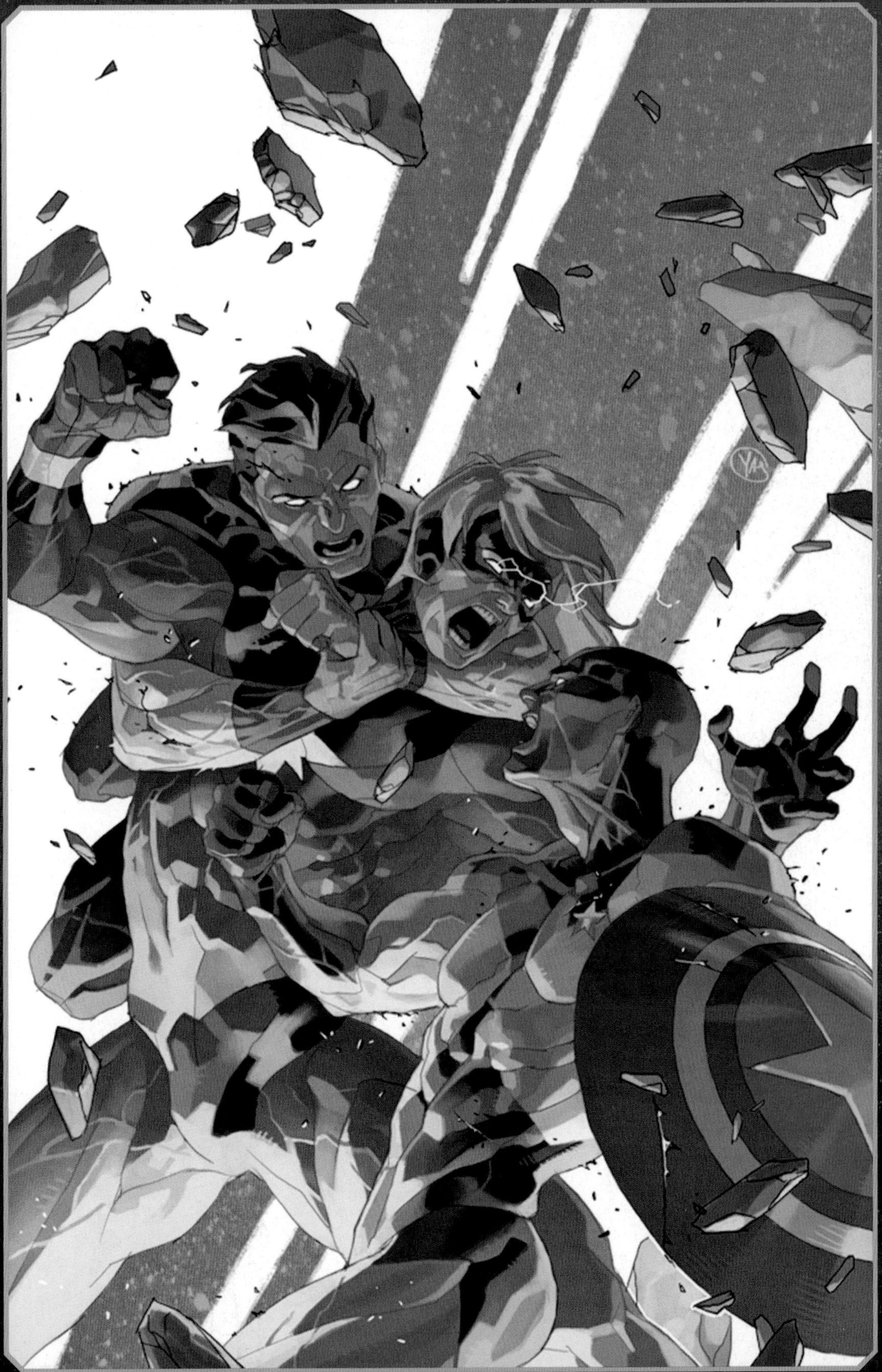

KORVAC SAGA #3 VARIANT
BY YASMINE PUTRI

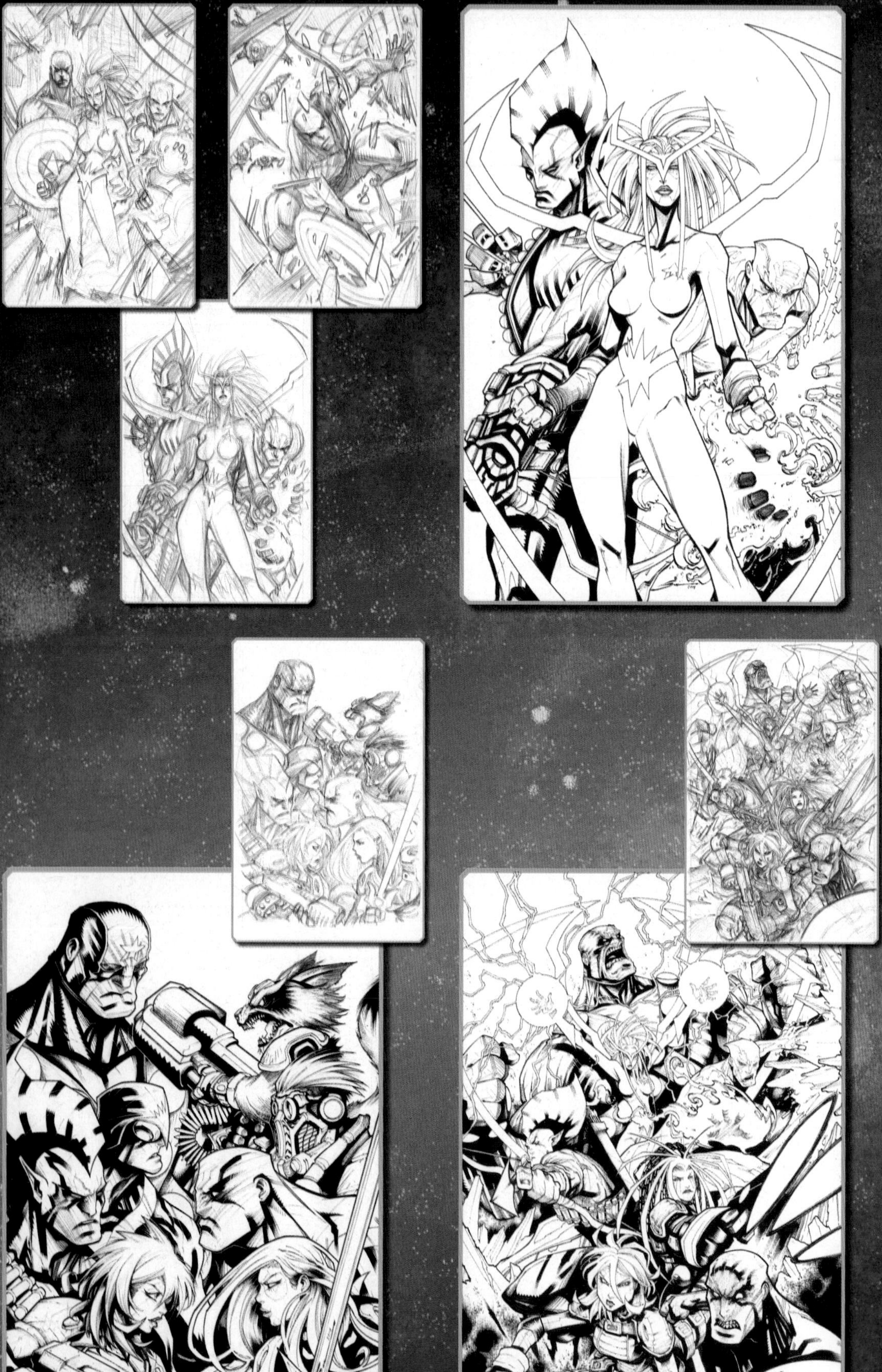

GUARDIANS 3000 #6-8 COVER SKETCHES & INKS BY GERARDO SANDOVAL